Airbrush Bible

Timothy Remus

Published by:
ArtKulture
An Imprint of Wolfgang Publications

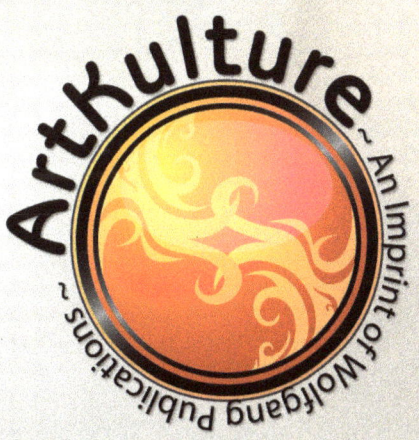

PO Box 223 • Stillwater, MN 55082
www.ArtKulture.com

Legals

First published in 2010 by Wolfgang Publications Inc., PO Box 223, Stillwater MN 55082

©Timothy Remus, 2010

All rights reserved. With the exception of quoting brief passages for the purposes of review no part of this publication may be reproduced without prior written permission from the publisher.

The information in this book is true and complete to the best of our knowledge. All recommendations are made without any guarantee on the part of the author or publisher, who also disclaim any liability incurred in connection with the use of this data or specific details.

We recognize that some words, model names and designations, for example, mentioned herein are the property of the trademark holder. We use them for identification purposes only. This is not an official publication.

ISBN-13: 978-1-929133-86-4
ISBN-10: 1-929133-86-3

Printed and bound in USA.

Airbrush Bible

Chapter One
    Leah Gall 6

Chapter Two
    Tom Nguyen 22

Chapter Three
    Keith Hanson 44

Chapter Four
    Luca Puganica 56

Chapter Five
    Steve Wizard 70

Chapter Six
    Ken Simonson 86

Chapter Seven
    Lenni Schwartz 100

Chapter Eight
    Susan Heidi 114

Chapter Nine
    Vince Goodeve 138

Chapter Ten
    John Nicholas 160

Sources 180

Introduction

Airbrush Bible is designed to provide ideas, instruction and inspiration to anyone with an interest in airbrushing. Whether your interest is pin-ups, illustration, body painting or vehicles, the sequences found in this book will help to expand your horizons.

At Wolfgang Publications, we published our first airbrush book in 1997, and since then we've produced an additional six airbrushing titles. Airbrush Bible is a compilation of all that work. The sequences include the most recent pin-up and body painting work, done with non-toxic water-based and acrylic paints, as well as some of our earlier automotive and motorcycle work.

No matter the media or medium, each chapter is a start-to-finish painting sequence. For this book we let the photos tell most of the story. The stories start with the first sketch, and finish with the completed art. Each chapter is the work of one artist, and includes an interview that explains why they like a particular brand of paint, how they learned their skills and where they find inspiration.

Seminars held by experienced airbrush artists provide a good learning opportunity for anyone with the inclination. Think of this book as ten seminars, each with a different artist, each with a different focus, all held in the privacy of your own home or shop.

Acknowledgements

Though I've spent the last twenty years leaning over the shoulder of various artists, the job never gets boring. Whether the job at hand is a pin-up painted on a panel, or a set of flames laid out on a motorcycle gas tank, excitement builds throughout the process. The buzz in the air starts when I walk into the shop and comes to a bang when – sometimes suddenly – all the steps, masking, mixing and spraying come to a conclusion.

Like a good athlete, the artists in this book make it all look easy. For most, the creative process is so intuitive that they don't seem to think, they just do.

And for allowing me to hang out while they do what they do, I give thanks. Thanks to Leah for making time in her busy schedule to give me a class in basic airbrush techniques. Thanks to Tom Nguyen for allowing me into his private domain as he creates a lovely pin-up image of model Jacki Morrison. Thanks to Keith Hanson for letting me hang in the shop every time I come to Boston, and for rearranging his schedule to accommodate mine. Thanks to photographer Doug Mitchel for the work he did with Luca Puganica and Ken Simonson.

I'm grateful to Steve Chaszeka (aka Wizard Paint) for showing me not only how to do reality flames, but also how to add embellishments as only he can. Lenni Schwartz is one artist who can do it all, from pinstripes to airbrushing. Heck, Lenni does complete paint jobs, and old-skool sign painting as well. No matter what the job, Lenni always makes me welcome in his shop.

Susan Heidi and I spent most of four days in her small studio, while she created on extremely beautiful pin-up image – thanks. For Vince Goodeve, it was a little easier, both because we are old friends, and because his studio and shop space is big and spacious.

I'm grateful to John Nicholas, and his boss, Kim Suter, for giving me the opportunity to document the creation of one very complex piece of motorcycle art.

Yes, I have a great job.

Chapter One
Leah Gall

School is in Session

Leah Gall is a talented airbrush artist, one who often teaches classes to both beginner and experienced airbrush artists. For this sequence we decided to simply let Leah "teach" a class to everyone who reads this book. The curriculum includes everything from how to stand, to keeping the tip of the airbrush clean, and all the basic strokes as well. Leah stresses the point that even though most of us want to skip the basic strokes and go right to making art, the basic strokes are a necessary component of

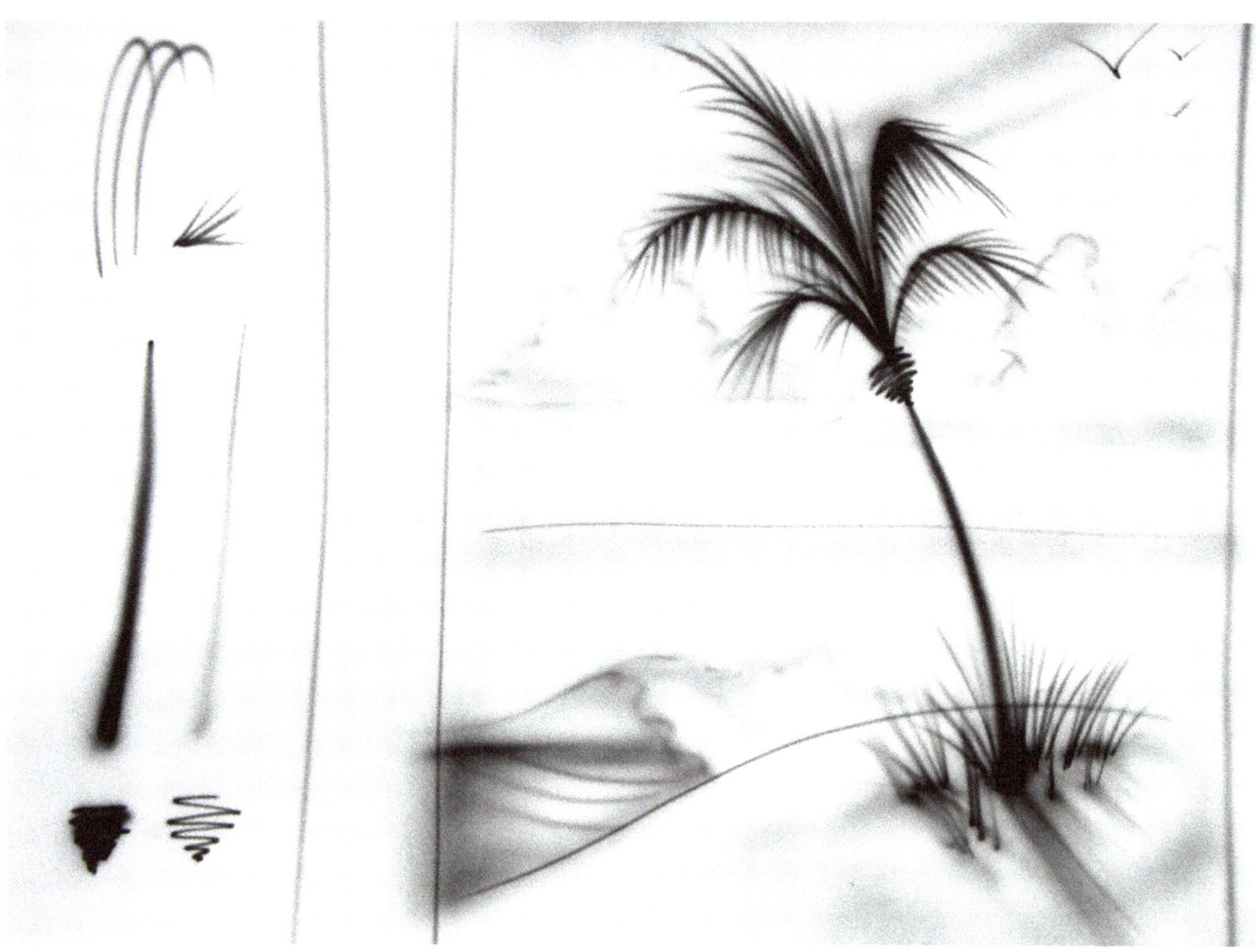

We are going to practice some of the basic moves, or essential airbrush strokes, that are used in almost all airbrushing. You will eventually see how what may seem like lines and circles, soft fades and dots, are all potential parts of an image. By combining these in varying patterns you can produce amazing things.

Photos: Timothy Remus, Captions: Leah Gall.

almost any art you're going to do. So don't skip to the end of the chapter.

THE AIRBRUSH

First, everyone has to understand that good airbrushes have a two-stage trigger, and the trigger does two things. First, it controls the flow of air. Second, it also controls the flow of paint. Start by holding the airbrush like a pencil, then press straight down on the trigger. With a good airbrush, there will only be air coming out and no paint. Now, with the trigger pushed down, you can pull it back a little to spray a thin line of paint. The more you pull the trigger back the more paint is released by the airbrush. The hard thing is to keep the air on while moving the trigger back and forth for more or less paint, while changing the gun-to-subject distance at the same time.

You always push the air on first and last. This sequence needs to become second nature. First, push the air on, then pull the trigger back for paint. Now, after you've made the stroke or painted an area, you push the trigger forward to shut off the paint, only then do you let up off the trigger so the air stops.

I always insist that my students work through simple painting exercises again and again. These exercises are building blocks. Each dot, each circle, and each dagger stroke will be part of a whole image you create tomorrow or next week. You can't run until you learn how to walk, and the learning exercises that follow will take you from baby steps to complicated dance moves. Don't be in a hurry, just practice, practice, practice the basic strokes first.

DOTS

I like to start students on a medium size dot, like the end of a pool stick, and then work on bigger and smaller dots. It's best to start subtle, you can always add more, let it build to size. The brush should be about 1-1/2 inches away from the paper. It's good to practice the spacing as well. Be sure to leave the air on between the dots. For smaller dots the tip gets closer and the trigger is pulled back less for less paint. Include soft or fuzzy dots in this exercise as well.

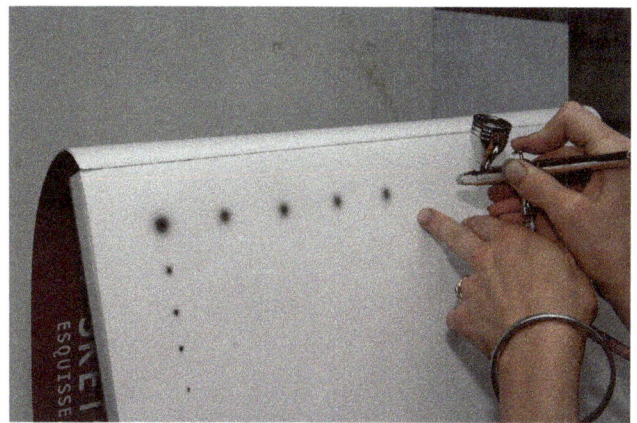

To start, press the trigger down to get air only. While air is flowing pull back until you see a soft dot of paint, now push the trigger forward to stop the paint, but keep the trigger pressed down for air only.

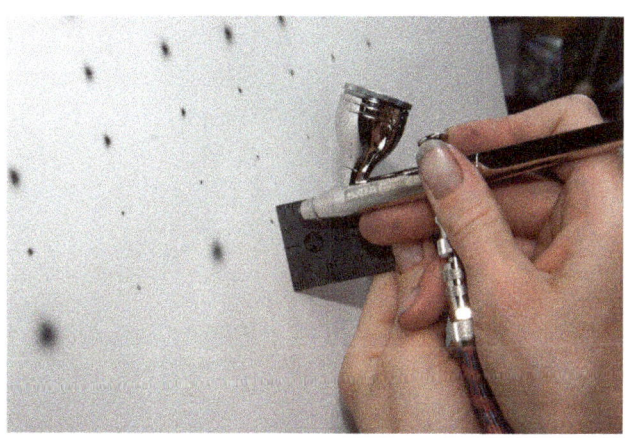

After the soft medium dots, move to the smallest solid dots you can make, by getting close to the paper - maybe 1/2 inch. Again; air first, then paint, then back to air only, then stop.

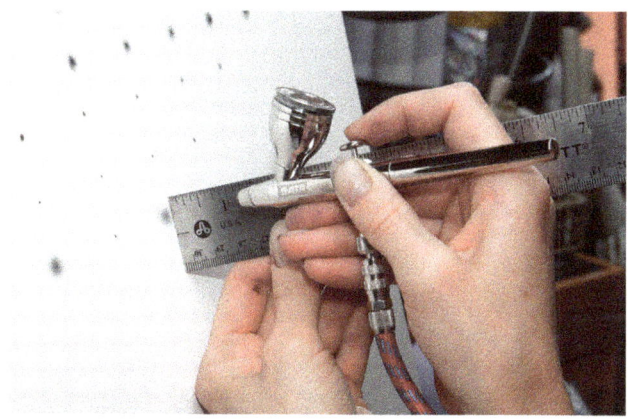

Be subtle - this is a fine instrument - treat it that way. Now alternate from soft dots to tiny dots. Always start lighter and softer - then you can gradually increase the flow, adding more paint.

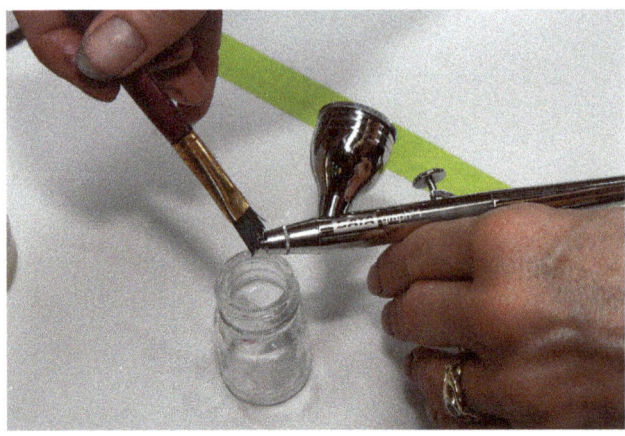

Quick tip: for cleaning the tip use a firm old paintbrush or tooth brush. For water based paint use water or airbrush cleaner, for solvent-based or automotive paints use a lacquer thinner.

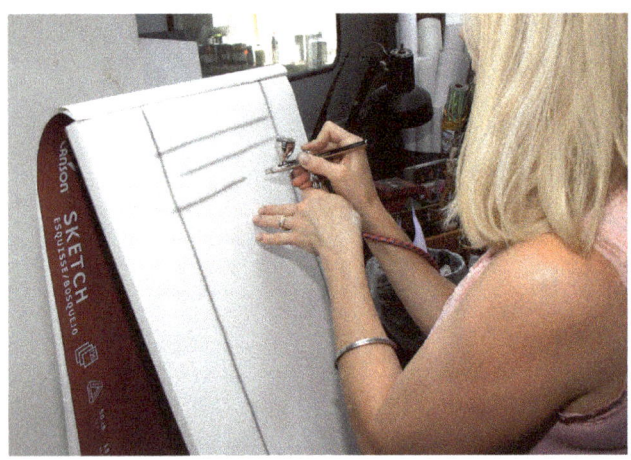

Spray two vertical lines, one on each side of your practice sheet, not too close to the edge. These borderlines are your target…

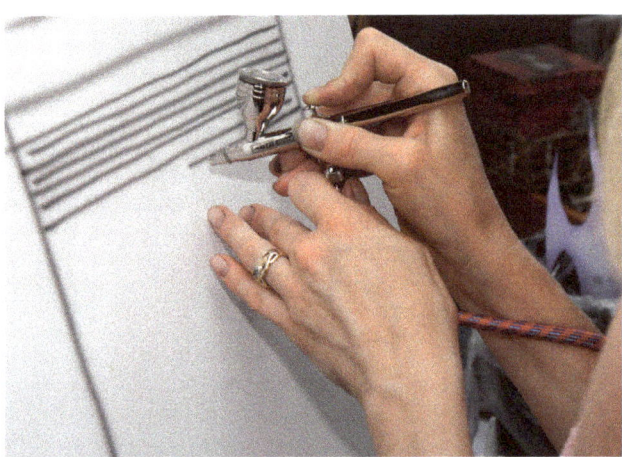

…stop the paint when you reach them, but continue your motion and let air flow past the borderlines - this will help you gain control and accuracy.

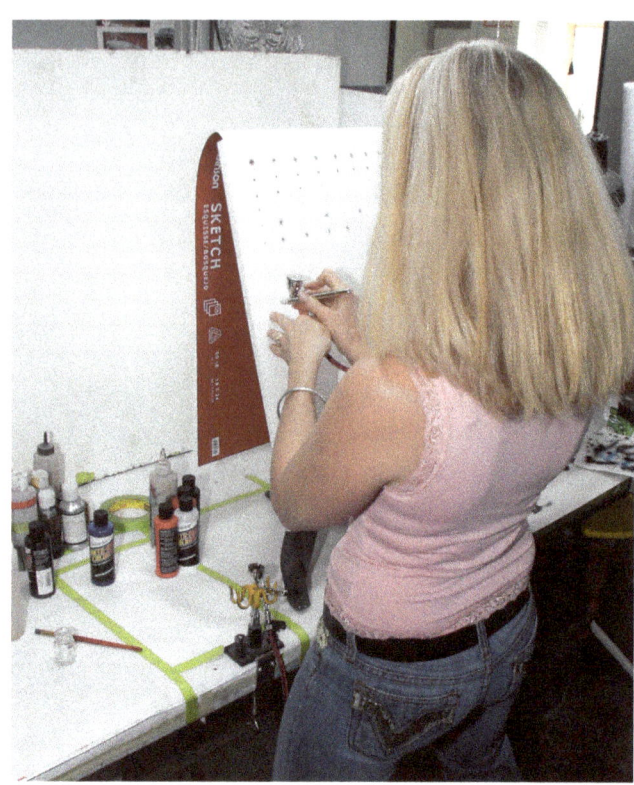

When standing in front of your work surface use your whole body, stay flexible at the knees, keep your arms at your sides…

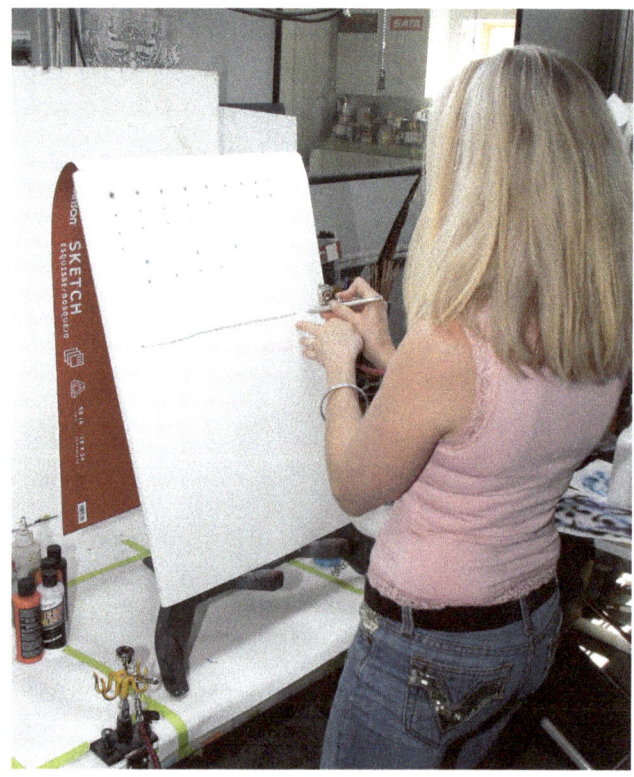

…try to keep your paint area directly in front of your chest/midriff - so that you don't have to raise your hands above your shoulder level.

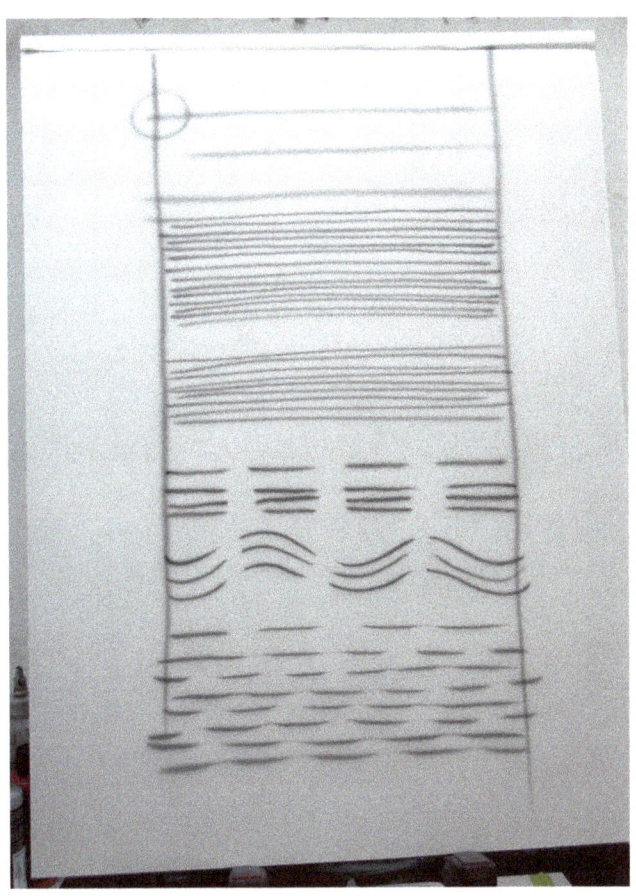

3. Here's a typical practice sheet of varying lines. Keep working from soft to sharp and back again.

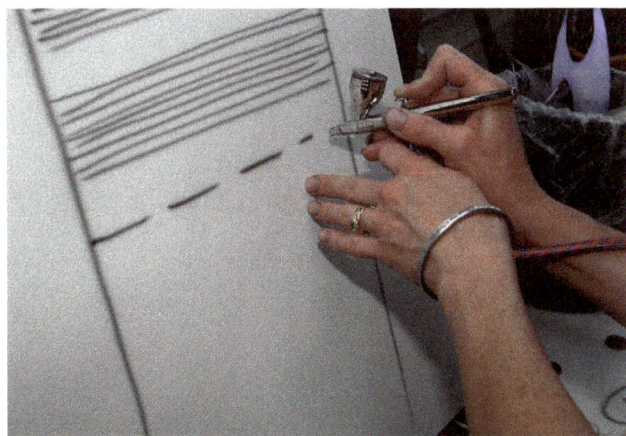

1. Learn intermittent lines, they will pull up your abilities. At the end of a line keep the air flowing and press the trigger towards your surface quickly to stop the paint flow.

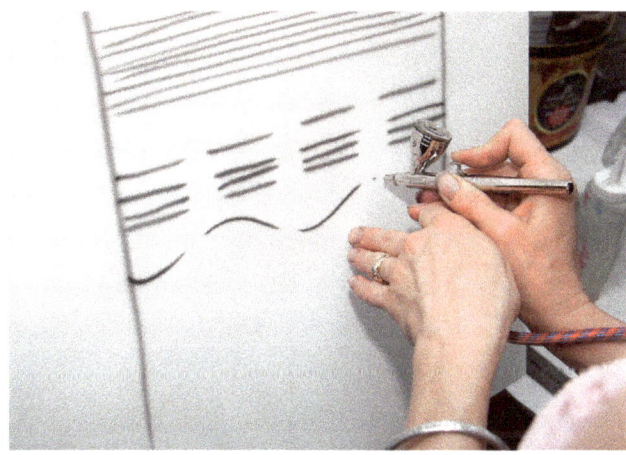

2. Add curves, making a curved dashed line, repeat! Practice this for accuracy. Paint on, paint off, paint on, paint off.

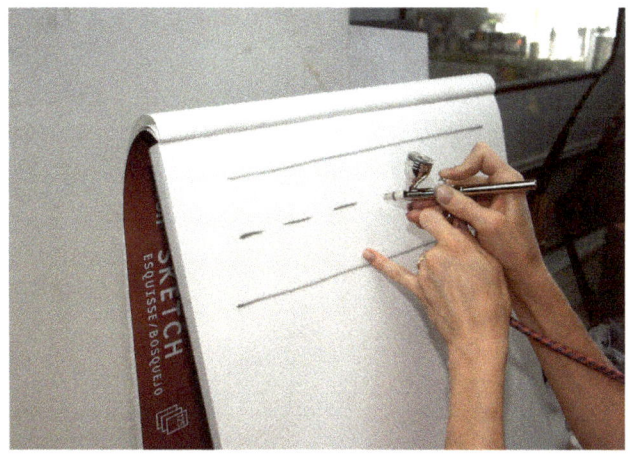

4. Spray guidelines for the next drills. Like your grade school lined paper when you first learned cursive writing.

LINES

With lines it's extra important to move with the hips (note the Posture section farther along) so the brush to paper distance stays constant. You start with the air on, then add the paint while the airbrush is moving, then shut off the paint, not the air, and keep the brush moving past the point where the painting stops. The idea is to stay inside the lines, you have to be robotic about it. As the lines get tighter I get the tip closer with a medium amount of paint.

DASHES

For dashes, keep moving - don't worry about the individual dash, just repeat, repeat, repeat. They don't have to be perfect, keep moving. Dashes are important, you are learning to turn the trigger on and off. Now make them curved.

LOOPS

Make a grid first. Use any old paper for this, you don't have to burn up expensive paper. Learn

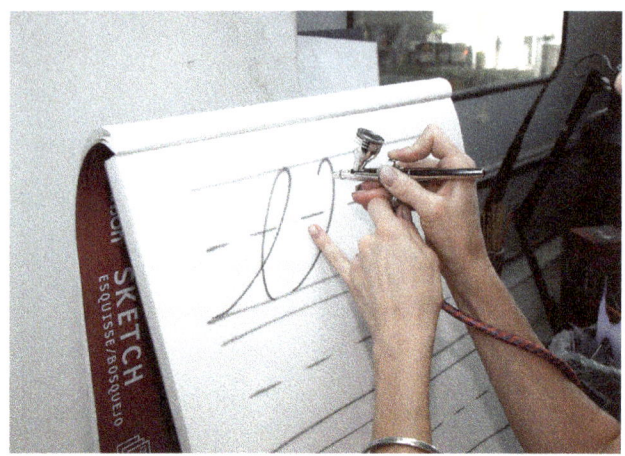

Loops. Use a medium-focus line somewhat close to the surface. At first keep the lines even and consistent.

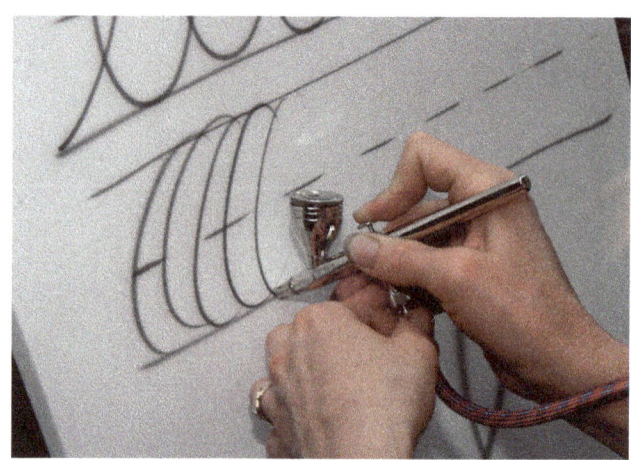

Add to your loops. Try "C" curves, the important part here is focusing on the guidelines, starting and stopping with accuracy.

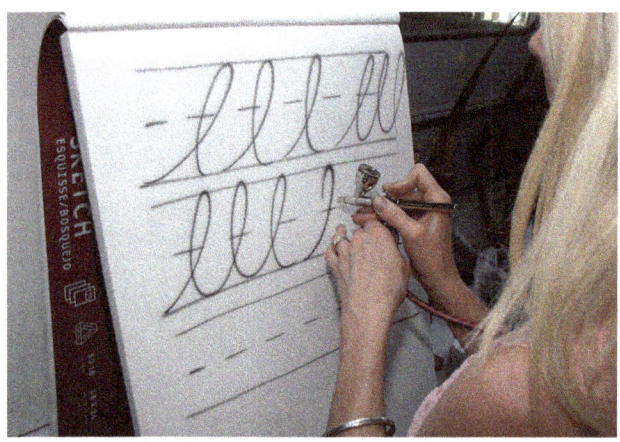

Practice a few rows of loops, then vary your distance to the paper, making the lines thicker and thinner as you go. Try them upside down as well.

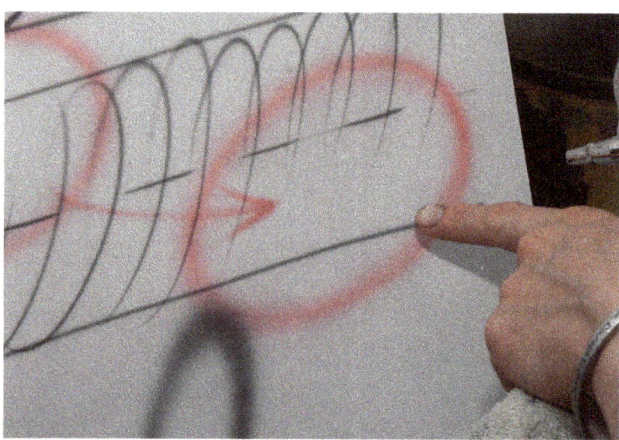

Spraying inverted loops. Continuing the motion, bring the paint to nothing, but continue your motion through the loops. We are eventually shooting for a dagger stroke, with a sharp point.

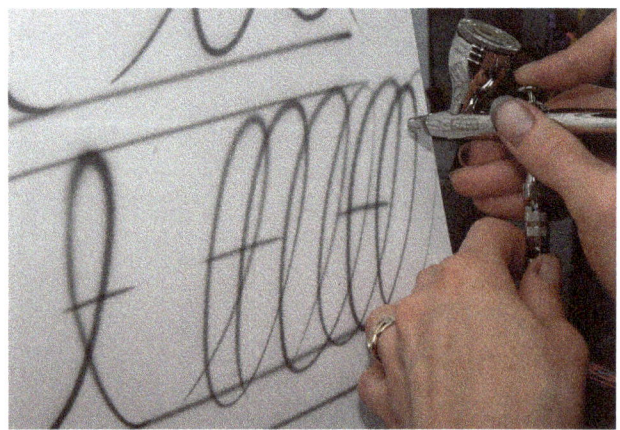

Try these and you will see what I mean by altering your brush-to-surface distance. Make sure that your fingers follow suit and that you spray less paint as you move closer to the surface.

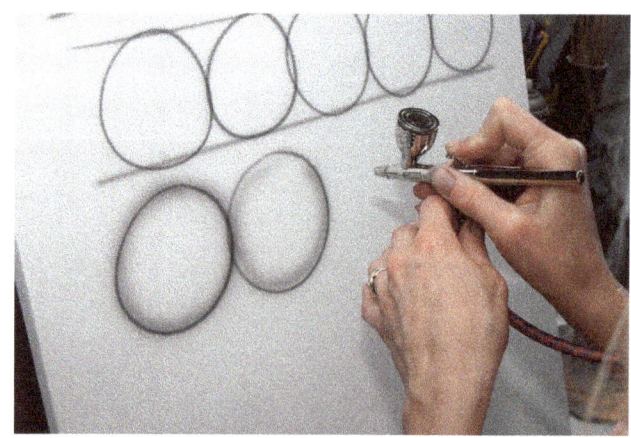

Circles help with accuracy - don't stress if they don't turn out right at first, just keep doing them. Keep them in even rows. Now, spray a softer shadow circle on top of the circles you have already painted.

to do them at a constant size and style first. Then learn to do variations by changing the distance from the gun to the paper. You need to do a lot of both types.

CIRCLES

Learning to paint circles is going to help with control issues. Next we go to half circles and then add some shadowing. All these exercises, circles with both hard and soft edges, will help you learn the various components necessary to create a complete image. Try half circles. I want you to be able to come from each direction and still hit the target area. Practice going from skinny to fat lines, and back and forth.

MORE COMPLEX SHAPES

From circles I like to move students through a series of more difficult shapes. Notice the examples of swirls and stars. Stars provide good practice for stopping and starting. Then try going over them again with shadows. Learn how to do clouds, they are often used in images and they're made up of a series of half circles. And that's the whole point, you have to get good at each of these shapes because each is essential.

POSTURE

I tell my students to always keep their back straight. You might call it working in the Tai Chi zone, you have to keep your arms between your hips and shoulders. Your knees need to stay flexible so the whole body moves. The idea is to be able to move with your legs and hips so the airbrush says 90 degrees to the paper and the airbrush-to-subject distance stays the same.

THE FINAL ANALYSIS

Each one of us is unique. We all have our own talents, strengths and abilities. Each of us have certain things that come easier. Work to strengthen the things that are hard for you and you will go far. In time, what you set your mind to do, if you stick with it that is, is what you will do well. Practice. Go for it! In airbrushing overcoming your short comings is your strength. Enjoy the things that come easy, work hard at the things that don't.

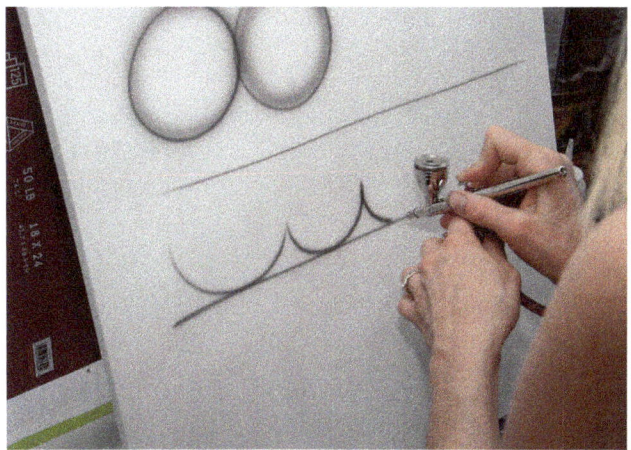

After the circles try scallops, work on starting and stopping your paint to form half circles from every direction.

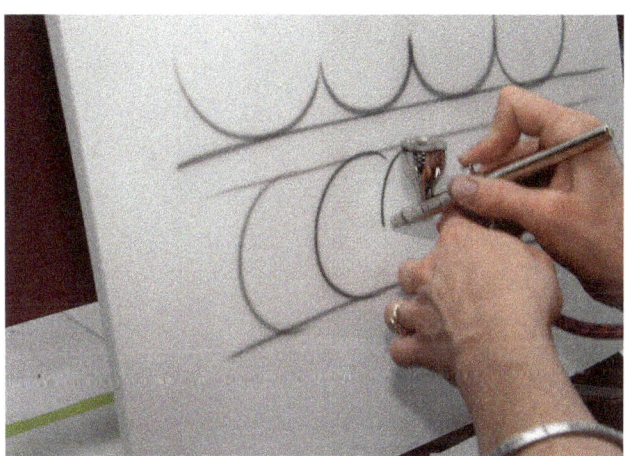

Continuing with the circle theme, paint many on top of each other. Very lightly now, faster and more evenly...

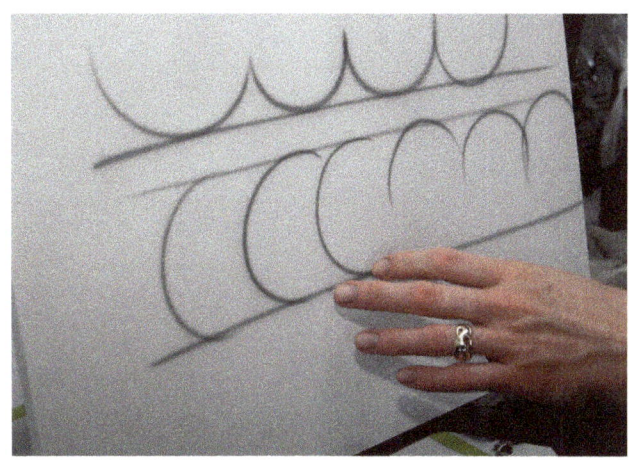

...spray a couple of pages, lightly and subtly. Even allowing the line to disappear at times. Work on subtly here!

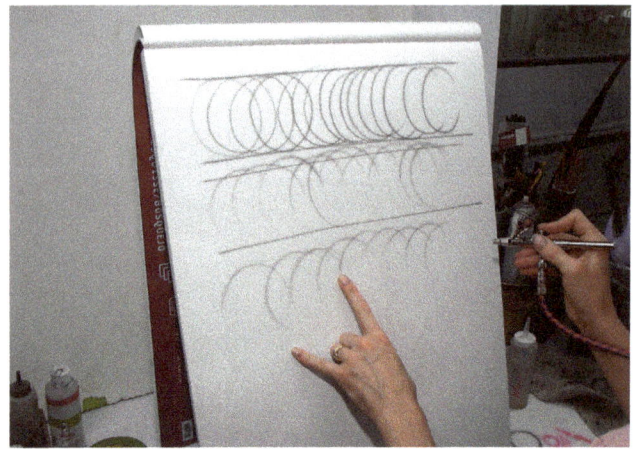

1. Here's my practice sheet...

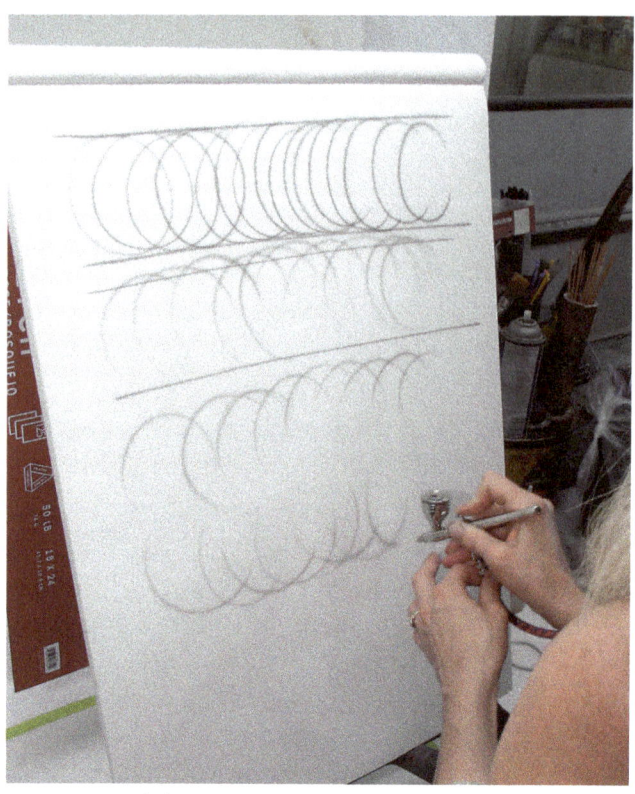

2. ...most of these are sprayed lightly. Again, I sometimes allow the line to fade away completely.

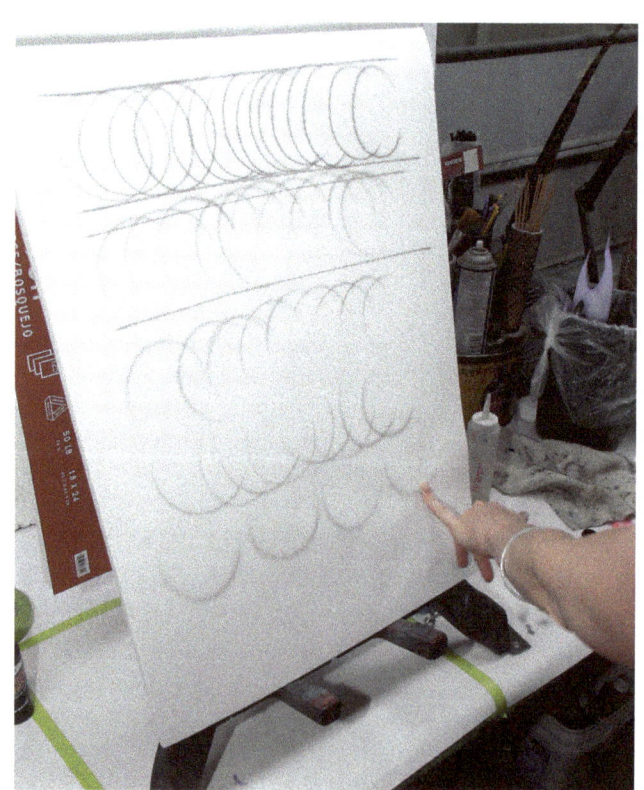

3. Here I'm starting into another series of partial circles.

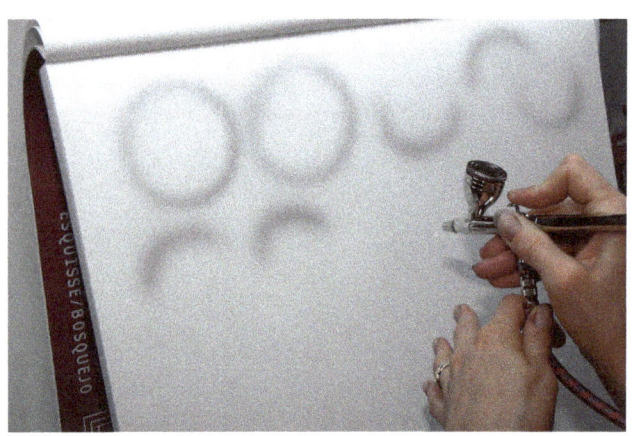

4. Now do shadow circles only. Vary these into partial circles. For the softer fade you are holding the brush farther away from the surface and using a medium amount of paint - up to a few inches away.

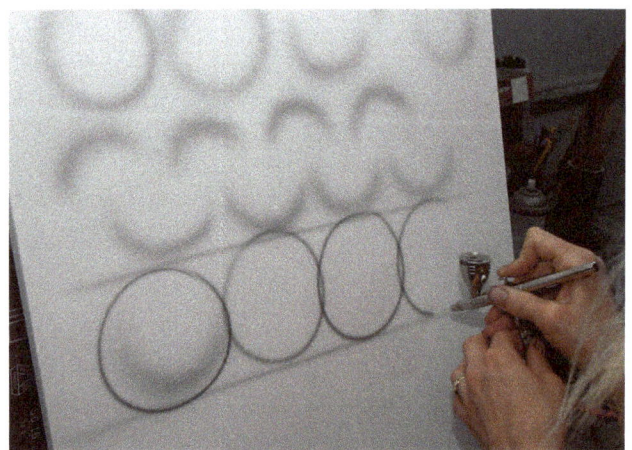

5. Now go back to your circles and add the shadows to the solid circles, which make them simple spheres.

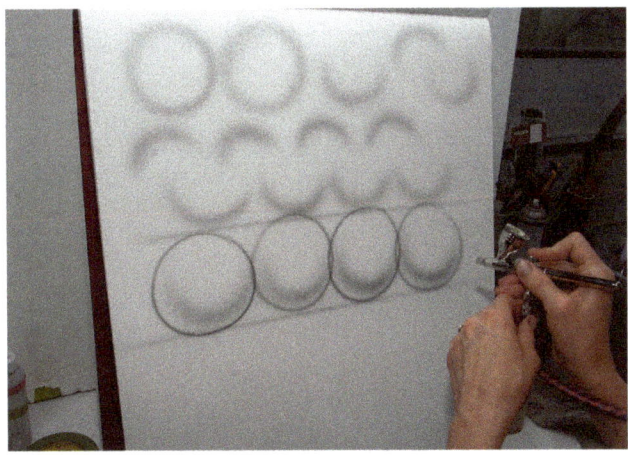

To make it appear as if they are lit from the top, spray your thicker shadow just above the bottom edge.

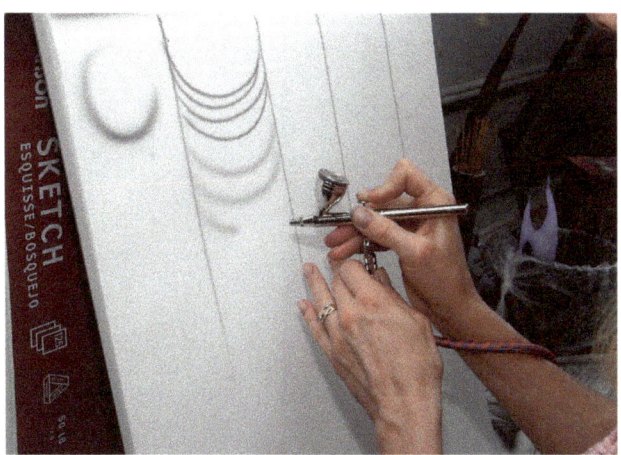

Spray a series of vertical guide lines. Do semi-circles this time, don't continue the motions into a full circle.

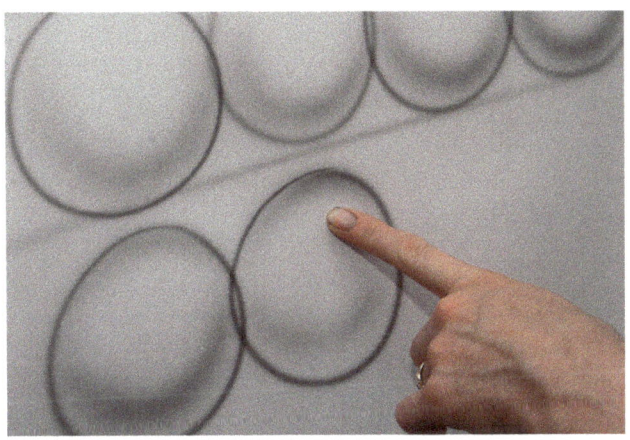

For an extra detail, spray right at the top, creating a little shadow directly on the line.

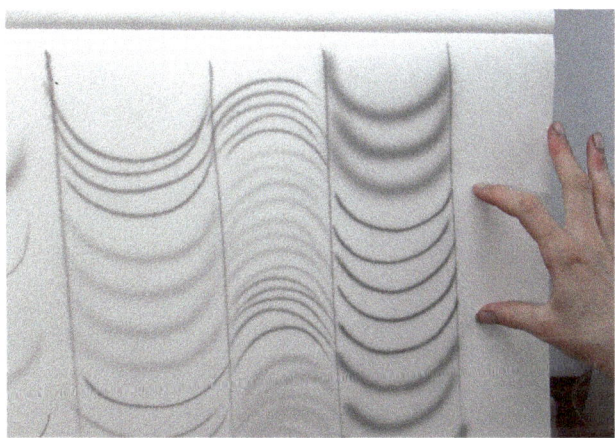

Make these targeted semi circles, starting and stopping paint flow (leave the air on). Vary from light sharp lines to soft, fatter lines, and to hard solid lines. Do a repetition pattern of 3 or so at a time.

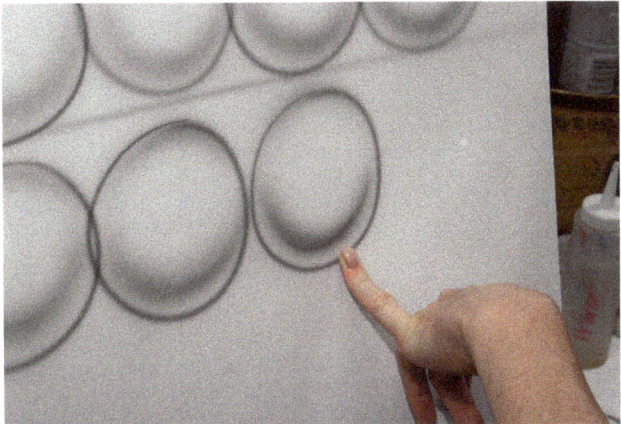

Keep painting a few of these and play around with the details.

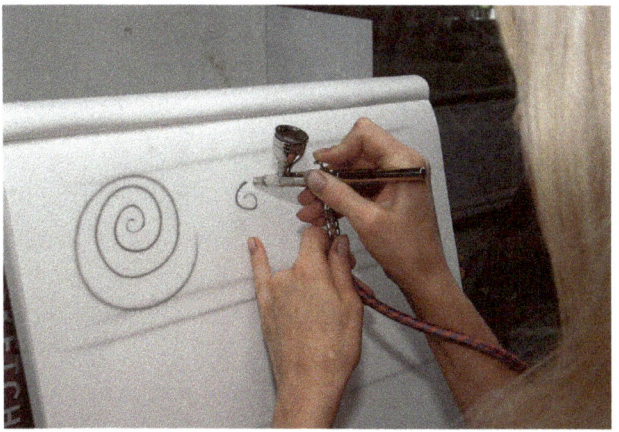

Swirls. Starting as subtly as possible, do these swirls clockwise and counter clock wise. Now do it again. Paint some coming in from the outside to the center - those are harder for me.

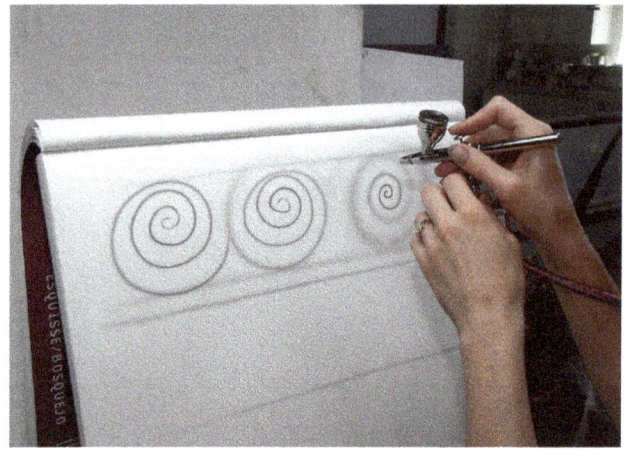

Relax and enjoy, do you have some great music playing?

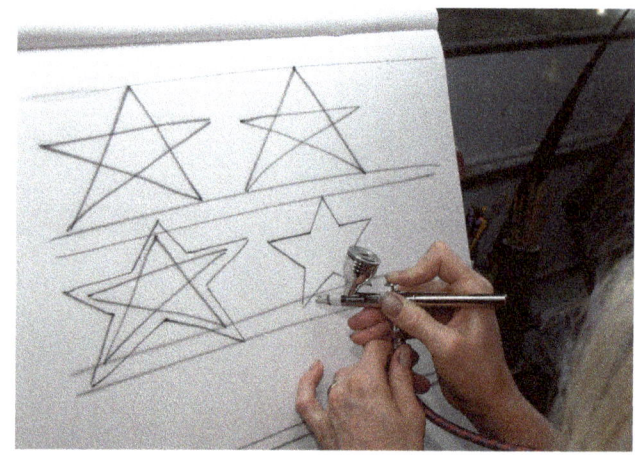

Here are a few things you can do with the star pattern to hone your start-stop skills. For the first ones, make each segment a separate line.

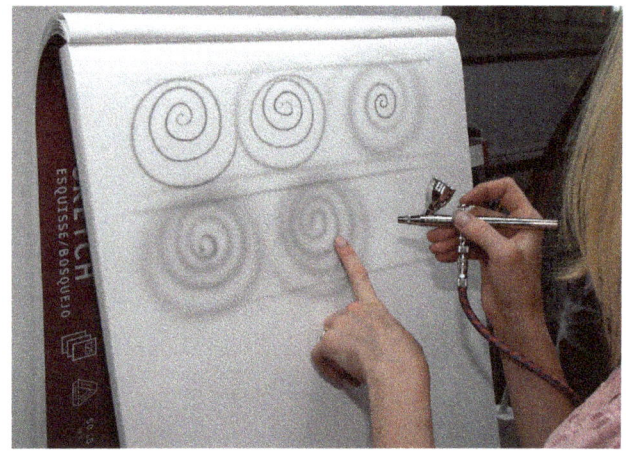

Spray these in a soft even shadow color as well.

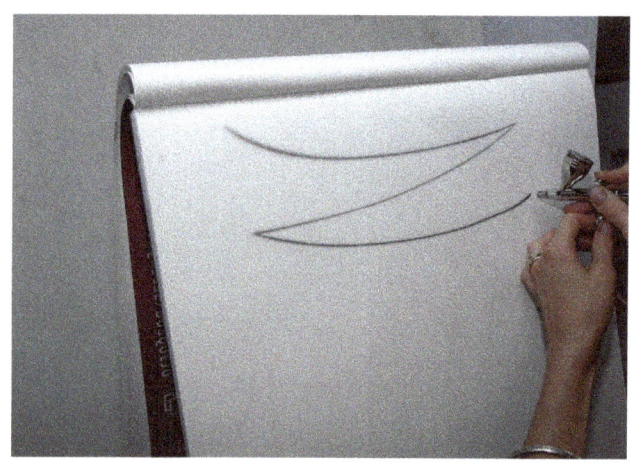

Try ziggy zaggies. Pick up speed on these as you go.

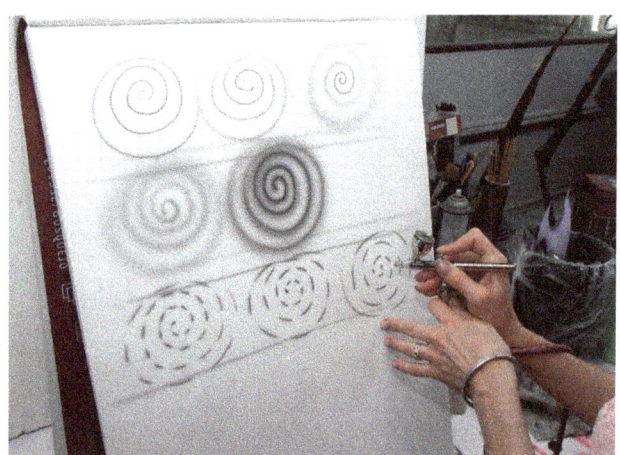

Now that you have this pattern down, try it with dashes, paint on - off, on - off. Keep the air on at all times though. Like walking and chewing gum.

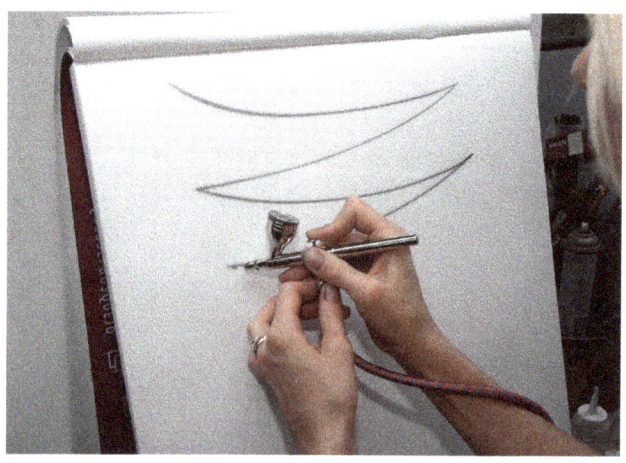

When you reach your turning around point, make it a point or a dagger tip. Then start your next segment. Get close and use less paint.

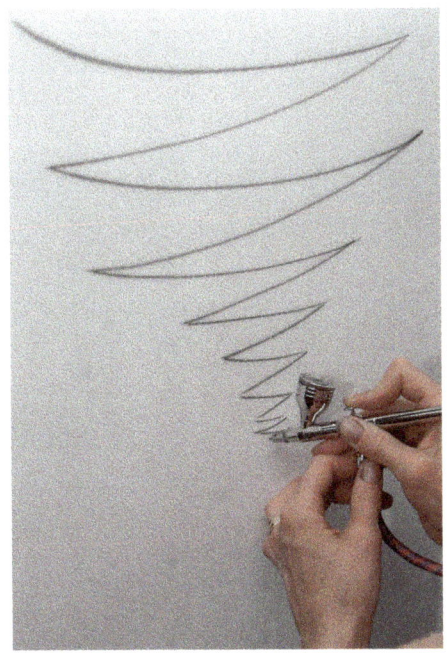

Start large, get smaller, and then turn that around - small to large.

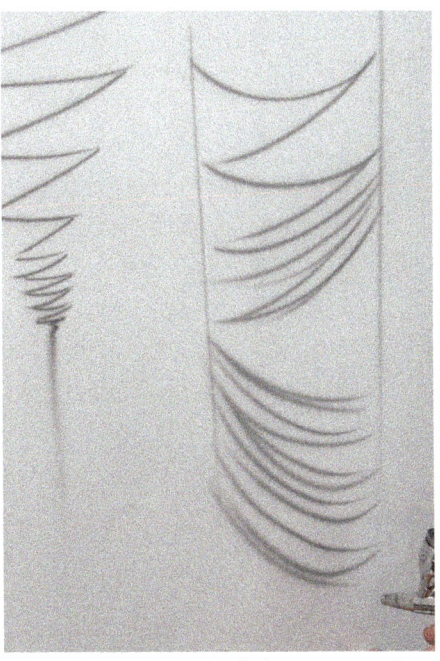

On this picture, and the one on the right, you can see how I went back and forth. Tighter zig zags...

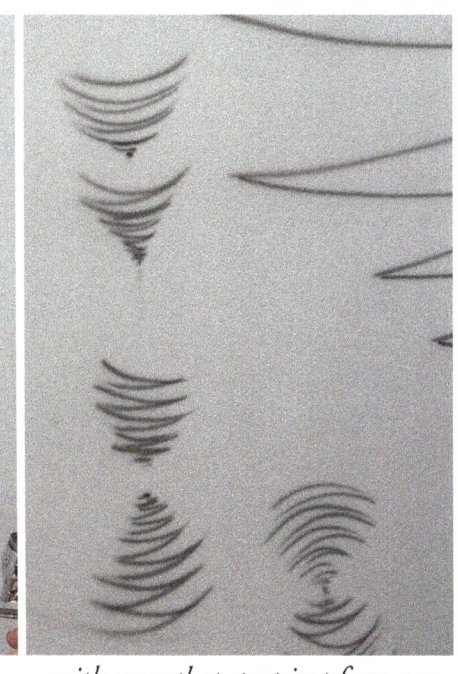

...with some that start just from one direction, and variations done with curved lines.

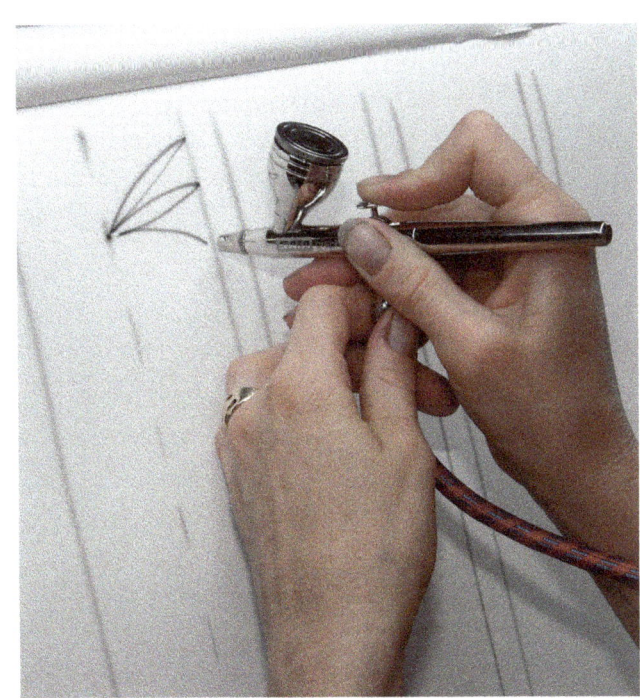

Now try curved lines, wider to a small dot and back again. Stay within the guidelines.

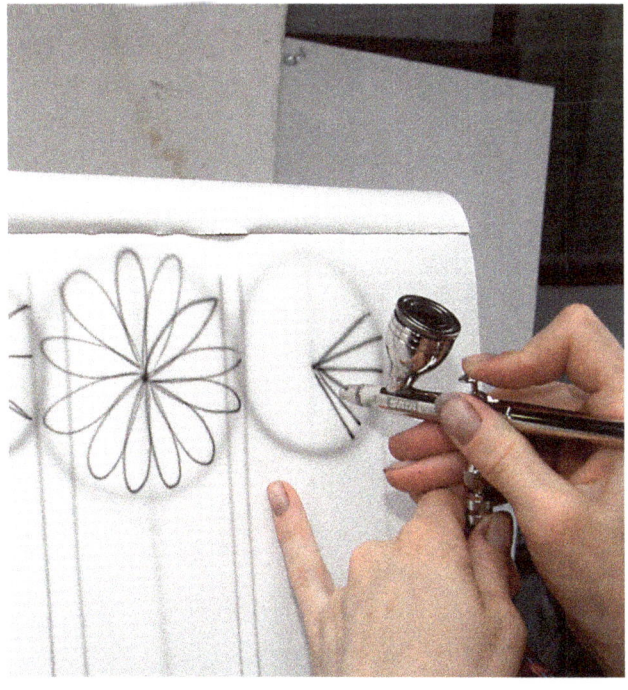

Starting with a center dot, make a daisy-like pattern, returning to that center point. Now you are really getting the hang of it.

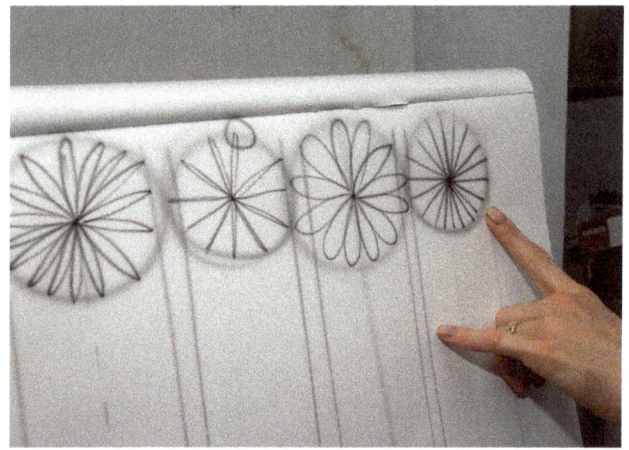

Here you can see the daisy pattern I made using alternating loops and lines.

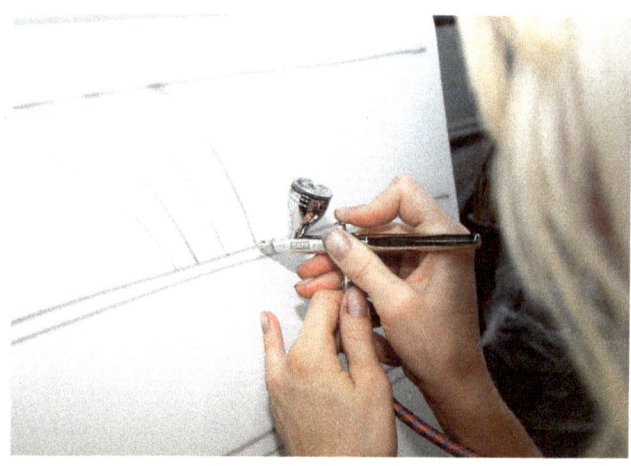

...and gradually get very close at the bottom before I stop my paint. I am looking for a dagger-like end to these strokes.

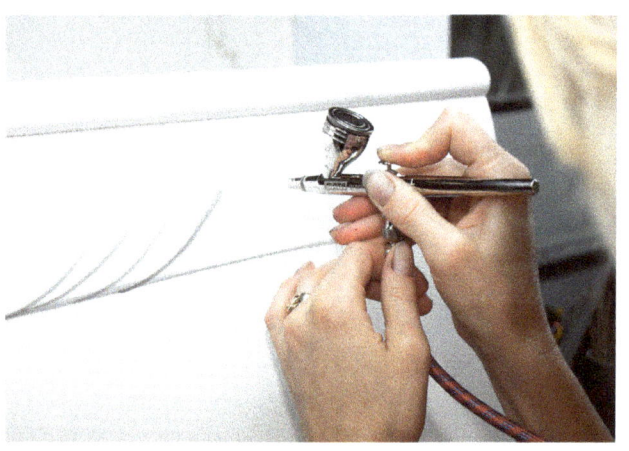

Back to one direction using a base line. Spray from the line up, using continuing motion, stopping the paint while keeping the air on. Good trigger control needs to become second nature.

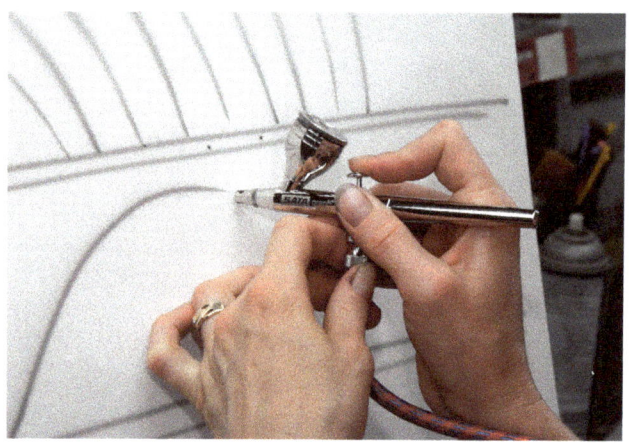

Try one big long loose arch. You know these are a lot of practice drills I am showing you. Take your time with these, split the lessons up into sections that you can do over different days or separate sittings.

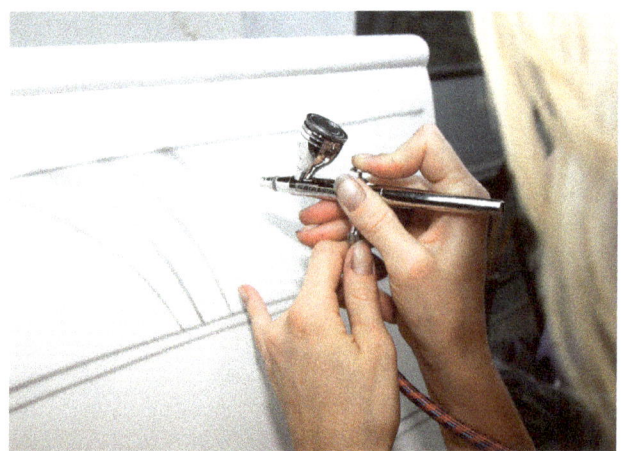

Here I go from the top down, staying within the guide lines. I start out holding the airbrush farther away from the paper...

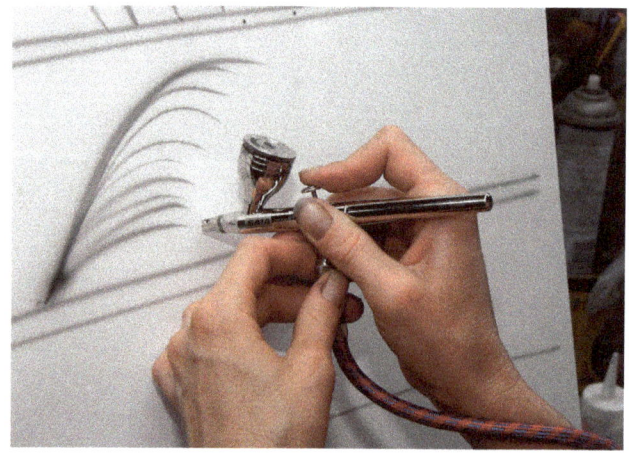

Now, pull a series of dagger stokes out of this line.

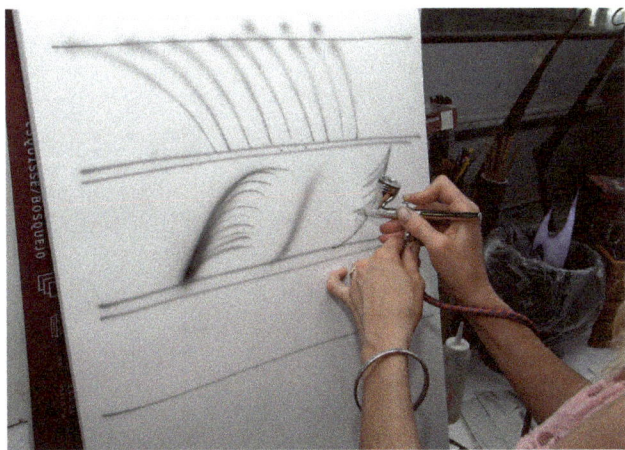

These are starting to look like thick hair or lashes, or barbs of a feather.

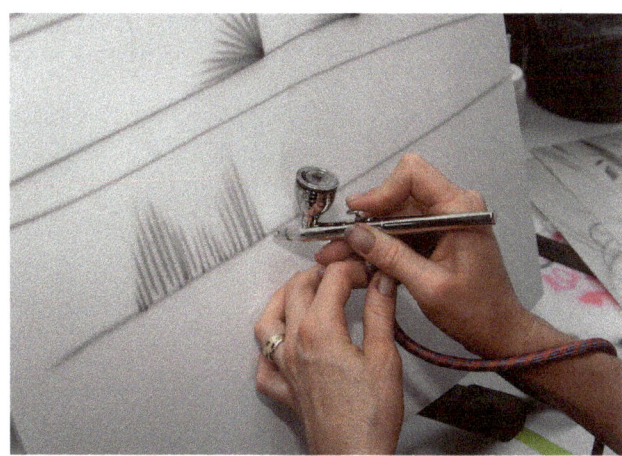

Now work from a a horizontal line going upward, varying the height in a systematic pattern. You are getting there.

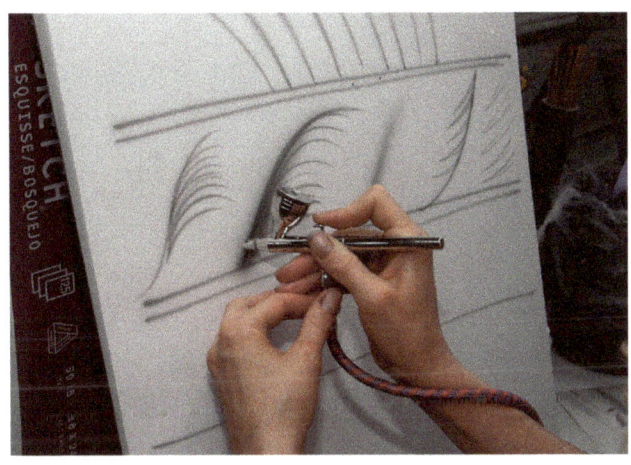

Practice these from many different directions, with and without shading.

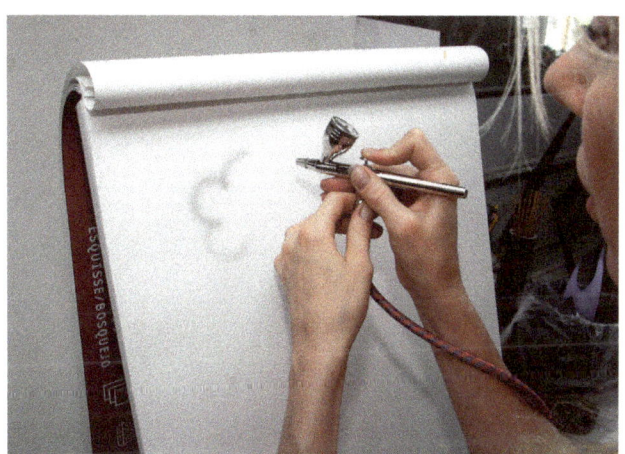

Time for something different - you know changing it up stretches your skill.

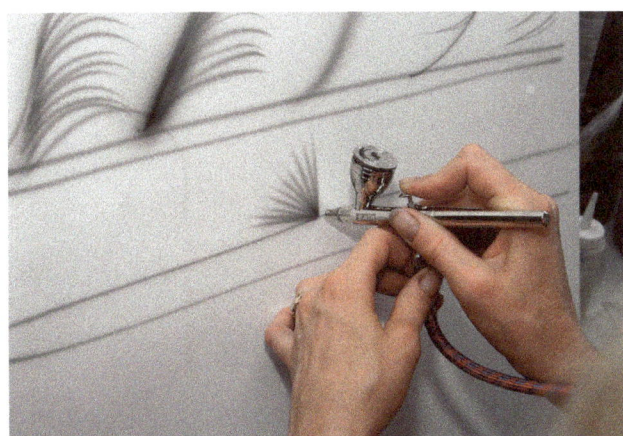

Now start from a point and fan out - you have to vary the distance and the amount of paint. Good trigger control is essential. Reducing the paint (keeping the air on) while moving closer to the surface gives us that dagger stroke.

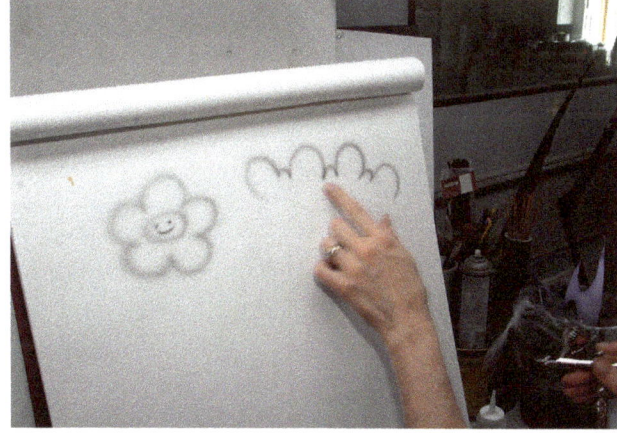

Soft scallops please, we are looking for evenness and a softer feel, but also a fair amount of color. Vary these soft scallops from small to larger.

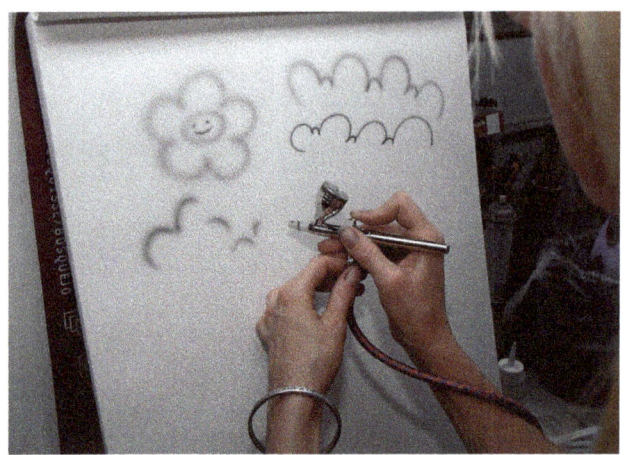

Break these up into soft, but even dashes.

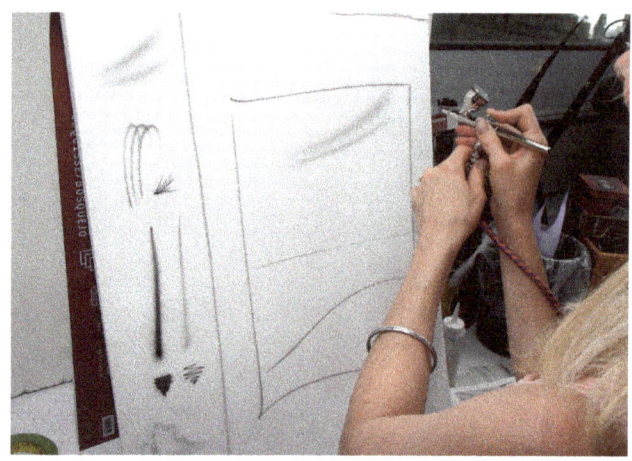

I have my individual elements on the left, take a look. We are going to combine these into a composition.

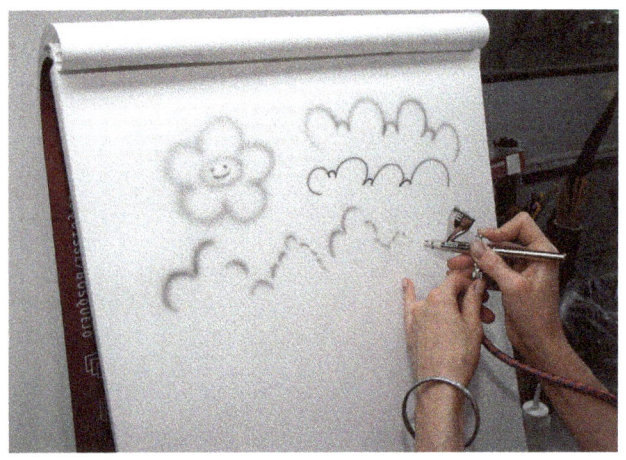

Work in ranges from dark to very soft, to the point where they're almost not there.

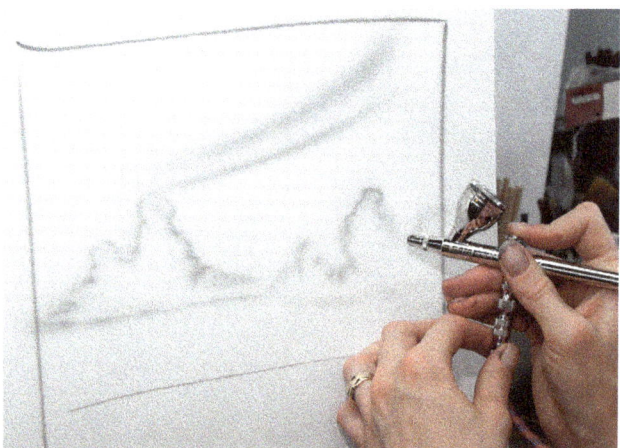

Two soft dashes form soft clouds. Under that make some semi-circle thunder clouds and under that a straight horizon line in about the middle of the page.

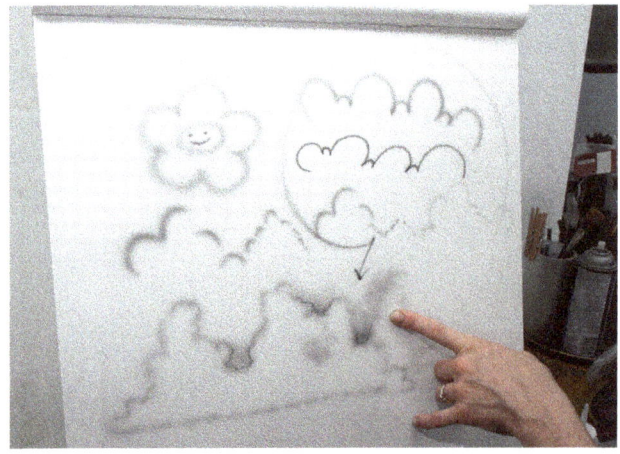

Form the components into soft cloud-like patterns, now come back and fill in the background with some color.

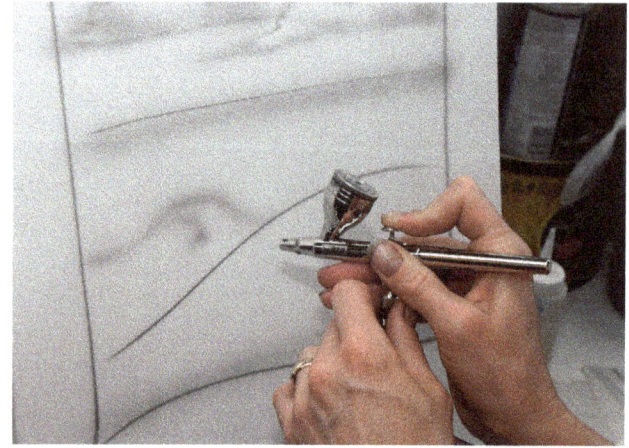

The curve represents a dune. Behind that I create a soft, rough wave.

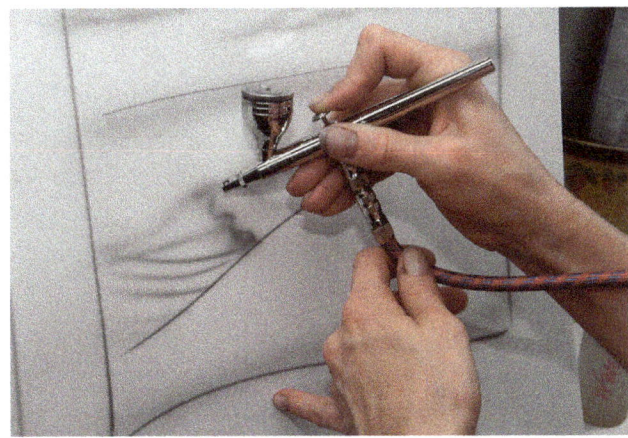

Working on the wave, I painted a few wavy lines and shadowed them. Then a darker horizontal line with ripples coming under that.

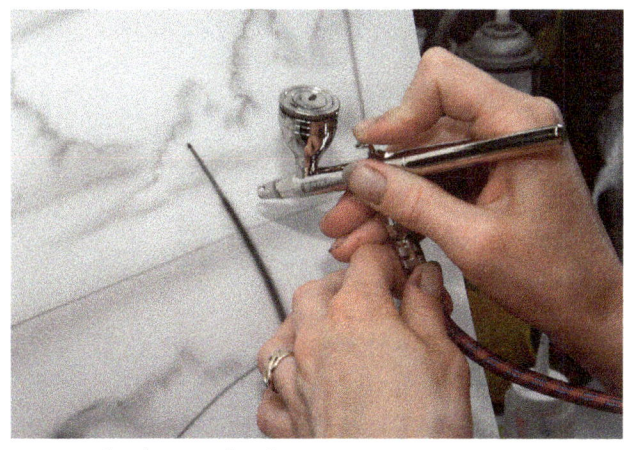

I come back over this line one or two more times to darken and thicken it. Some people work in heavier lines, I would suggest starting lighter and building the line up gradually.

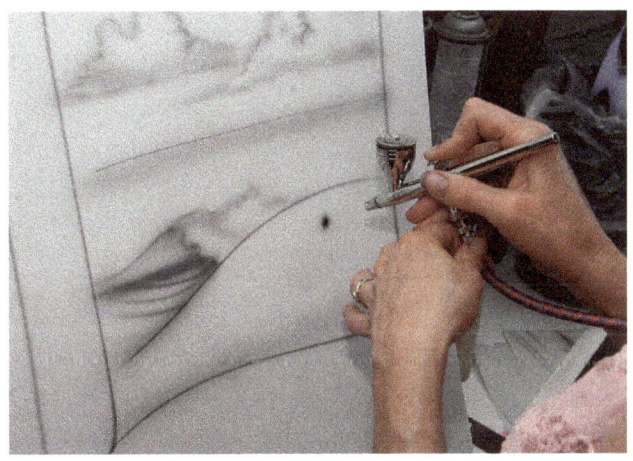

On the right of center of my dune I start with a dot, then spray a fairly heavy line...

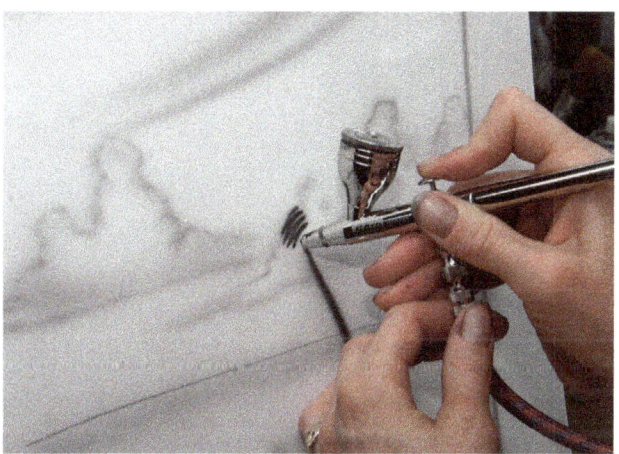

Next, spray a tight small zig zag triangle at the top of the stalk.

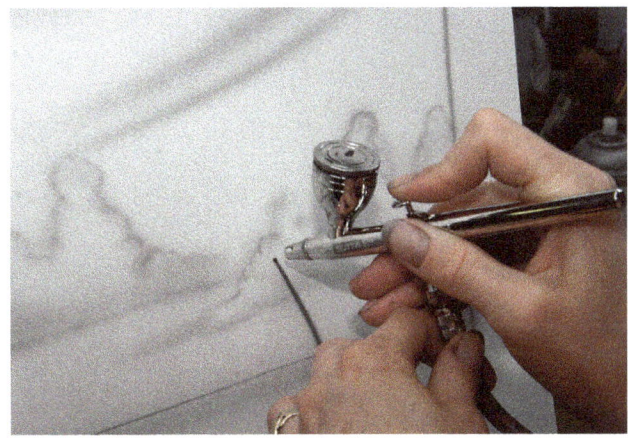

...leading up to a tiny dagger tip.

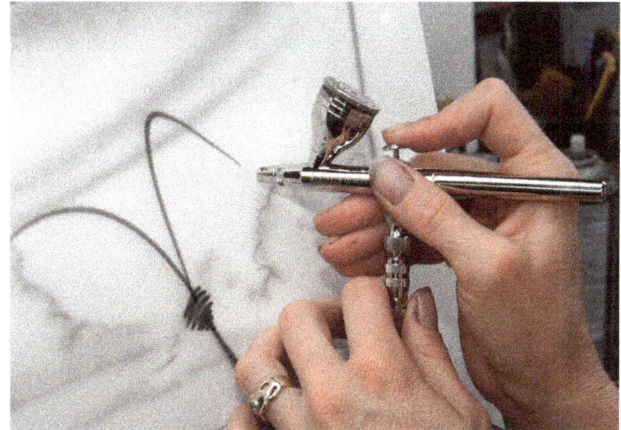

Spray about 5 front stalks out of our zig zag triangle at the top of the palm tree trunk. I won't tell you what this stuff is until after we do it so you concentrate on line and technique - rather than "object."

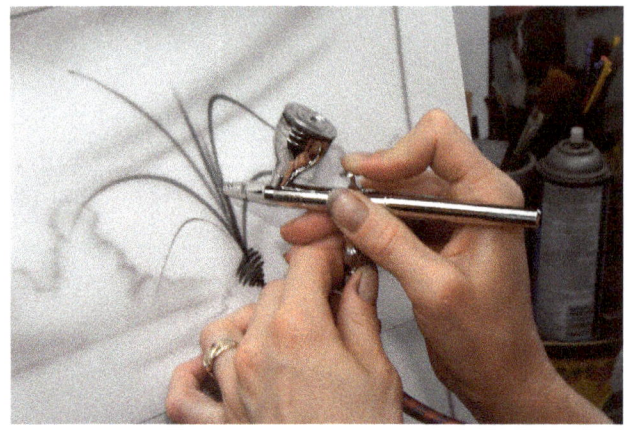

Now that we have our stalks we will add many little dagger stokes as palm fronds...

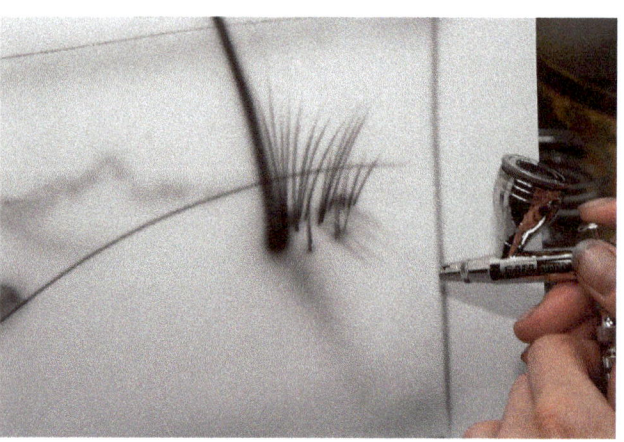

In the sand dune I sprayed a soft shadow coming out from the tree trunk to the right. In the sand next to the tree I add daggers coming up out of the sand, and I shadow this grass as well.

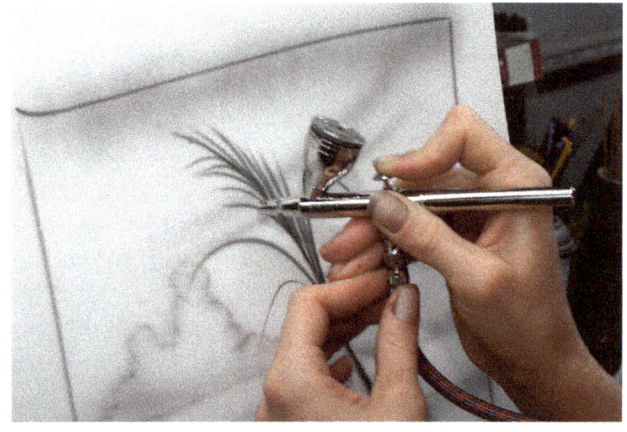

...on this first stalk spray, many small lash lines from the center of the stalk. Give it some personality, balanced with control and consistency. Balance of opposing elements is something I emphasize.

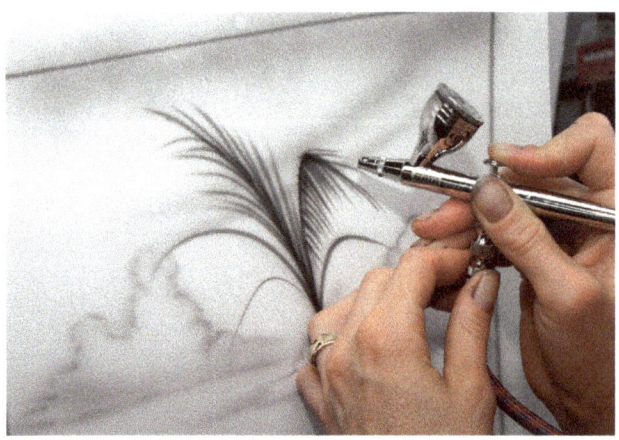

On this second stalk I mostly spray downward hanging dagger strokes with a few accent ones on the top side.

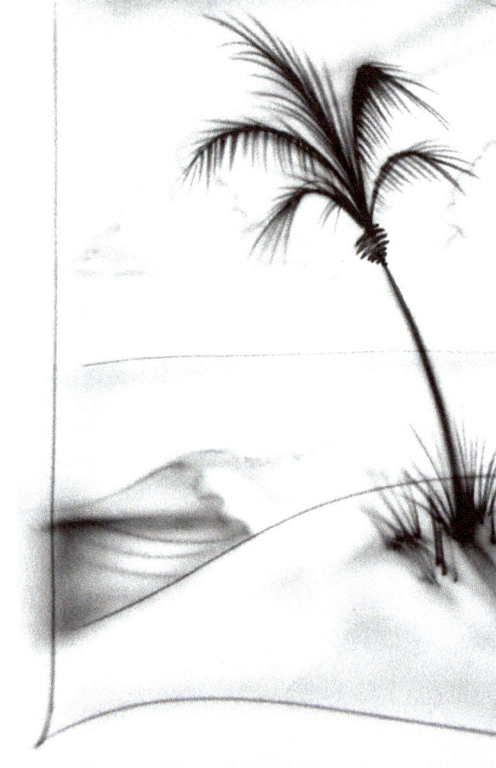

Continue with a shadow softly across the top. Stand back and take a look. The basic skills we picked up are all a part of this picture. Now you can practice all of the strokes without relying on just drills and exercises.

Leah Gall Q&A

How long have you been doing, airbrush art?

I've been doing this for 19 years.

I started at a flea market in Florida, airbrushing all kinds of images onto almost anything. That evolved into a lot of T-shirt painting, and then I graduated to working booths during Bike Week in Daytona doing lots of helmets and jackets. Eventually, I ended up in the Twin Cities.

What kind of painting experience did you have prior to airbrushing?

My mom helped me out with finger painting as a kid. And it was my dad who bought me the first airbrush. I did paint in high school, and my Dad had a body shop so I got some automotive experience there. In fact I used to mix paint for my Dad, and I still like to create my own colors.

What's the biggest job you've done so far?

The classes that I teach are the most important thing I've done. They are important because I like to help people and I like to share what I know.

What inspires you?

Renaissance art, classical art, the old Roman and Greek architecture, the sculptures on the buildings, human body sculptures, and all of God's creations.

Any tips for the beginner?

When you fall down, get up again and again and again.

What brands of paint do you prefer?

For cars and motorcycles I use urethane-based automotive paint, mostly the X-otic brand. For water-based work I like paint from Auto-Air.

How long have you been teaching the classes and do they take place at your studio?

I've been teaching for three years. Sometimes I travel and sometimes I do them here. A class can be as small as one student, or it can be a typical small group, but I really do enjoy them. It's nice to have interaction with the students.

Any final words of advice for a novice airbrush artist?

Stick to your guns.

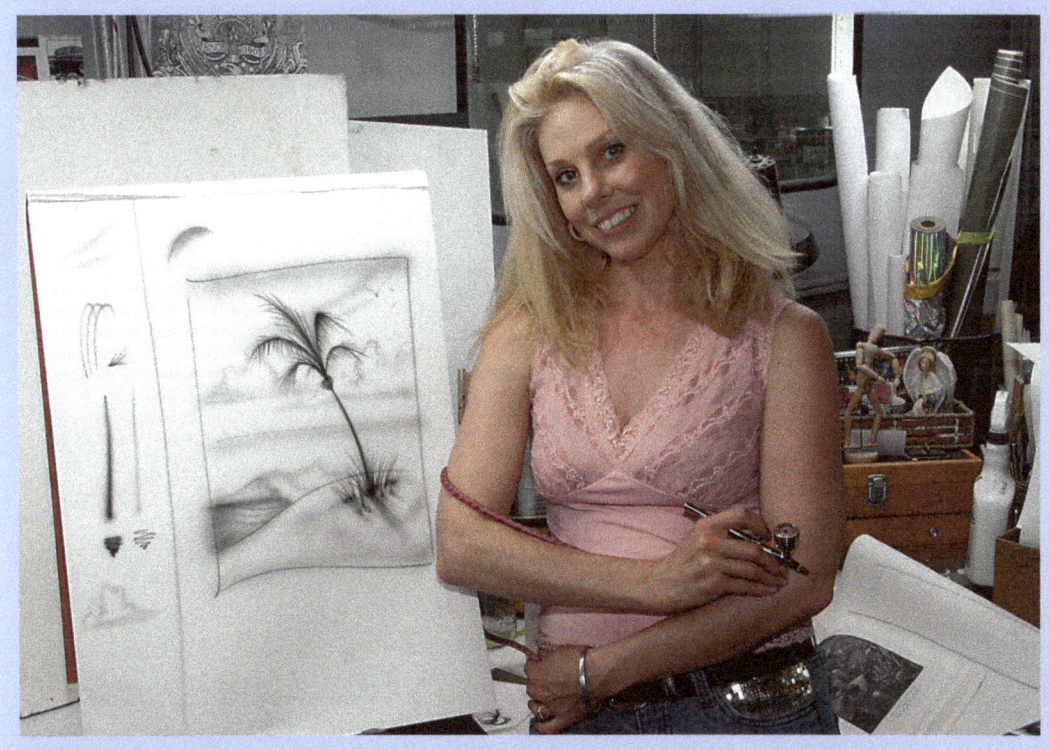

A very versatile artist, Leah Gall is as comfortable working on an art print with water-based paint as she is doing a mural down the side of an old hot rod with urethane.

Chapter Two

Tom Nguyen

A Pencil Drawing with Color

Until a few years ago, the closest Tom Nguyen came to doing pin-up work was drawing Wonder Woman panels for DC Comics. Creating comics requires great drawing skills, and it is these drawing sills that underlie Tom's pin-up images. Less than ten years ago, Tom decided to combine his drawing skills with his airbrushing skills to create a unique pin-up style.

While some pin-up artists do only a cursory outline of the image, Tom's images are fully

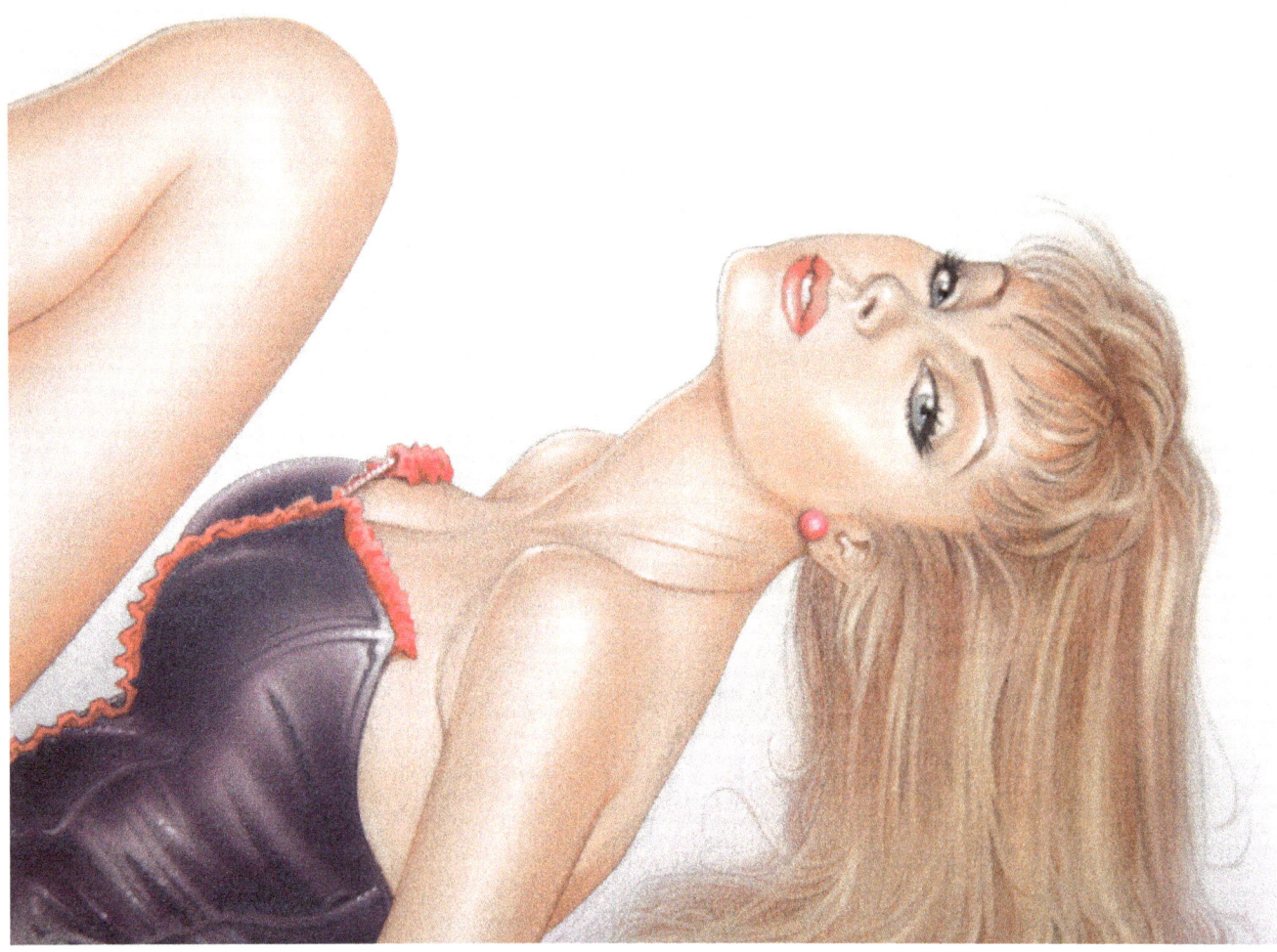

To create a sexy pin-up image you need photos of a great pin-up model - Jacki Morrison in this case.

drawn pin-ups before he starts in with the airbrush. And, instead of completely covering the pencil work, the use of transparent paint means some of the drawing can be seen under the paint even after the image is totally finished.

Like a lot of artists, Tom spends long days in his small studio. The release in this case is the gym in the garage. "I was a regular at the local gym," explains Tom. "When they announced they were going out of business I asked if I could buy some of the equipment." For Tom, body building is not only a healthy alternative to long hours at the drawing board, it also gives him a very good understanding of what muscles really look like. "Being a body builder helps me to understand body structure and muscles, and how they change as the body moves. The understanding helps with both my cartoon and my pin-up work."

Despite Tom's success with pin-ups, painting the winners of various beauty pageants in both Minnesota and Wisconsin, in addition to images like that seen here, cartoon work still forms the foundation of his work. Currently, the pin-up work is only twenty percent of Tom's work.

If body building helps Tom draw and paint the perfect pin-up body, it's three summers spent doing caricatures at the local amusement park that serve as the foundation for his ability to capture the magic in a model's face. "Working summers at the park was really good training," explains Tom. "When it comes to the faces, I don't have to be a slave to that projected image, I'm able to simply draw the image, and I can embellish it slightly if I want to."

Working with Tom for four days as he developed this image turned out to be a pretty easy assignment. With the TV in the corner providing a quiet soundtrack, Tom works with a certain ease. Though multiple deadlines loom on any given day, there's a nice vibe in the studio, a sense that this is what Tom is good at, what he is supposed to be doing – drawing cartoons and pin-ups, one panel at a time.

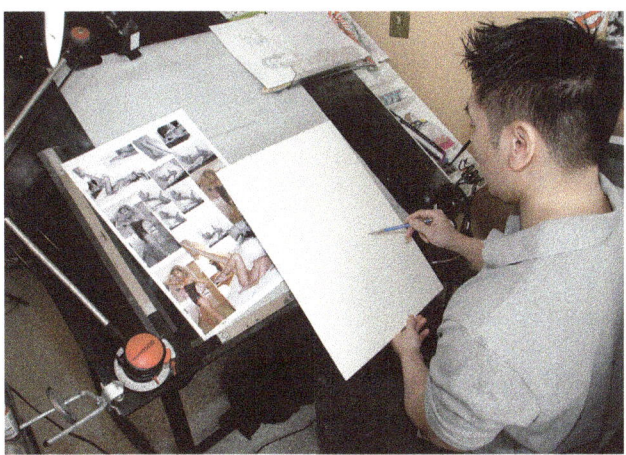

I begin by printing out the reference material on one sheet. Then I begin roughing in the figure on the cold-press illustration board, picking out the best elements from each photo. Drawing lead is normal HB.

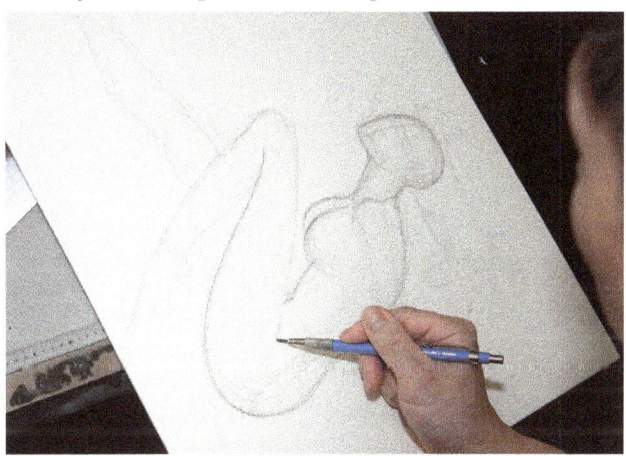

Here I focus on proper construction of the figure and curves. It's important to capture the overall essence as opposed to worrying about little details here. At this stage I can exaggerate certain aspects.

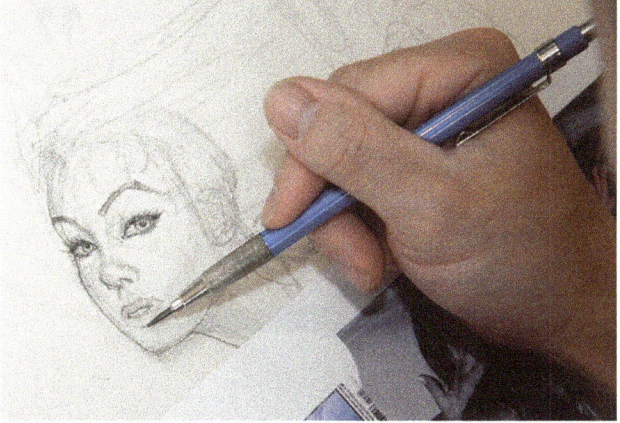

The most important things to me are the face and hands. If I don't get these right, the drawing is as good as dead. Here I'm refining Jacki's face to get a good likeness and proper proportion.

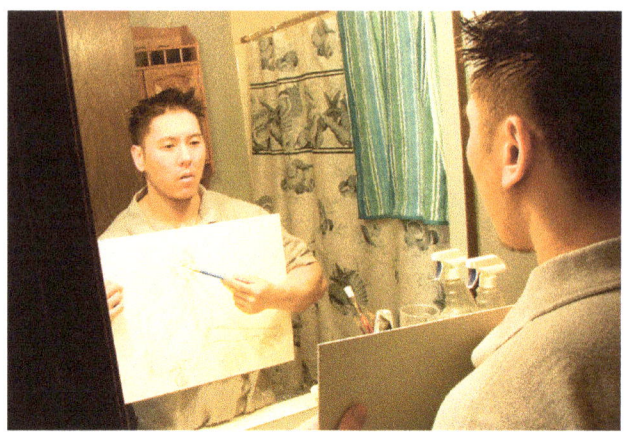

I'm using the good old trick of looking in the mirror to help me spot glaring errors in my drawing. Reversing your art will give you a different perspective, one that your eyes aren't used to.

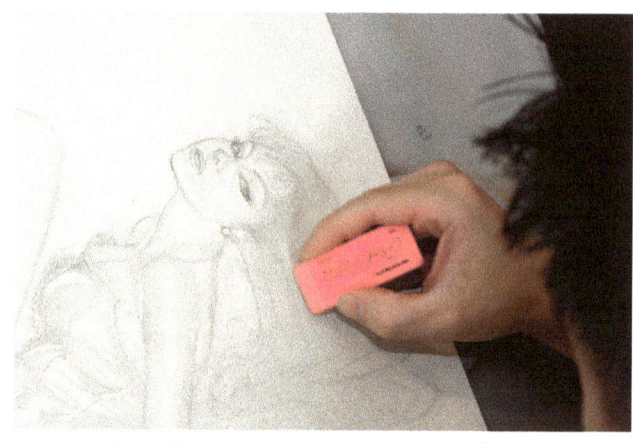

For the hair I'm using the edge of a Pink Pearl eraser which is a good compromise between the abrasive hard electric eraser and the gentler kneaded eraser.

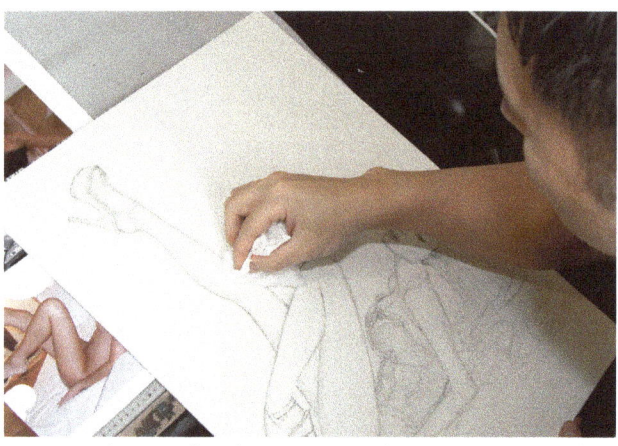

Using a lump of toilet paper (toilet paper!), I gently wipe it all over the drawing in order to purposely smear the graphite around. Although this knocks down the contrast, it also creates a soft gray "wash."

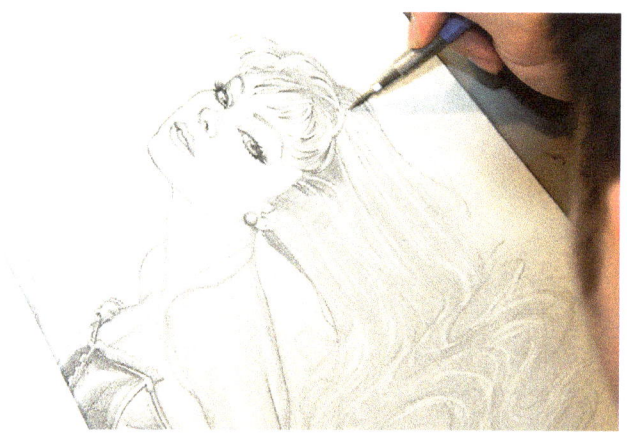

Here I'm going back in with pencil to redefine sharp, dark details that I lost during the smudging stage. At this stage you can really begin to see the pencil art "pop" as the contrast is enhanced.

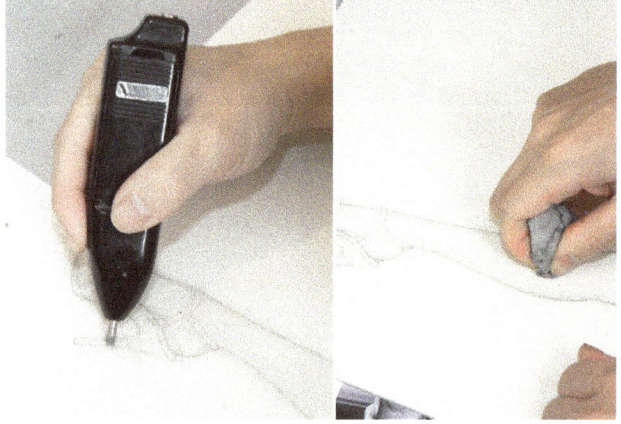

Because of the previous step, I can now use various erasers to create light/highlighted areas on the figure. The electric eraser is good for small details; the kneaded eraser is better for broader, softer highlights.

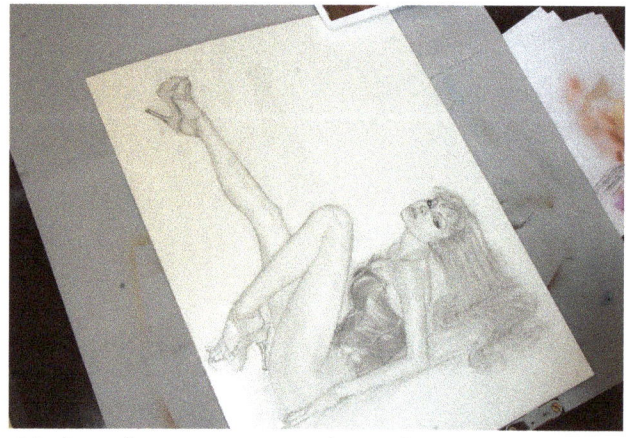

My least favorite stage: applying the matte, low-tack sheet of frisket film and cutting out all the pieces necessary to create masking. Masks are cut for each leg/shoe, the corset, and the entire upper body above the corset - the hair and arm are not separated.

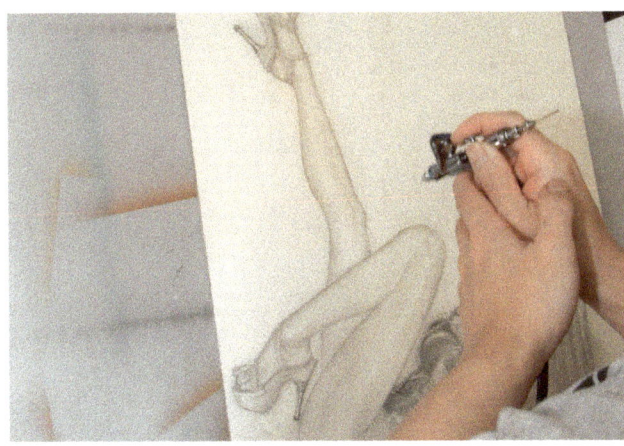

Revealing the back leg first, I spray a very light coat of my pre-mixed flesh tone color. It's important not to get too involved and heavy-handed now - I'm just trying to get some semblance of color on the work.

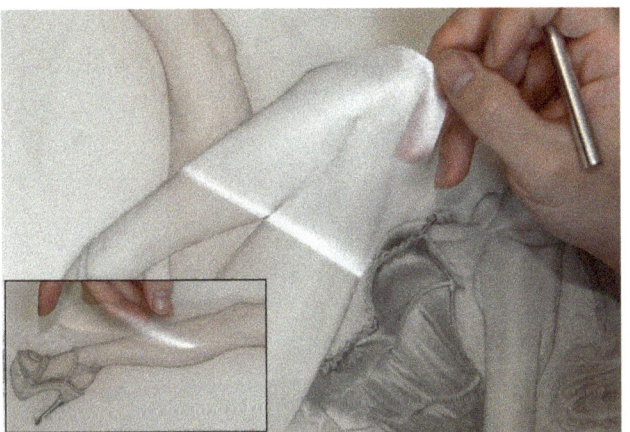

I remask the back leg (to prevent overspray from painting other areas), and reveal the front leg...

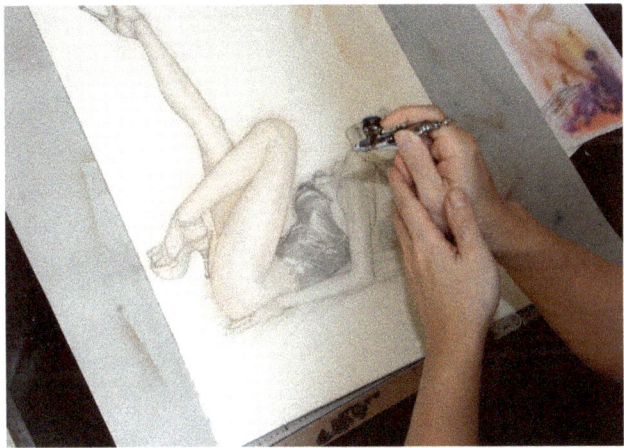

...I now spray the front leg in the same manner as the first leg - with a very light general misting.

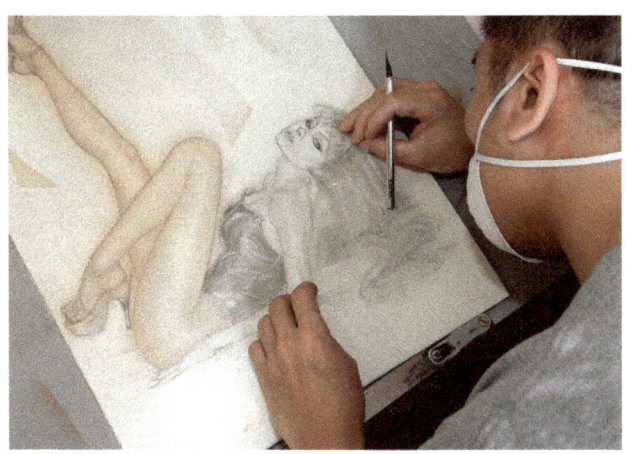

After I remask the front leg, I move on to the upper body and uncover the entire upper body skin areas. You can see that I'm wearing a dust mask so as not to inhale the paint spray.

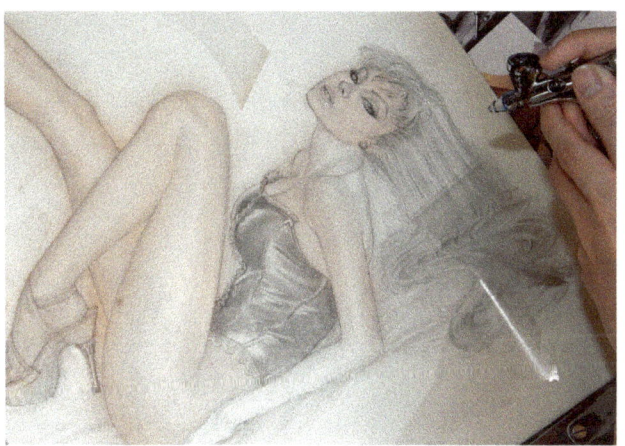

Again, I'm doing a light general spray over the face and shoulders. Remember that I didn't cut a separate mask for the hair to separate it from the skin. This way I don't get a hard transition at the hairline.

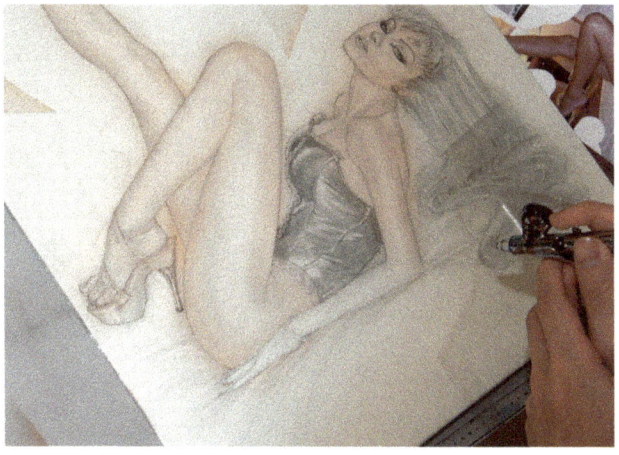

Still working on the upper body, I proceed down to her supporting arm to add a light coat of color.

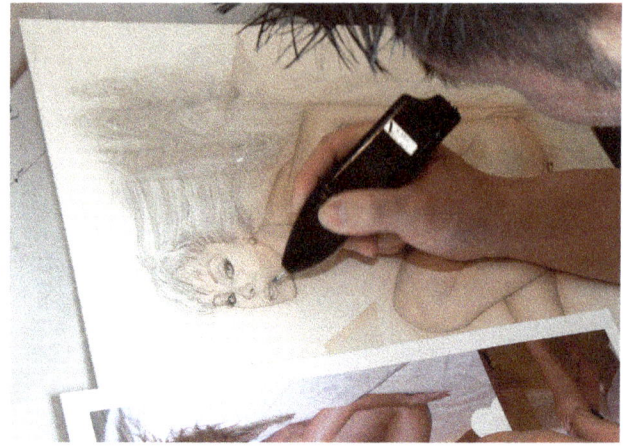

After the first layer of flesh color is applied to the entire piece, I begin erasing highlights. This is like erasing highlights after smudging the graphite.

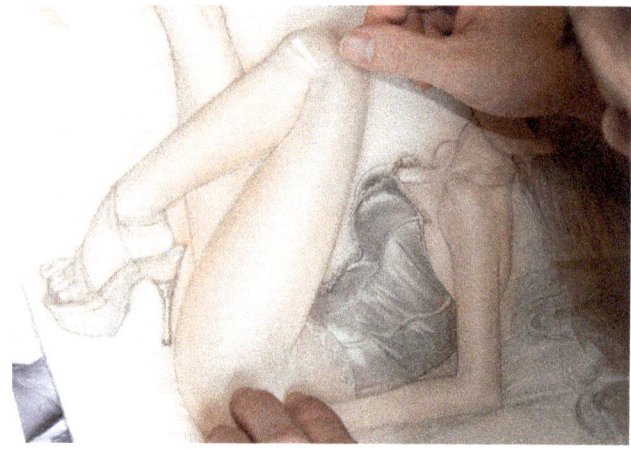

Moving on to peeling the frisket off the front leg again to repeat the erasing.

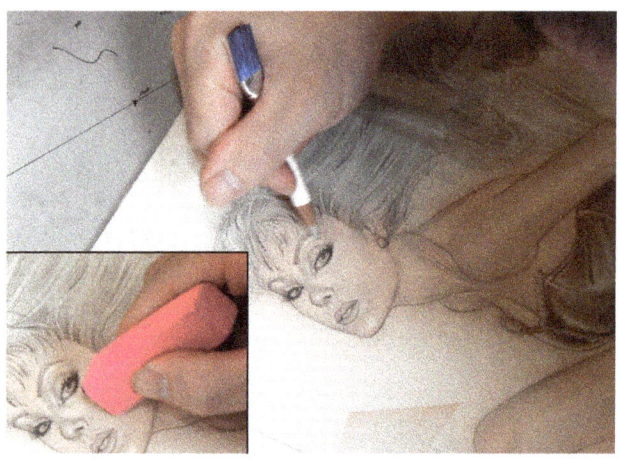

In the main photo I'm using a typewriting eraser called an Eraserstik. It's very abrasive and takes small areas of paint off well, especially in faces.

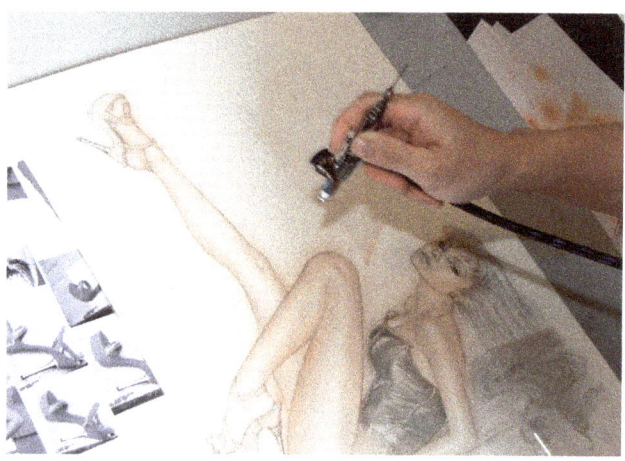

I've remasked the painting except for the back leg. Using my flesh color again, I begin spraying my second round of paint. This time I'm a little closer and more particular with where I'm spraying.

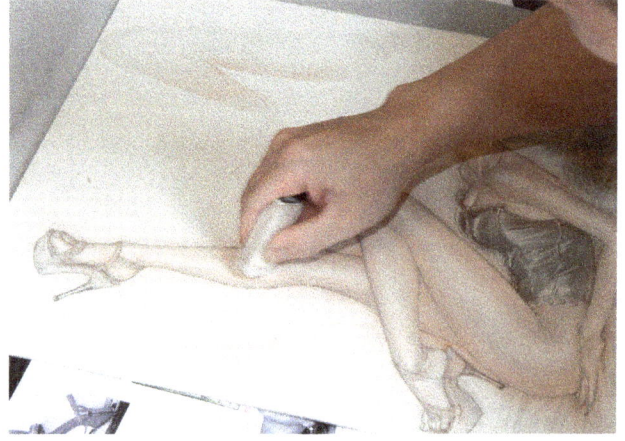

For the long, broad highlights of the leg, I employ yet another type of eraser, a white drafting eraser. This is the least abrasive one in my arsenal, and takes paint off very slowly - perfect for soft highlighting.

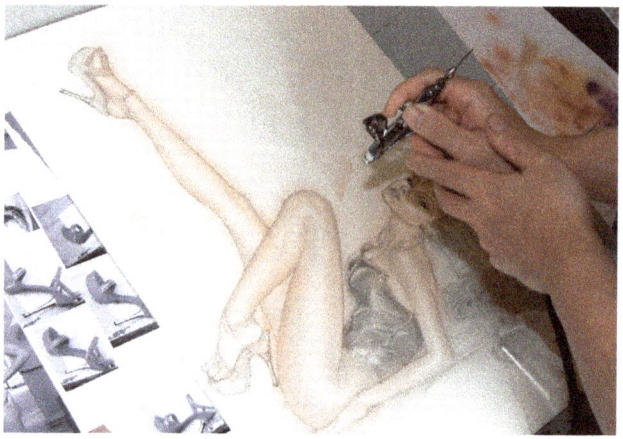

I'm still on the back leg, but working down to the butt.

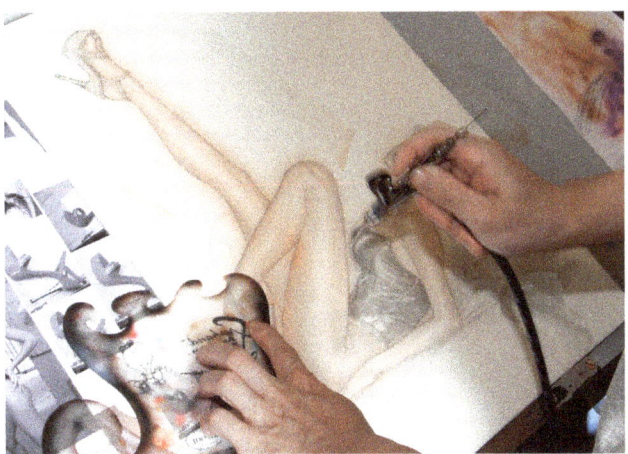

Here I'm just adding a little color to the front leg.

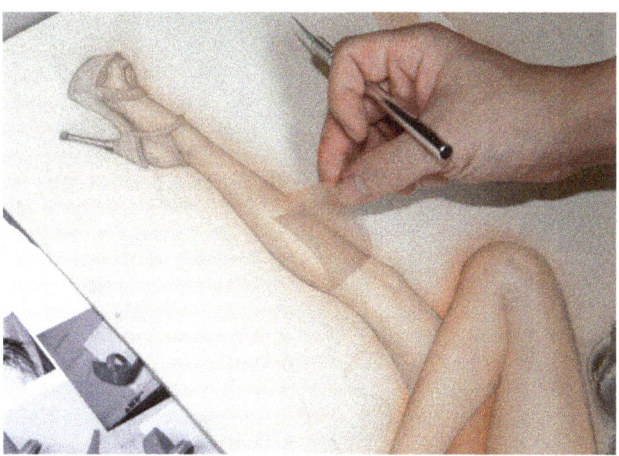

I peel back just a little of the masked, previously-painted back leg in order to check the color contrast between the two legs. Gotta keep things consistent!

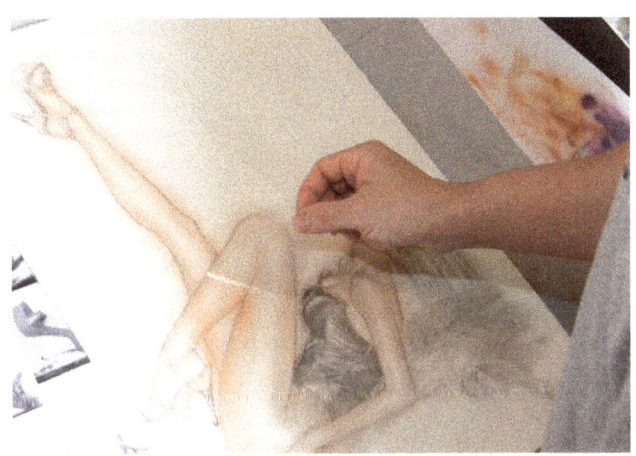

I'm peeling the mask for the front leg as I'm about to attack it next.

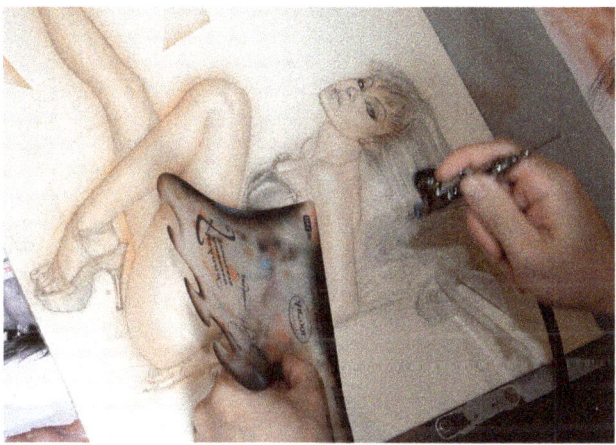

Both legs are completely masked, I move to the skin parts of the upper body again. I'm using a free hand shield to block the area by Jacki's armpit that's right next the area of her arm that I'm working on.

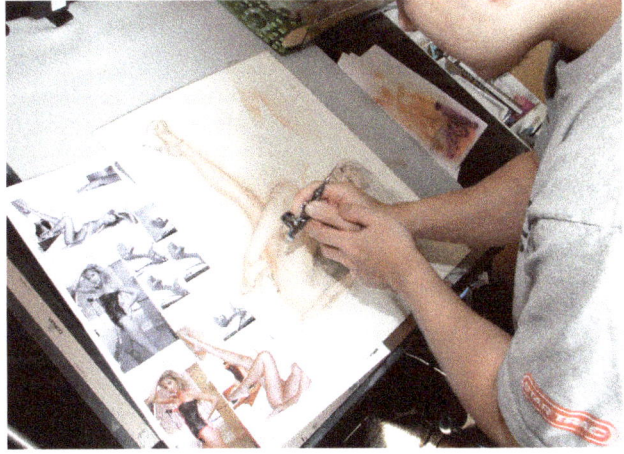

I look at the reference material every few seconds in order to maintain accuracy. I'm working on the near foot.

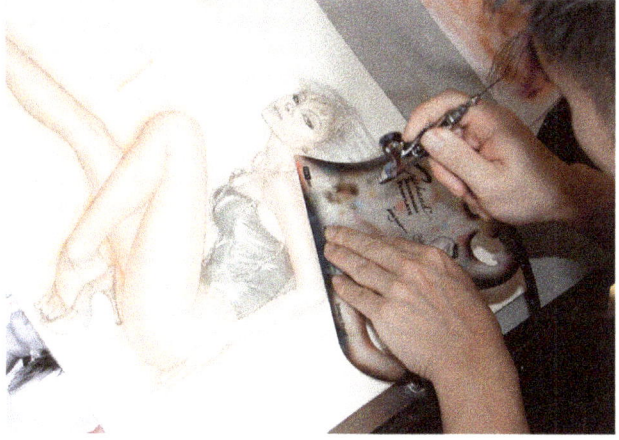

The opposite side of her arm is sprayed in the same manner, as I shield the shoulder blade area. This creates a clearer separation of the arm from the rest of her body since we're dealing with the same color.

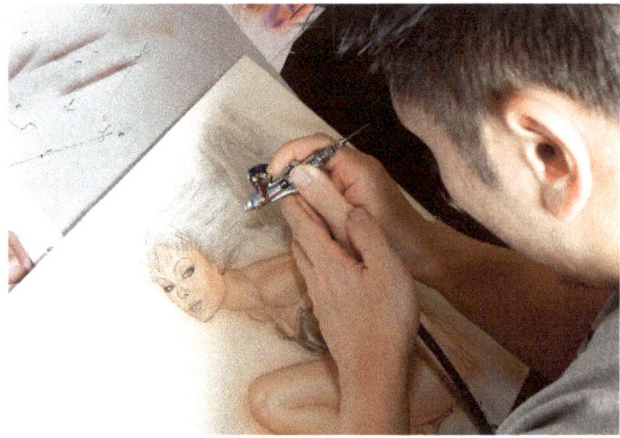

I'm working on the face, adding more color and depth. The hair is unmasked, so I'm more careful getting near it with free hand airbrushing. A little overspray is inevitable, and gives a nice soft transition.

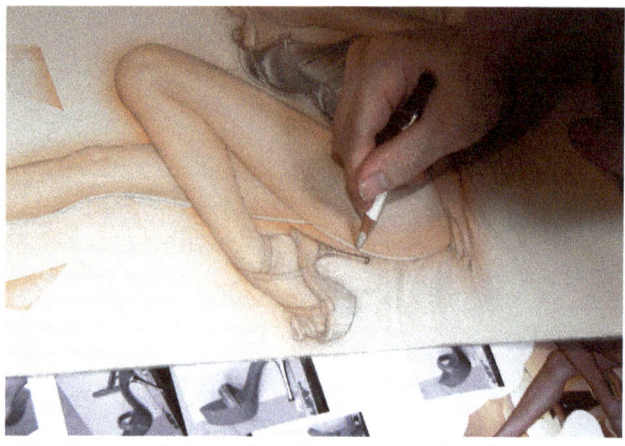

The Eraserstik is perfect for creating thin bounce lighting on the back of the leg. The bounce light is my artistic license; it helps make the figure in the painting more dynamic.

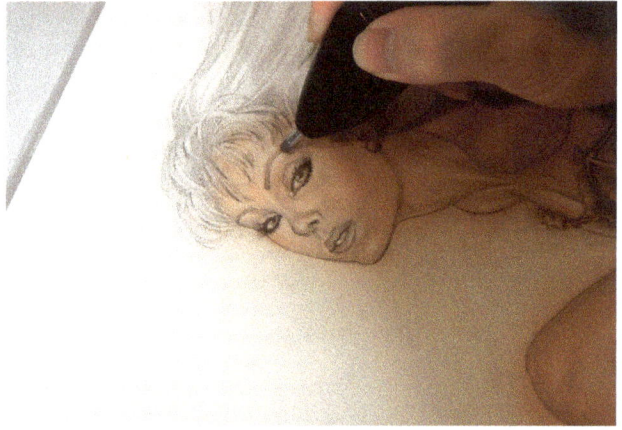

Going back in with the erasers now. This erasing is also a little more fine-tuned and particular, we're gradually getting smaller with the highlight sculpting. Working in layers the way I do helps add depth.

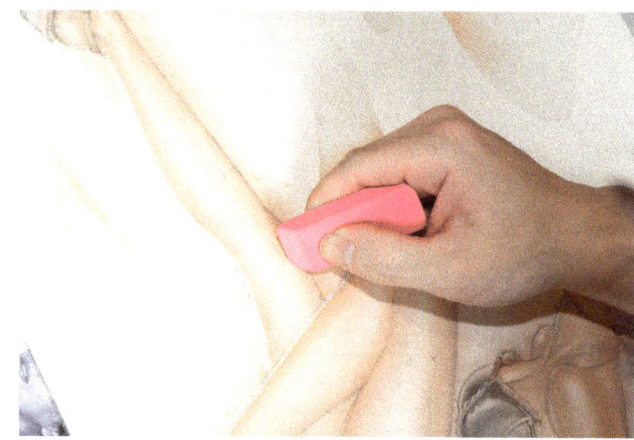

Using the corner of the Pink Pearl eraser, I do some more sculpting on the knee area of the back leg.

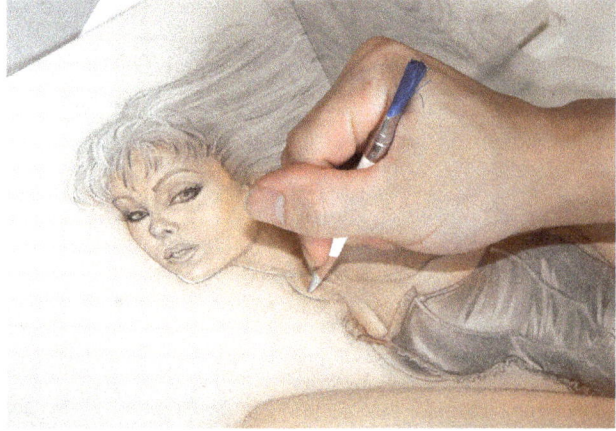

I'm using the Eraserstik again, this time for the smaller highlights on the rear shoulder. The electric eraser would be too small, and the pink-white kneaded erasers would be too big.

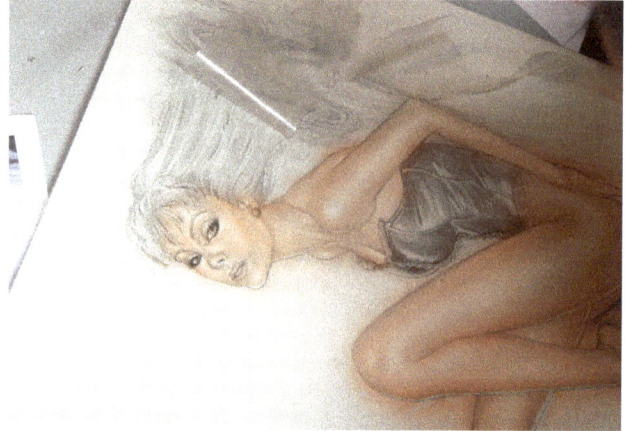

An overview look of the upper body skin area to see that it looks alright, especially compared to the legs.

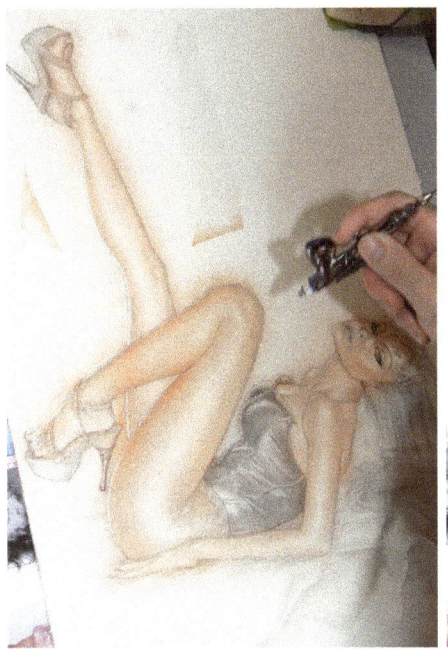 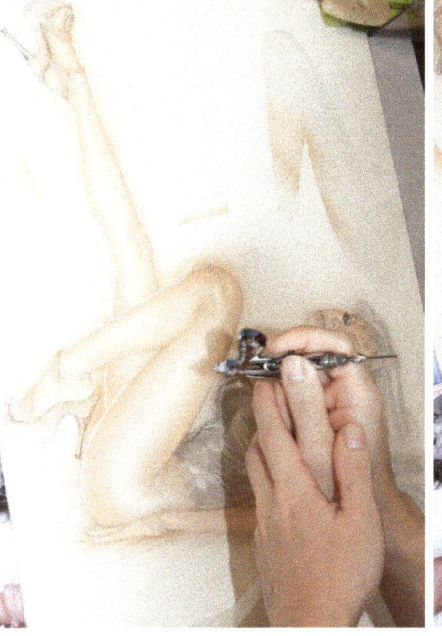 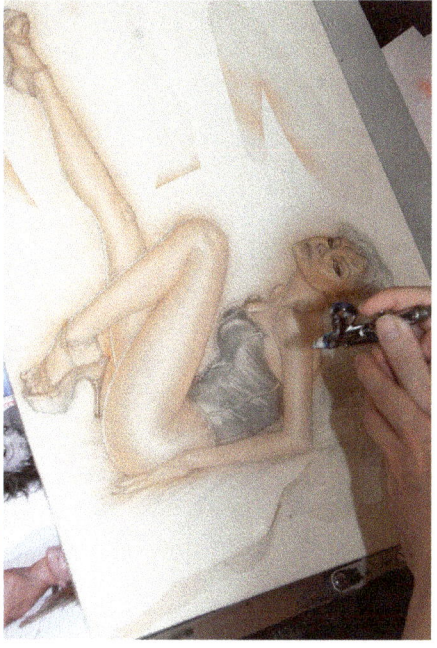

This is my final round of attacking the skin, and this time it's with a darker and dulled down version of my flesh tone. Shadows are the last step to make the skin really "pop." Here I am starting again at the legs.

Working down the front leg, I try to beef up the darkness near the edge. The area between the edge's bounce light and the main highlight is always darkest, and helps bring out dimension.

Still working on the front leg, I'm gradually moving towards the upper body.

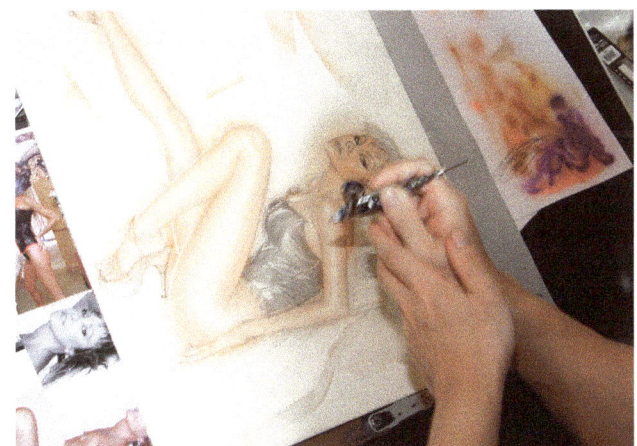 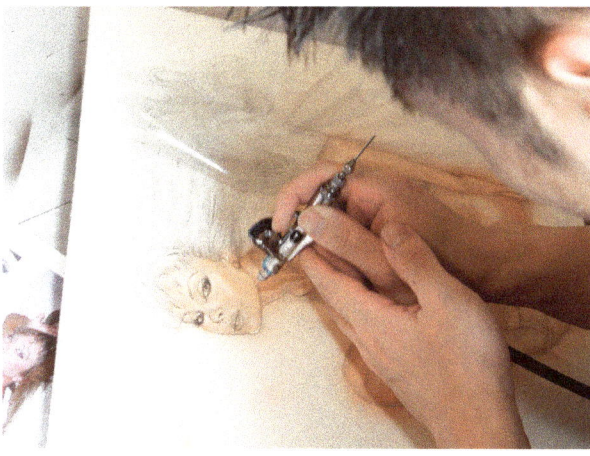

Sculpting shadows around the breast area, being careful not to overspray into her arm and shoulder.

Moving on to the face, I deepen the shadow under her cheek bone.

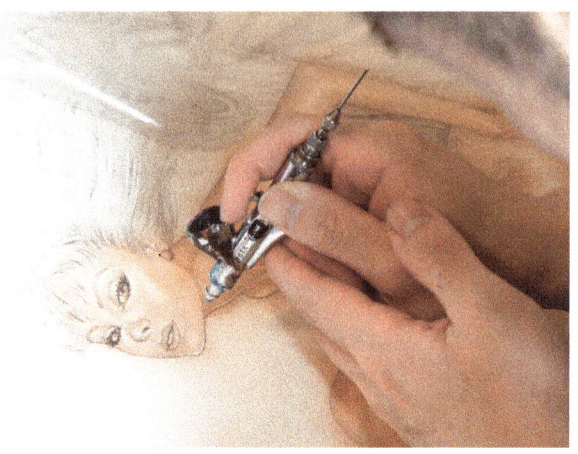

I have to be very delicate here as I'm working the shadows of her chin. My Custom Micron airbrush, along with low air pressure and thin transparent paints, helps me achieve fine, controllable sprays.

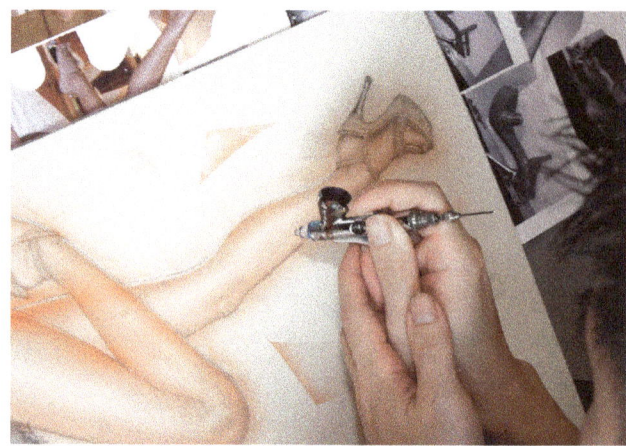

I am fixated on her calf at this point.

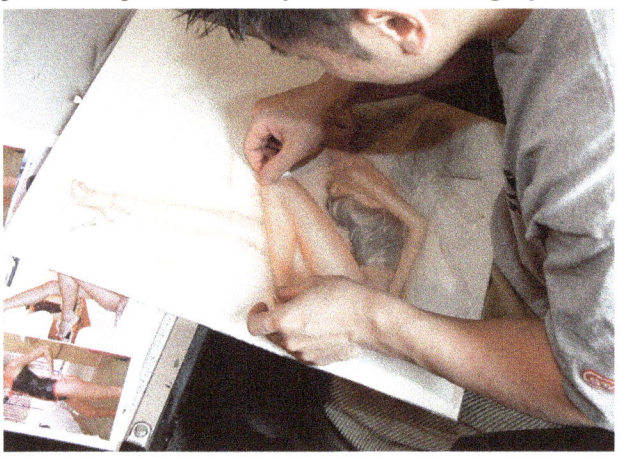

I should go darker on the skin. So I remask the front leg before spraying the back leg. When working with a light background, your eyes tend to get fooled into thinking that tones are darker than they really are.

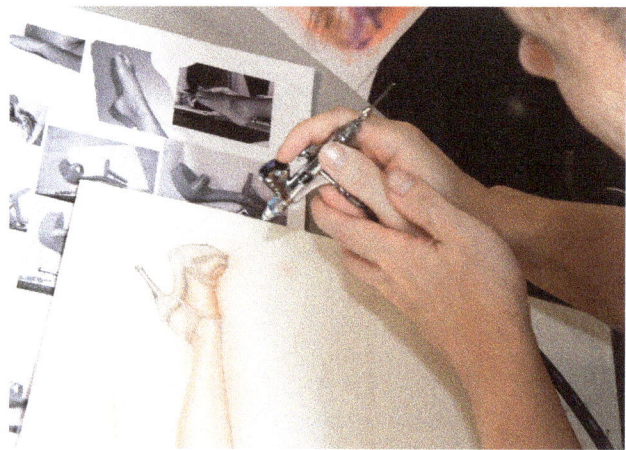

Now I'm working her foot. Close attention is paid to delicate areas such as the feet, hands, and face. As mentioned before, if I mess up on any of these parts, then the painting is ruined.

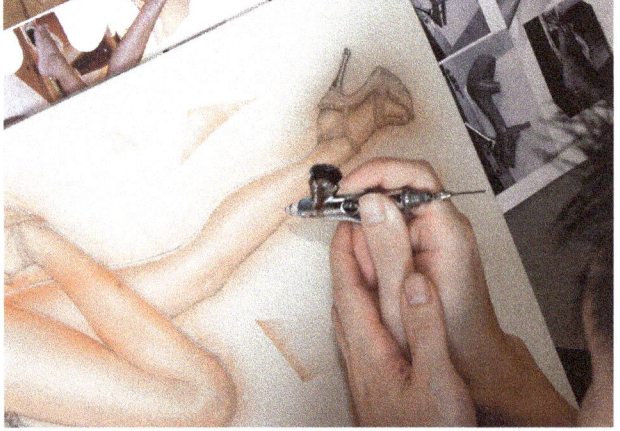

Now I spray the back leg again, attempting to beef up its tone. At this point I'm just concerned with the receding edges of the form and avoiding the highlight. This will enhance the dimensional effect.

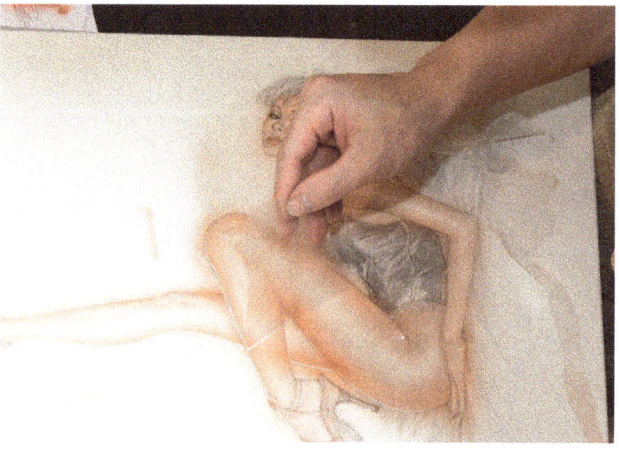

Once again I pull the mask on Jacki's front leg as I get ready to paint it...

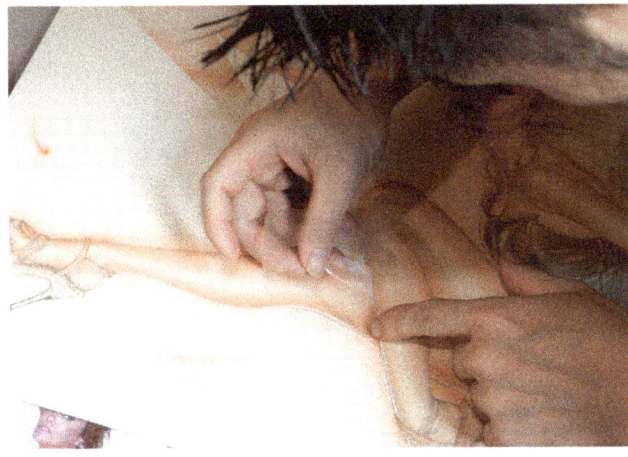

...but not before carefully remasking the back leg that I've just finished painting!

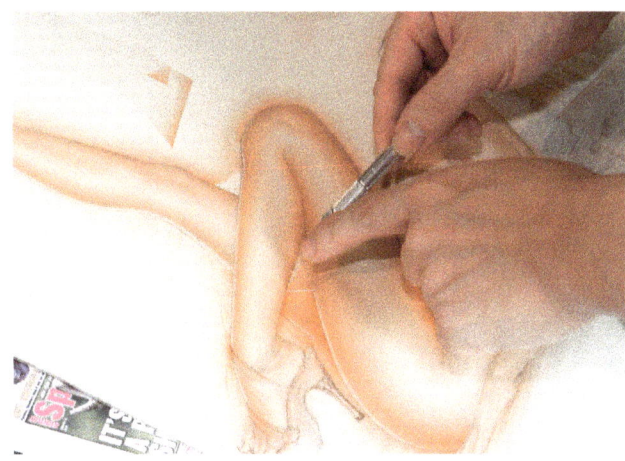

I'm just peeling a corner of the frisket to reveal the back leg in order to make sure the skin contrast is consistent in both legs.

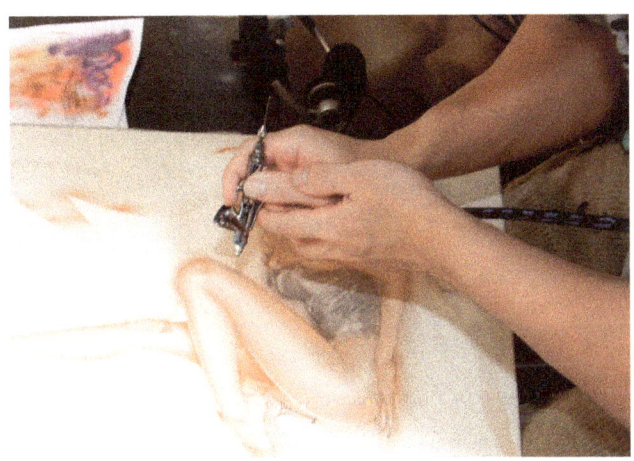

And now the final sculpting begins on the near leg.

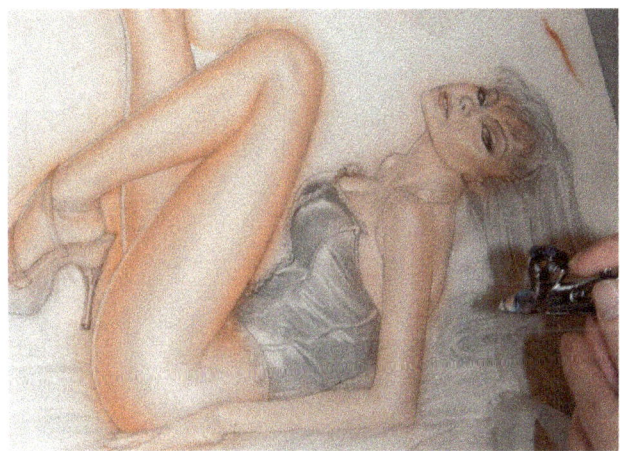

Here I'm working on the upper body, specifically adding more shade and depth to Jacki's arm.

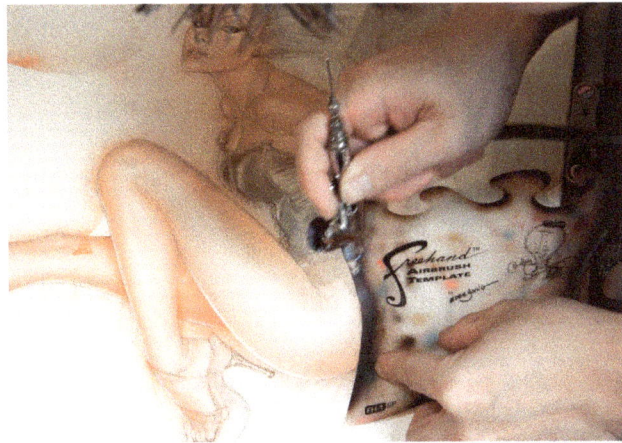

With the aid of the freehand shield, I block the hand as my shadow spraying rounds downward toward Jacki's butt.

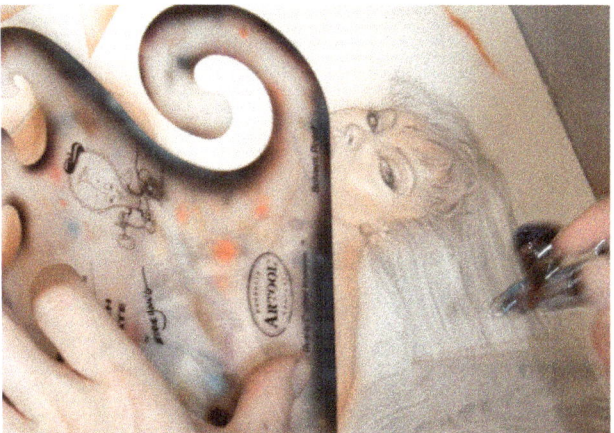

Finished with the arm, I use the freehand shield once again as I work on the rear shoulder area. I pay careful attention not to spray too high or heavily as it would create a line running up her neck.

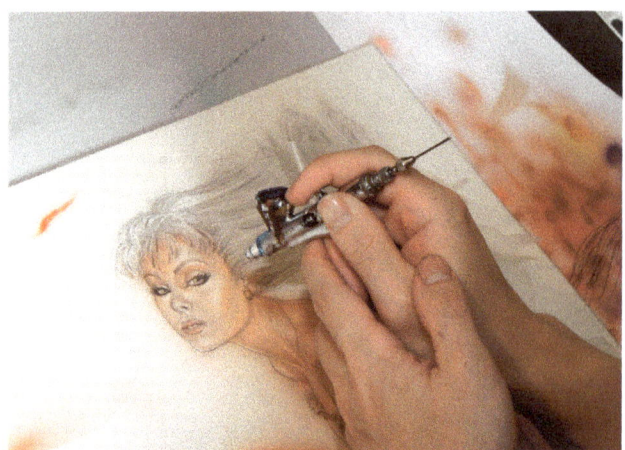

Final shadows are added to the face, particularly around the eyelids and under her bangs. And the area under her cheekbones is darkened slightly.

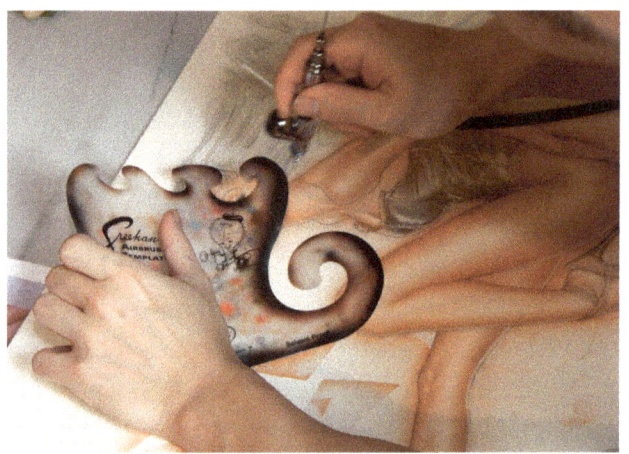

Jacki's face is shielded as I enhance the shadows on her neck.

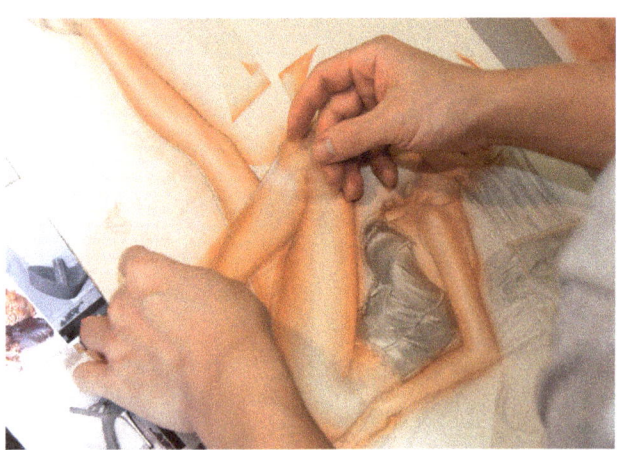

I peel the frisket off of the previously masked legs in order to do my final round of erasing on the brightest highlights.

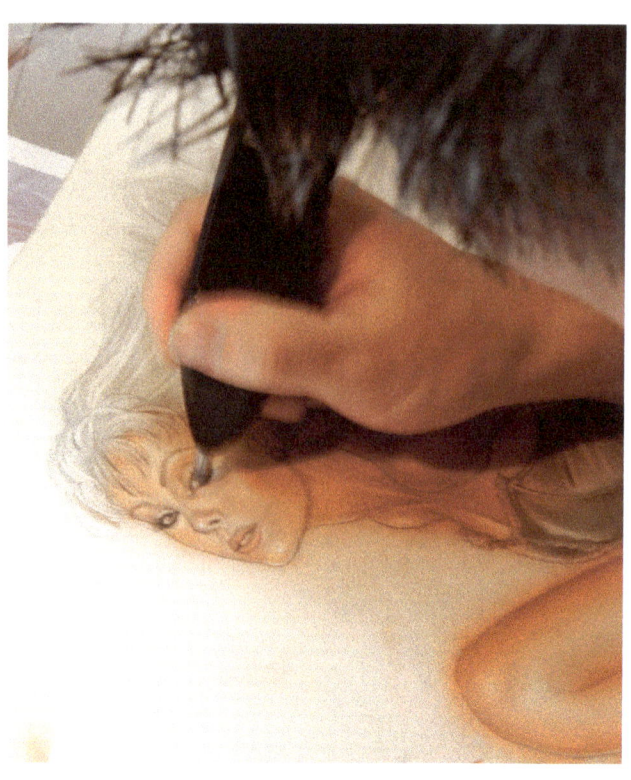

I now add the smallest, brightest highlights in the face (called specular highlights), particularly in the whites of the eyes (shown here), right underneath the eyebrow, the tip of the nose, and on the chin.

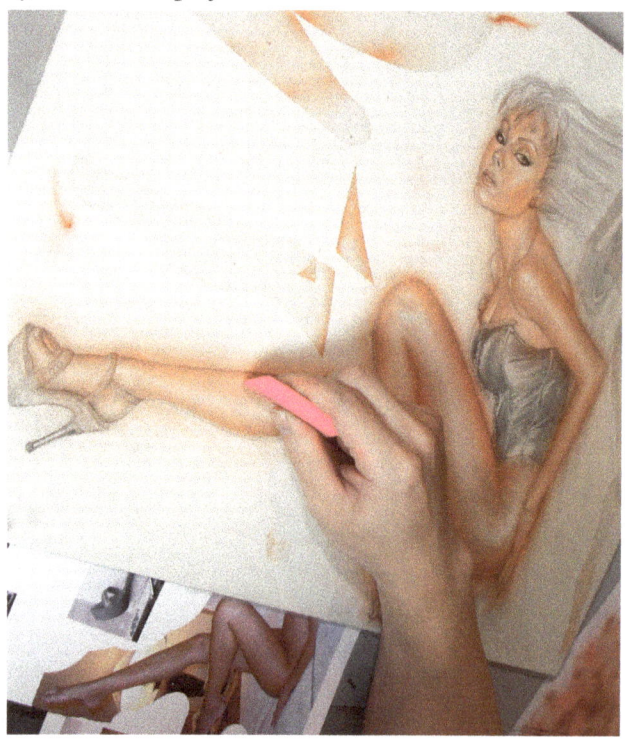

I do the same thing with the rest of her body. Here I am using the pink eraser to work the final middle gleam of highlight on the leg. It's important to note this highlight isn't as strong as a specular highlight.

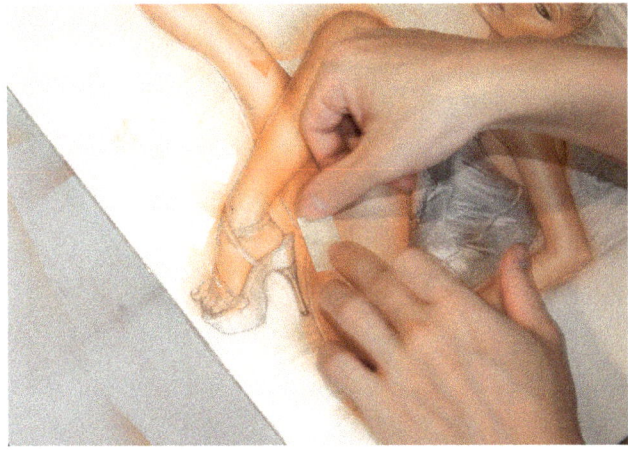

I'm done with the airbrushing portion of the skin. So I recover them and begin sealing the edges with masking tape.

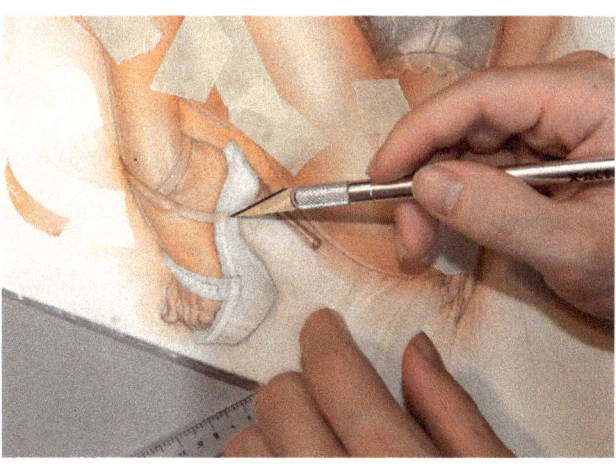

An Xacto blade (the same one used to cut the frisket) is used to more easily lift off the tiny pieces.

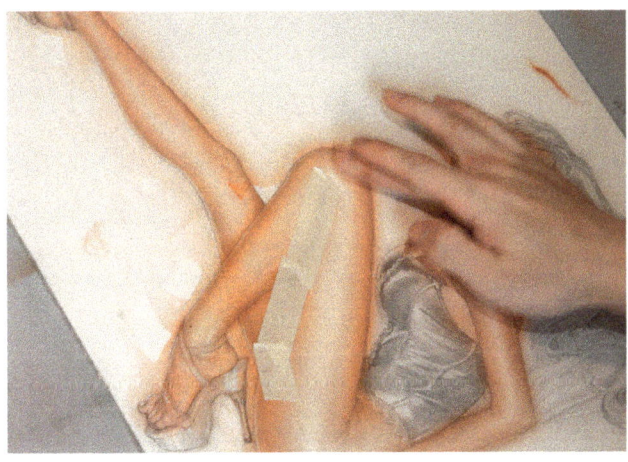

By sealing the edges of the frisket, I'm assured that any upcoming paint won't leak into the hard work already done.

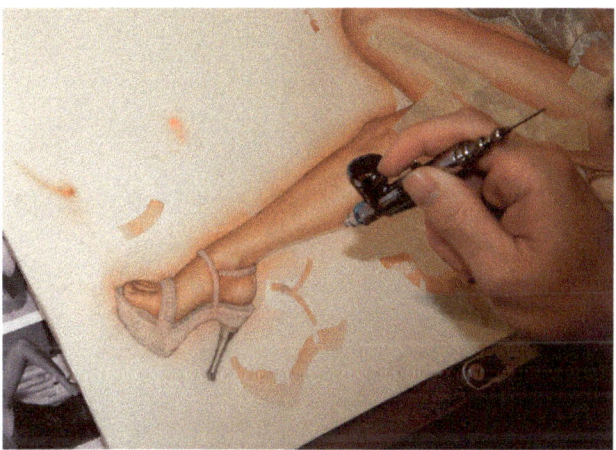

I begin spraying a light tone of red on the shoe. Spraying too heavily right off the bat will inhibit effective erasing.

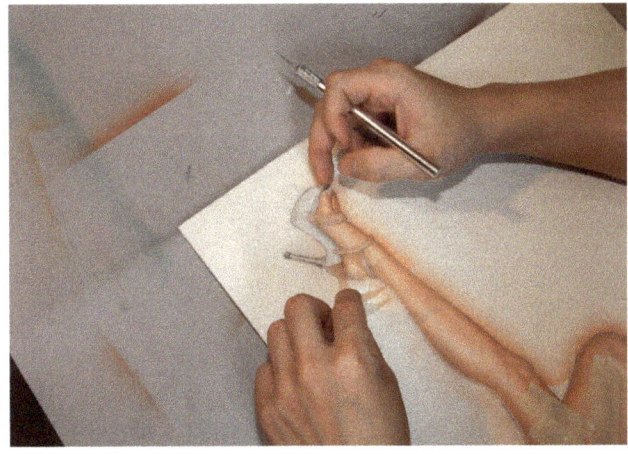

I begin peeling the frisket off of the heels prior to painting.

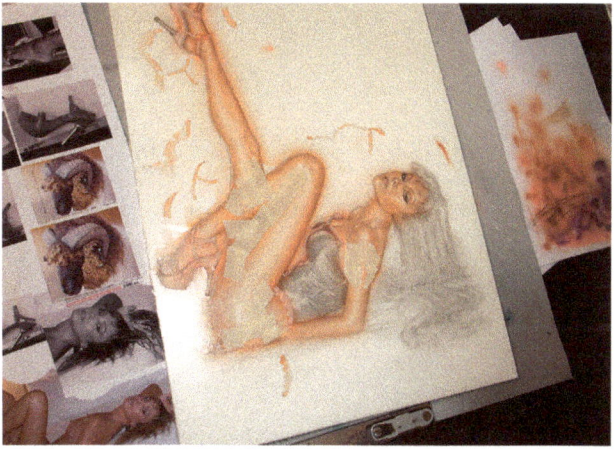

A broad overview of the heels after the initial spray. Again, reference material is always right next to the piece, as I'm constantly looking back and forth.

Tom Nguyen Q&A

Give us a little background on you, how did you get started in art, and are pin-ups the main focus of the work you do?

I am self-taught, no art classes other than what was required in school. I followed artists and I always liked comic book art. In my early teens I did portraits and caricatures. Eventually I developed the ability to capture a likeness, it forces you to study the features of the face. It's a nice skill to have and means I don't have to rely on a projector to get a good likeness. I didn't pick up an airbrush until I was 15. About a year later I applied at Valley Fair, the local amusement park, to do caricatures. They started me out doing face painting, then I did caricatures. I worked every day in the summer for three years, and it really pumped up my skills. In 2003, Steve Driscoll and I went to Glamourcon just as spectators, even though I had done some pin-ups before that. After Glamourcon I decided to use my skills as a comic book artist to develop my own pin-up style.

Who inspires you, who do you look up to?
Sorayama, he is my favorite, Olivia, is the best female illustrator. I owe a good chunk of my knowledge to Steve Driscoll, he and I met at Valley Fair. I took his advice and put my own twist to it. Steve is The Man as far as I'm concerned. My paintings are heavily drawing based, his are heavily paint based. He has unbelievable control with the airbrush.

What do you use for an airbrush?
I use an Iwata, Custom Micron B. It can create fine lines, the trigger is super smooth, and it feels good in my hand, very solid, never had a problem. Handles all the paints, the line quality is impeccable.

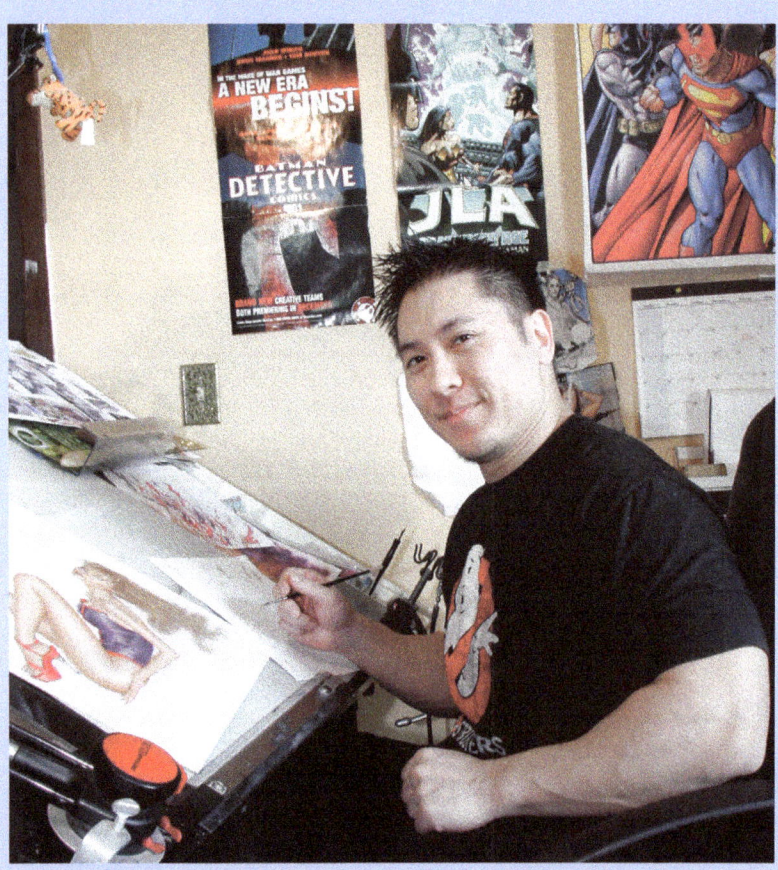
Tom at work in his small studio, surrounded by some of his comic-book posters.

And what do you use for paint?
Com.art usually, mostly transparent, some opaque. Transparent because it's less likely to clog up the airbrush, also because my illustrations are so based on the drawing, I want the pencil work to show through. You do have to be careful with transparent paint, it's hard to cover up a mistake.

Do you always mix your own colors?
Yes, I studied color theory when I was young. It takes practice and you really have to know and understand the color wheel.

Can you talk a little about your method of creation: the fact that you sketch the image out first, and then come back in with the airbrush?

I think I was always good at drawing. I feel it is one of my strengths. Even before pin-ups I wanted to add color to my drawings, I liked the effect of blending the two methods. This is a good method for me because it utilizes both of my skills. This method allows me to add

Q&A continued

a lot of detail because of the drawing underneath. It's mixed media.

How do you create believable skin tones?

For basic generic skin colors I start with a yellowish or ochre color, and slowly build it up. Adding a little magenta or sienna brown is a good way to darken it. If it's too saturated then I try dulling it down with some green or blue. A drop of purple is a good way to create a darker, shadow version of the skin tone. You can modify the skin tone with a little of something from across the color wheel. So if it's on the orangy side, add a cool color for the shadow. Then mix the color to taste. You also have to consider the color of the light source and the surrounding colors of the environment. Realistic skin tones will pick up color from their environment.

How do you find models, and do you do your own photo shoots?

My first model was a friend of my sister. At Glamourcon 2005, I found Jacki Morrison (the model seen here). Every time I go to Glamourcon I meet more models who are anxious to work with me. And I've worked with a number of top pageant winners and competitors. For example, I'm a prize sponsor for the Mrs. Minnesota, Mrs. Wisconsin, and Mrs. Iowa pageants. I paint the winner each year, and that networking provides more models from the pageant area.

Any tricks of the trade, something you've learned over the years?

A little change in posture can help a lot. I use an old drawing technique, the S curve, it makes for a much more interesting image that way. For example, avoid using straight, stiff posing in the figures. With women, you want to utilize a lot of slants and angles - something that is already naturally appealing in their figures, as opposed to the male physique. Because of this, I use a lot of "S" curves when constructing the figure, and even use it to exaggerate the female form.

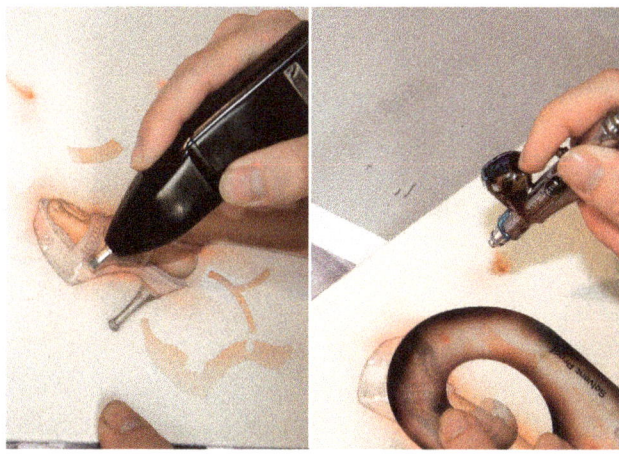

The highlights are smaller and harsher on the shoes, so I whip out the electric eraser to do the job. Right: The freehand shield allows me to cover the lip at the top of the shoe while I add more tone around it.

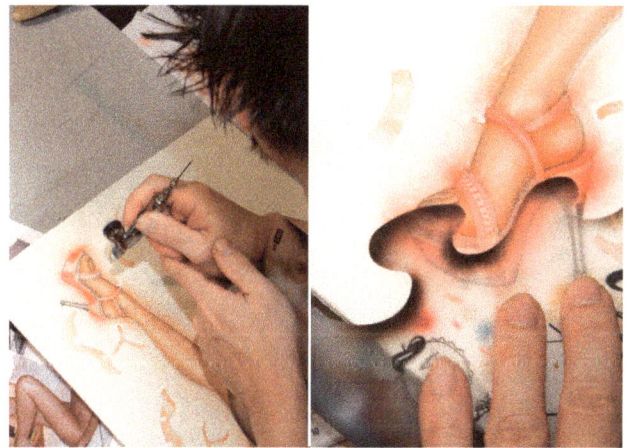

I took several reference pictures of the high heels so that I can pick the best elements from each. Right: Some parts of the freehand shield match up with the curves of the shoe to make my job a little easier.

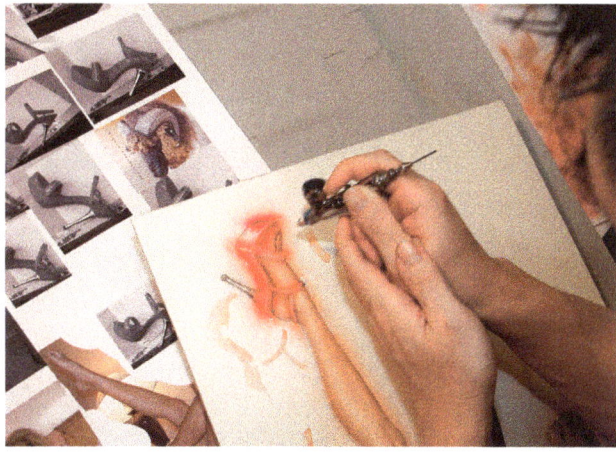

Going deeper with the red so that it's not so light and pink. Again, building up the red with erasing in between makes for good depth.

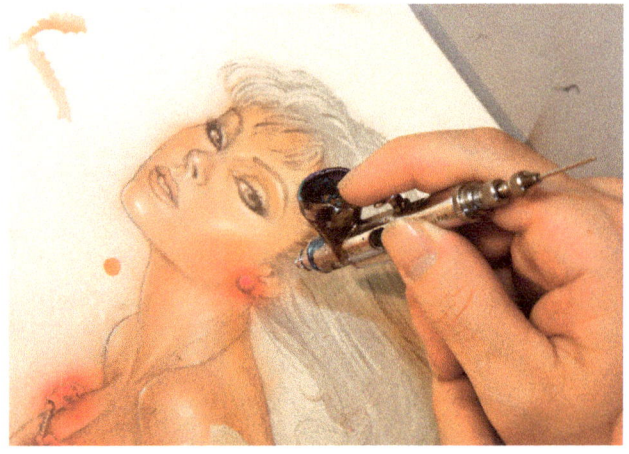

Using the same red, I remove the previously cut masks from the earring and red lace and begin laying down color.

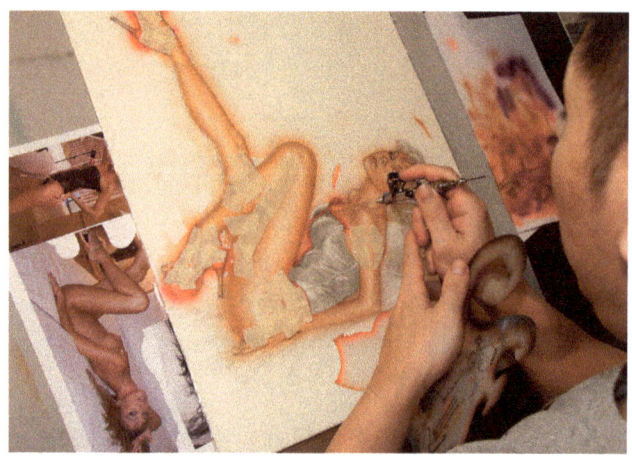

After sealing the edges of the heels with masking tape, I peel the mask off her corset and begin to lay down its color.

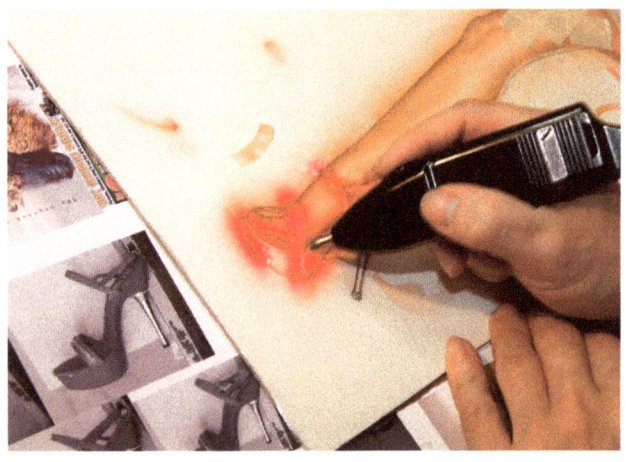

I'm now doing the final specular highlighting on the shoes before I cover them up for the last time.

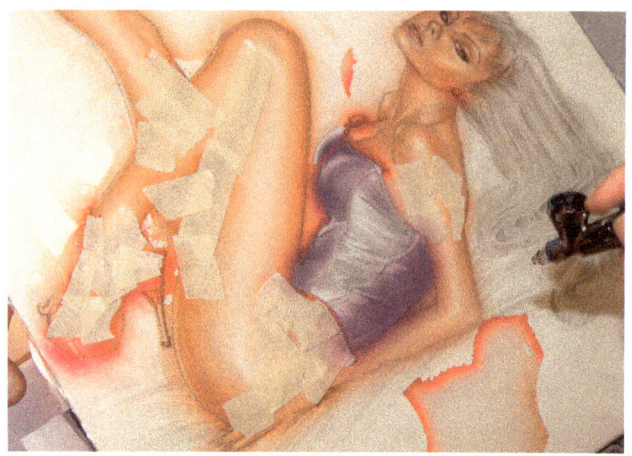

The first light layer of my pre-mixed dark purple tone is sprayed gently. It's not a flat wash to start, there is a soft highlight that I left.

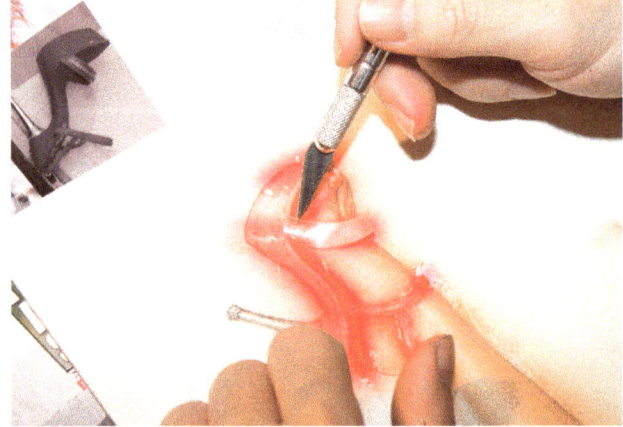

I carefully remask the high heels now that I'm finished with the airbrushing part. The razor blade helps me align the masking a little better than I can with fingers alone.

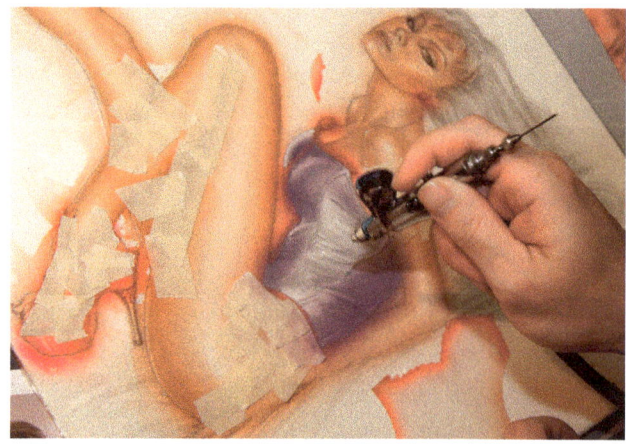

I move in just a bit closer to loosely sculpt some of the wrinkling, but I'm still not going too dark.

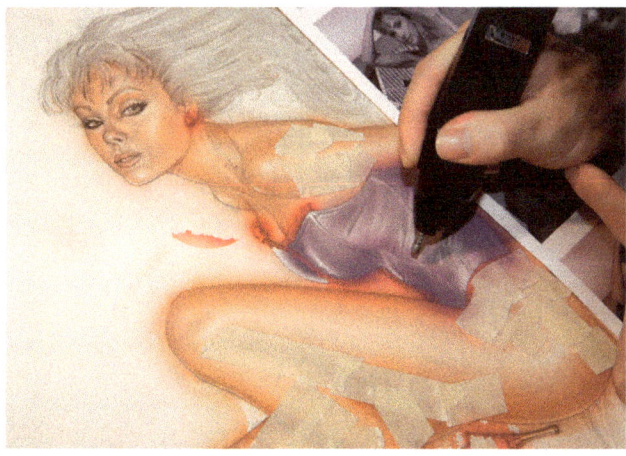

The highlights on this texture are small and particular, so I use my electric eraser to do the job.

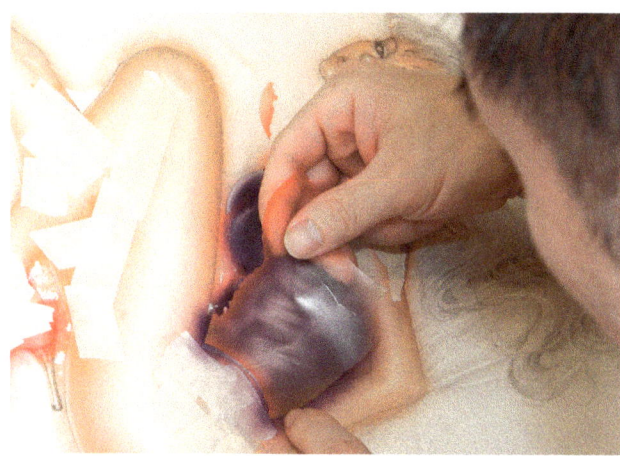

When I'm done with the corset, I remask it and will eventually seal its edges with masking tape again.

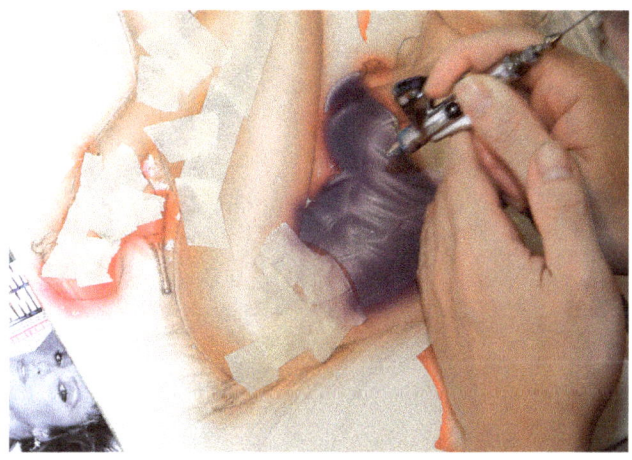

I go in with another blast of dark purple to deepen the corset.

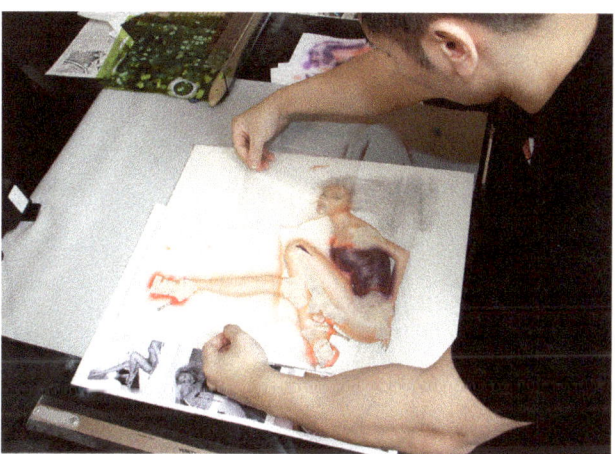

Remember how the mask for the hair was all one piece with the upper body? Well, it's actually connected to the whole background, too. Here, I remove it.

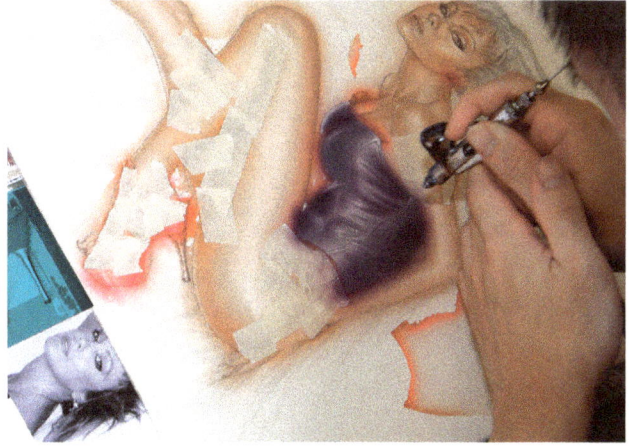

Focus is placed on the darkest of darks as I now avoid the highlight areas.

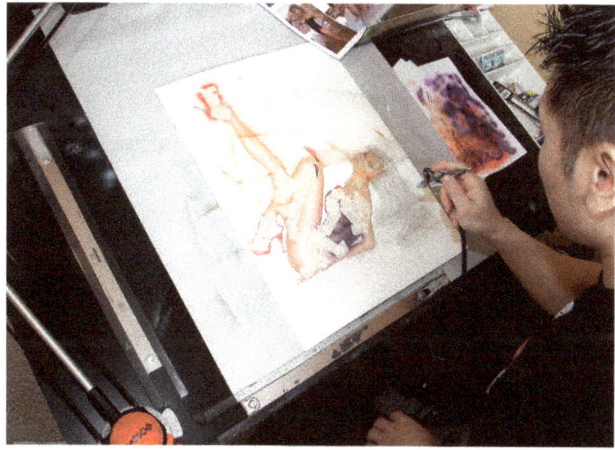

A broad, light-purplish wash is applied to the sheets that Jacki is lying on.

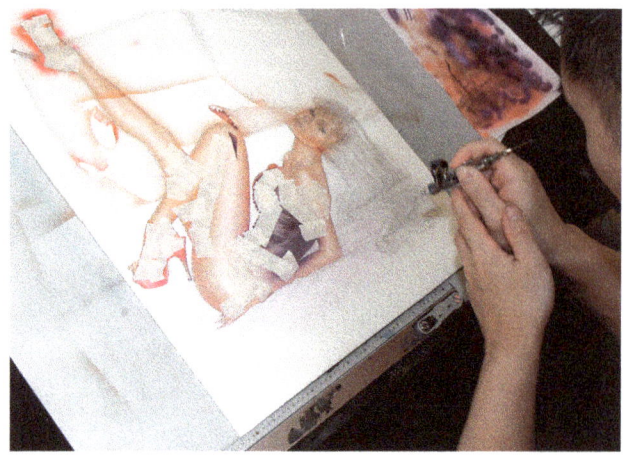

I'm still working underneath her arm and building up the color.

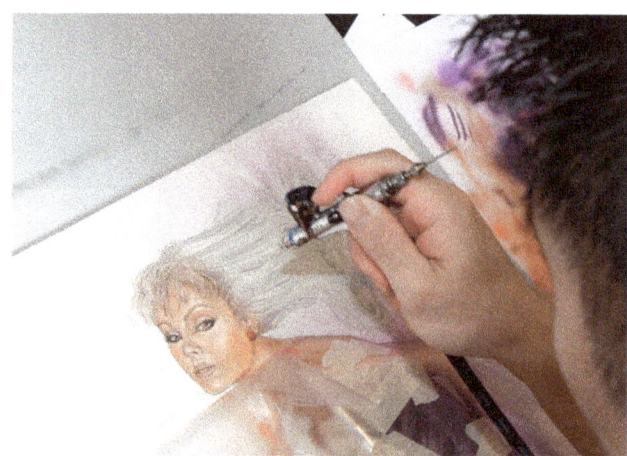

Finished with airbrushing the sheets (it was light and easy), I move on to the hair. The sheets are still unmasked.

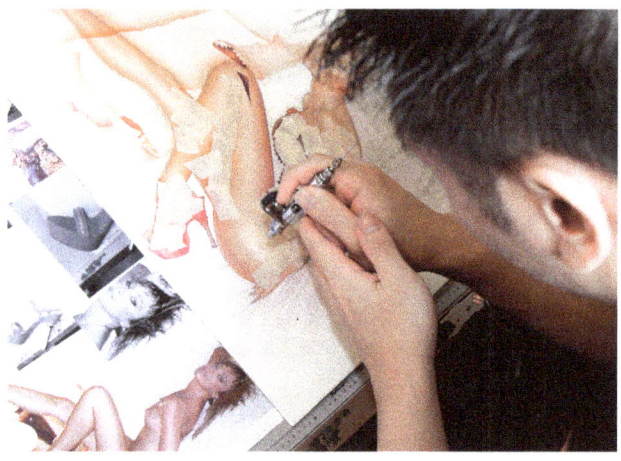

I'm working on the other side by her butt now. I pay careful attention to fade the purple off behind her.

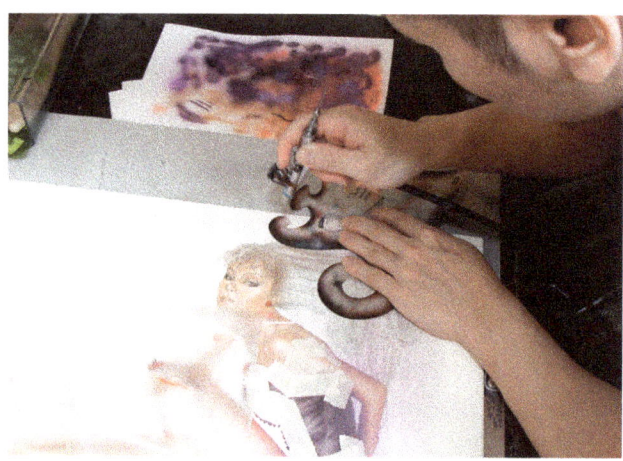

I'm careful with the area of her bangs as it's right next to Jacki's uncovered face. I do want the soft transition, but not too much overspray.

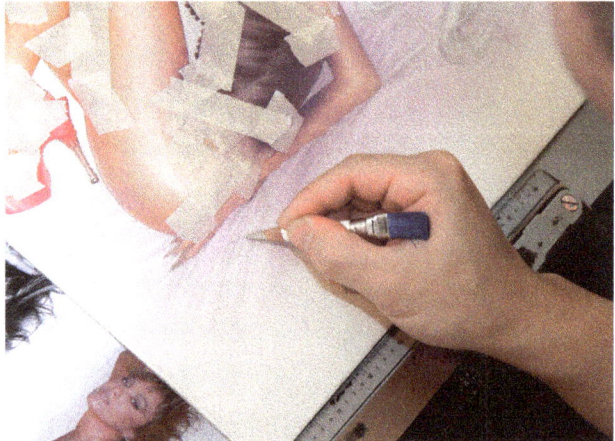

The first layer of purple is done. Here I'm using the Eraserstik to scratch out highlights and begin bringing out the wrinkles.

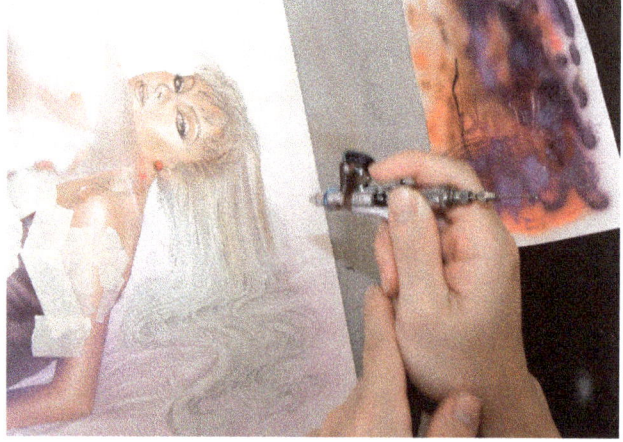

I move down the length of her hair with vertical strokes. Again, I do want to control the overspray that spills onto the sheets.

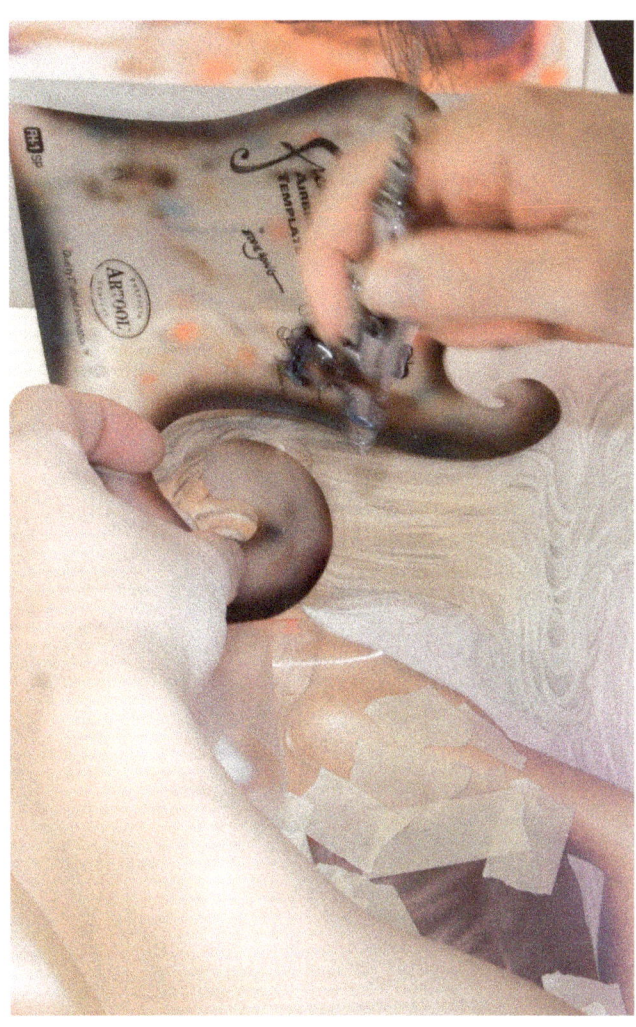

The bottom of the ear is shielded while I focus on the darker part of the hair that flows out underneath.

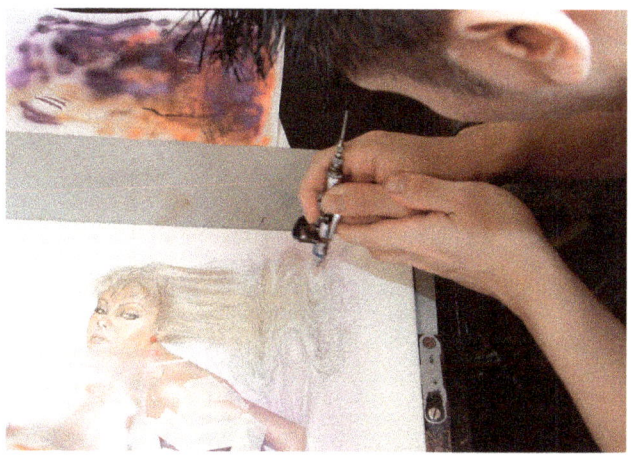

The swirly bottom part of the hair flowing on the sheet is carefully sprayed. These strokes are finer and more deliberate.

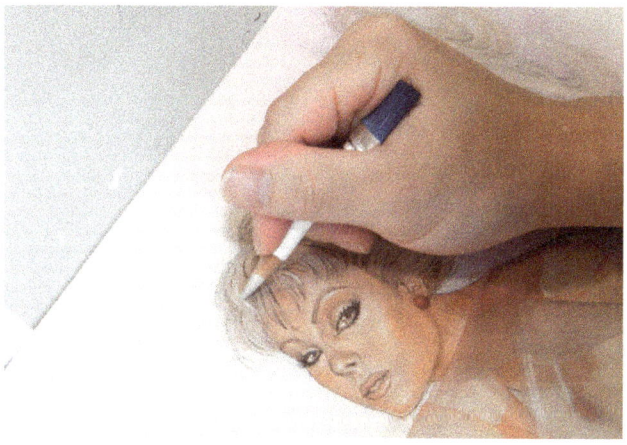

Done with the first round of hair spraying, I now go in with the EraserStik to bring out highlights in the bangs.

Continuing down the hair, I keep picking out my highlight areas, while trying to be careful so I don't overdo them.

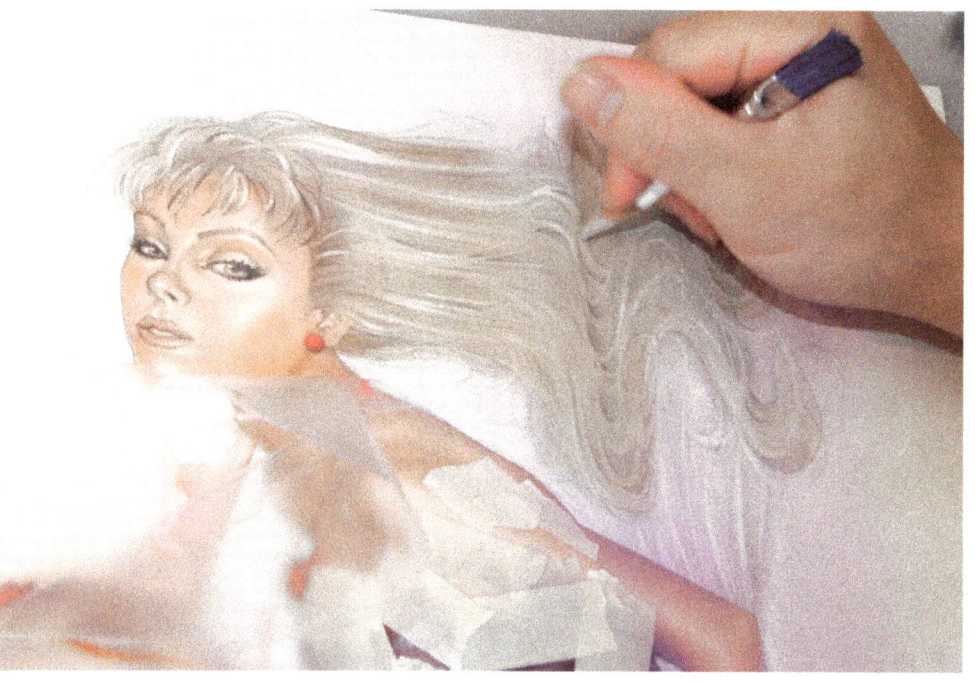

39

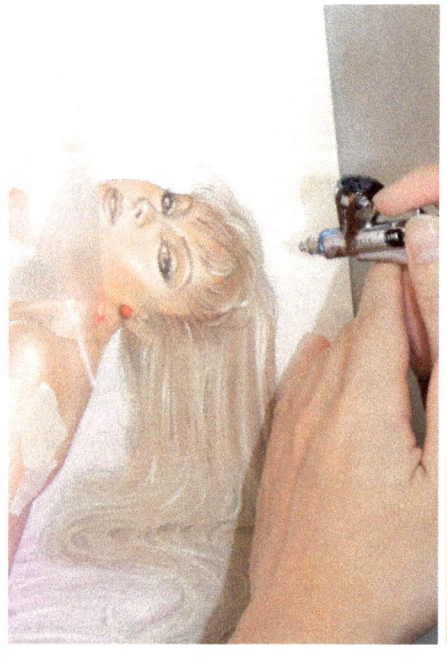

Going in with another round of light brown, I deepen the tone of the hair to help give it depth.

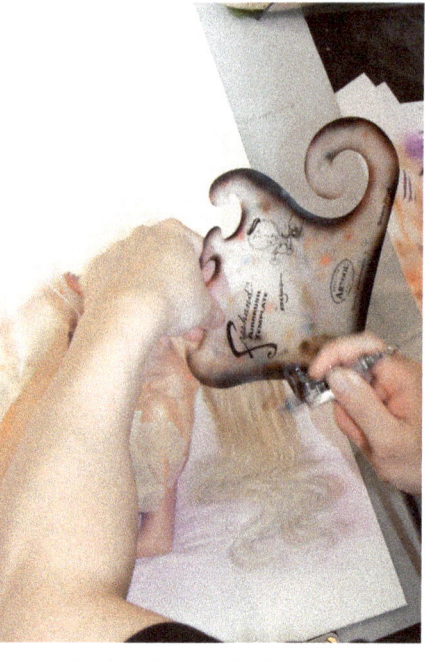

I use the free-hand shield again to protect the ear from the heavier spraying.

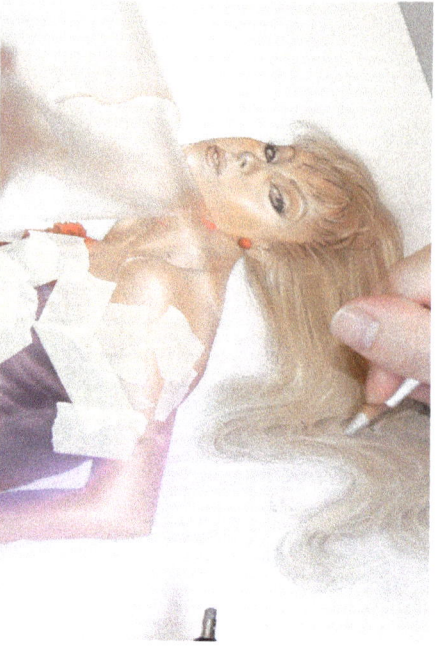

Redefining the highlights again with the EraserStik. Later I'll actually use a sable brush with white for the specular highlights.

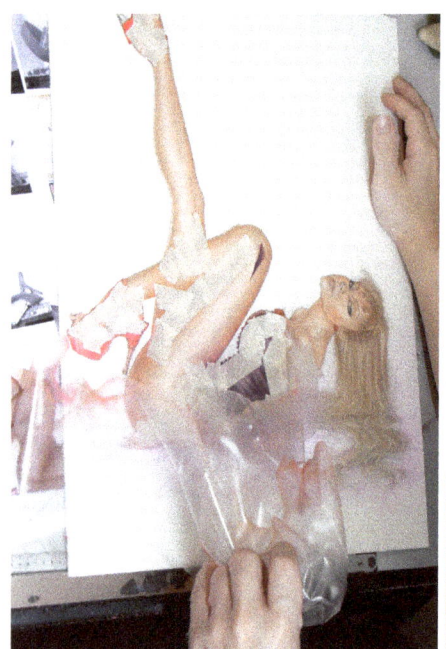

Feeling fairly done with all of the actual airbrushing, I start to peel off all of the frisket (my favorite part!).

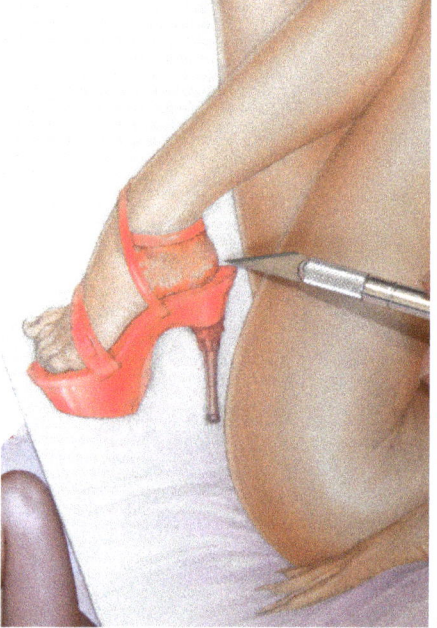

Again, the Xacto knife is used for removal of the smaller pieces.

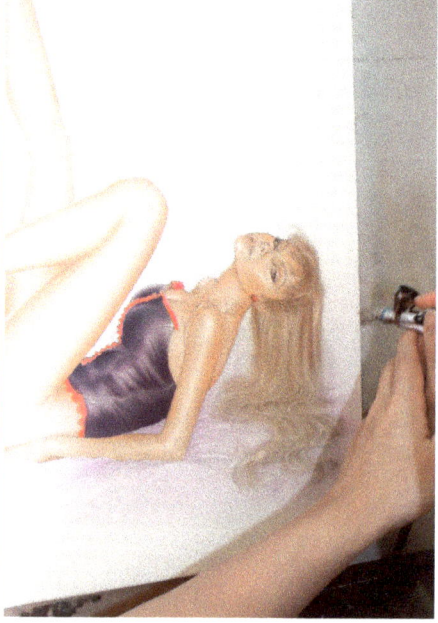

I decided that the hair could be even darker, after looking at the whole piece. So, in I go again with the airbrush.

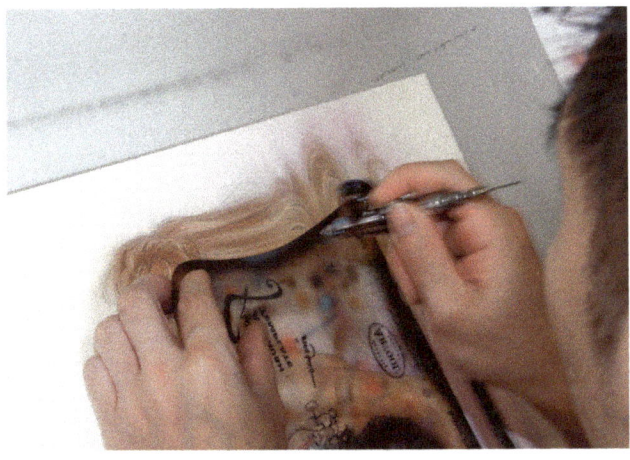

The free-hand shield helps me make random defined lines...

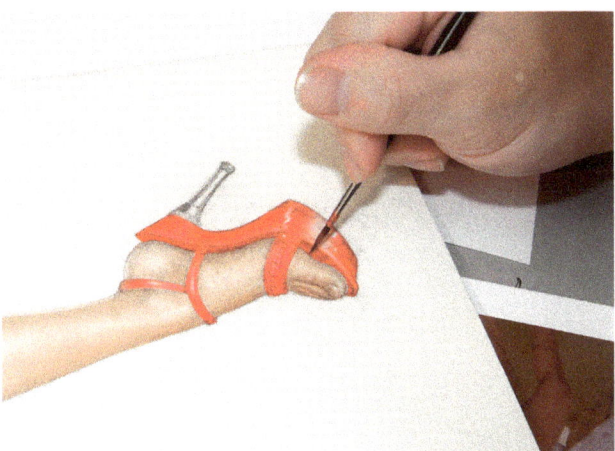

The final step in the painting is the brushwork to bring out the final details and finishing "pop."

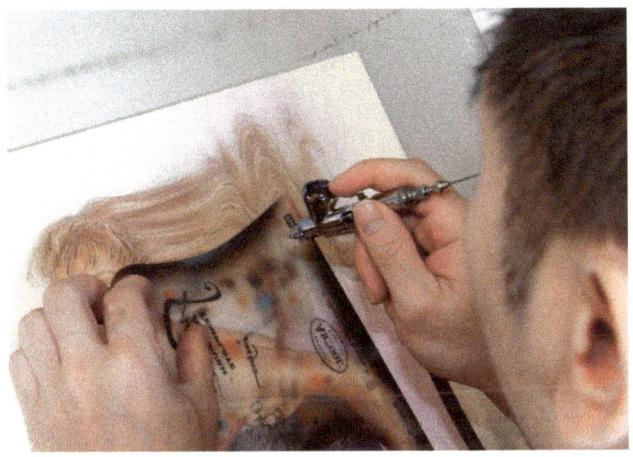

...within the hair to break up the softness.

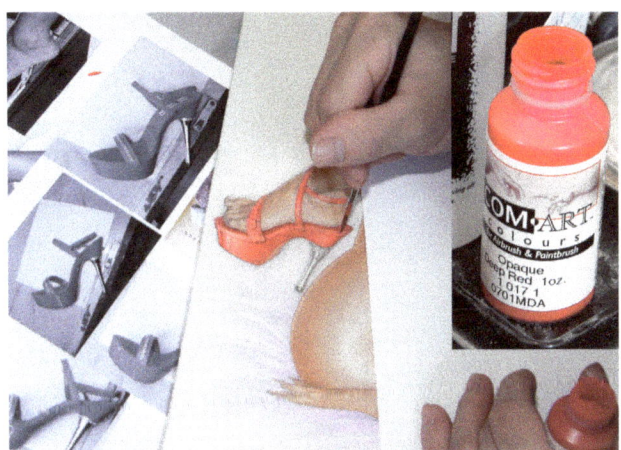

Here I'm using the red straight out of the bottle to bring out the deepest parts of the high heel. But, I'm watering it down just a bit.

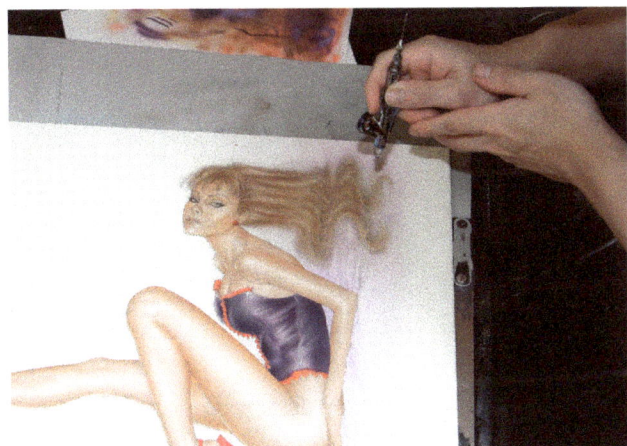

Of course I have to move right down the hair to keep the overall tone even with what I just sprayed in the previous step.

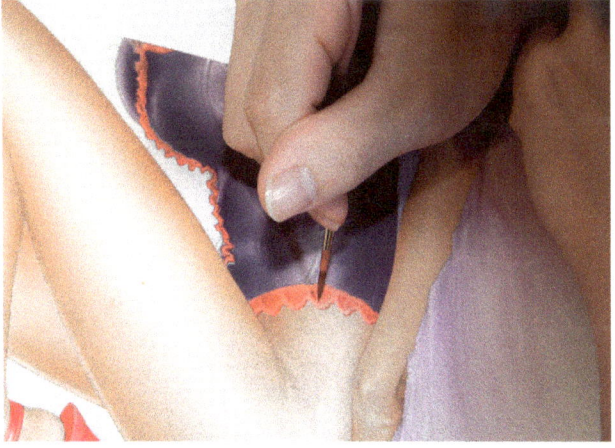

To keep things consistent, I'm using the same red to detail the lace. At this point I'm making up the detail as the photo was too small.

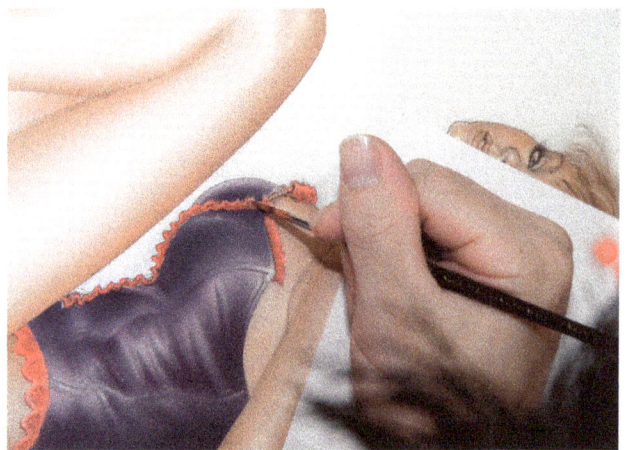

I concentrate on keeping the textures consistent throughout the lace pattern of the entire corset.

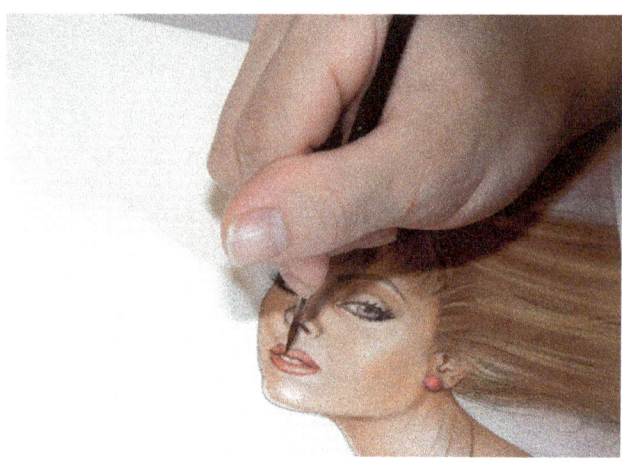

I return to the lips to do more refining, particularly around the gums/teeth. I must have missed it before.

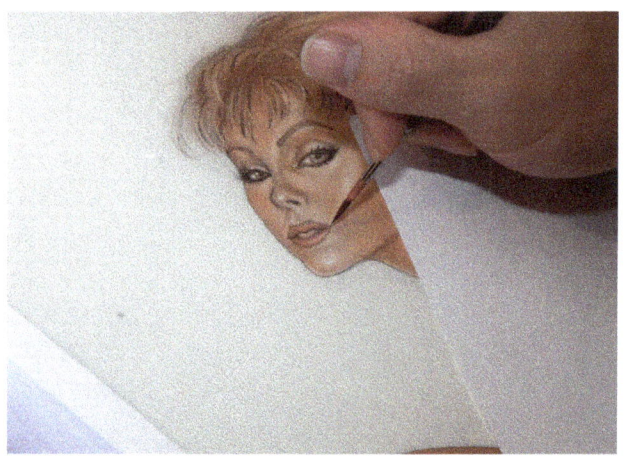

I water the red down in various shades to hand paint the lips.

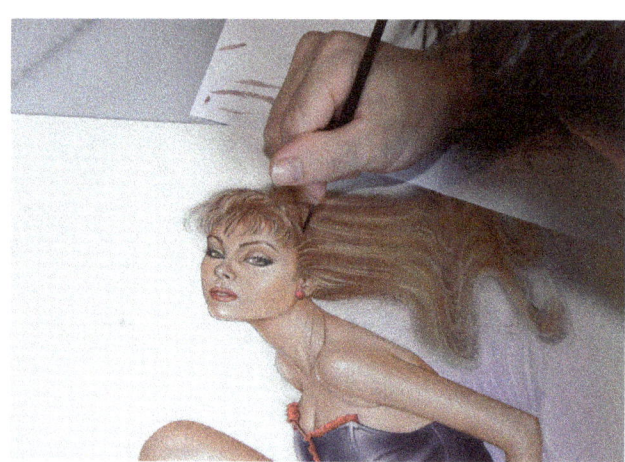

Now to bring out the hair. I'm using a dark mixture of my hair tone to hand brush in individual strands.

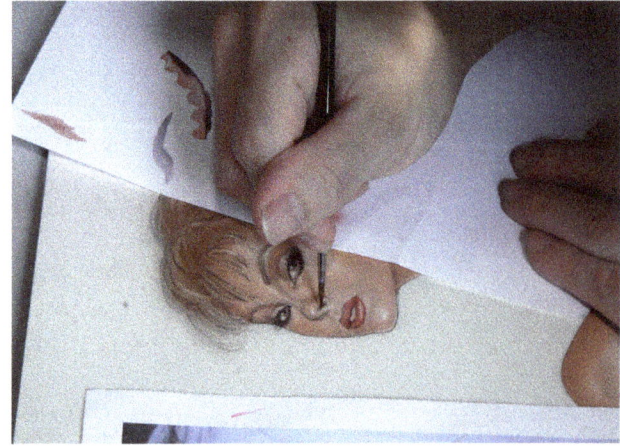

Using the previously mixed shadow flesh tone, I water it down a bit and carefully begin sculpting the nose.

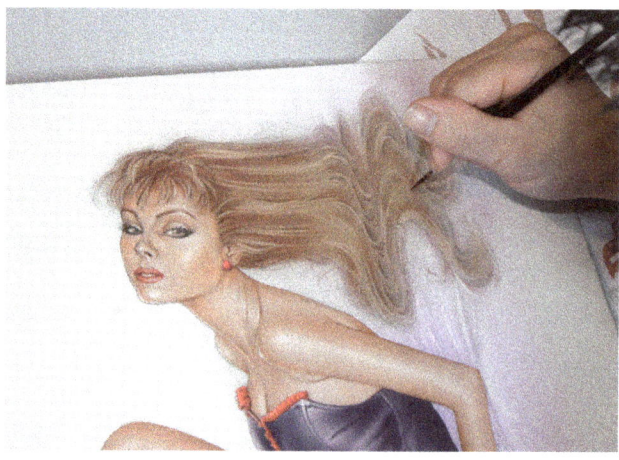

Working down the hair and into the swirlies. Free hand airbrushing can't get lines these sharp; I have to keep the pattern random.

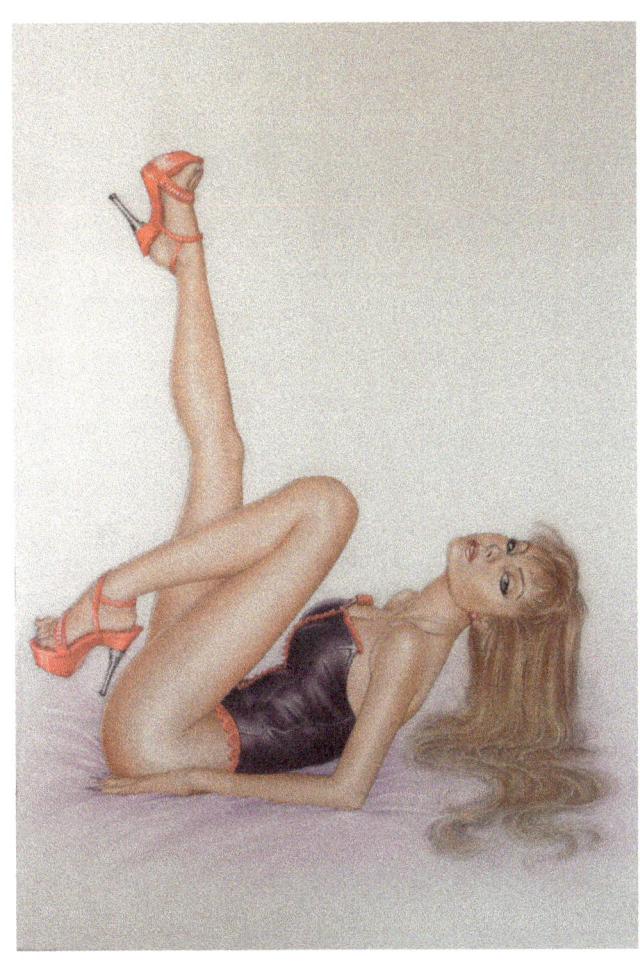

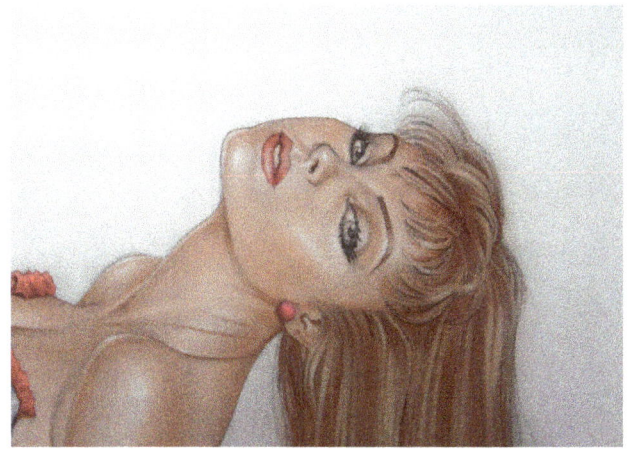

An overview of the face area to see where I'm at, and whether I need to put more work into it.

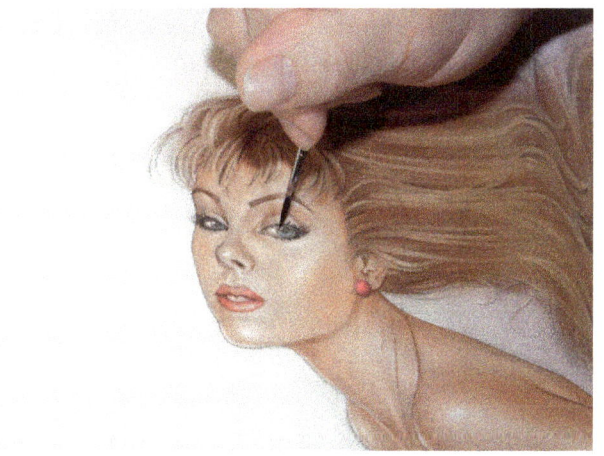

The eyes are very important since they draw the viewer in. Here I'm applying a bright royal blue to Jacki's eyes.

For final specular highlighting I use my sable brush with opaque white on the lips and earring. I think it's time to call it good with this painting. Thanks to the beautiful Jacki Morrison for posing for me!

Still on the eyes, I use Smoke (it's not as strong as straight opaque black) to define the eyelashes. Don't overdo and outline every single little hair!

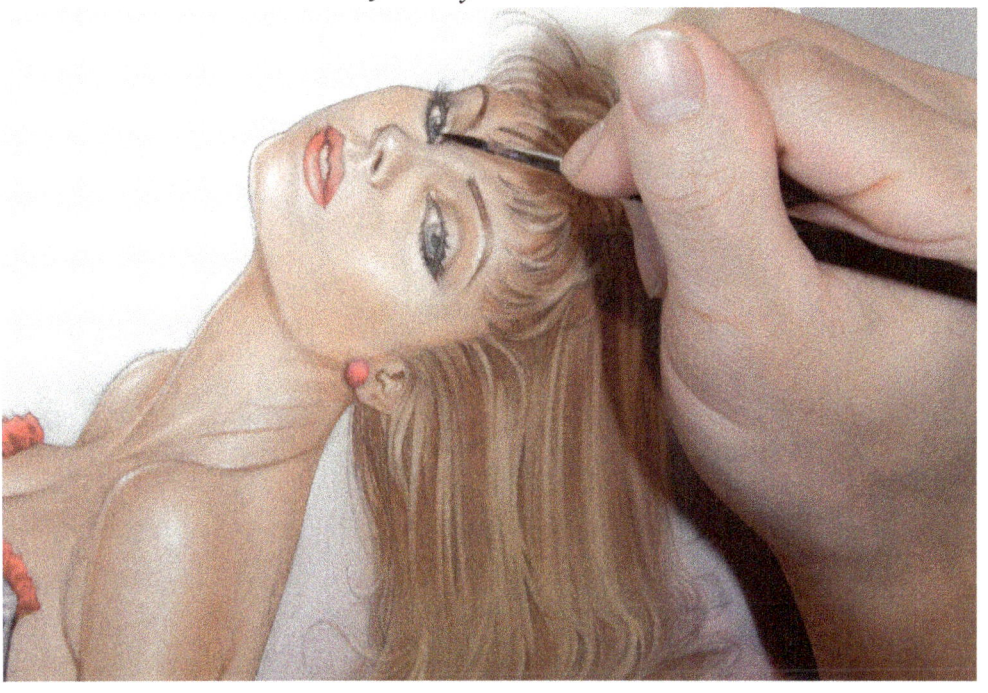

43

Chapter Three

Keith Hanson

Throw Out The Rules

Best known as the graphics artist for bike-builder Dave Perewitz, Keith Hanson is a man with a fresh approach. After nearly thirty years doing pinstripes, airbrush and paint work, Keith likes to disregard the rules of convention. Don't ask him how he gets the two sides of the tank exactly the same, because he doesn't even try. "Each piece is different," explains Keith. "It gives you a reason to go and look at the other side. I try to balance one side with the other,

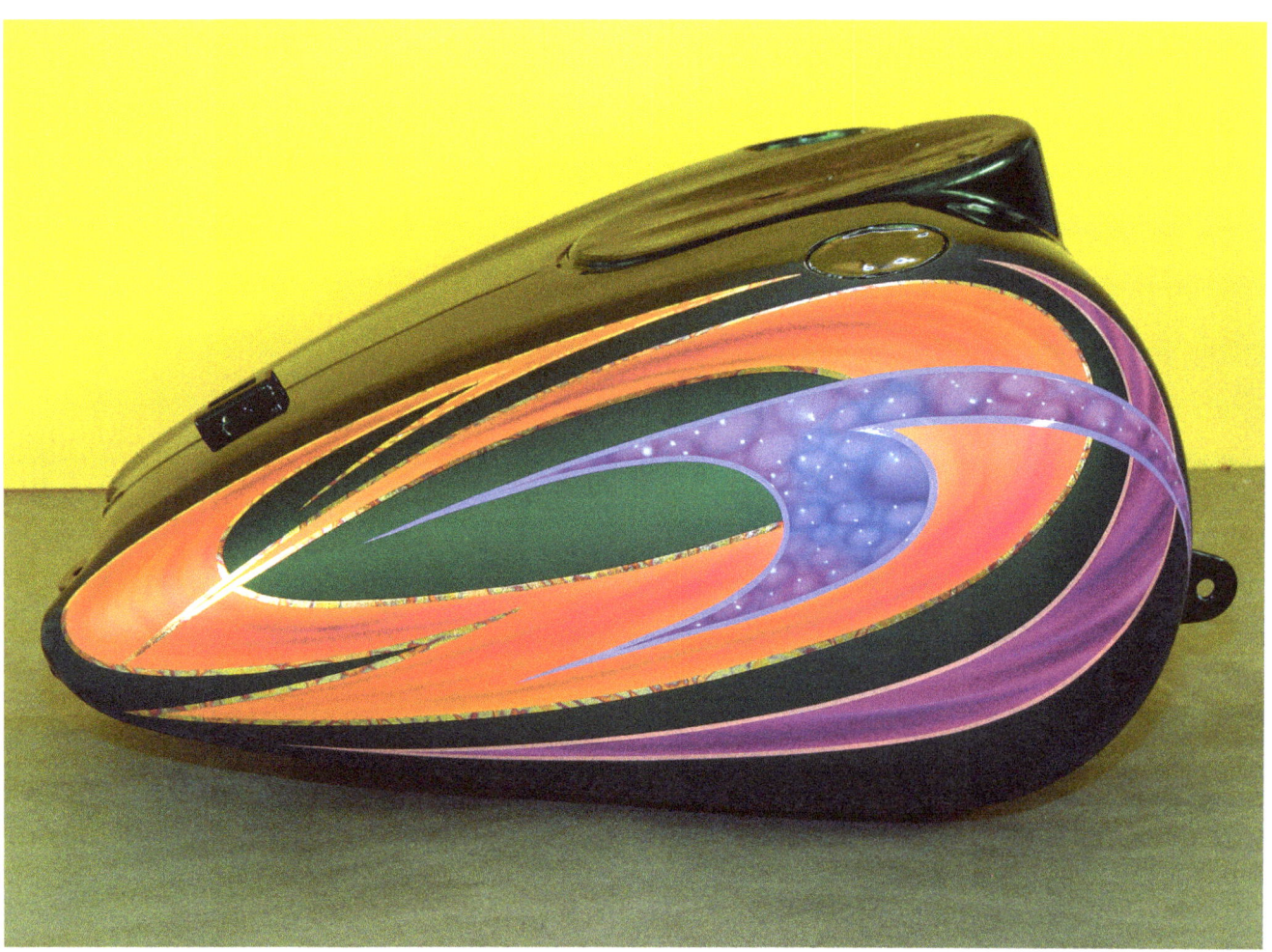

Keith Hanson has his own ideas about graphic design. One of which is the idea that the right and left sides of a motorcycle tank do not have to be identical. In fact, Keith often works to ensure the two sides are similar in a design sense, but not even close to being the same.

you can do that by using up about the same amount of space on one side as the other, or you can use color for that. If the graphic is brighter on one side than the other, I might use a real bright pinstripe on the other side." And if you wonder why some of his pinstripes look so much like gold leaf, it's because they are gold leaf.

THE INITIAL LAYOUT

Rather than work from a sketch, Keith works out the design right on the tank, explaining as he does, "I tend to just do it, because if I think too much about the art, I get too tight."

With the green basecoat already finished and sanded, the layout evolves right on the tank, done with green fineline tape. The layout takes time, each side needs to flow with a similar design. The next step is to cut out the overlapping pieces of tape.

The rest of the masking is done with wide masking tape cut out with the Xacto knife, then more tape and masking paper.

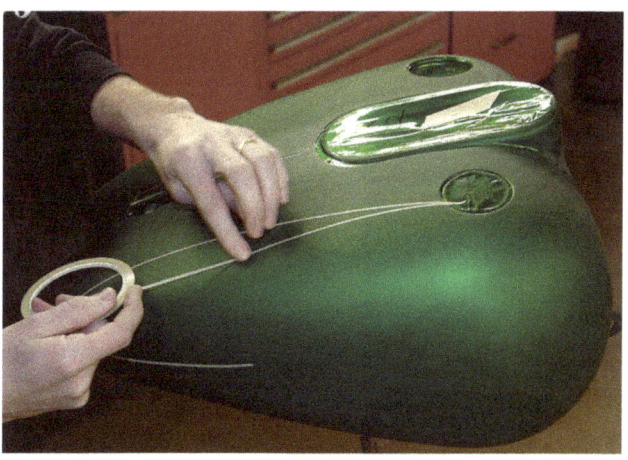

The layout is done directly on the tank, working without a sketch and without much in the way of preconceived ideas.

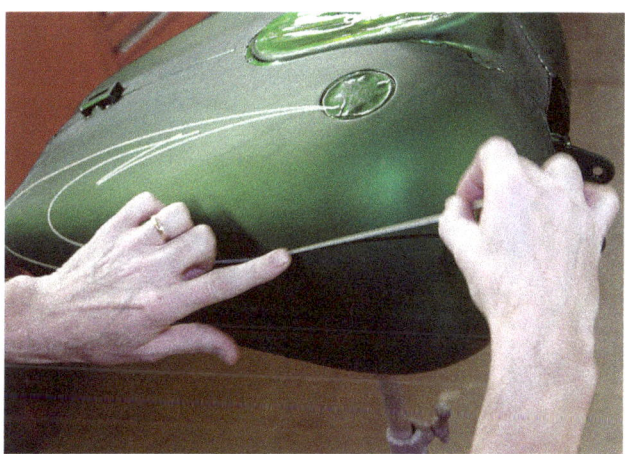

The design flows from Keith's head to his hands.

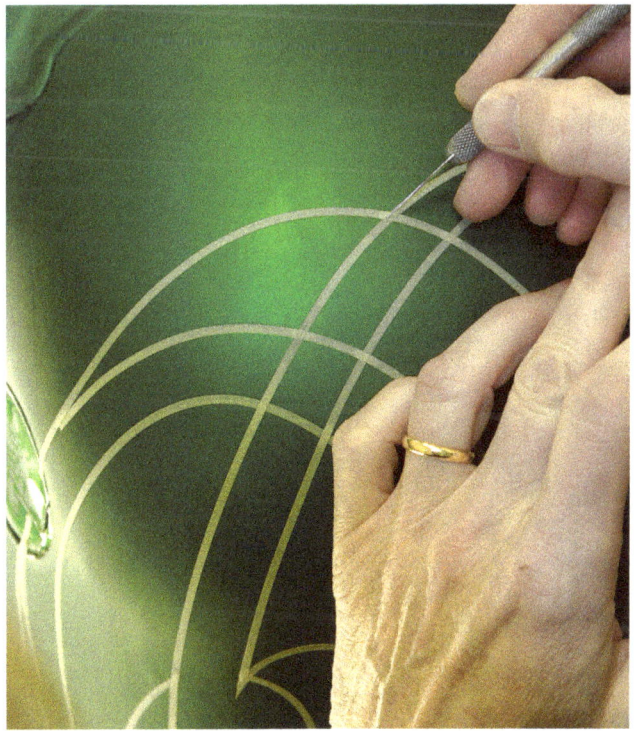

Before the actual masking can take place, Keith cuts out the overlapping fineline tape.

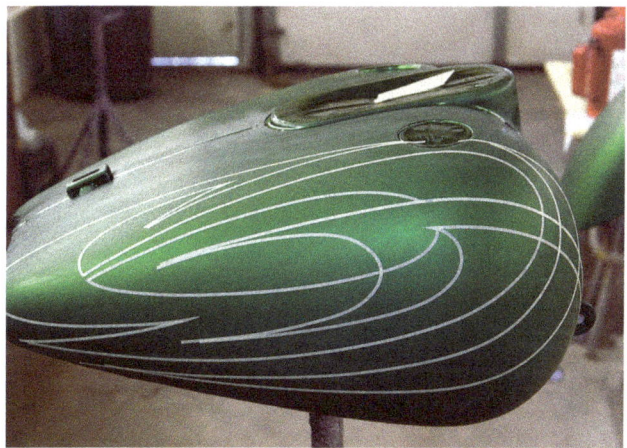

Here, the outline of the graphic appears on the tank. The two sides will be "balanced" but not identical.

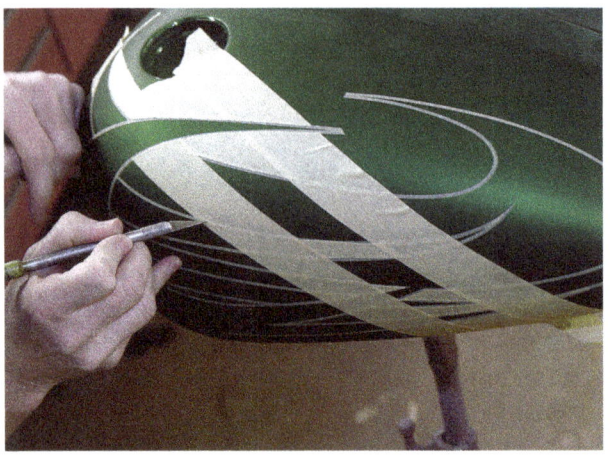

Once the design is finished, the masking is done with wide tape...

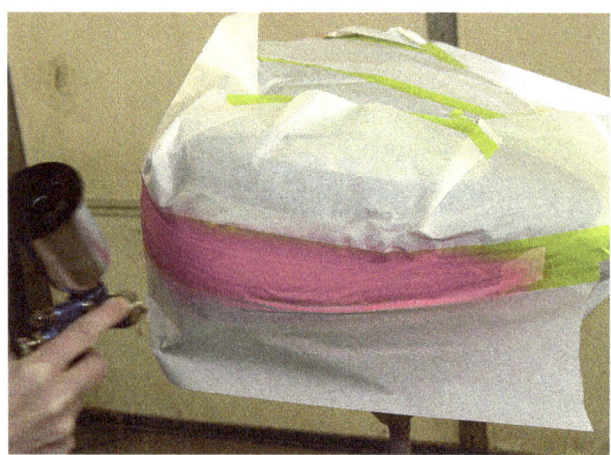

The light pink goes on first, in two light coats.

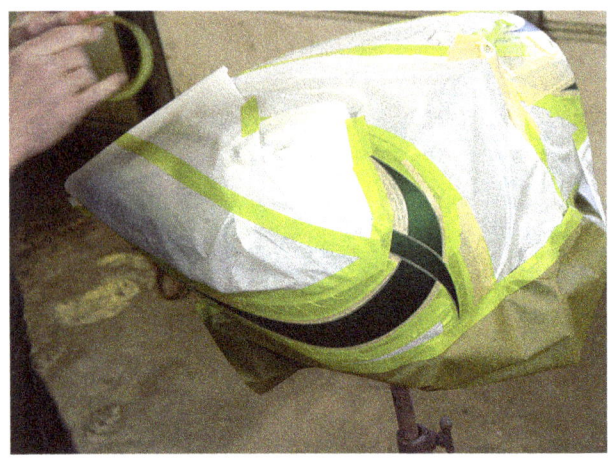

...and paper.

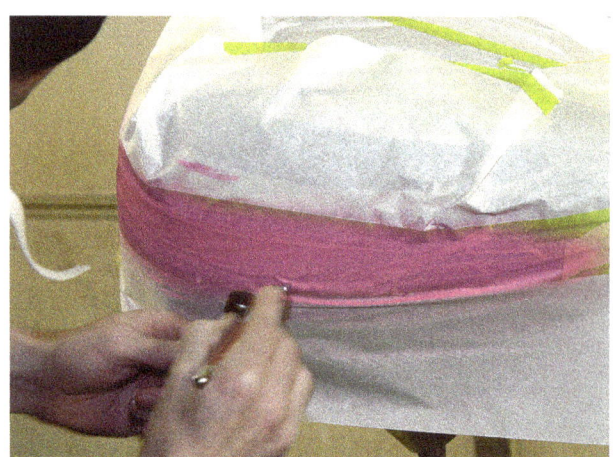

Once the basecoat is dry, Keith starts with hot pink, applied as streaks or a series of passes using the airbrush.

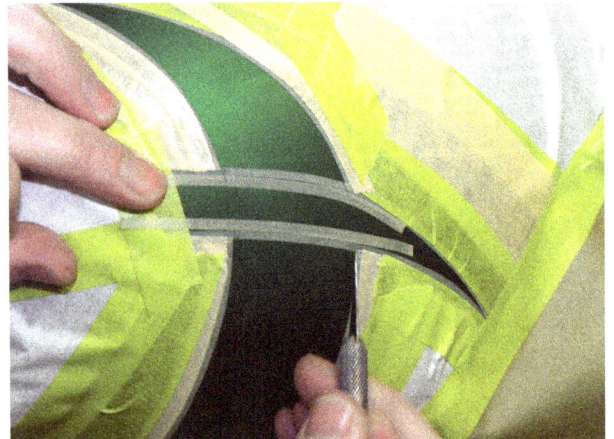

You have to know which spear goes over or under. In this case, the horizontal spear goes over, which is why the 2 outer pieces of tape will be pulled off.

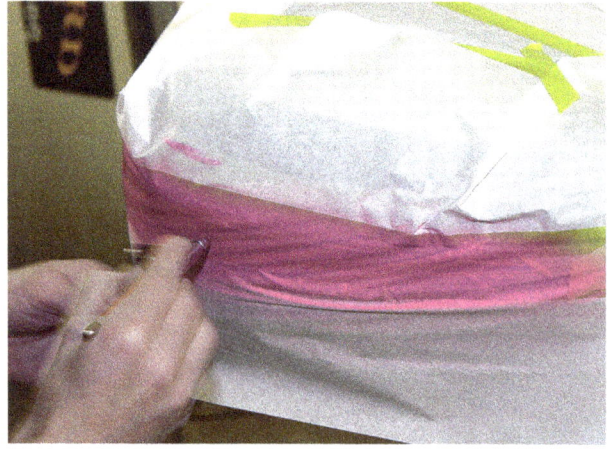

Passion pearl is next, sprayed on top of the hot pink to darken the streaks.

START SMALL

"I start with the smallest graphic," says Keith. "The one with the least amount of color in it. By doing the smallest areas first, it keeps me moving faster. Smaller areas dry faster and can be taped over faster, so I can move onto the next step quickly. During layout you have to be sure to modify the tape out where one spear runs under the other so you get the right effect."

The first color Keith applies is PPG light pink basecoat (DBC51589), applied to the entire spear in two coats. This is the base for the darker colors to follow. One of Keith's rules is to start light and go darker.

A PROGRESSION OF COLORS

In this case, hot pink pearl from House of Kolor (PBC 39) is the first accent color applied over the light pink. The hot pink is applied in a series of passes, (note the photos). Keith explains that, "I like to flush the airbrush with reducer between each color, to ensure the next color doesn't get mixed in with the previous color."

"As you go along with the project, applying various colors, you apply a little less of each color in the progression. In this case, passion pearl (PBC 65) is the second color. If the first color is 50%, the passion pearl is 30% and the final color is 20%."

Blue intensifier from PPG (DMX 220) is color number three. Sticking with Keith's plan of applying less and less paint with each step, the white is applied last, in a series of small, running highlights. To protect his airbrush work, Keith applies two coats of DBC 500 intercoat clear using a SATA pistol-grip airbrush. This brush is bigger than most airbrushes, but still smaller than a touch-up gun.

"I always pull the tape carefully," explains Keith, "so I don't pull tape underneath that I would like to leave in place. Usually, by the time I have the tape pulled the paint I've just done is dry enough to tape over and I can move right along with the project."

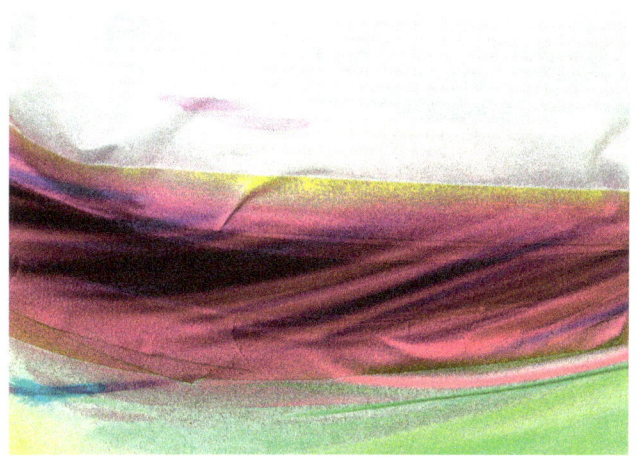

This is the panel after the blue intensifier (the last, and darkest, color) is added to the streaks.

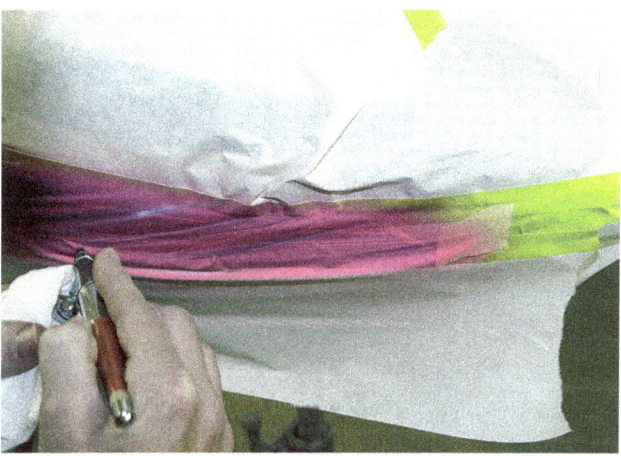

A few white highlights are added as the final touch...

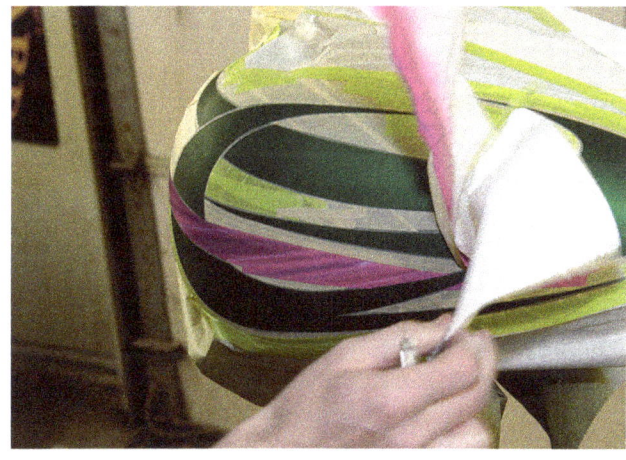

...and the work can be unmasked.

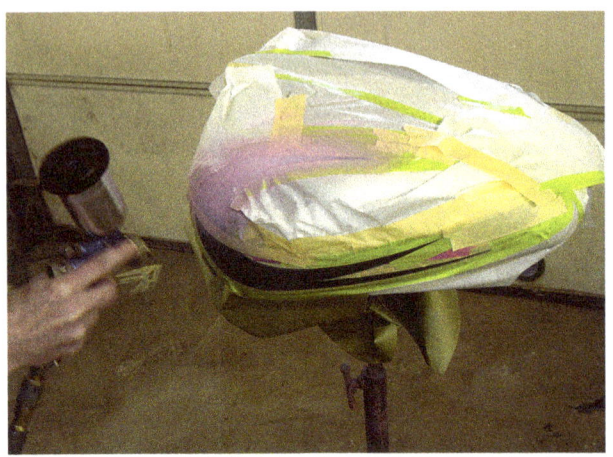

Another spear, another color, dark lilac in this case.

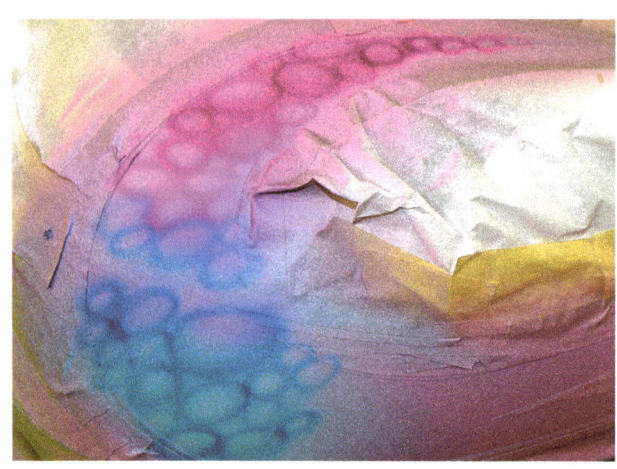

...then in hot pink (BC 39)...

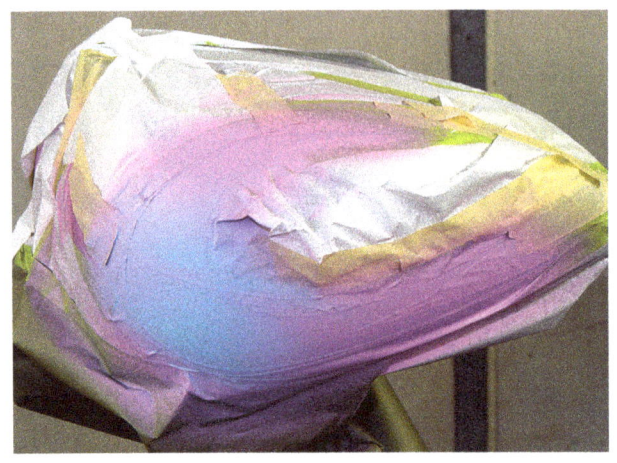

Two coats of the dark lilac are followed by green blue (DBC 17709) on the front of the spear.

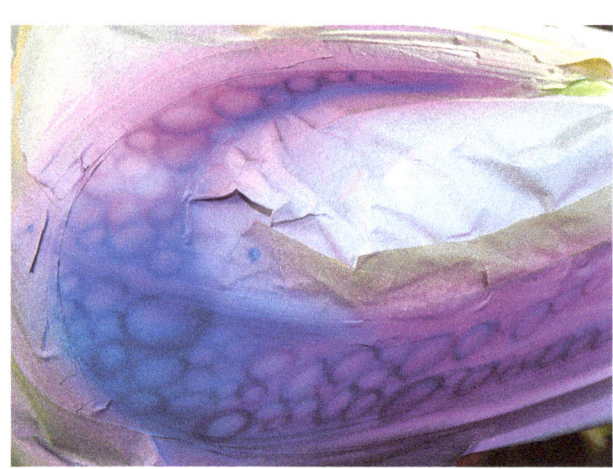

...which is darkened by blue intensifier (DMX 220)...

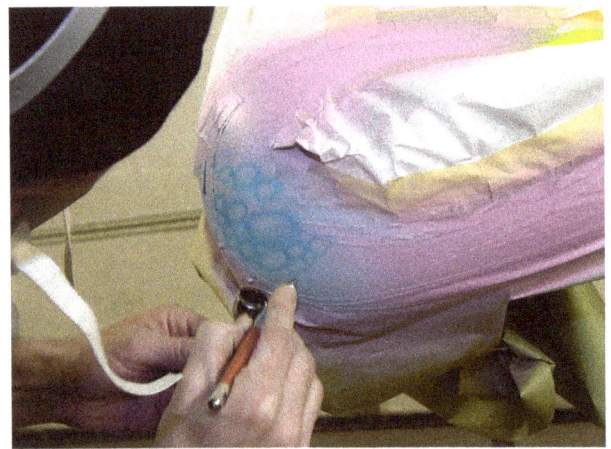

Abstract circles come next, done first in light pink pearl (PBC 57)...

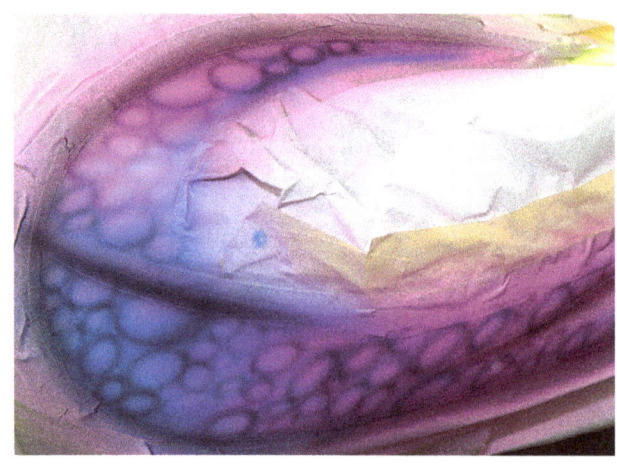

...and then a little black (DBC 1683).

Retape and Start Anew

After retaping, the next spear is coated first with dark lilac (DBC 51598), applied with a touch-up gun to the entire spear. Next, comes green blue (DBC 17709), applied in a series of small passes at the front of the area.

Light pink pearl (PBC 57) is next. This color is used to create a series of small circles. Sometimes Keith keeps the gun close for tight lines and detail, other times he moves it farther away for a softer edge.

Hot pink pearl (PBC 39) is next, used to create more circles surrounding those already there. These are created at random, with no apparent pattern. Blue intensifier, the darkest color of this series, is used to tone some of the circles already created and help to give them dimension. Black is next, used to darken some of the circles and to create a shadow line along the top of the spear.

Keith applies pearl (PPG PRL 89 mixed with DBC 500 intercoat clear and reduced 1:1) over the black to soften it a little bit (all references to black are DBC 1683). White highlights come next. Keith explains that, "these precise little pinpoints of white are used to separate the surfaces from the background."

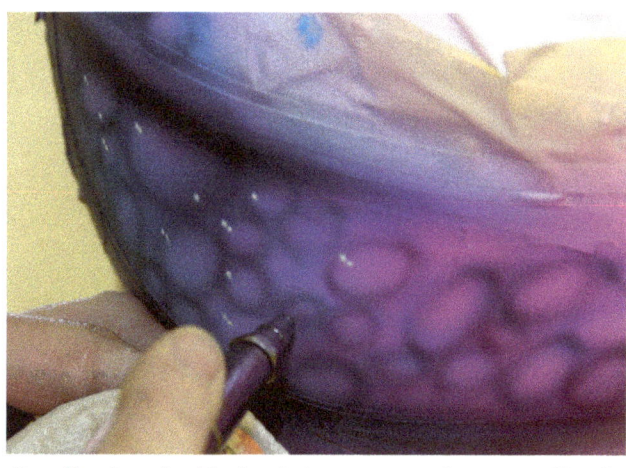

Small white highlights help to create the 3-D effect by making the highlight seem like it's the highest point...

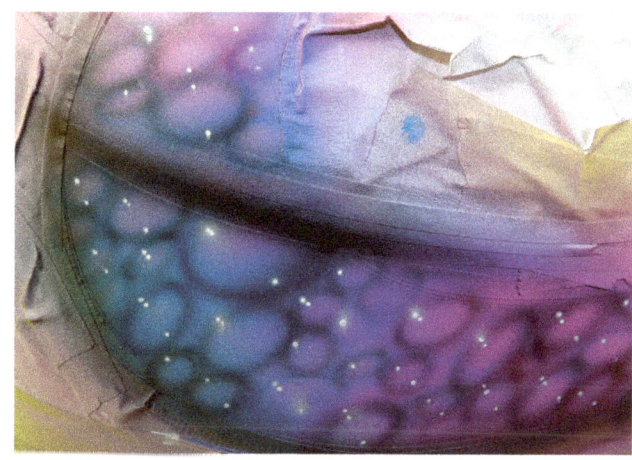

...the point that catches the light.

...Keith begins to re-mask and prepare for another series of colors.

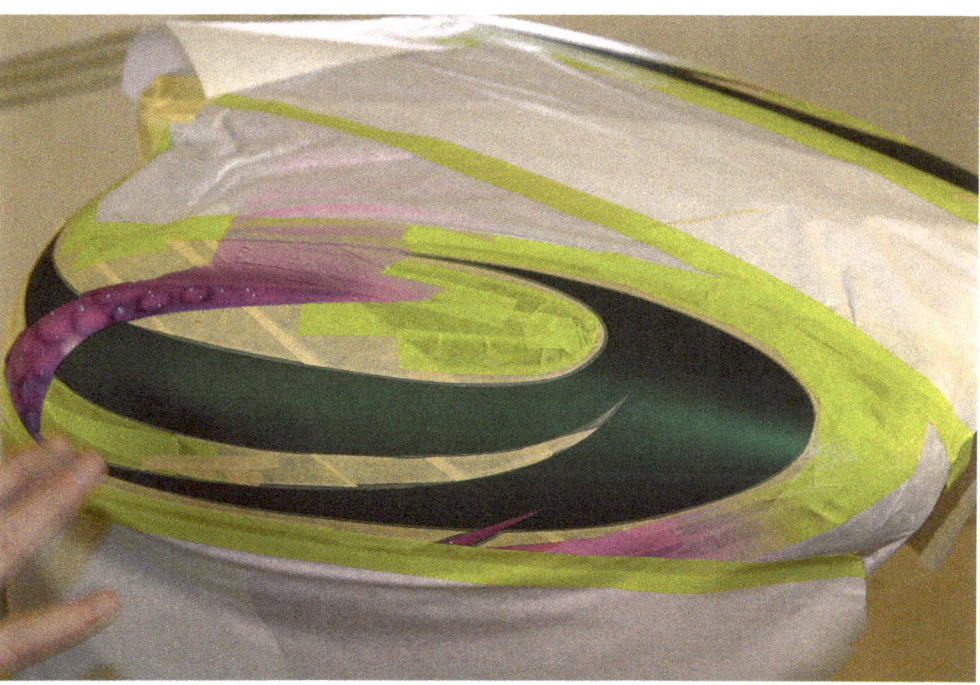

49

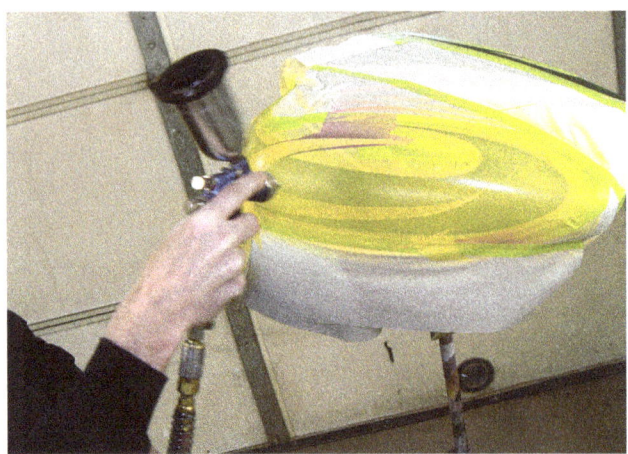

"I like to run 35 to 40 psi at the gun, and the same for the airbrushes."

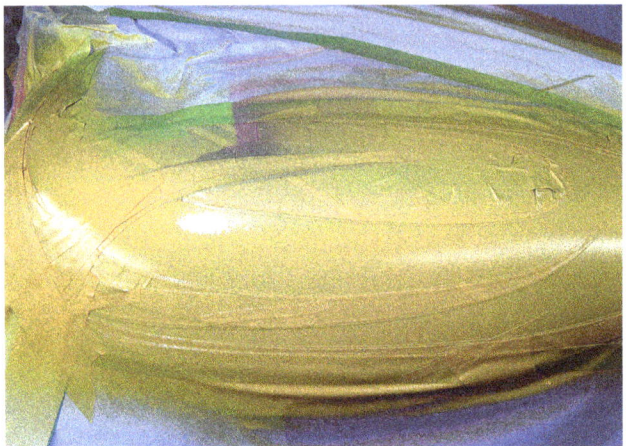

The biggest part of the design is the brightest, seen here after 3 coats of sunburst yellow.

"The white creates the illusion that the light is reflecting off the part that is closest to you. Again I moved from dark to light, and even though we didn't use very much white, look at the effect it has. After the white is finished I apply two more coats of intercoat clear to protect all this work."

THE MOST IMPORTANT AREA

"This progression is working really well," explains Keith. "Now we're at the biggest part of the design, the largest area and the one that will have the most color. It's more efficient to work this way. As I work, I don't worry too much about the edges. A lot of these don't have to be perfect, you're going to have a pinstripe to cover any roughness."

Work on this next area starts with sunburst yellow (DBC 83032). The yellow is applied to the entire area in three light coats using a touch-up gun. Sunrise pearl (PBC 30) is next, applied in two light coats, used in this case to tone and richen the sunburst yellow.

THE NEXT DESIGN

What might be called the accent colors start with sunset pearl (PBC 31), applied with an airbrush to the perimeter of the area, and in subtle streaks that follow the overall shape of the spear.

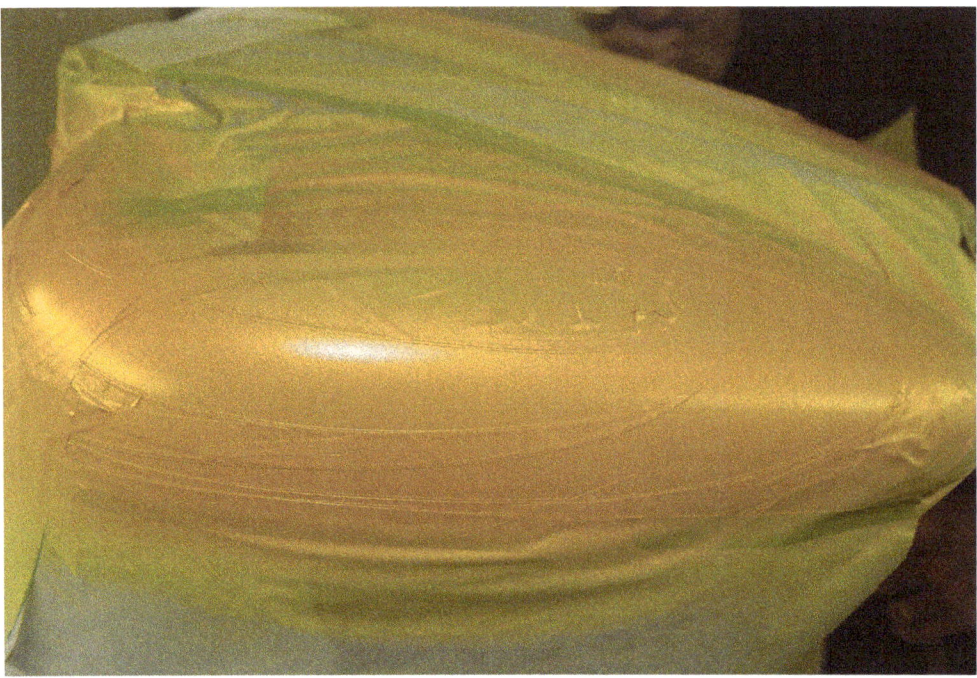

Sunrise pearl is applied on top of the sunburst yellow. The combination produces a totally new, and much richer, color.

Q&A: Keith Hanson

Keith, how did you get started doing airbrush work?

I remember the moment I developed a fascination with paint. I was seven years old and my sisters were starting a fan club. They needed a sign and I asked if they would let me work on it. My dad was artistic. That isn't how he made his living, but he always encouraged my artistic endeavors. My mom wanted me to go to art school, but I hated school so much that I couldn't see that. I didn't really start doing art work professionally until I was about 23. I've been on my own since 1978.

I started out pinstriping as a hobby and then it progressed. People say if you can stripe you can letter, so I started doing sign work. Then they started to ask, "Can you do gold leaf?" When they would ask about some skill I didn't have, I would go practice and then take the job.

I came into contact with motorcycles through a local painter, John Hartnett. Many of the people I met then are still customers and friends, including, and especially, Dave Perewitz. I learned as I went along. The equipment, the paints and all the rest. For about nine years I painted and lettered funny cars, dragsters and show cars. Of course I did motorcycles too. But at one point I decided to switch, to work on motorcycles instead of race cars.

Where do you get your ideas?

I try to come up with new ideas so my work isn't so repetitive, I don't go to bike magazines for my ideas, that's the last place I look. I get a lot of ideas from the fashion industry, they are in the business of making you buy things you don't need. I like to look at their textures, their use of color.

The idea for the "circles" used on this tank came from a stone wall, that's where it started and look how far it's gone.

How do you pick colors and designs?

I let the design tell me what it's going to be, I don't pick colors ahead of time.

Which paints do you use?

I use H of K and PPG both, almost interchangeably. I don't use any water-based paints.

Which airbrush do you like?

My work horse airbrush is a Paasche VL 1. For more detail I use a Richpen 213C. To get automotive paints to go through the airbrush the paint needs to be over reduced by about 50%.

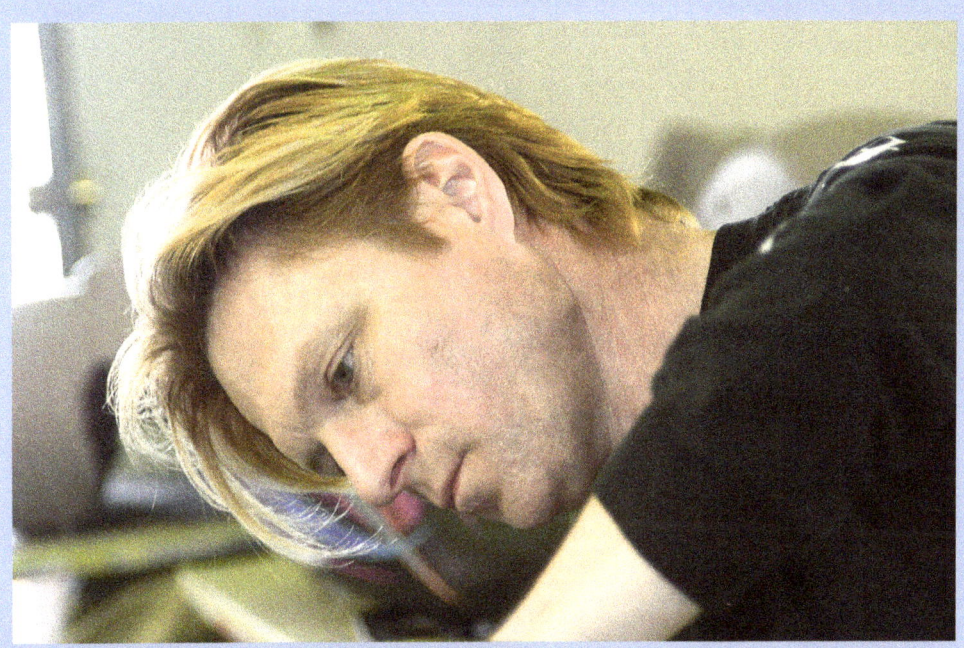

Talented and innovative, Keith Hanson is the only motorcycle guy to subscribe to both Cosmopolitan and Easyriders.

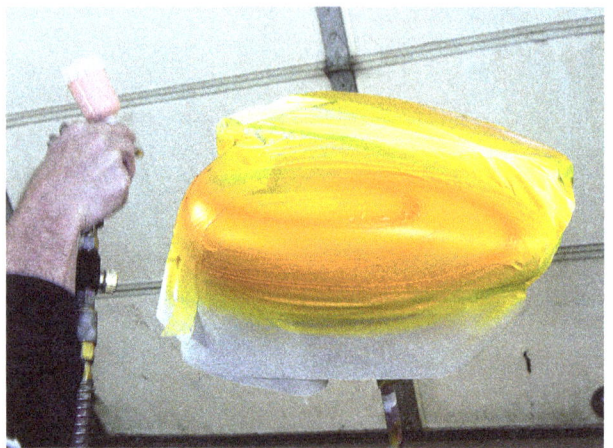

You can see the design develop as Keith applies swirls of sunset pearl.

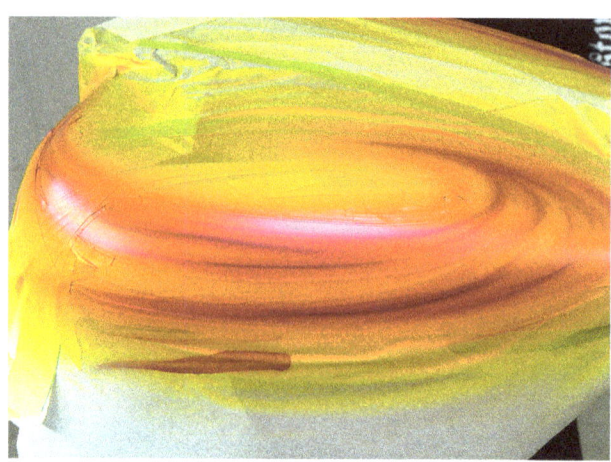

A little hot pink, and a dusting of blue intensifier, adds brightness to the swirls.

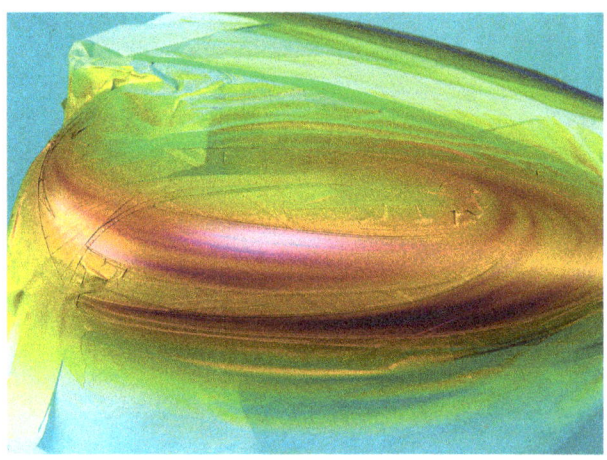

The sunset pearl is followed by multiple light passes of hot pink.

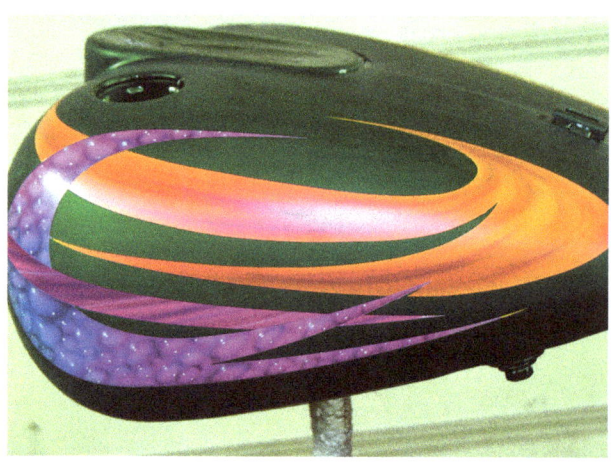

A look at the three separate, but interacting, areas before the pinstripes.

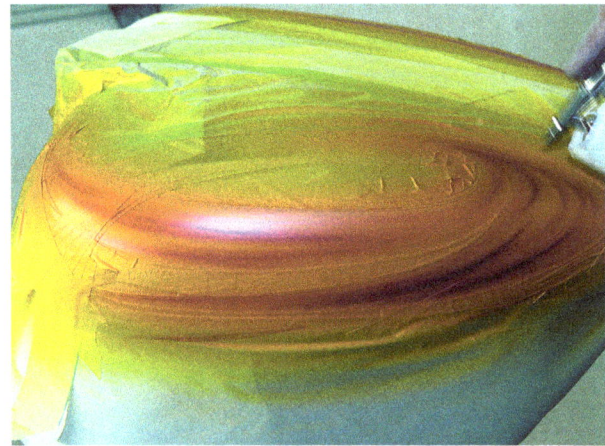

The effects are subtle, the next color to be applied is passion pearl.

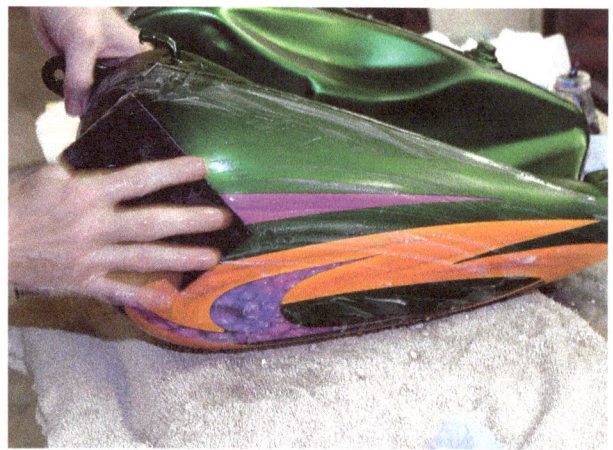

After applying a quick coat of intercoat clear and allowing that to dry, Keith scrubs the tank with 800 grit wet paper, "to take down the edges."

The sunset pearl is followed by hot pink (PBC 39). Using an airbrush, Keith does more swirls, overlaid on top of what was done with the sunset pearl.

Passion pearl is next (PBC 65), more swirl patterns are laid down on top of previous patterns. Moving back and forth, Keith adds a little more hot pink for a subtle effect, followed by some blue intensifier. Next comes a quick coat of intercoat clear.

Keith's Color Theory

"You can put almost any color with any other if you have the right colors in between, so the pinstriping is very important. Using leaf for a pinstripe draws a lot of attention to the panel. Pinstripes are an easy way to add more punch."

Keith advises that overspray can be eliminated with some wet 1200 grit. Before doing any pinstriping the tanks are clearcoated with final clear and allowed to sit overnight. The clear is then wet sanded with 800 grit paper. "I don't use a sanding block," explains Keith, "basically, I'm just taking down the edges of the graphics."

Pinstripes

Keith outlines each panel with fineline tape, this tape is a guide, which is why he leaves 1/8 inch between graphic and the tape (note the nearby photos). All the pinstriping, except the leaf of course, is done with H of K striping urethane mixed with their reducer (U 00) and no catalyst. For mixing paint and reducer to the right viscosity, Keith uses a non-porous palette. The brush is a Mack brand, size 00 made from squirrel hair. "This is a bright job, says Keith, "I want bright stripes. I want a lot of contrast so I can see this job from a distance. It's important that the paint be evenly distributed throughout the brush, even if it means using your fingers to smooth out the bristles."

"I start with simple stripes first, as I did with the graphics. And mentally, when I do the easy steps first, by the time I get to the really hard parts, to me it looks like I already have the job almost done. I also use a Mack scrolling script,

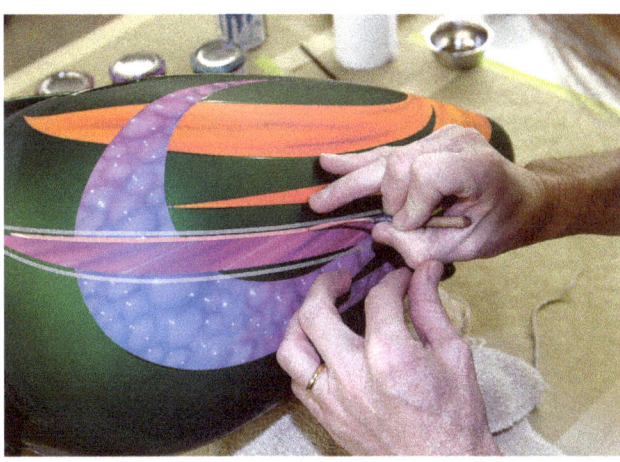

A piece of fineline tape run just off the edge of the graphic is used as a guide for Keith.

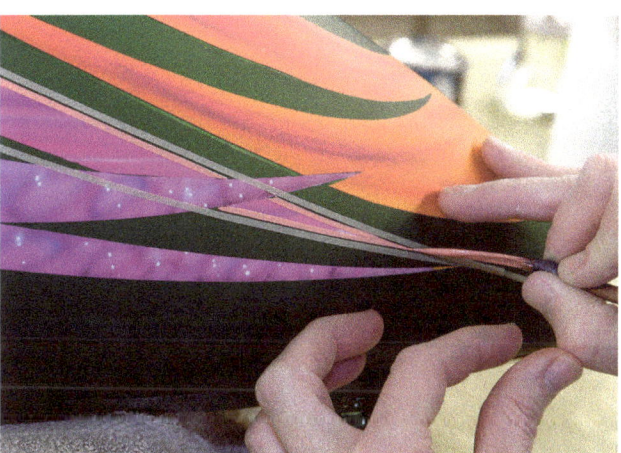

At the corners, "the pinstripes can be used to elongate and exaggerate the shape."

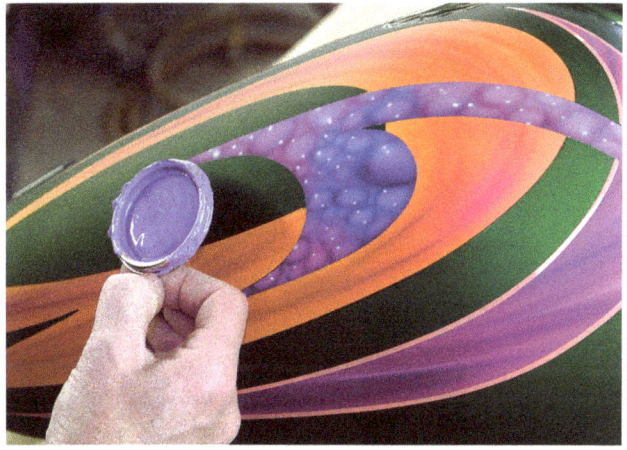

Colors are picked on the fly.. But be careful, because the urethane striping paints can't be easily wiped off if you don't like the effect.

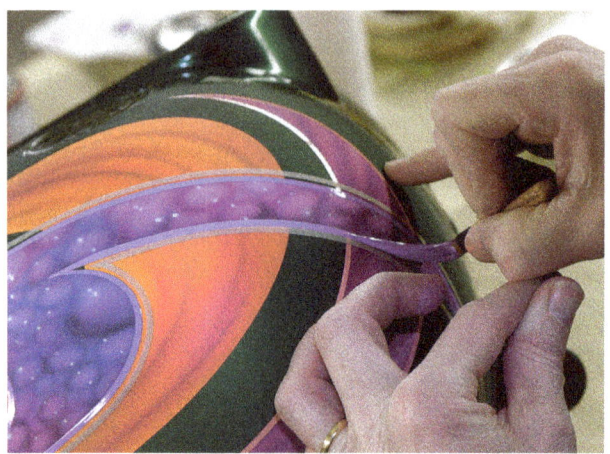

Most of the stripes are done with a conventional Mack number 00 pinstriping brush made from Squirrel hair.

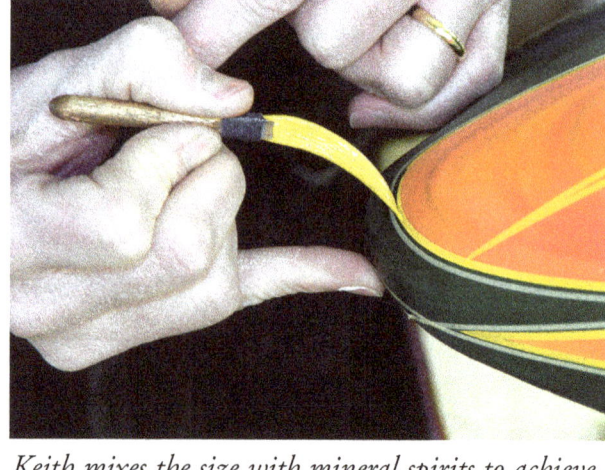

Keith mixes the size with mineral spirits to achieve the right viscosity. One-Shot gives it the color. A pinstriping brush is used for application.

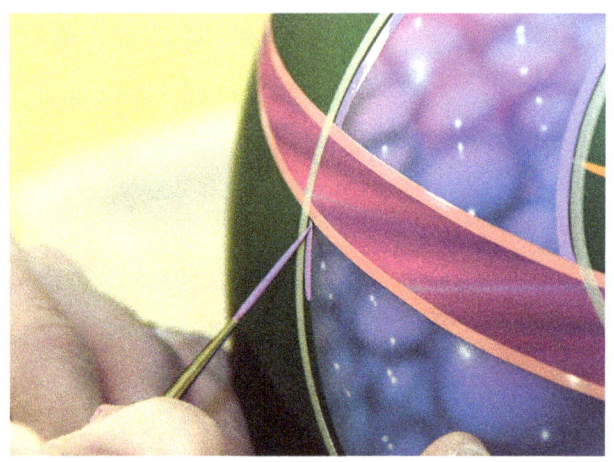

For tight detail work and intersections, Keith likes a small lettering brush. Brushes are cleaned in regular paint reducer from H of K, not the U 00.

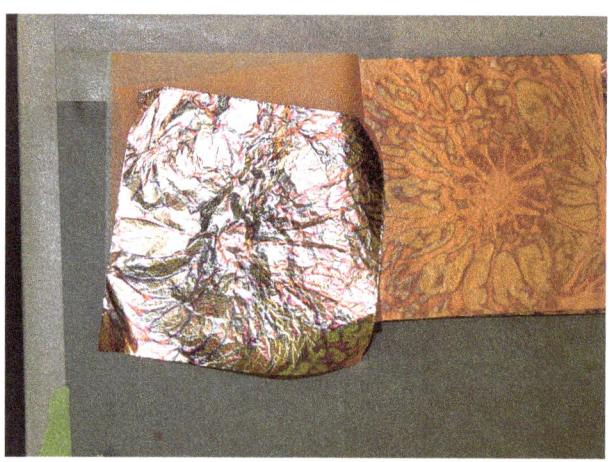

The leaf is variegated red, available from Sid Moses.

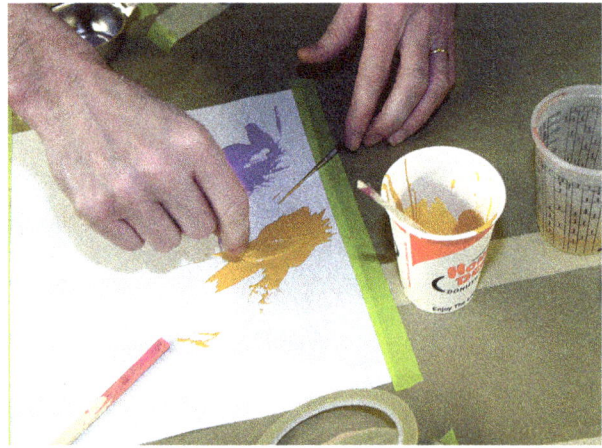

The size, or adhesive, is mixed with paint so it's easier to see.

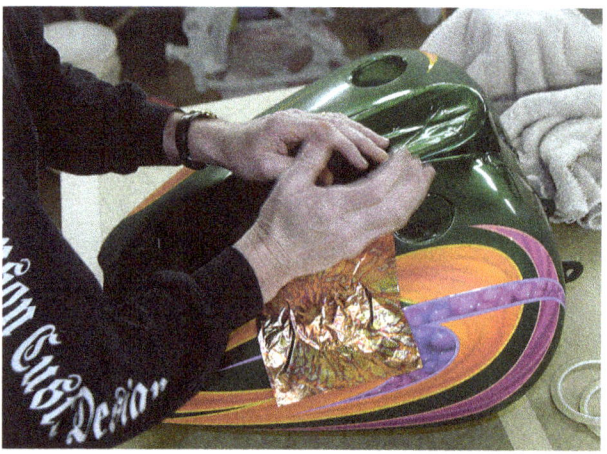

Keith uses soft taps from the heel of his hand to fully seat the leaf onto the size.

it's like a small lettering brush. I use it for intersections and small areas. Peach (U 28) is the first color. I always try to use the stripes to exaggerate the shapes you already have, the stripes help to elongate the tips for example. I look at pinstriping as an extremely important part of finishing any job. The second pinstripe color is violet (U 29)."

Keith prefers Rolco sizing mixed with imitation gold paint from One-Shot, just a little to give it color. "When thinning the size I use mineral spirits," explains Keith, "as little of it as possible, just enough so the paint doesn't drag. Like I always say, 'I like to let the design talk to me.' And it seems in this case that the orange section is dominant, so I should use the brightest pinstripe around that area to keep it dominant, thus the use of variegated leaf."

The size is applied with a pinstriping brush. "As soon as you can touch the size and none comes off, that's when it's the right time to apply the gold," explains Keith. "I like variegated gold, it has more color and more going on. "

The main sheet of leaf is attached to the tank, large and small excess areas are torn off and moved to a new area, then tamped down again with the heel of Keith's hand. This process repeats until all the size is covered in gold leaf.

"This leaf is from Sid Moses (see sources), it's got the most color of any of the variegated products," explains Keith. "I knock off the big chunks by hand, then rub it down with a soft rag to eliminate the rest of the excess, then wipe off the gold dust with a damp rag. The size never really does dry completely."

Keith advises doing the leaf last, "because if you do it first you might have to tape over it, and you can't. And once the leaf is on, don't wash the surface with anything stronger than soap and water. I clear it immediately. As you would anything else."

The final clear Keith uses is PPG 3000, because it's affordable, works and dries fast, and offers good UV protection.

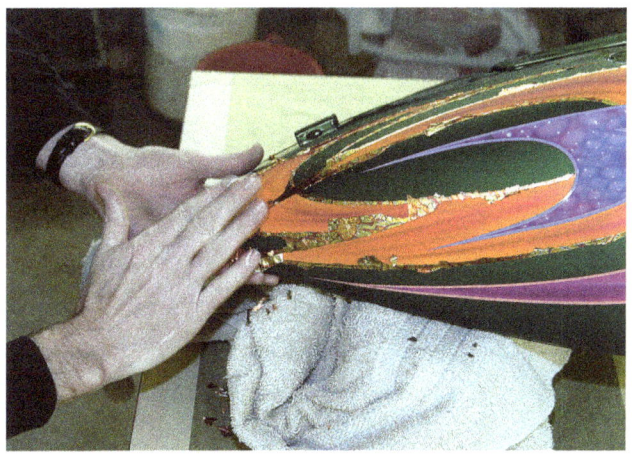

Once the leaf has adhered to the size, Keith gently pulls off the excess material, which is moved to a new area.

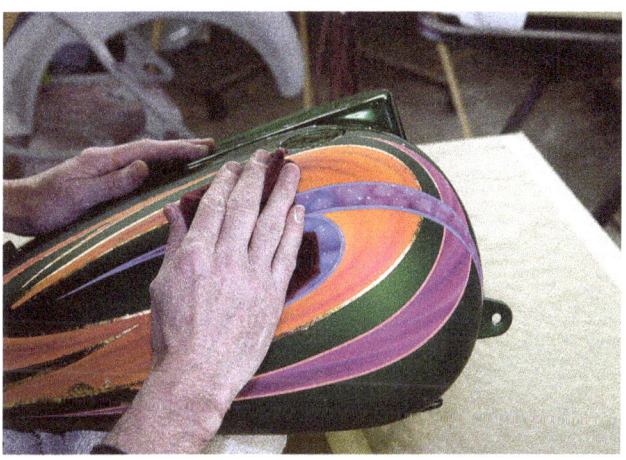

By rubbing the area down with a soft rag the rest of the loose leaf is pulled off.

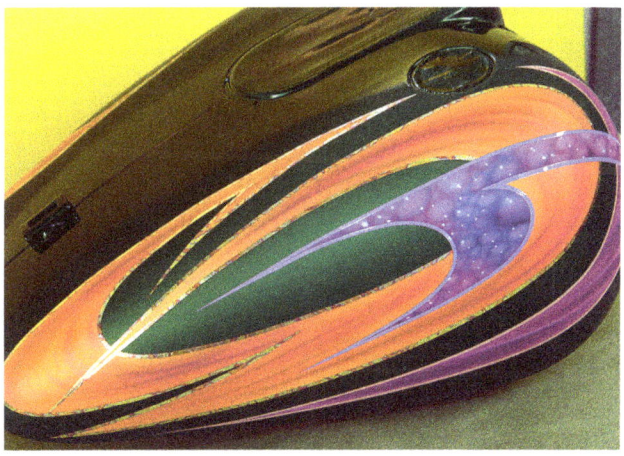

The finished tank, minus the final clear. Compare this to the picture on page 52 and note how much impact the pinstripes have on the overall design

Chapter Four
Luca Paganico
Formal Attire

It all started way back in the first grade when Luca picked up a pencil for the first time. Like so many of the artists in this book, his initial taste of the art world only made him hungry for more and soon his desire to create was overwhelming. Not only was his passion to draw growing, but his ability to do so kept pace. There are many like myself who enjoy the art of drawing but lack the talent to go beyond stick. Makes for a mean game of hangman.

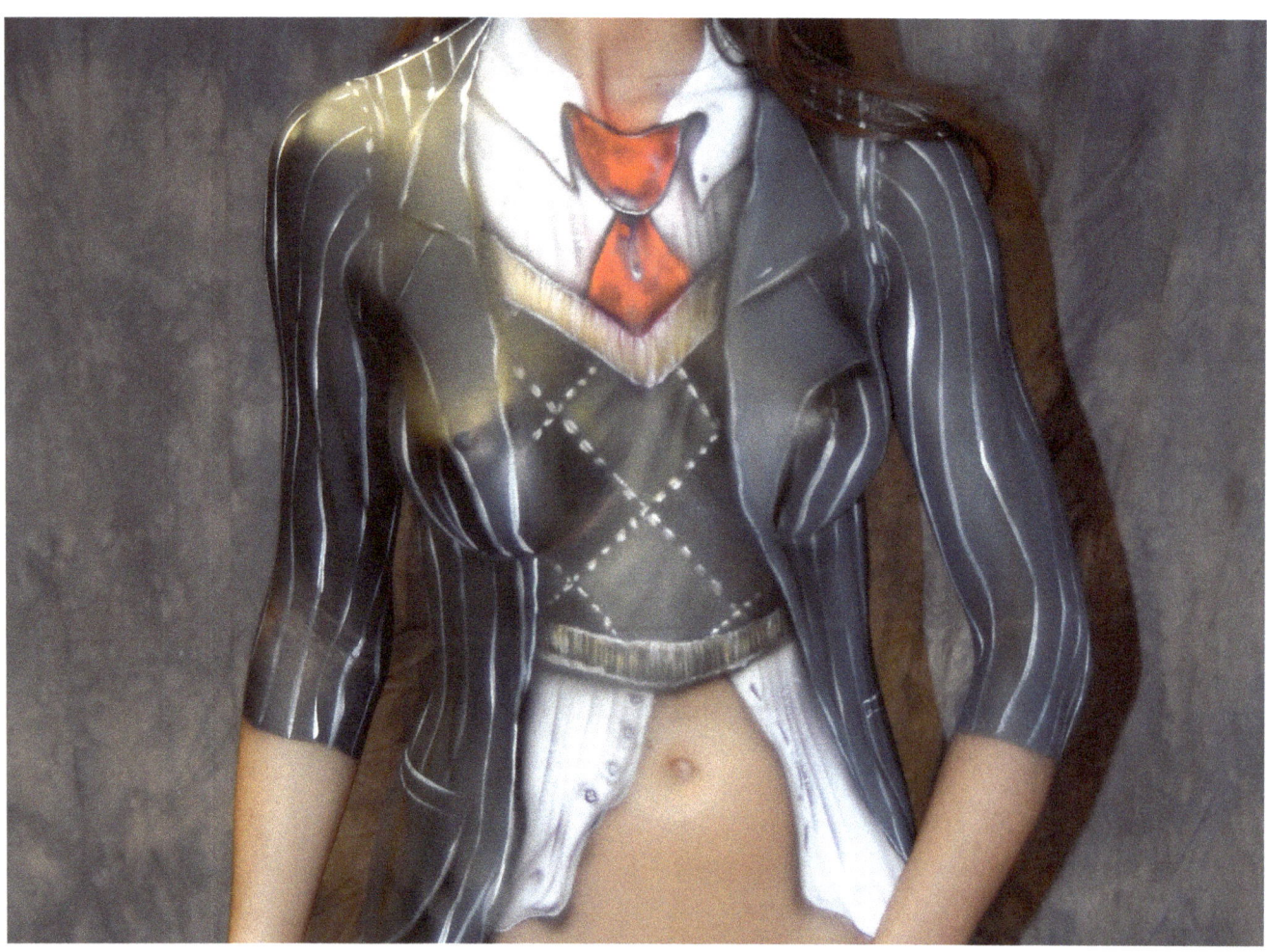

All dressed up and nowhere to go, Jennifer looks like she's ready for an interview.

When he reached the college years, he turned his attentions to industrial design and spent most of his time on specialized technologies. His newfound interest led him to become a successful nightclub and restaurant designer. He was able to use both his industrial and artistic visions to bring new life to existing structures, or to create brand new facilities that won him awards and new clients. He is not only capable of designing the stylish interiors demanded by clients, but can apply an expanse of faux finishes to create the illusion of wood and marble on simple surfaces.

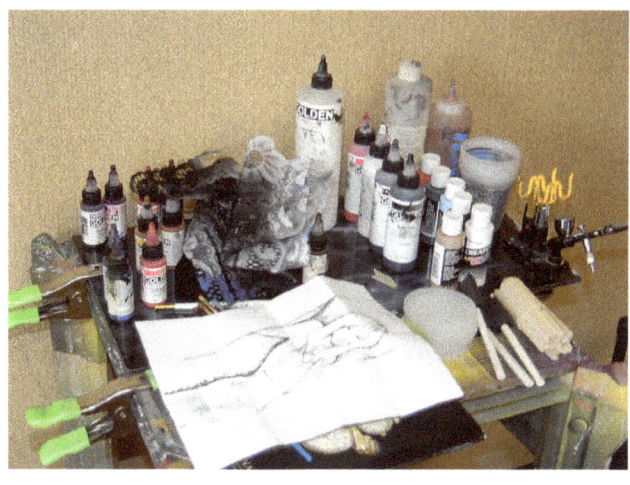

Nearly every inch of his portable table is covered with materials needed for the job at hand.

As satisfying as designing interiors was, he continued to keep his brushes wet in the art world. His airbrush experience leads back nearly two decades and has taught him many tricks of the trade. Unlike many others who operate their airbrushes at a lower rating, Luca runs his under 65-70 psi for the control he seeks. This higher pressure works best with the Golden brand of paint that has become a staple for him.

The joining of his airbrush skills and the new field of body painting happened about six years ago when he painted himself for Halloween. The effect and response were terrific and sent him off in another creative direction. This first foray into the body painting fold led him to a number of commercial and entertainment assignments. He is often tapped to create promotional human art, with the models walking around displaying his art at public venues.

One thing Luca has in common with most of the featured artists in this book, he sees the body painting universe expanding every day. As more talented people join in the parade, I'm also certain that this trend will grow to become far more mainstream and accepted as a fresh form of art.

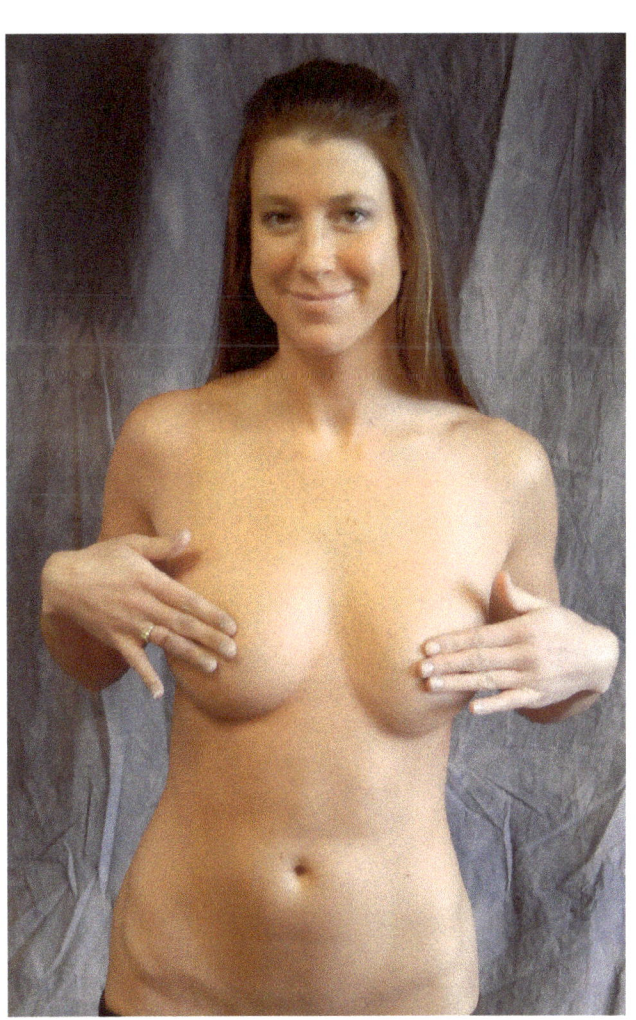

Jennifer has worked with Luca several times in the past and was ready for her latest set of painted clothes.

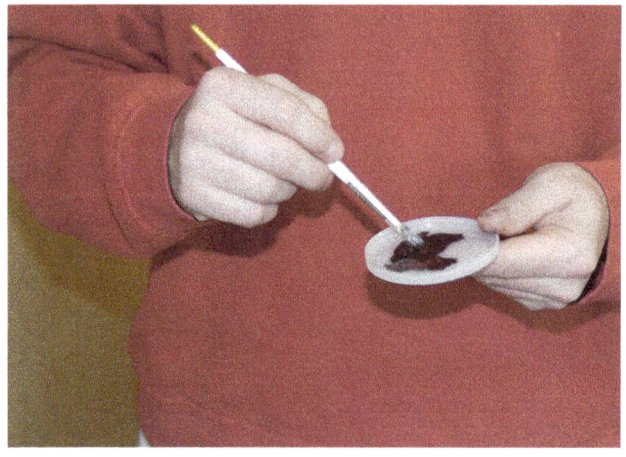

Luca will begin the process with painted lines, and starts by placing some raw material on a mixing surface.

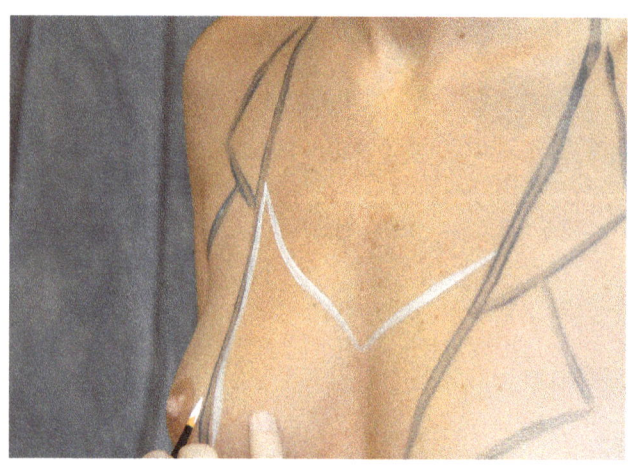

By using lines of appropriate shades, Luca can soon see the position of his future work.

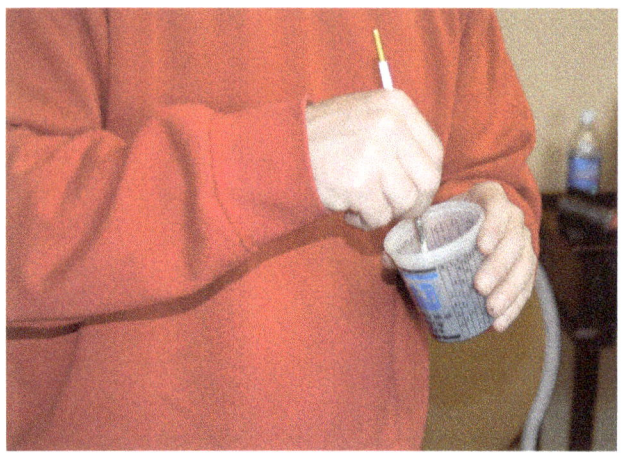

Satisfied with his blend, Luca prepares to put his first brush into action.

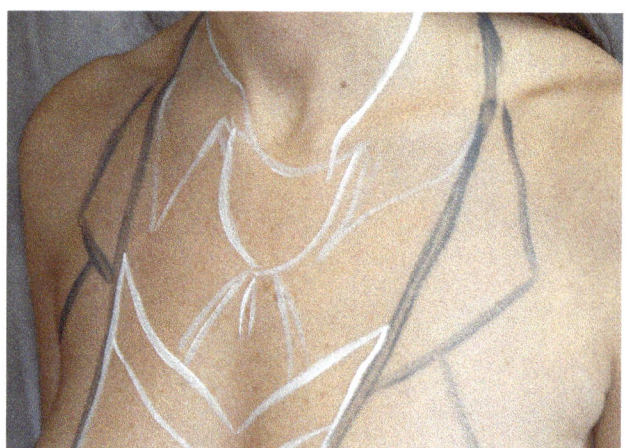

In only a few minutes we can see the shirt collar, sweater and jacket lapels taking shape.

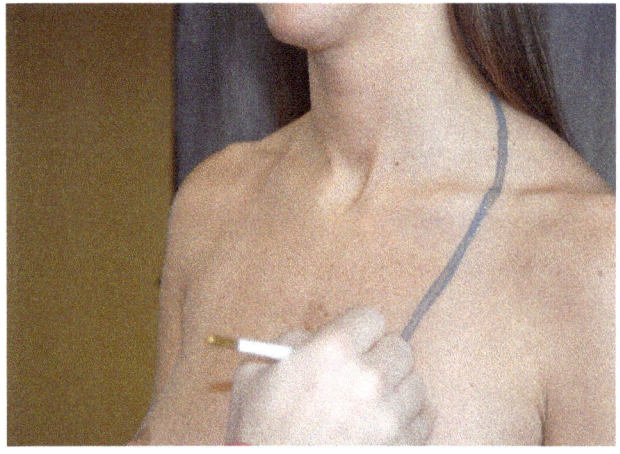

The neck line of the jacket is the first mark made on Jenn's chest and will soon be followed by much more.

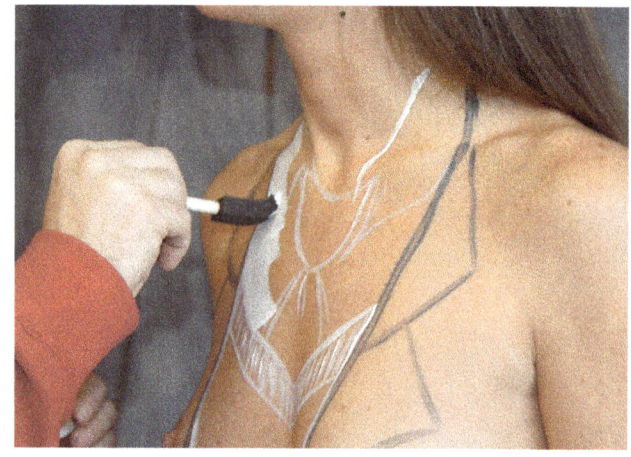

With the guidelines complete, Luca uses a wide brush to fill in some larger areas with a white base.

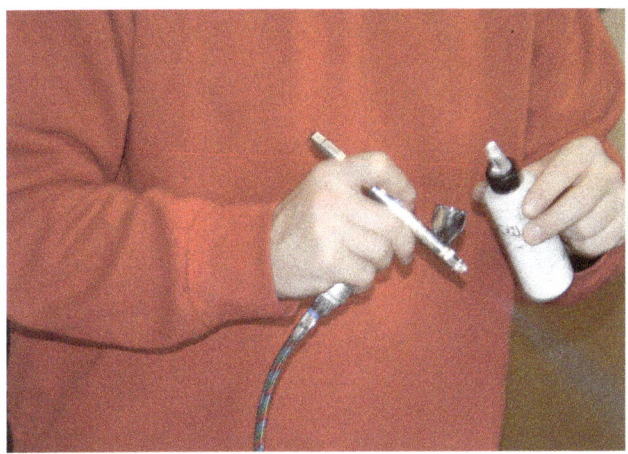

Picking up his Iwata Eclipse airbrush, Luca gets ready to add the first color so work can begin.

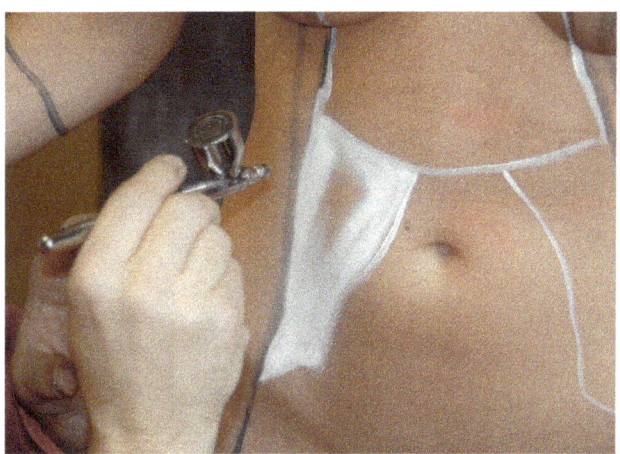

The tails of the shirt will be visible beneath the sweater jacket and are filled in with their base coat.

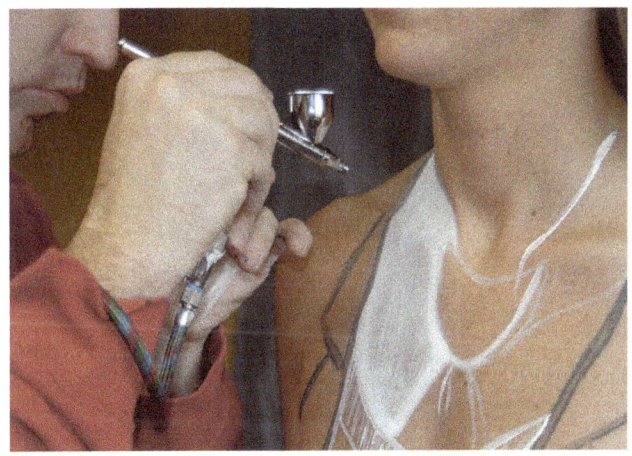

The airbrush makes quick work of filling in the white spaces that will soon become the dress shirt.

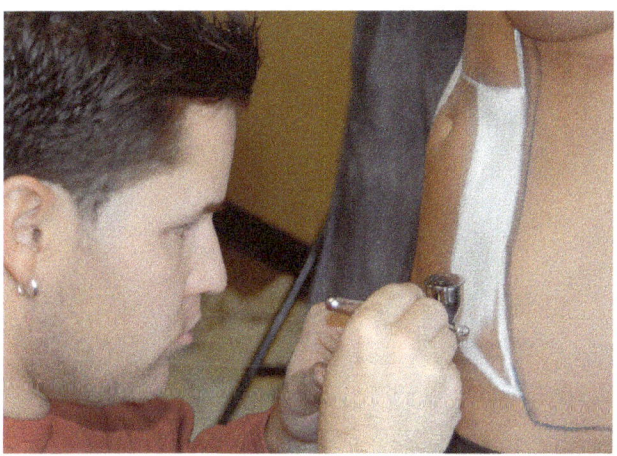

Running his gun at 65-70psi gives Luca the control he demands and allows him to put the paint only where he wants it.

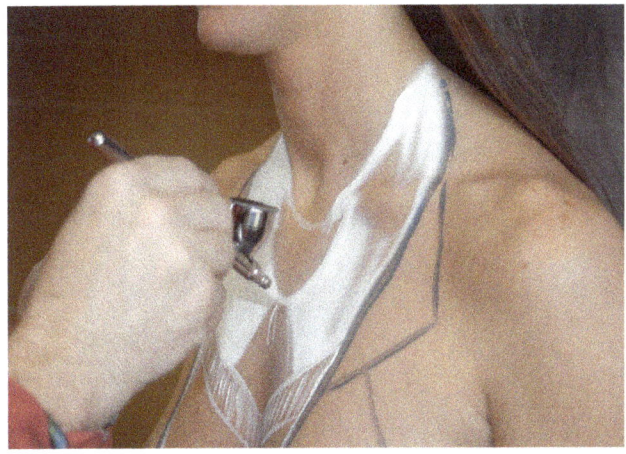

Quick hands with precise motion, and a complete control of his airbrush, deliver a swift and consistent application of paint.

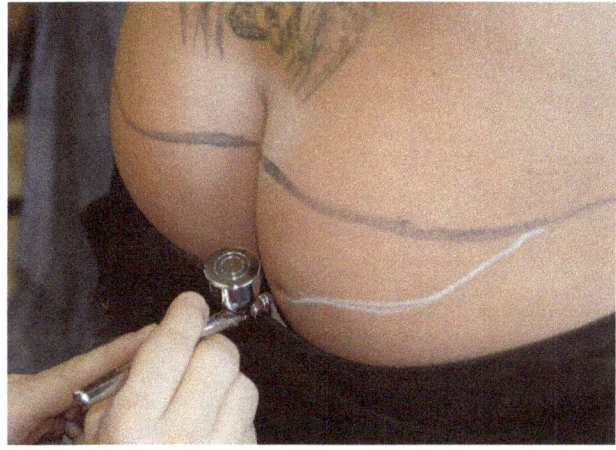

The rear tail of the shirt will also protrude from the suit jacket and those initial forms are now outlined.

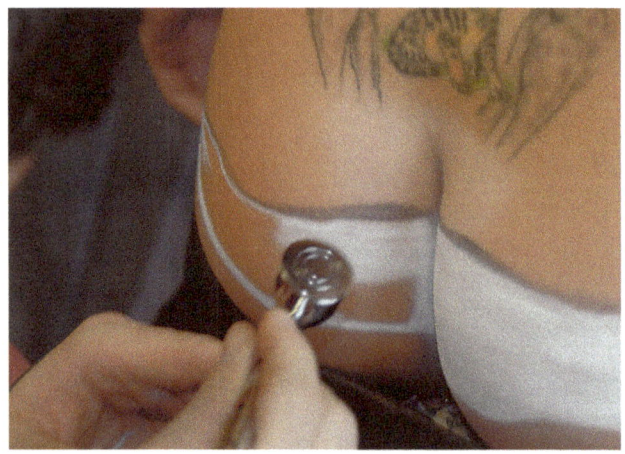

Staying in the lines, Luca uses the airbrush to quickly fill in the spaces that will become the shirt tail.

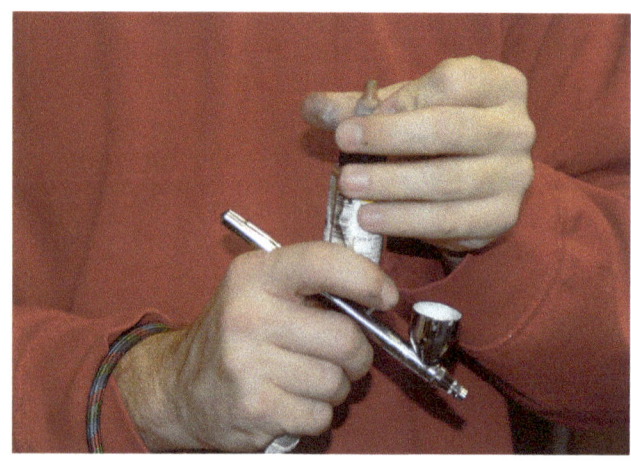

Luca readies the airbrush for the next color which will be a dark shade of green.

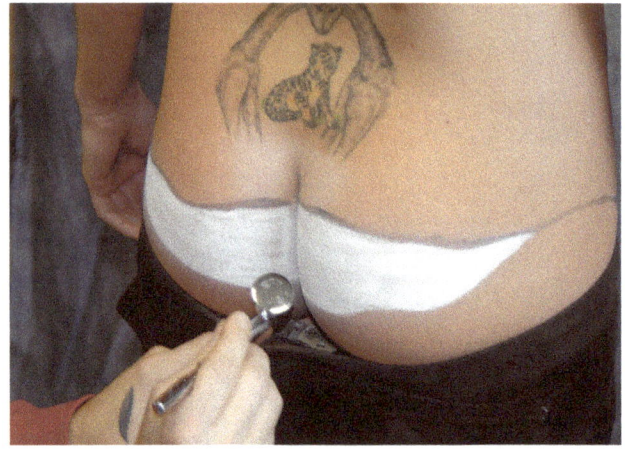

The opacity of the paint increases as additional passes are made and allow Luca to contour the fabric.

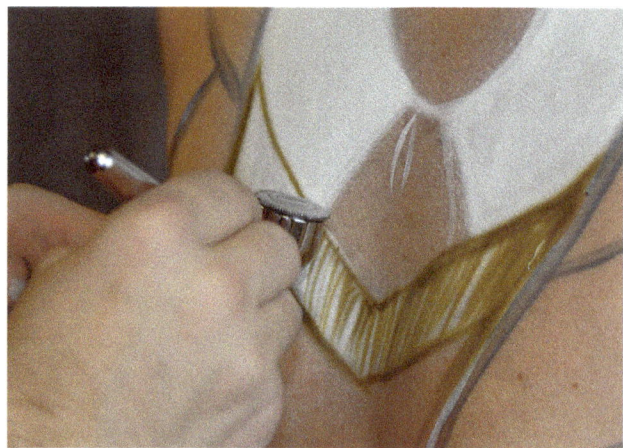

The first vertical lines of the sweater vest appear as Luca places precise lines of paint in position.

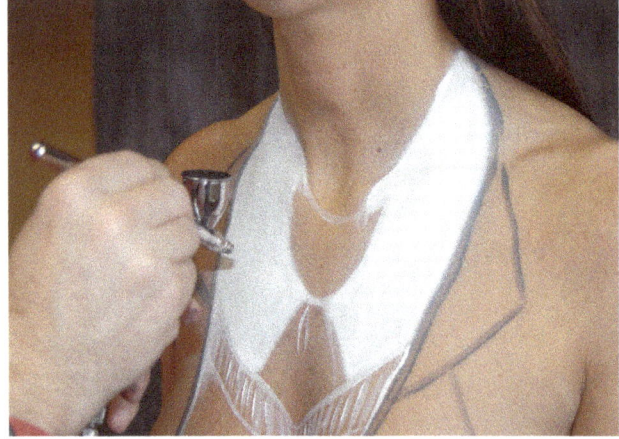

Wanting a deeper white on the shirt, he returns to the scene to spray on another layer.

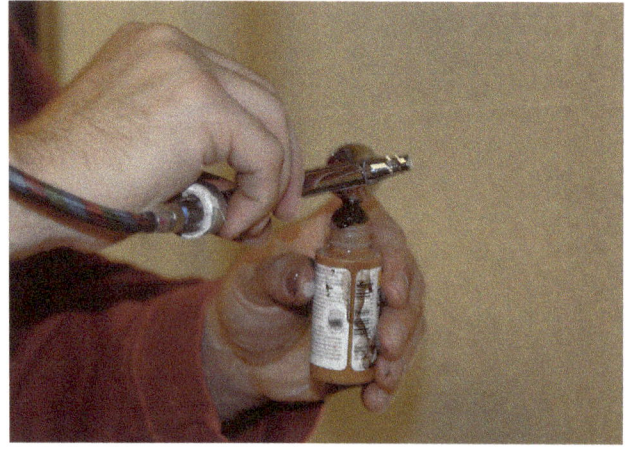

When he is done with a color, the unused paint is returned to the original bottle for use later.

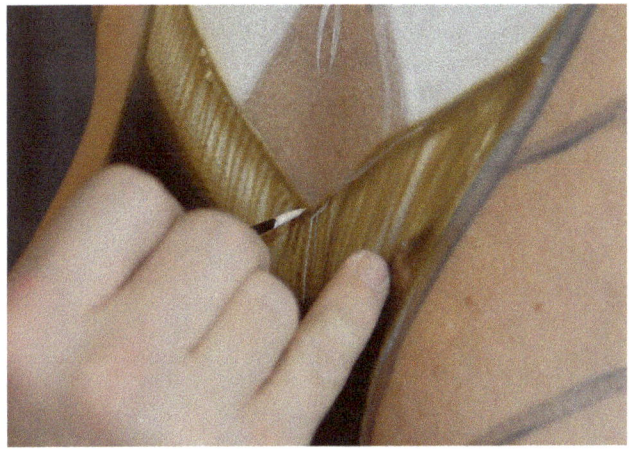

Turning again to the brush, he adds additional detail to the elastic of the sweater.

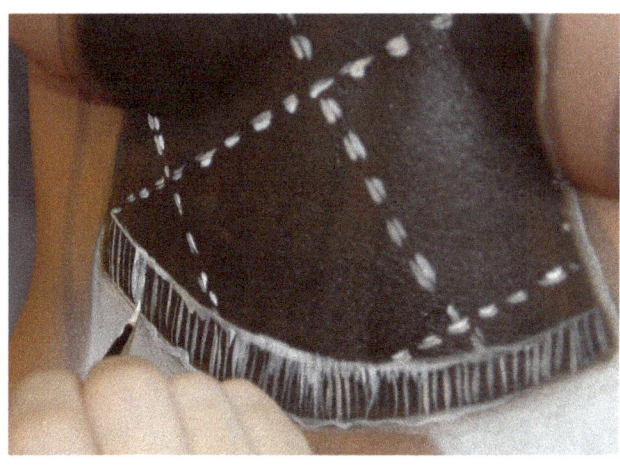

More brush work is employed to enhance the realism of the sweater.

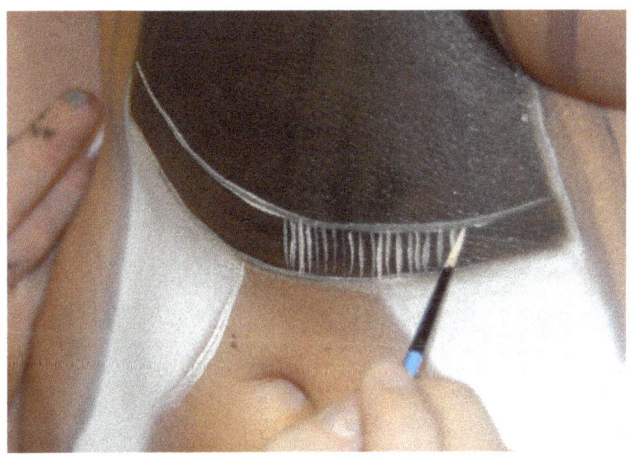

The lower edge of the sweater vest now gets its own lines that define the elastic portion of the garment.

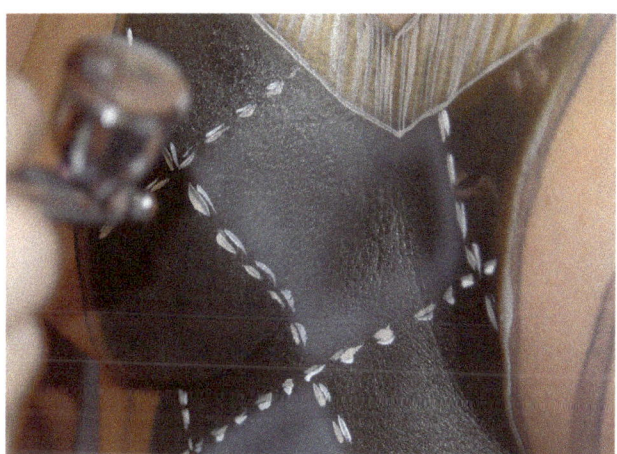

Returning to the airbrush, alternate panels of a lighter hue are sprayed on to further shape the sweater's realism.

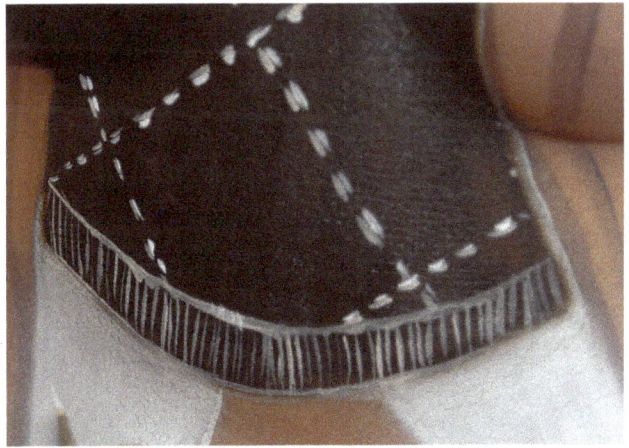

A slightly wider brush was used to add the first of the argyle pattern to the front of the sweater.

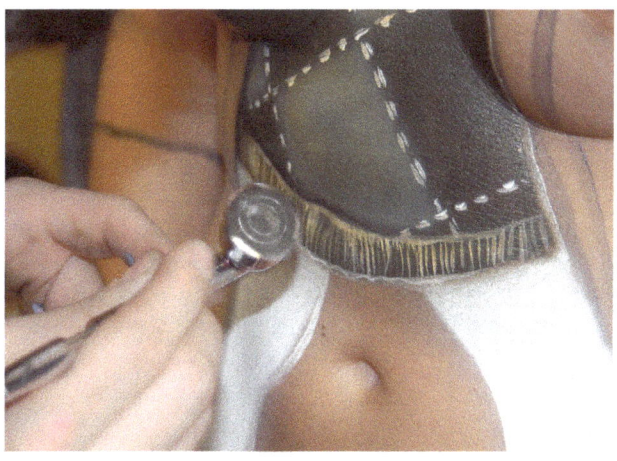

The subtlety of the second color selected really adds a strong feel to the piece.

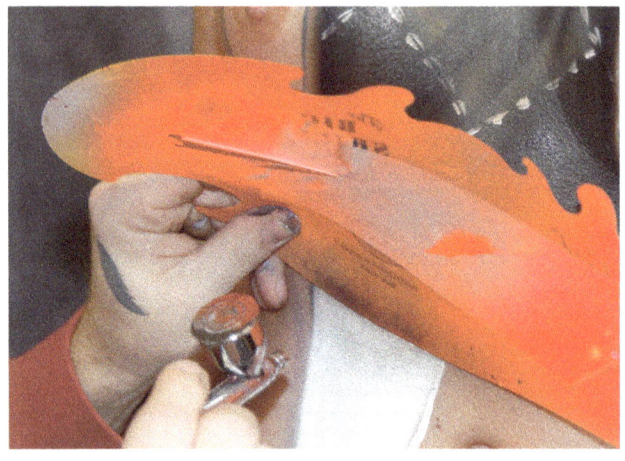

When he needs to add a crisp line with the airbrush, a plastic frisket is used to block the spray.

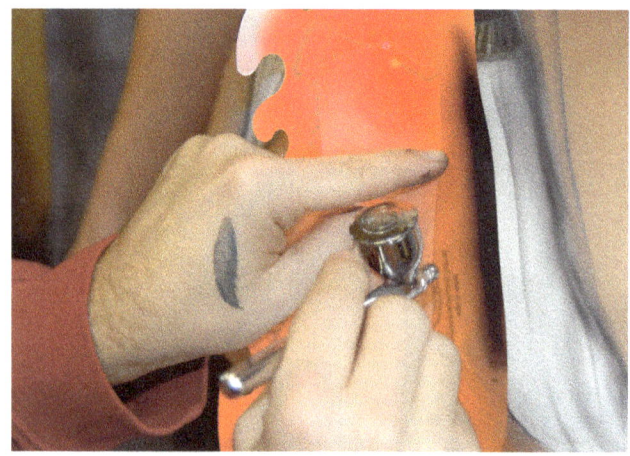

Additional wrinkles are sprayed on using the airbrush and the masking frisket.

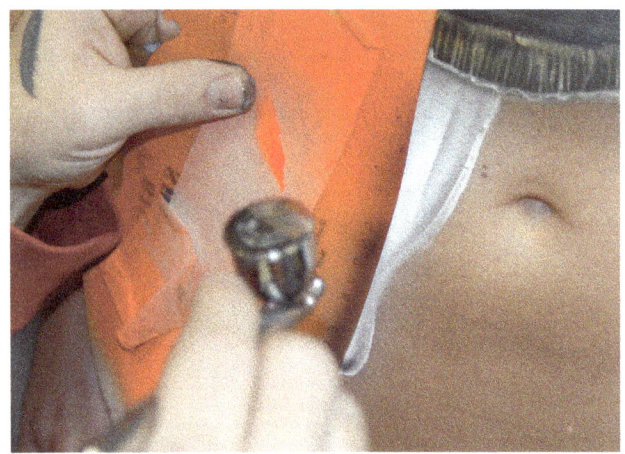

Each move of the frisket exposes the newly painted surface to a new wrinkle.

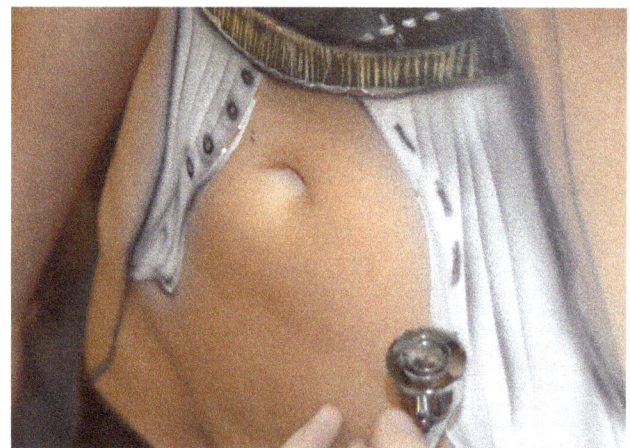

Buttons need button-holes and they are now added to the opposite tail of the shirt.

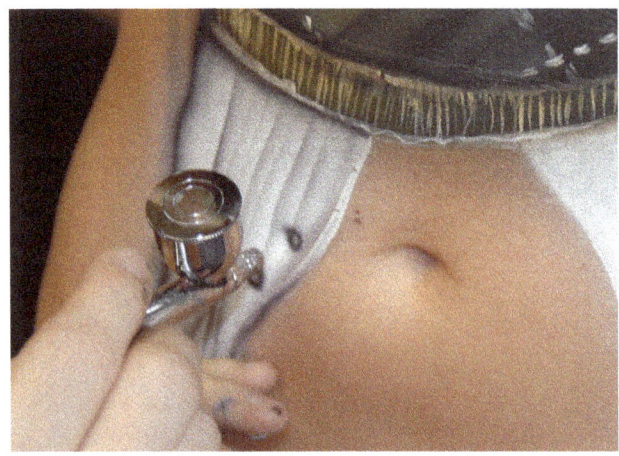

The exposed buttons of the shirt tail are now created with a quick burst of paint while holding the airbrush in one place.

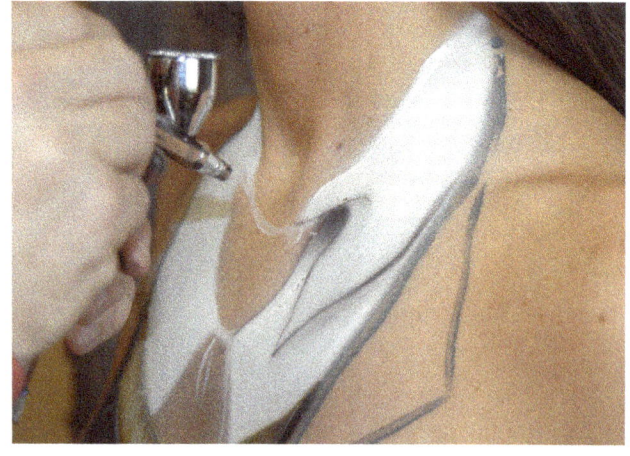

Moving north, Luca begins to add information to the collar of the shirt.

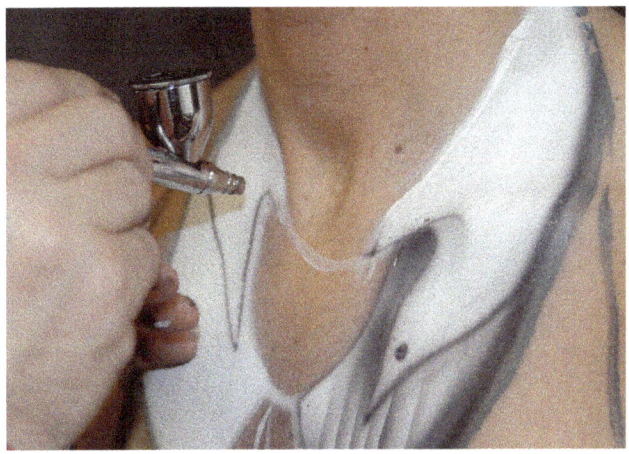

It was amazing to watch as the quick movements of his hand revealed such fine details in a short period of time.

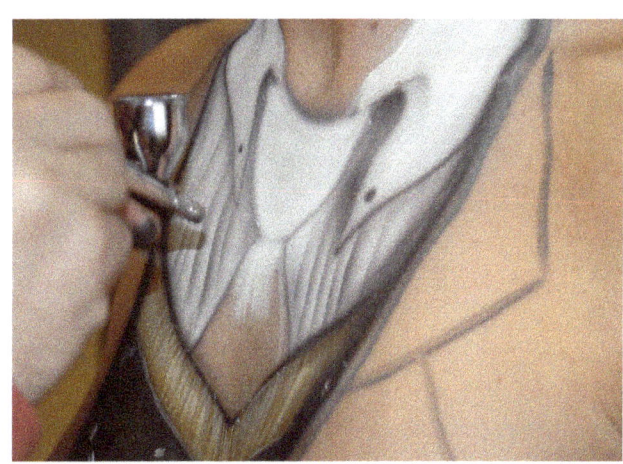

Some overall shading is now added to the crisp lines to bring out more realism in the fabric.

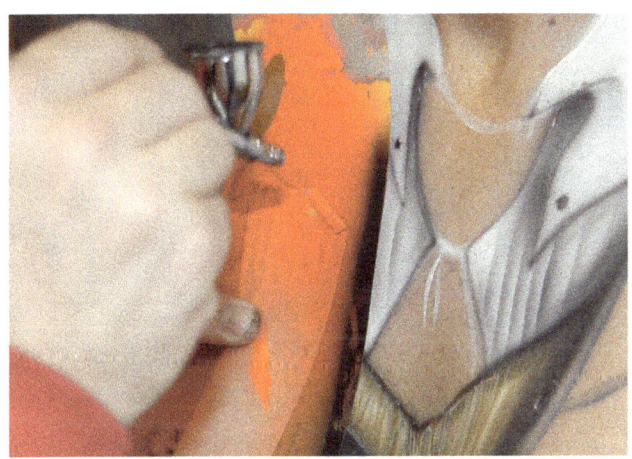

The plastic frisket is used again to add some ruffles to the shirt.

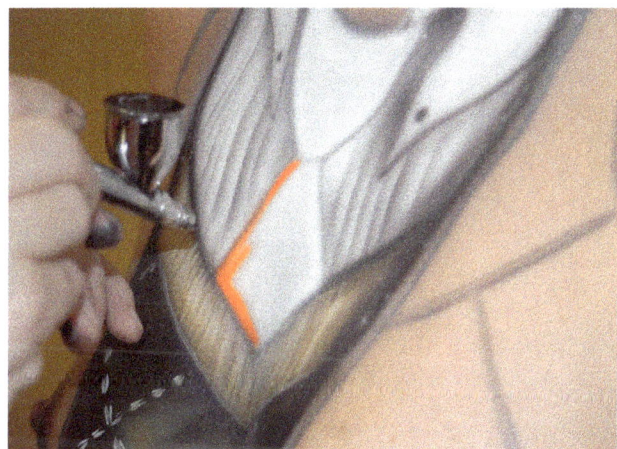

The cravat will be red with spots, so the base color is now added to the theme.

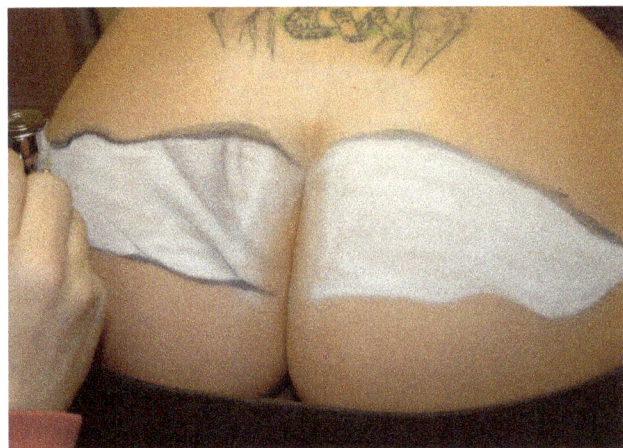

Giving the front of the shirt a moment to settle, he turns his attentions to the shirt tails on Jennifer's derrier.

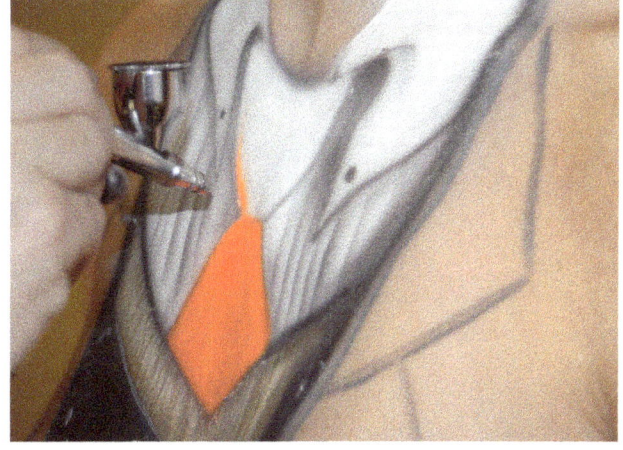

It takes little time for Luca to complete the portion of the tie that is visible.

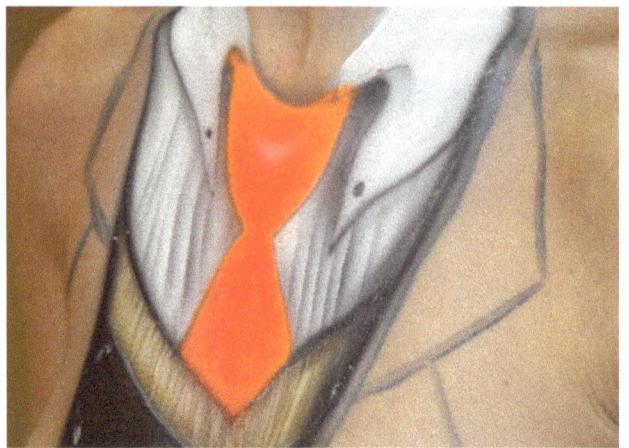

The necktie now painted red...

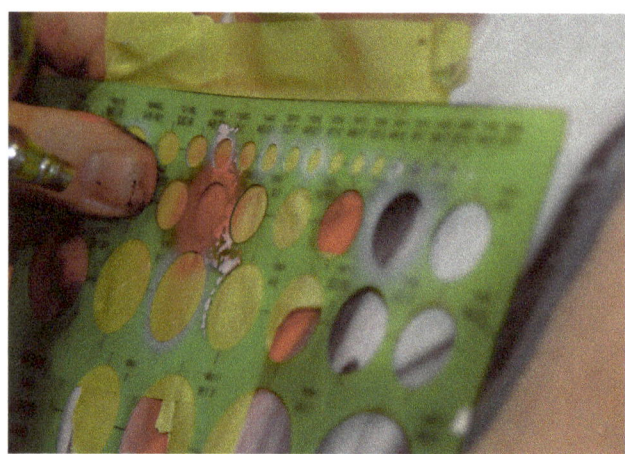

By placing the taped template right on top of the skin, the resulting circle of color will be sharply defined.

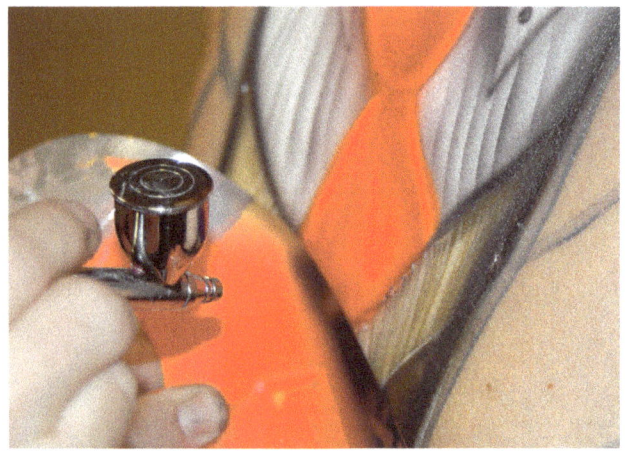

...this plastic mask allows Luca to add precise lines to the piece without disturbing the existing colors.

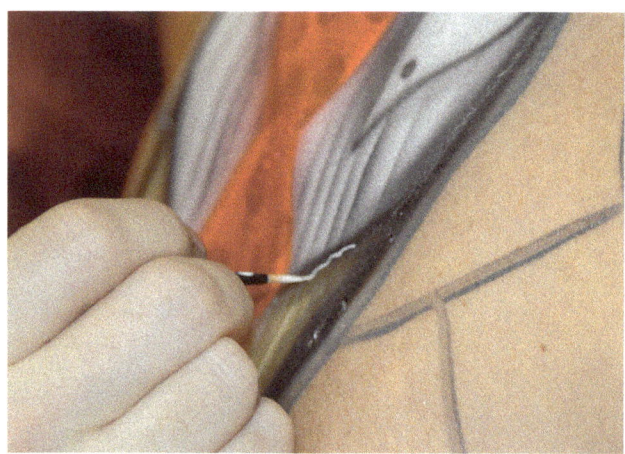

A small brush is used to add some further details to the sweater.

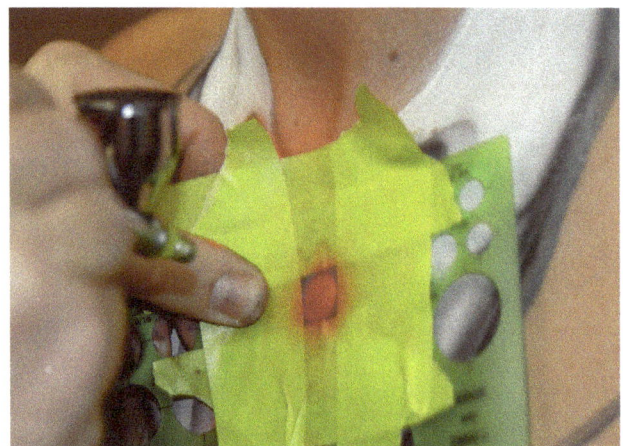

By taping off the desired hole in a plastic template, he can add consistent circles of color to the tie.

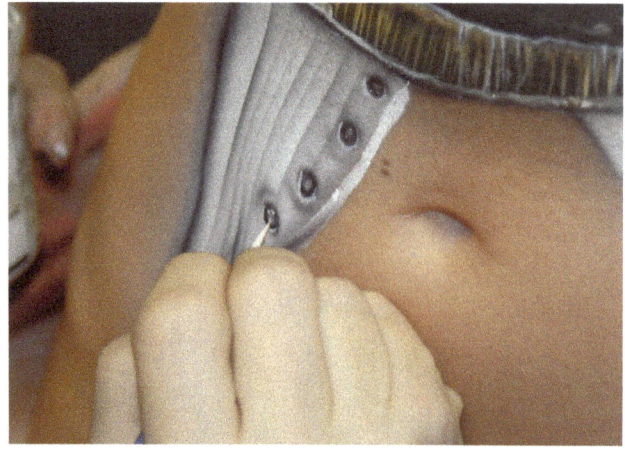

Having added the buttons earlier, Luca returns to the scene to bring more life to the tiny accessories.

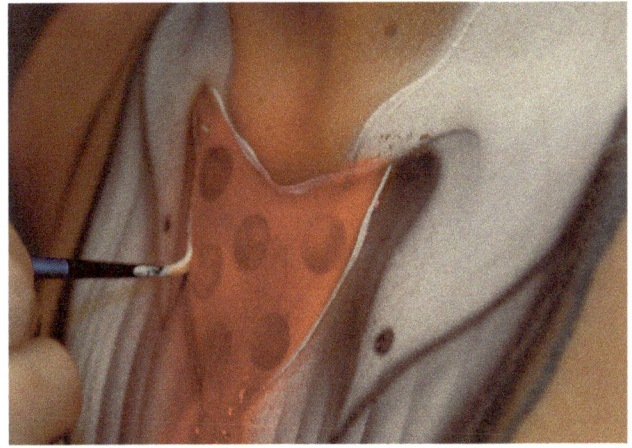

The necktie is now touched with tiny flecks of white to bring out another level of detail.

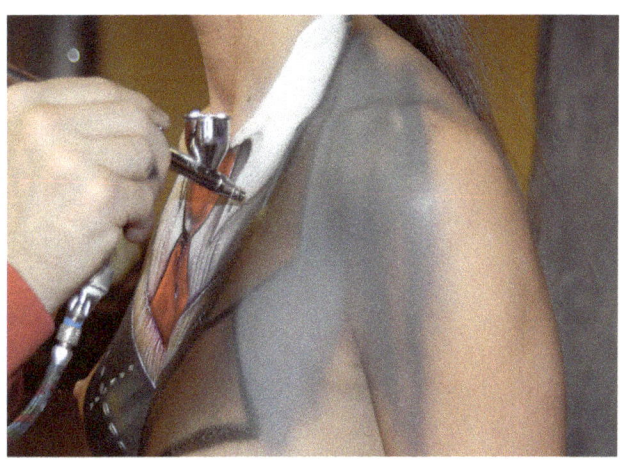

Time for the suit coat as Luca loads his gun with gray and begins to cover the remaining portion of Jenn's torso.

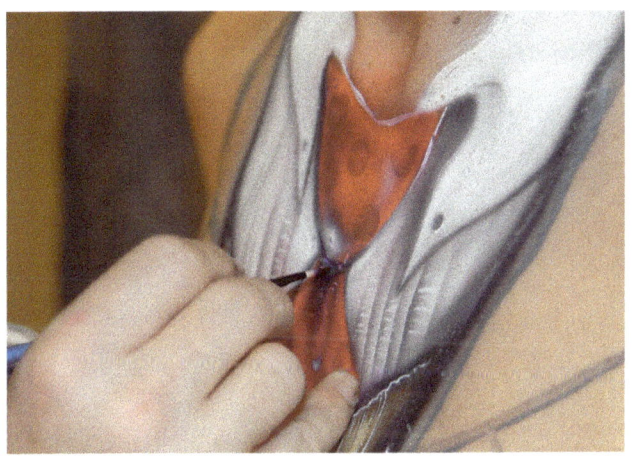

Each small touch of the brush adds a detail that was not seen before and gets closer to looking like the real thing.

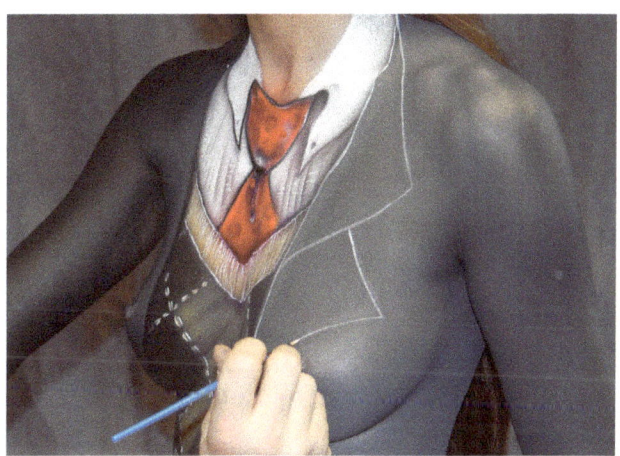

Once wrapped in gray, Luca returns to begin adding the pinstripes to the fabric.

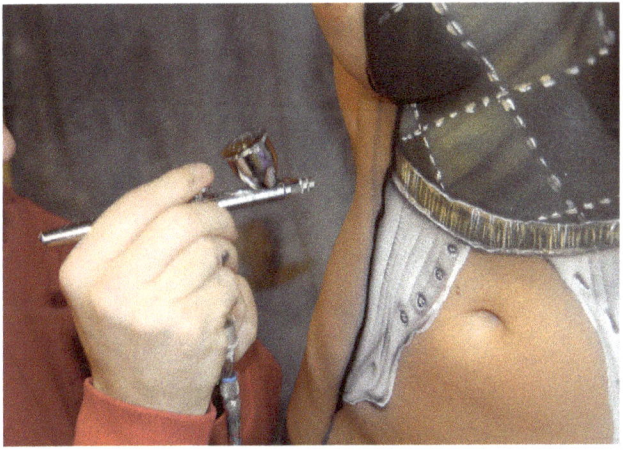

Diagonal lines are airbrushed into the panes of the argyle pattern to simulate twisting of the fabric.

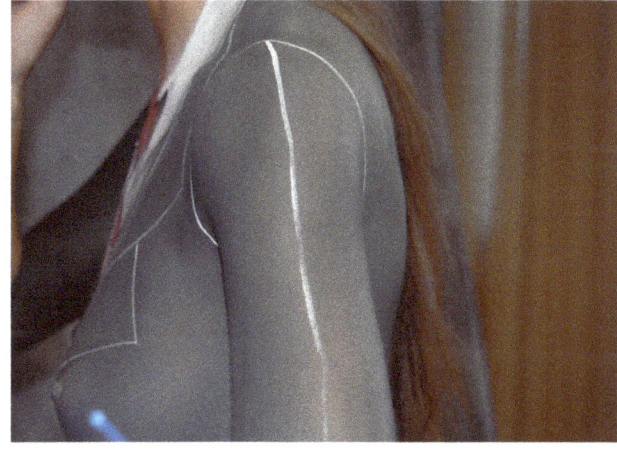

The lines are applied by brush and appear uneven and broken but the final piece will reveal the genius of this technique.

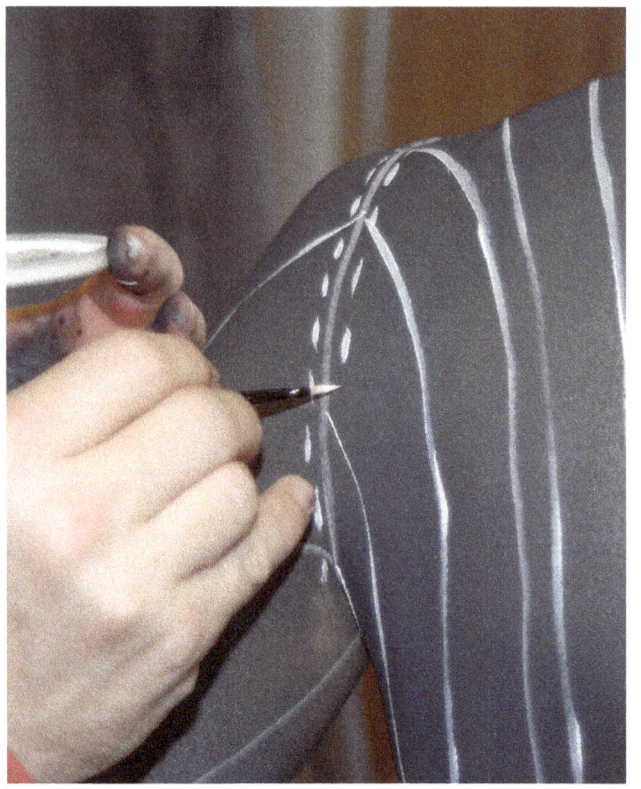

Stitches of the sleeve are now a part of the design and look right at home.

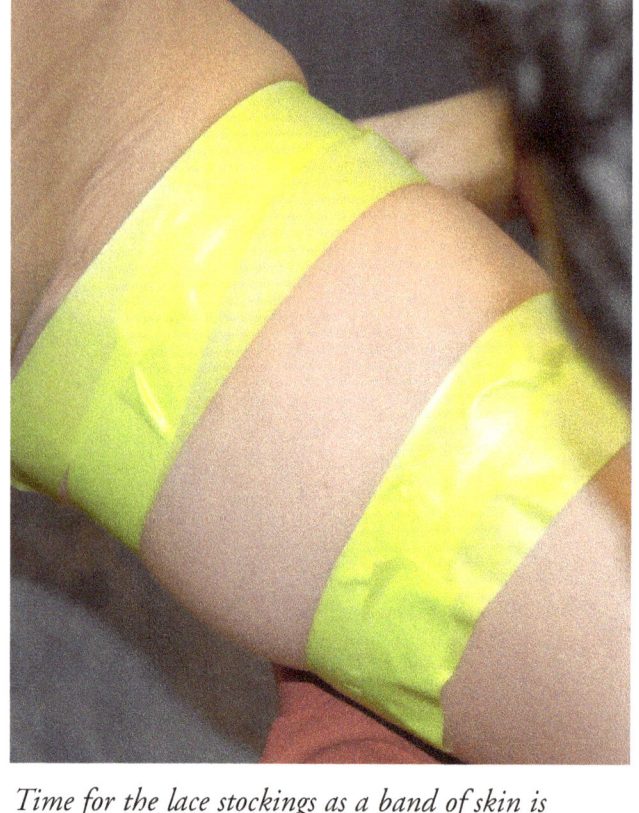

Time for the lace stockings as a band of skin is masked off with tape.

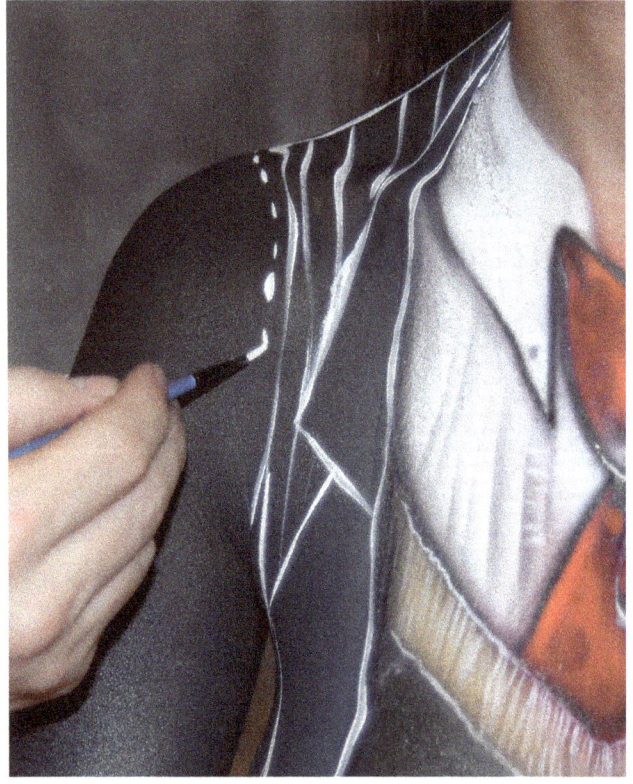

Collar details are added and also do their part to create the illusion of realism.

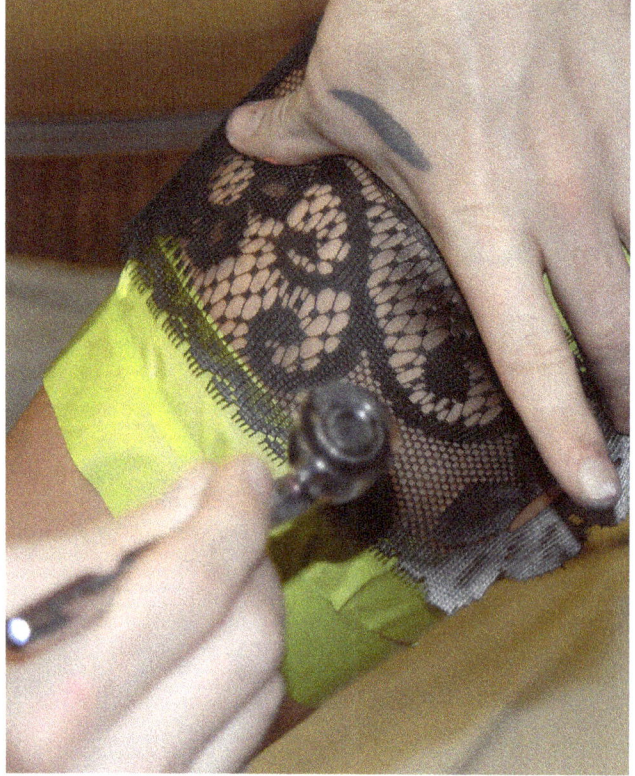

By holding a section of actual lace over the skin and spraying through it, a replica, in reverse will appear.

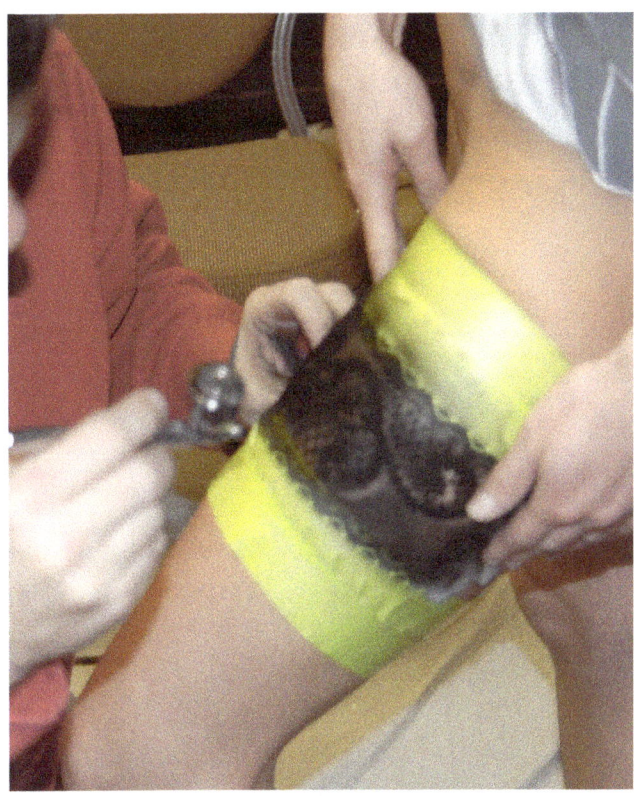

The section of actual lace is sprayed through, to create a nearly seamless look of lace.

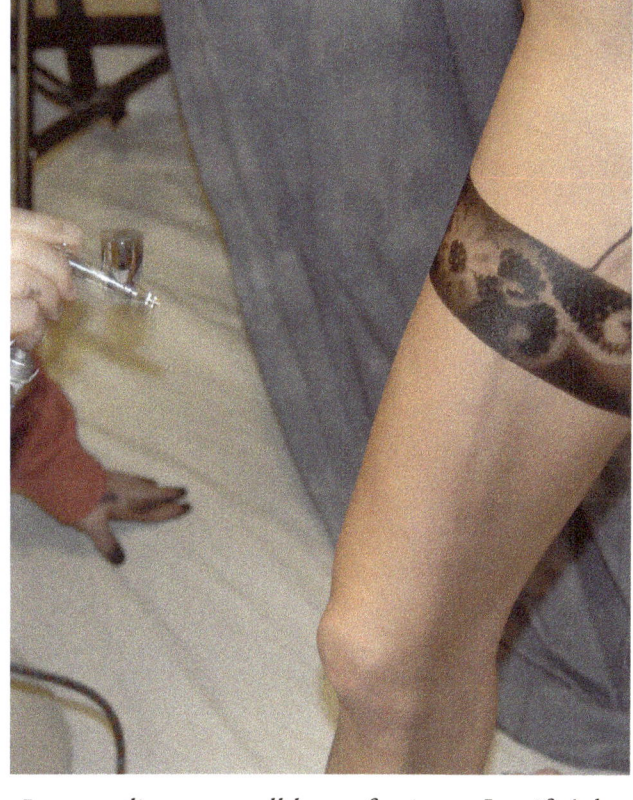

Luca applies an overall layer of paint to Jennifer's legs in an uneven pattern to replicate the silk stockings.

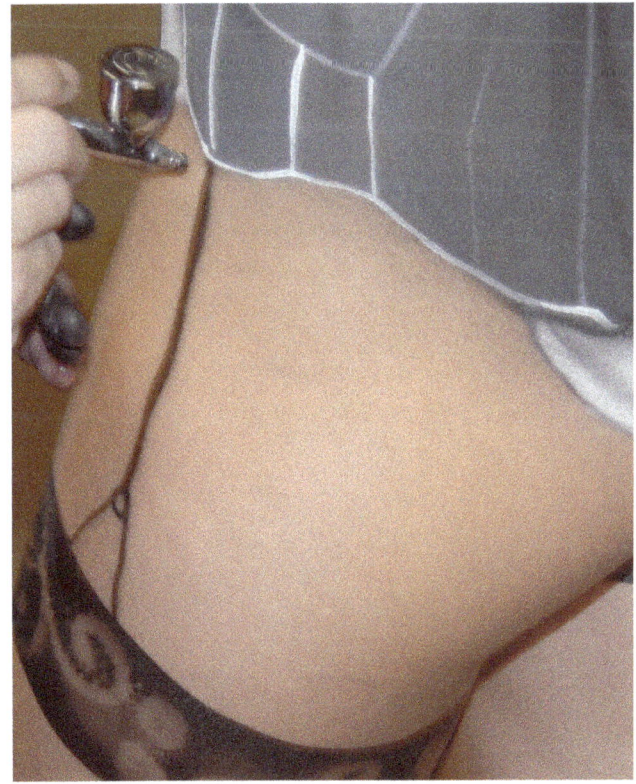

Holding the stockings up are a dainty set of satin straps.

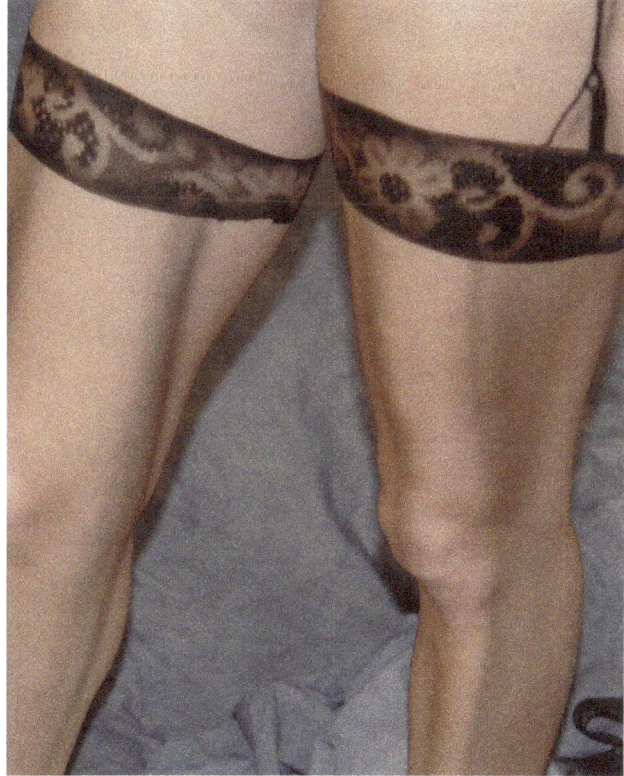

The depth of the illusion grows deeper with every pass of the airbrush.

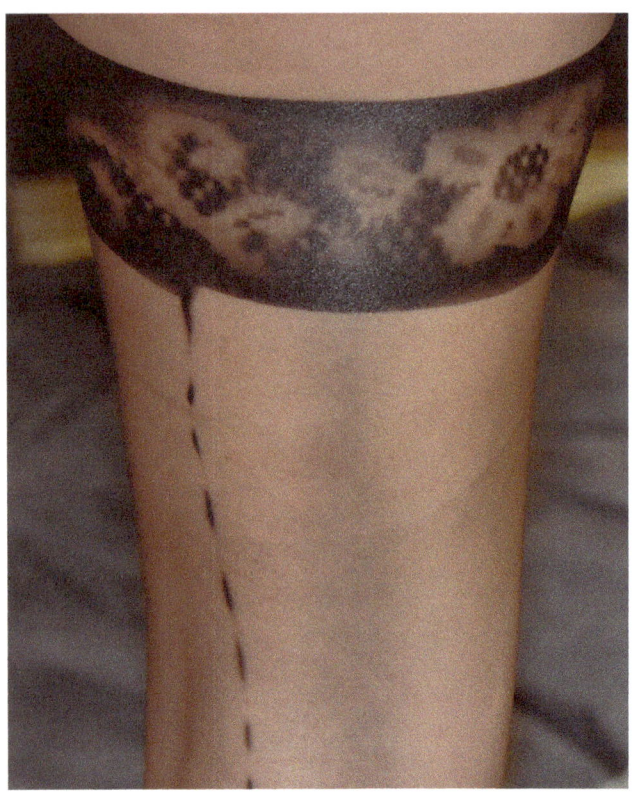

Proper stockings have the seam down the back and Luca has added them with a small brush.

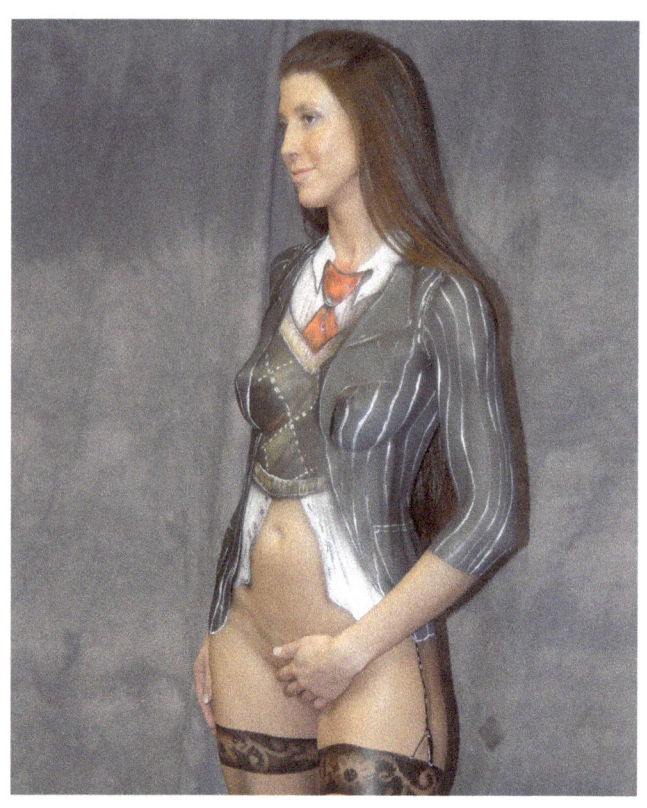

The finished piece from the side.

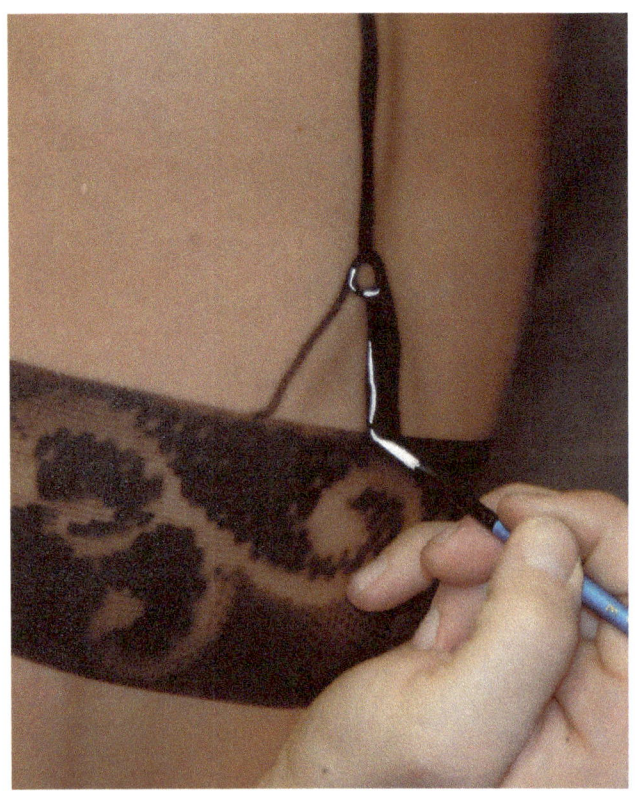

More detail of the support straps are added.

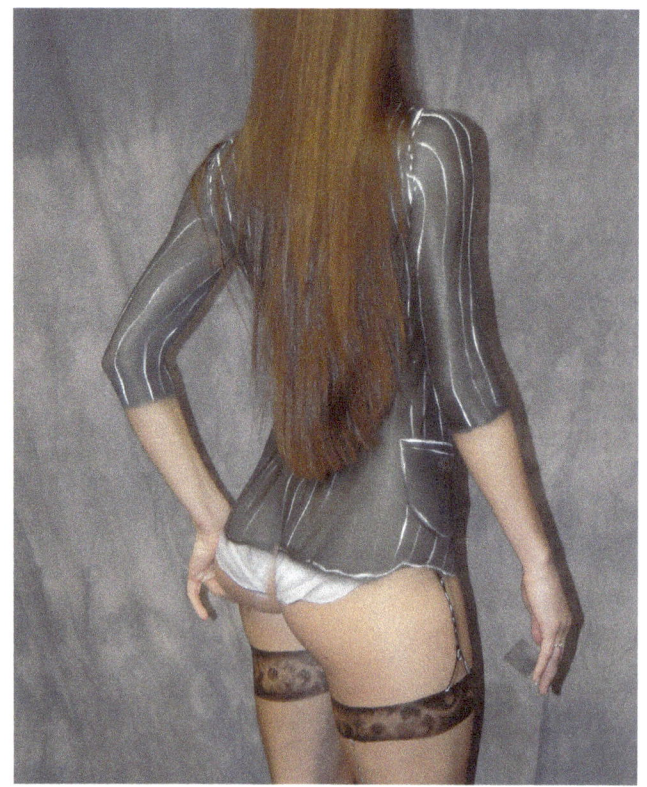

The finished piece from the rear.

Q&A: Luca Paganico

How long have you been creating body art?

About 5 years with 15 years of airbrush experience prior to that.

What was your first exposure to the medium?

Not sure what my first exposure was, but my first application was to myself for Halloween one year.

What kind of painting experience did you have before this?

In the 15 years of practice I have created all sorts of art including illustrations and wall murals.

How young were you when you started to dabble in art?

It was grade school when I first picked up a pencil and began to draw and things happened quickly after that

What do you enjoy most about body painting?

The fact that it's so different from my commercial work and that it gives me such freedom to create art of my own design.

Where has your body art been created, and for whom?

Much of my body art has been done for promotional purposes which forces me to work quickly while still creating colorful and accurate pieces.

How much of your body art is planned in advance?

A piece of this level required a bit of advance thought and sketches, while others are done by the seat of my pants using only a theme as my guide

What's your favorite type of body art?

No real favorite style has become clear and I enjoy viewing others work to get inspiration.

Any plans for the future?

I think the field of body painting is on the upswing and will grow into a more welcome form of art as the exposure to it grows.

What brand of paint do you use?

Golden Airbrush Illustration paint works great for me and offers plenty of colors.

How about brush and airbrush choices?

An Iwata Eclipse, dual-action airbrush does the job and I typically run my compressor at 65-70psi for the best results.

Luca Paganico
Pittsburgh, PA 15235
412-607-6363
lucapaganico@yahoo.com

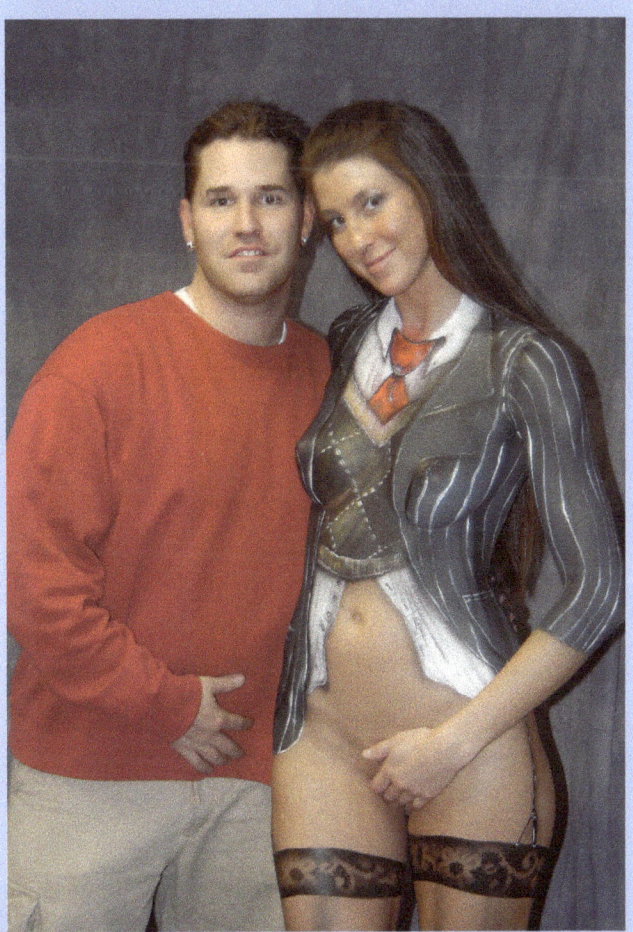

Luca poses with his model wearing his latest creation.

Chapter Five

Steve Wizard

Reality Flames Surround a Chrome Eagle

Like most of the airbrushing sequences in this book, the creation of the chrome tribal-style eagle is really a two-part affair. First comes the eagle, then the flames. Steve Chaszeyka (aka The Wizard), from New Middletown, Ohio, starts with a drawing of the eagle and a piece of chalk. The paint work is being done on a new motorcycle for Logic Motorcycles in nearby Youngstown, Ohio. The Eagle originated "in my head" explains Steve.

Next he applies premask masking material,

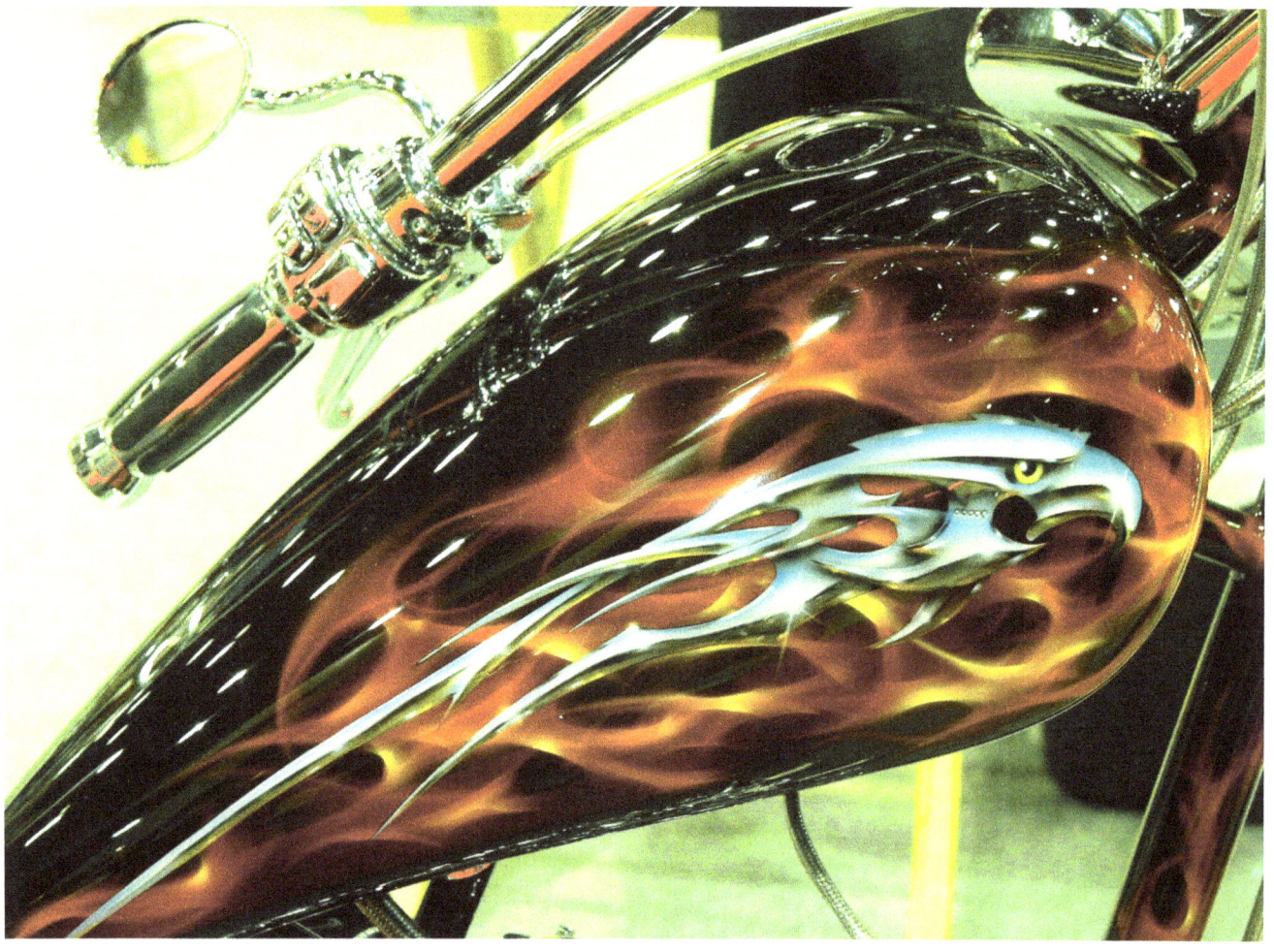

The finished design, done for Logic Motorcycles, is a nice combination of two designs: a chrome eagle laid out over a set of reality-flames.

designed to transfer vinyl letters to a surface, to both sides of the tank. "I like the transparency of it," explains Steve, "it allows you to examine the look of your work, what you're exposing and what you're hiding." (The tank has already been painted with urethane base coat, clearcoated, and sanded with 600 grit paper.)

Before taping the drawing over the premask material, Steve coats the back of the drawing with chalk. Now the sketch is taped over the tank so Steve can run a pencil over the design. As he presses on the pencil, the outline of the design is transferred to the premask material. A light chalk line is left on the premask.

"You have to have the right amount of pressure on the Xacto knife as you do the cutout," explains Steve. "Too much and you cut into the basecoat or you cause the clearcoat to lift, then you are back to the drawing board. Cutting in the corners is kind of like driving a Masserati, you have to let off in the corners or you miss the turn and have to go back." A non-transparent material is used for masking off the rest of the tank so that what's left is just the shape of the eagle.

A duplicate sketch for the right side of the tank is traced out on the light table after placing the first sketch "upside down" on the light table.

Steve warns that, "when you tape the designs onto the tank you have to make sure they're positioned exactly the same on both sides of the tank."

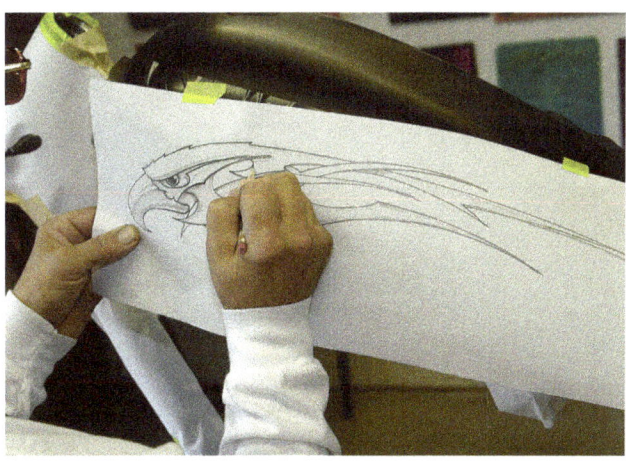

1) After attaching the premask to the tank, Steve lays the original sketch over the top, then traces the outline of the eagle with a pencil.

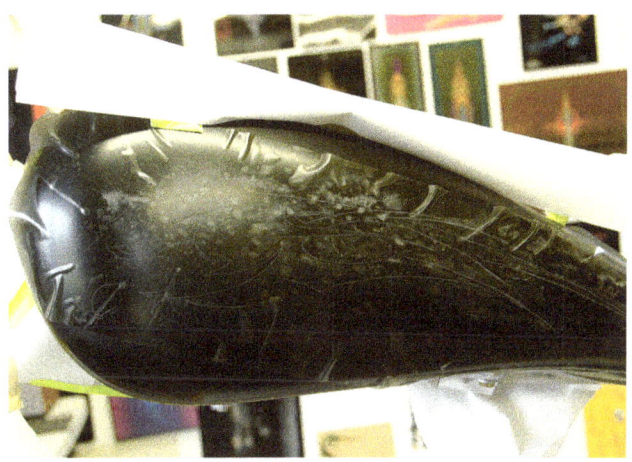

2) Because of the chalk on the backside of the sketch, the design is transferred to the premask material.

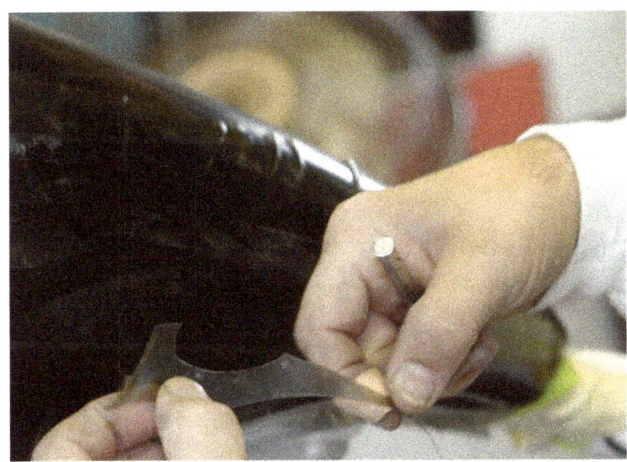

4) All the cut out pieces are carefully saved for use later in the project.

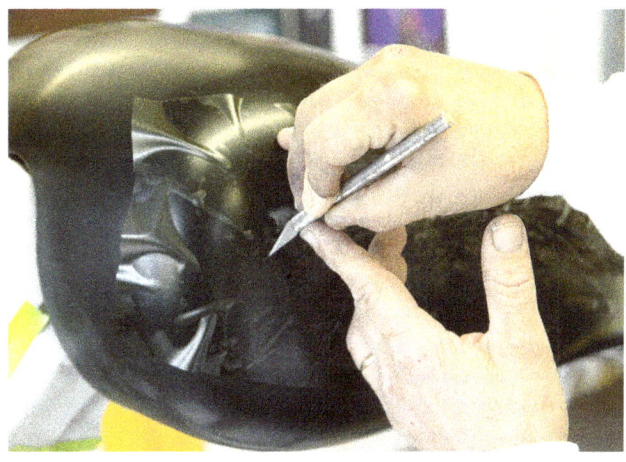

3) Cutting out the premask is very time consuming, as Steve says, "once you start to paint it goes pretty fast, but this part takes time."

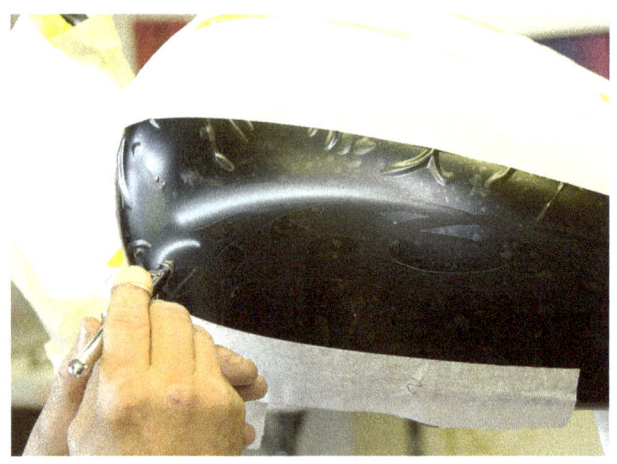

The actual painting begins with pastel blue. These are the areas that will be highlights in the finished artwork.

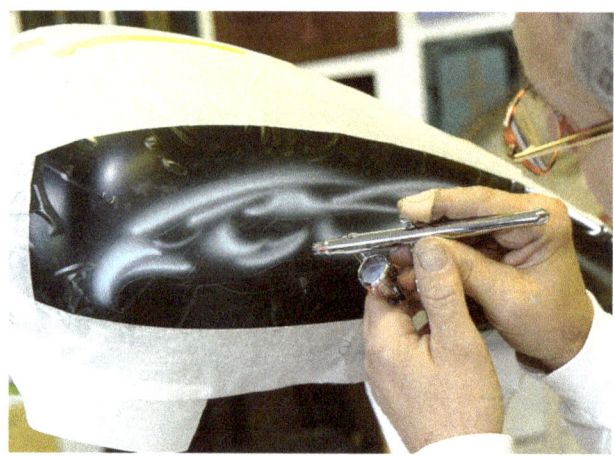

Gradually, the beginnings of the design emerge from a series of highlights.

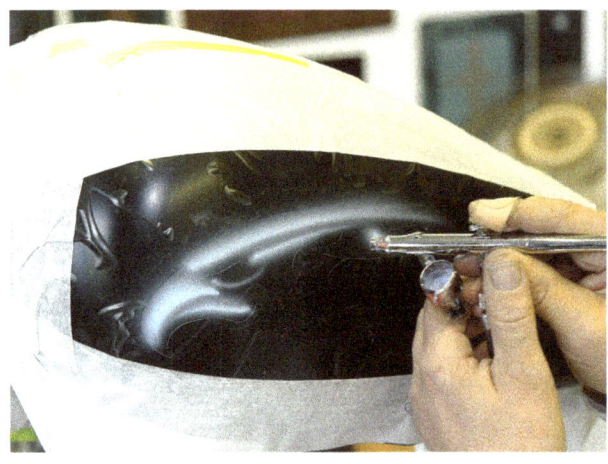

For many of these highlights, Steve starts with a small dot of paint...

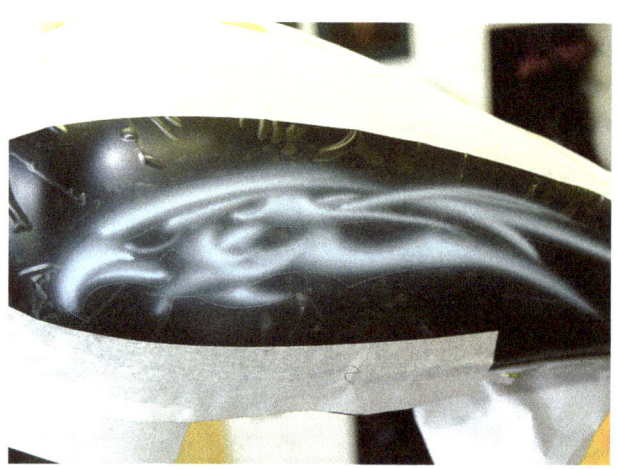

At this point it's easy to make out the stylized eagle.

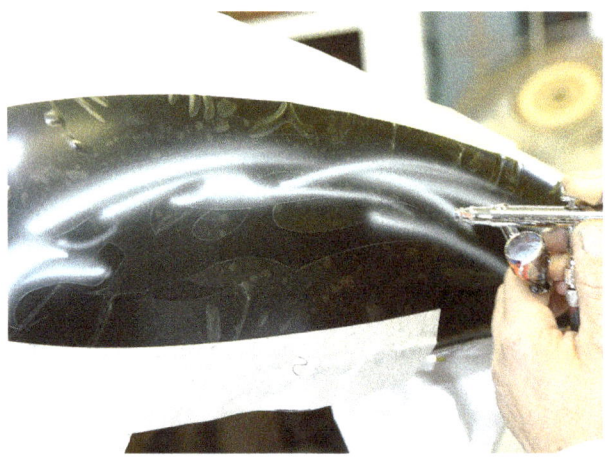

...and then moves the airbrush rapidly across the tank from the dot toward the rear.

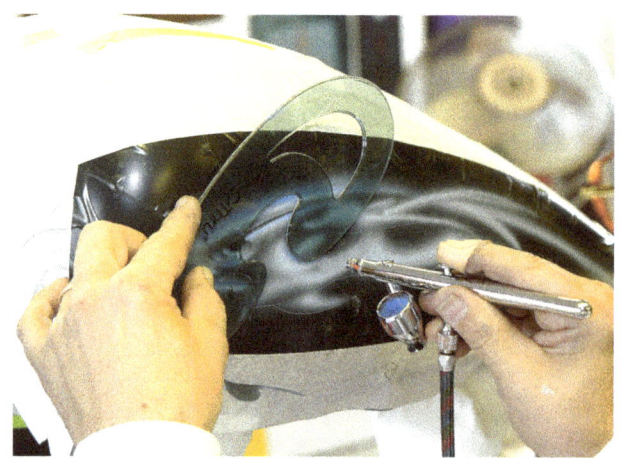

Masks or stencils are often used to contain the effects of one color (blue reflected from the sky in this case) to a small area.

Applying Color

The first color to go on is a pastel blue that looks almost white, "I'm putting this paint on in places where I imagine the highlights to be," explains Steve. The effect looks almost like a speed line on an illustration. Next, Steve mixes a darker blue. The idea is to duplicate the look of chrome by mimicking the mirror images that occur in chrome. "Chrome is only the reflection of things around it," explains Steve, "often blue from the sky with brown or green on the bottom depending on what the object is parked on. At the top I darken the chrome, because as a chrome object rolls around, at the top where it doesn't get as much light, it gets darker. That's the effect I'm trying to create. I'm a little ahead of myself but I want to go in here and make some highlights with pure white."

Lower Reflections

Now Steve uses a "more reflective color on the bottom," dark grey and orange in this case, with a bit of brownish green. These colors are reflecting the ground that the object is sitting on. Close to the horizon line Steve adds black to the brownish-orange mix. "If you look at the reflection on a piece of chrome there is a horizon line and it's typically black, or nearly black." Steve will come back later and add more highlights to the "raised" parts of the

Continued on page 76

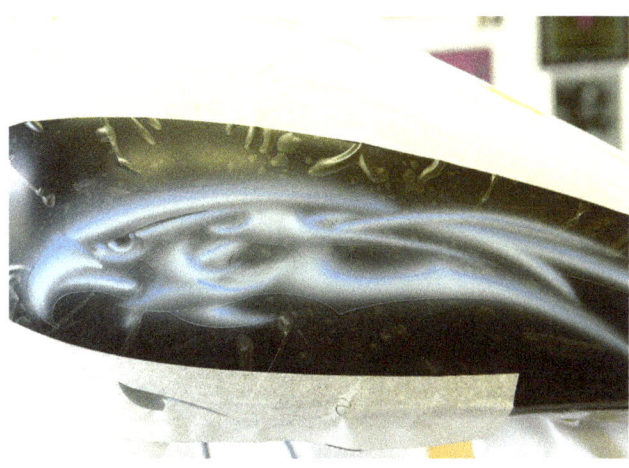

At this point you can clearly see the eagle's head and feathers done in light highlights and reflected blue.

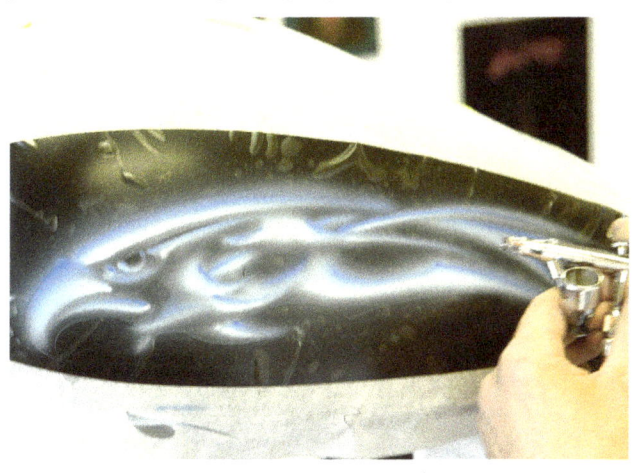

Now, Steve adds pure white highlights.

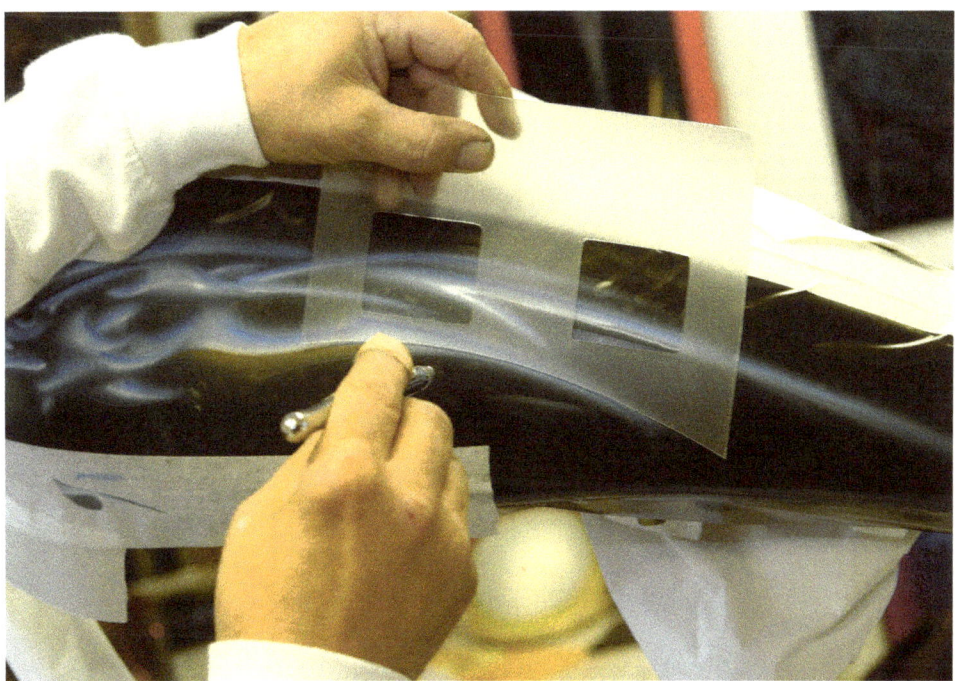

The lower edge of a chrome object reflects whatever it's sitting on - the ground in this case.

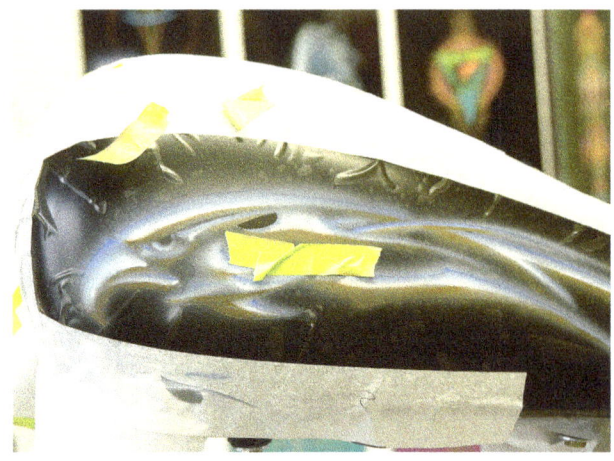

Masking tape is used to contain the effects of the "ground" colors to specific areas.

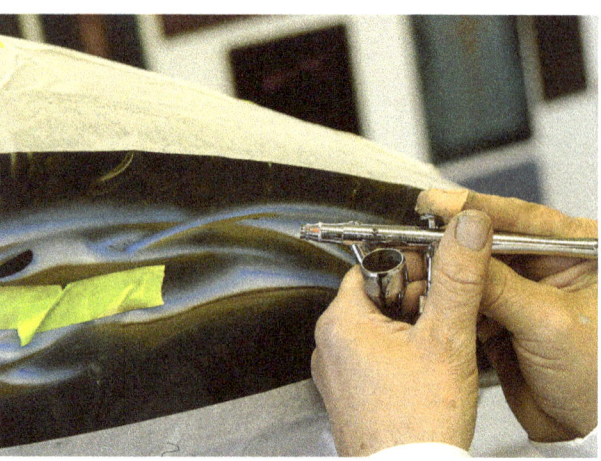

...a horizon line that flows along the chrome spear.

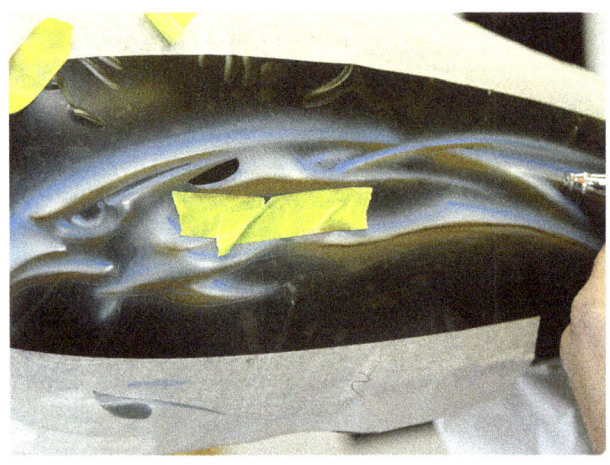

Close up shows how darker earth tones are used to create the horizon line.

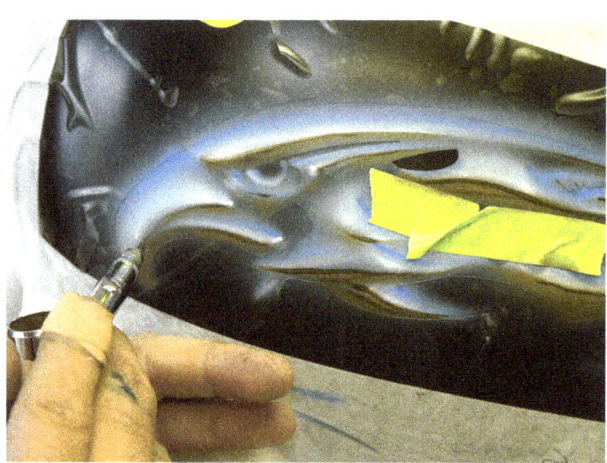

The same technique is used on the eagle's top and bottom beak.

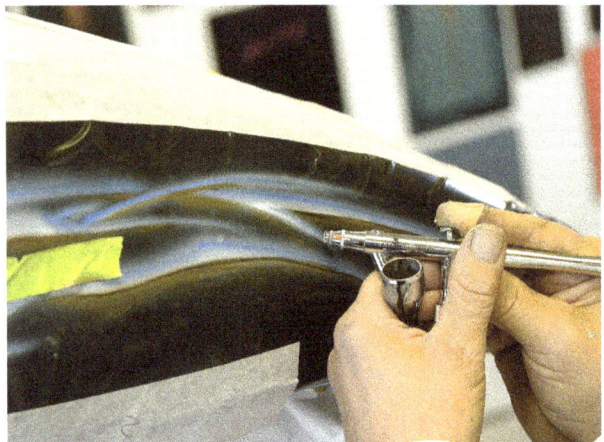

A two-handed grip and careful trigger pull make for a clean, smooth line...

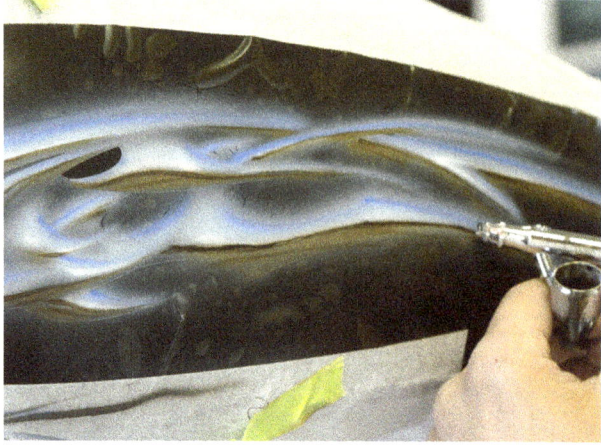

After creating the horizon line, Steve goes back later to darken it, by adding a small amount of black to the mix.

Q&A: The Wizard

Steve, give us a little background on you and how you became an airbrush artist?

I always had a knack for art, it always came naturally. There was this fella here in town, Guy Shively, he was my mentor. After seeing him I charged ahead and started pinstriping cabinets at home, the TV, cars in the garage. Over the years I developed a style. Airbrushing was my second pursuit. I thought I could make a dollar at that too. I'm self taught. At that time no one would teach you anything. Back then the big name was Greg of Akron, he inspired a lot of airbrushers, including me.

I did it part-time for years while I sold insurance or real estate. Then I went to work for a guy with a catalog company as an illustrator. And that was good. I learned I was good enough that this person would pay me, I had skills to contribute. In the meantime I'm going to car shows and making a thousand or two on a weekend. So I quit the catalog company and went out on my own. And it's been very fun and profitable since then. I've been on my own for twenty years.

What kind of paints do you like?

For striping it's One-Shot. I'm loyal to Mack brushes, they have a real feel for the artist. They are developing a brush with my name on it. A scroll brush. It suits my needs and style of striping. Other people think the magic is in the brush, it helps, but that's not all of it.

For airbrushing I like Spies Hecker paint, it's high pigmentation, light-fast with a lifetime guarantee. But nearly any basecoat system will work. House of Kolor has a great system too when you want unique colors. H of K has the tints you need for the reality flames.

Where do you get your ideas?

I have a lot of things in my head that are creative, like that eagle. Sometimes that flow is restricted 'cause the customer has an idea. He may want a wolf posed a certain way. I call that doing the dance, you have to reproduce the picture he gives you. The creativity is gone and it's mechanical at that point, but that doesn't make it any easier. And I have to give credit where credit is due. I'm really grateful to Mike Lavallee for sharing the formula for the reality flames.

When do you use a test panel?

I use them when there's a high risk the customer and I aren't on the same page as to how much the underlying marblizing or ghost-flames should show through. So I suggest he spend two hundred bucks and do "knock downs." These are three-part panels with the effect done three ways. Then the customer picks the one

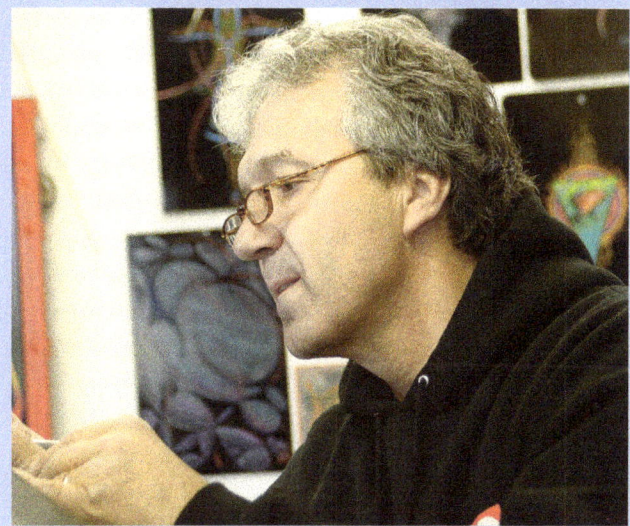

he likes. And if he or she doesn't like any of them, maybe it's not someone I should work for.

To what do you attribute your success?

I attribute my success to my wife and partner Carol. She's the driving force behind Wizard Graphics, and she keeps me "level." It also takes a lot of hard work. If you're waiting for that big break it ain't ever going to come. Back to the creative part, ideas that are new and fresh are hard to come by. A really successful artist like Chris Cruz can compose something unique, but still his style, and people love it, that's his strength.

You said earlier that this is a two-step process?

On a piece like this, the eagle and flames, you do them one at a time. Some guys do the flames, apply clear and then the eagle right on top, but I like working on black. Step one, work on the eagle, no distraction from the other art. Then cover that up and do the flames right over it, just "do the flames." Then when you uncover it, it's like MAN, this is great. But you do have to have the whole thing in your head when you start. You have to make sure the overall composition works together and fits the piece.

How much do you use the computer?

I use it when I have to cut lettering. And if something has to be repeated, like a logo. It's a wonderful tool for when you need an exact shape, it also saves you from razor-blading into a paint job, the computer generated mask saves all that.

You said something about the art of observation?

When you look at the reference, when you're trying to match feathers or chrome or whatever, you need to know when to use the airbrush versus the hand brush.

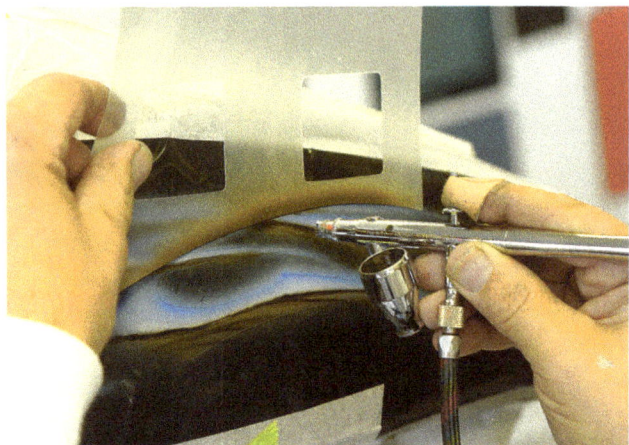

Steve keeps a number of masks and stencils handy for precision work.

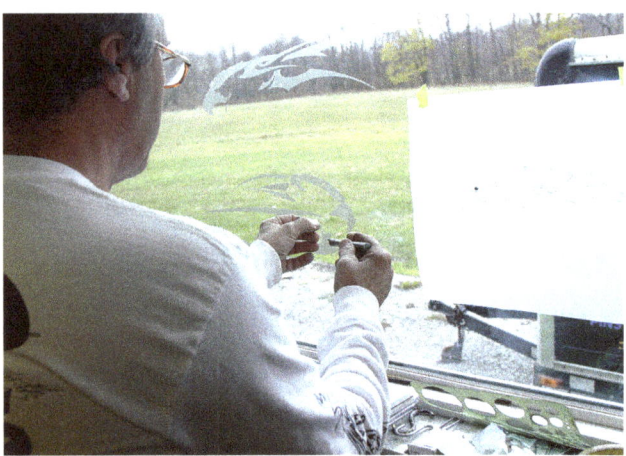

Pieces of premask, cut out earlier, were saved on the window...

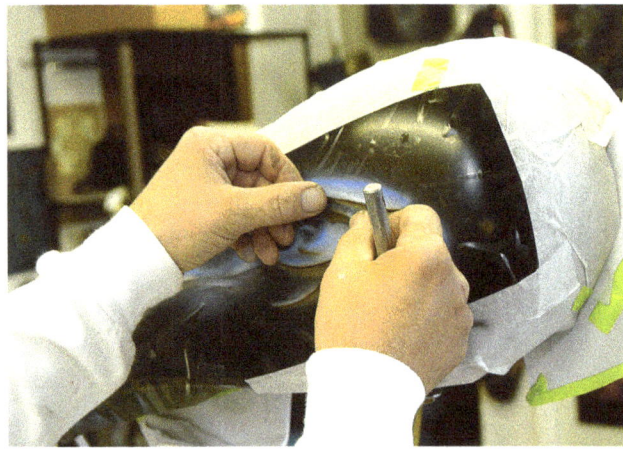

...and can be used now.

horizon line, so it looks natural (usually the part of the chrome piece closest to the camera, or eye, will be a highlight or a star of sunlight).

Small masks are used throughout the process (note the photos) to contain the effect of a color to one small area. Most of this job is done with what Steve calls a "middle of the road Iwata airbrush."

THE BEVELED EDGES

Pieces of the design that were cut out earlier are now used again as masks. The part of the mask that is laid down is then trimmed at the very edge, because this "new edge" will end up being a reflective surface (note the photos on the next page).

After pulling the edge of the masks off the areas that will be beveled, Steve sprays the area with white, with a few highlights. Light orange is used to create a gold-colored edge on the bottom of the bevel, this will be the reflection of the flames that will be added later.

A RIVETING TOPIC

Steve thinks a few rivets might be a good addition to the eagle, explaining, "They detract from the smoothness of the piece, but they add good mechanical detail." Just to be sure they're going to work Steve tries them on the test panel before putting them on the tank.

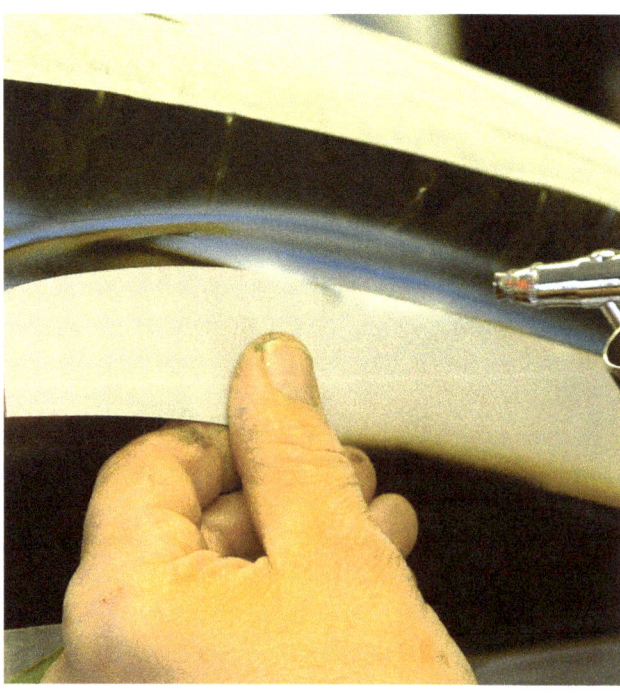

Using white paint and a stencil, Steve begins creating highlights on the uppermost area of the chrome.

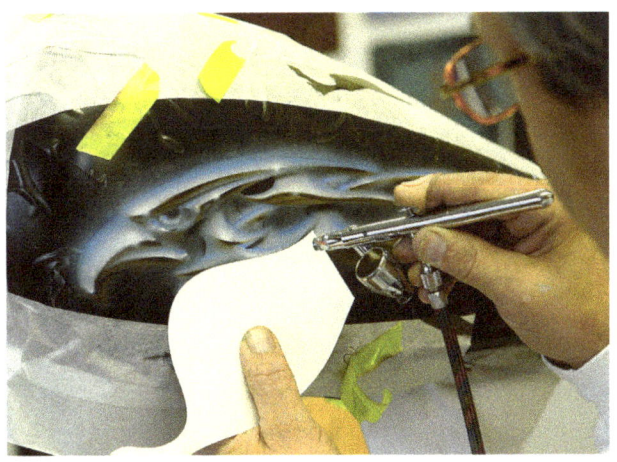

Here Steve uses another stencil as he creates one more highlight on the very edge of the chrome.

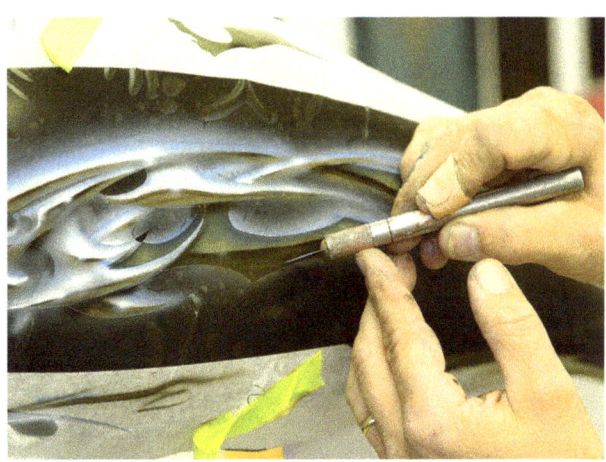

At this point part of the mask, cut out earlier, is put back down and the Xacto knife...

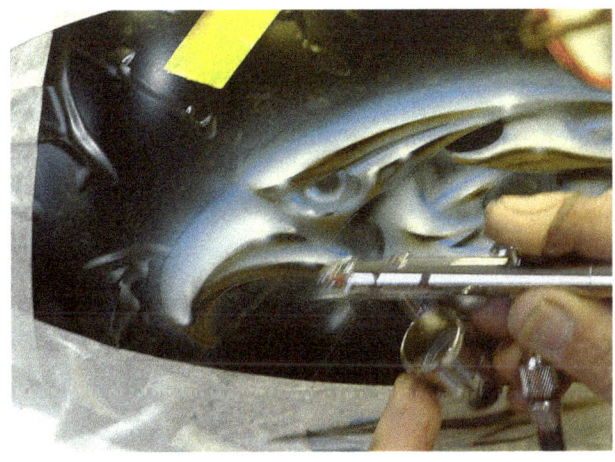

More highlights on the beak, done freehand this time.

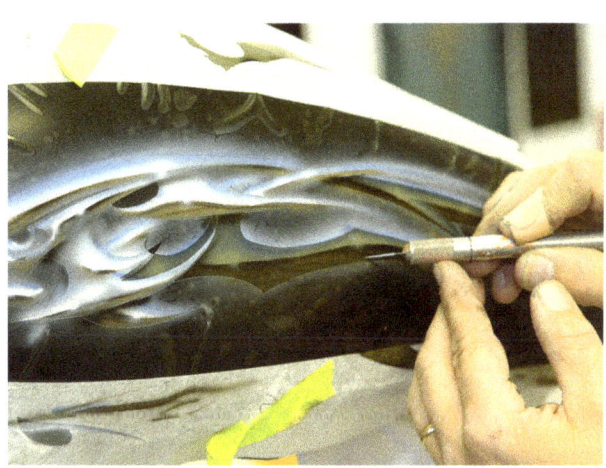

...is used to cut out a thin edge.

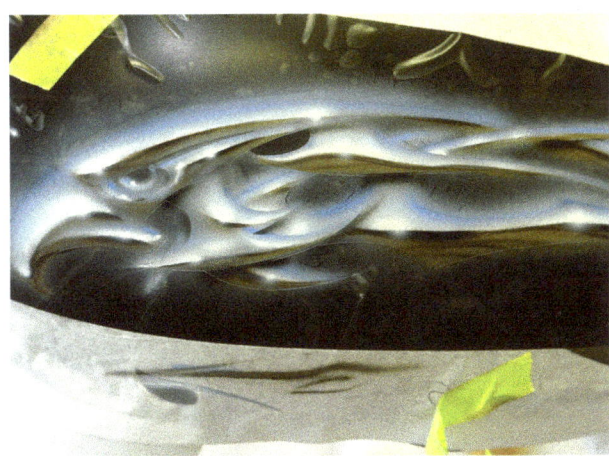

A progress picture, note how the highlights help to raise the chrome off the tank and enhance the 3-D effect.

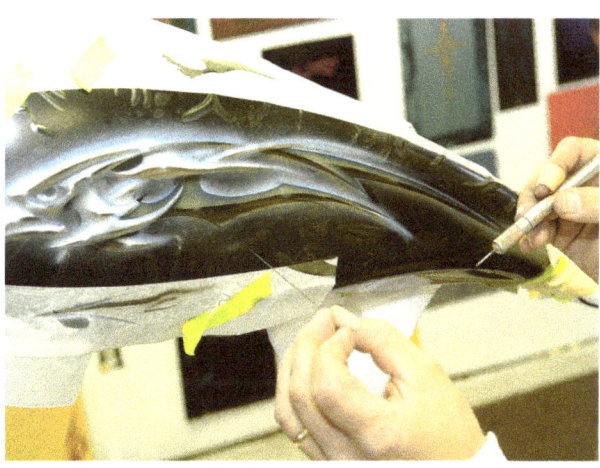

Now this piece of the mask is peeled away. This area will be the beveled edge.

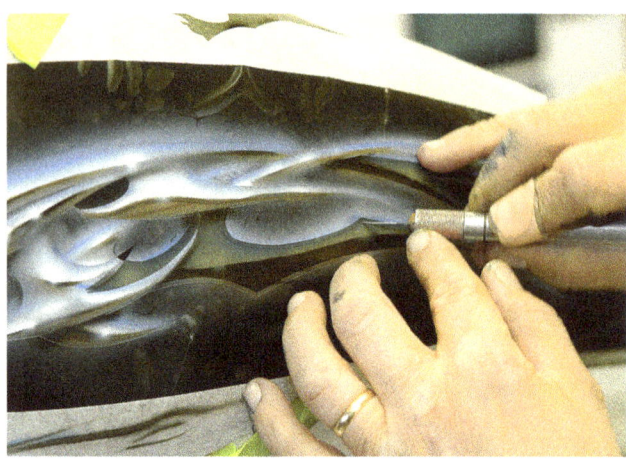

Now the upper part of the mask is trimmed to create another beveled edge.

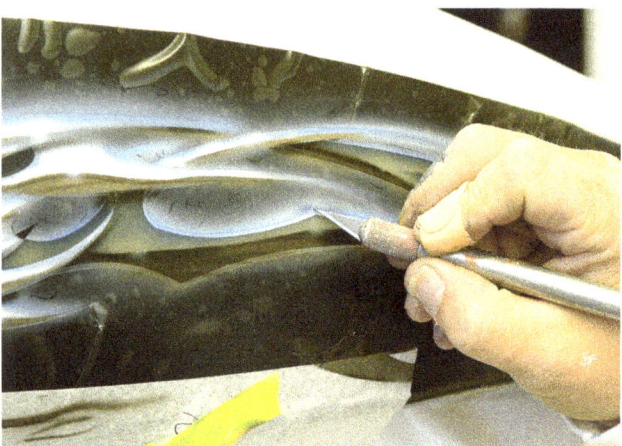

With the mask trimmed, the white/blue applied earlier shows through.

Happy with the test results, Steve puts the mask on the eagle. The first color is white, "we are doing the highlights first partly because that's the paint that's in the gun." Just because these rivets are small doesn't mean they aren't a lot of work. Next, he puts the dots back on the design and creates the highlights on the bottom of each rivet.

"When I want detail like this I turn the air pressure down to 10 or 15 pounds," explains Steve, "normally it's 35 or 40 psi. The gun I'm using is an Iwata revolution." Finishing the rivets requires that Steve mask and unmask the area a number of times so he can create the level of detail necessary to make these look like convincing rivets. The actual sequence of events is best explained by the photos and captions.

REALITY FLAMES

Before starting in on the flames Steve masks off the eagle with Transfer Rite Ultra made by American Biltrite Inc. As Steve explains, "I'm covering over the eagle (some call it back masking) so I can spray the flames without any over-spray on the eagle.

The process of creating the reality flames might seem intimidating. In fact, Steve recalls being, "terrified when I first saw these flames." Like most complex tasks, this one becomes less intimidating when it's broken down into a series of steps. In this case, there are ten steps to the reality flames.

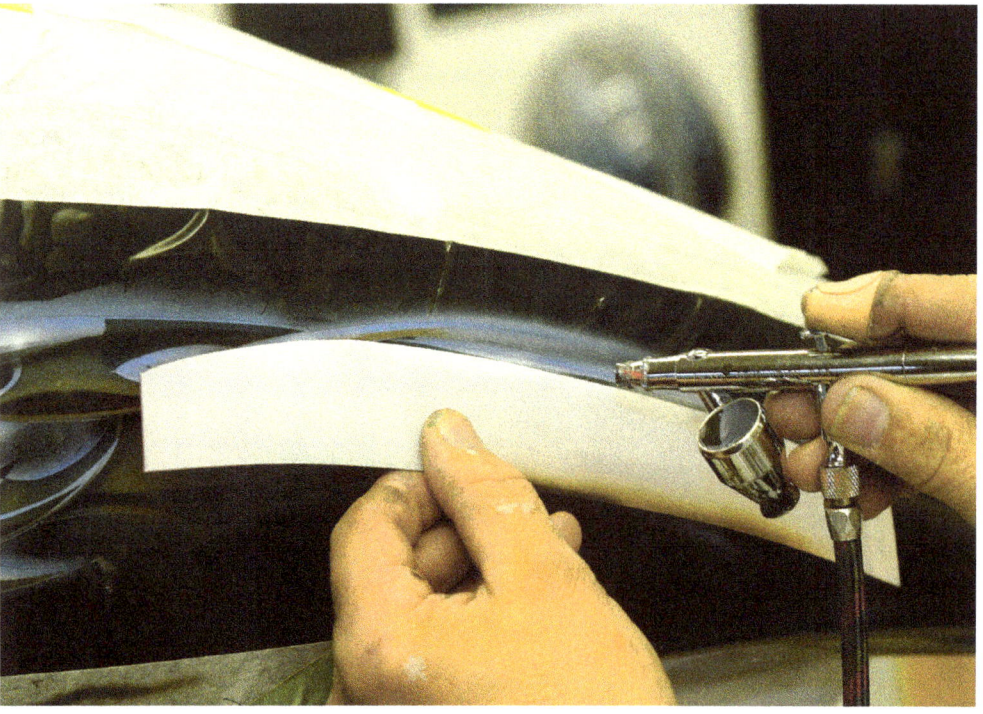

Now highlights can be added to the just-exposed beveled edges. Note: The eagle and most of the pre-flame work is done with Spies Hecker paints.

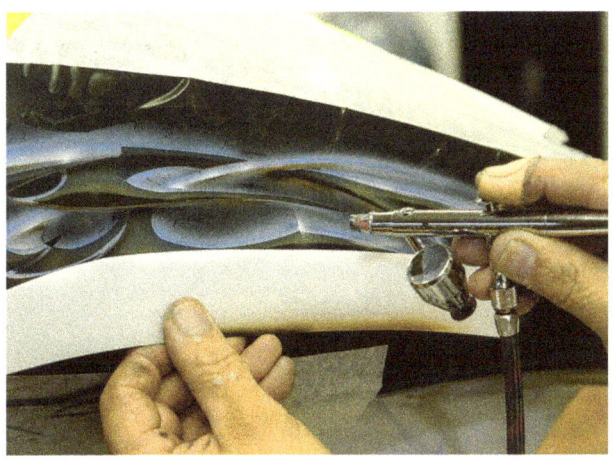

You can see how white paint and a stencil have been used to create a star at the intersection of two beveled edges.

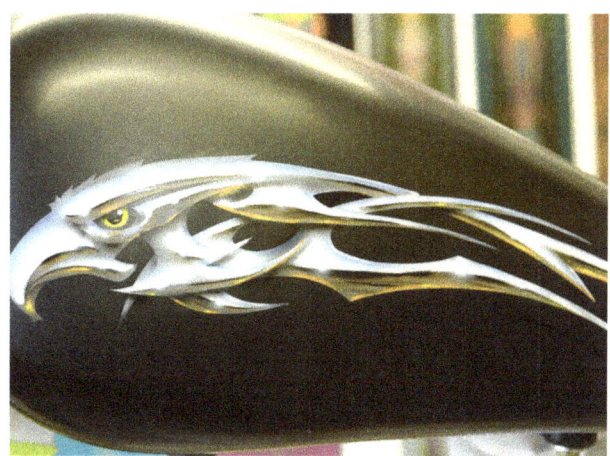

Progress photo of a chrome, tribal-eagle complete with horizon line and beveled edges.

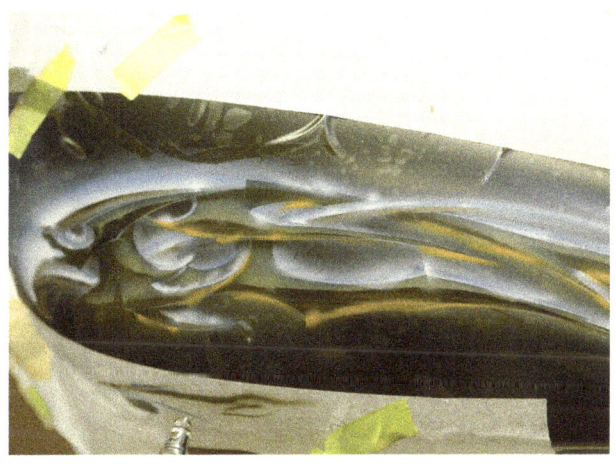

A progress shot. Note how the lower beveled edges reflect the red of the flames - which haven't been created yet.

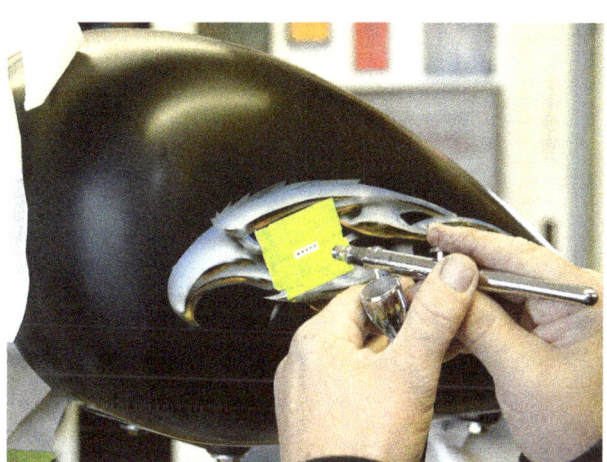

Steve decided to add detail, in the form of a set of rivets on the side of the eagle.

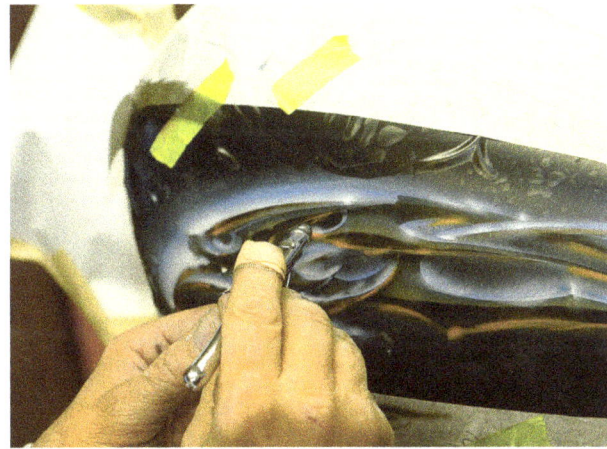

Before finishing this part of the project Steve adds a few more white highlights.

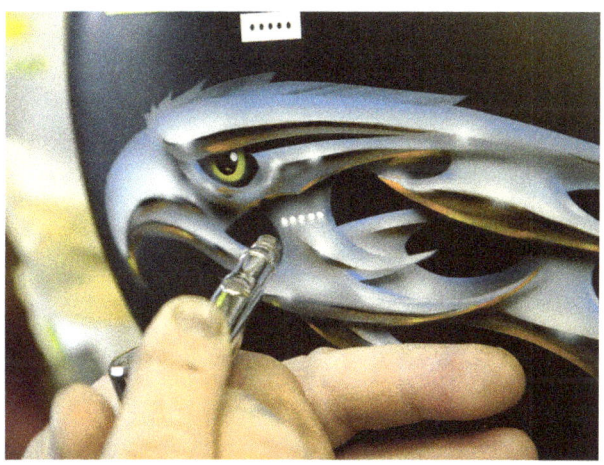

After spraying the basic white rivet, Steve masks each rivet and adds a highlight on the bottom.

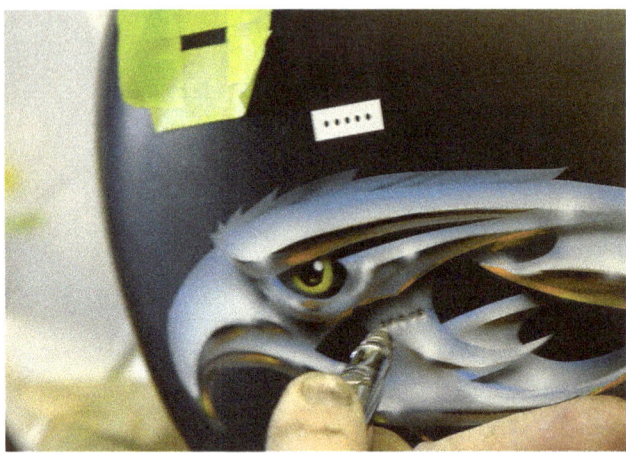

1) Before taking the masks off the rivet heads Steve adds shadows around each rivet to help "sink" it into the metal.

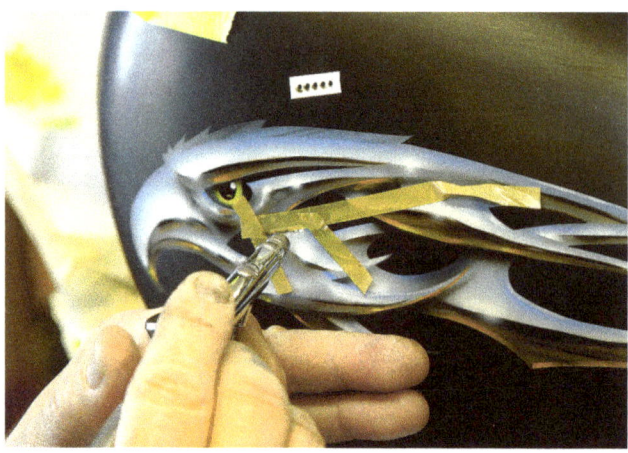

4) To create a seam Steve masks each rivet, then runs masking tape along the edge of the seam followed by a little dark paint.

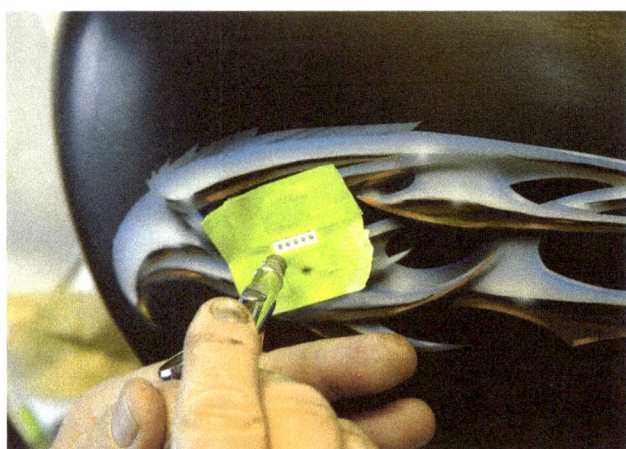

2) Now the masks are "swapped" and shadows are added to the lower edge of each rivet.

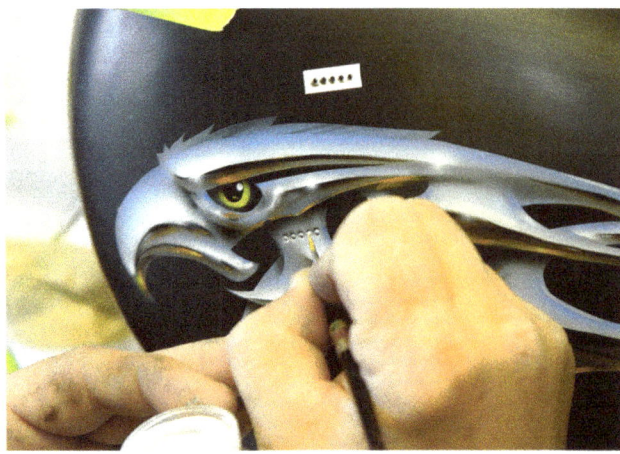

3) Next a bright highlight is added to each rivet with a drop of white paint.

Step 1: House of Kolor moly orange (SG 103 Q01) is the first color you put down. Steve calls this, "the foundation for all the rest, this will be the background for the flames." As the photos show, Steve puts this moly orange down freehand without the use of any masking or stencils.

Step 2: Steve calls this, "knocking it back" with candy apple red. "This makes the orange mysterious, enhances the highlights and darkens the shadows." The paint is kandy koncentrate (KK 11) from H of K mixed 3 to 1 (one part KK 11) with SG 100, an intercoat clear. "I put this on fairly heavy with a conventional touch-up gun (a Sata mini jet HVLP), running at 35psi."

Step 3: More moly orange. "I'm using a template to reinforce some of the shapes we did earlier," explains Steve. "And also adding new shapes."

Step 4: Candy tangerine (KK 08) applied over the moly orange.

Step 5: Chrome yellow (SG 102) reduced 25 to 50 % and applied with a template. Suddenly the reds are redder - partly by contrast with the yellow nearby. Steve warns that, "when you get near the end of the project it's easy to just rush through the last parts of the job. There's a lot of standing back and looking at a job like this, comparing one side of the tank to the other, or the front fender to the rear, to make sure the job is consistent."

Continued on page 85

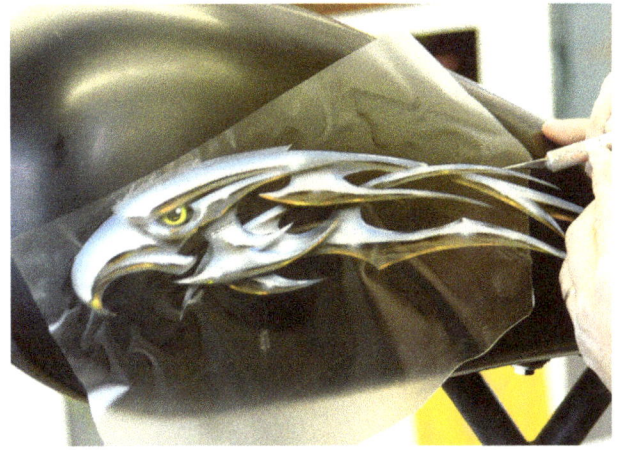

Time for reality flames, but first a little masking with clear material.

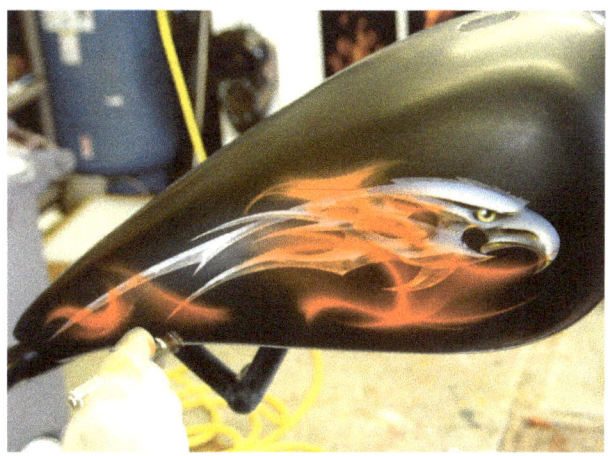

...in a pattern...

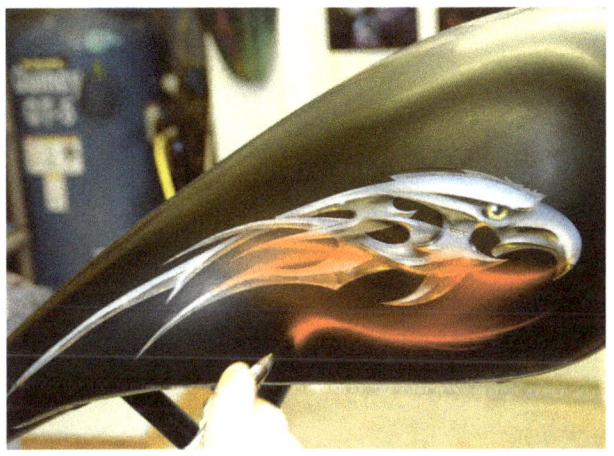

The first color is moly orange.

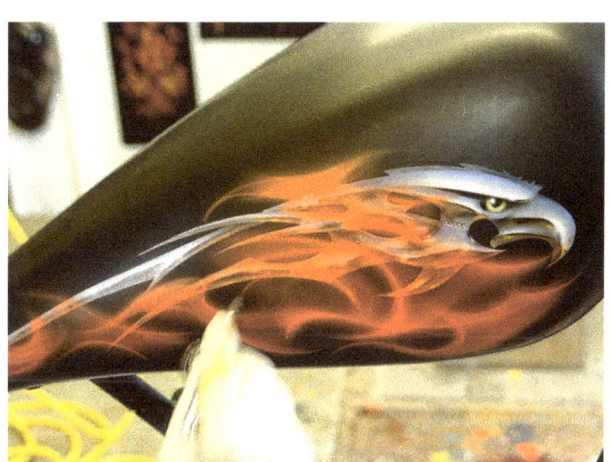

...that suggests the licks of a campfire.

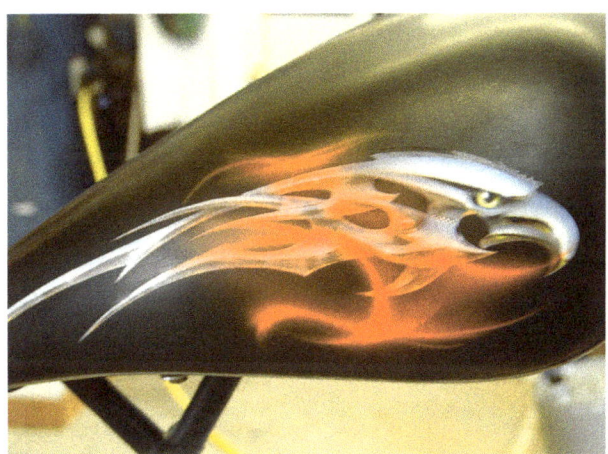

These early licks are applied freehand...

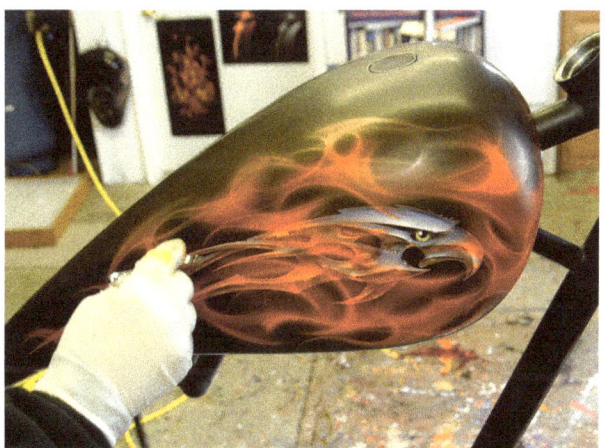

Steve keeps at it until the entire side of the tank is engulfed in random red licks.

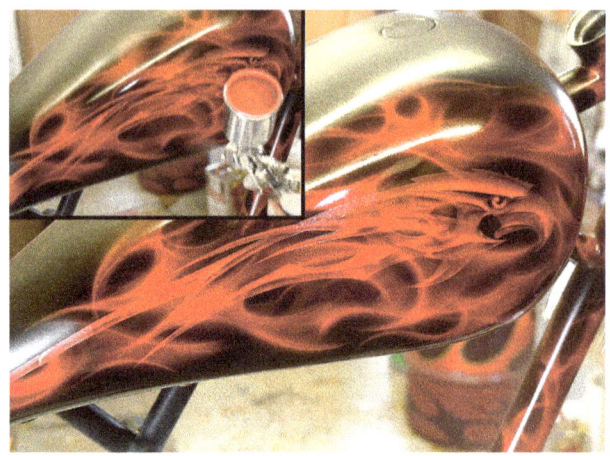

The candy apple red is next, applied over the moly orange, followed by a coat of intercoat clear.

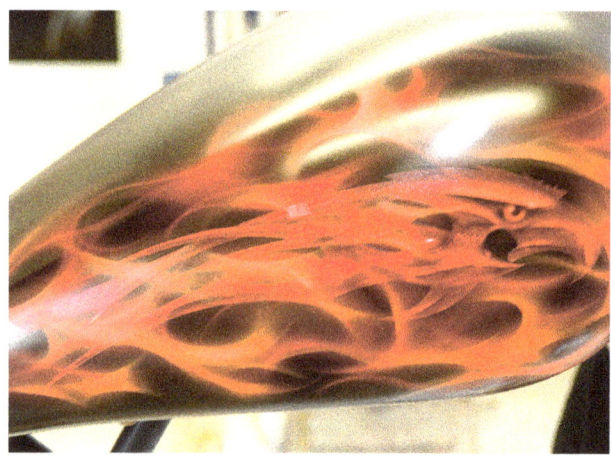

A progress shot at the end of the moly-orange-with-stencil step number 3.

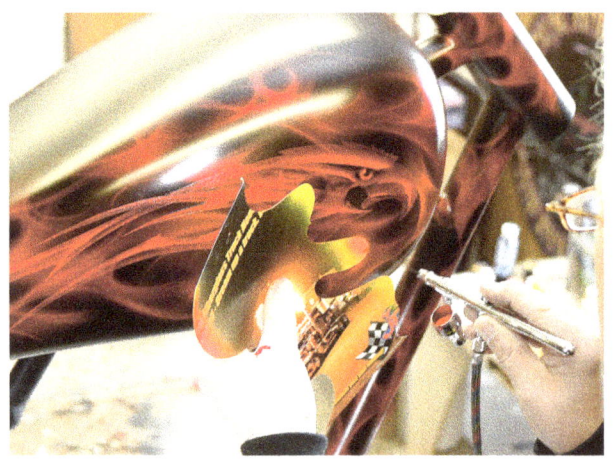

More moly orange follows, but applied this time with a stencil.

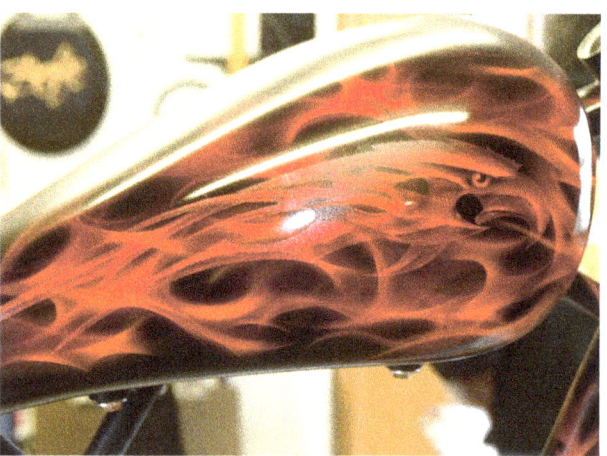

A mist of candy tangerine (step number 4) has been misted over the moly orange to richen the colors.

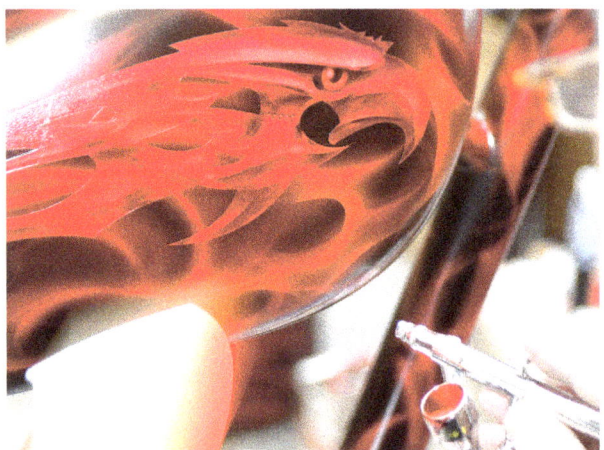

Note how the use of the stencil gives definition to the flames.

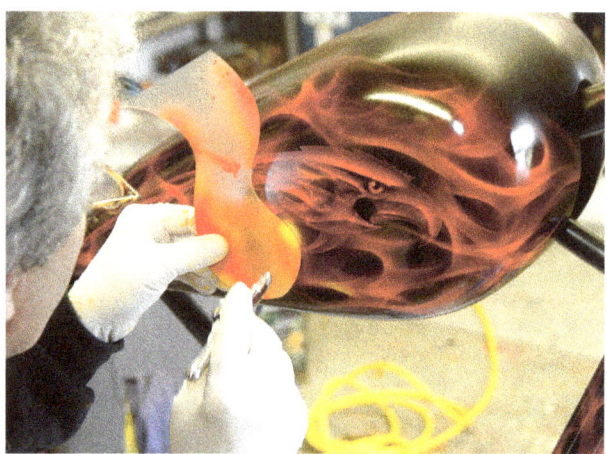

The chrome yellow (step number 5) is applied with a stencil to brighten the flames.

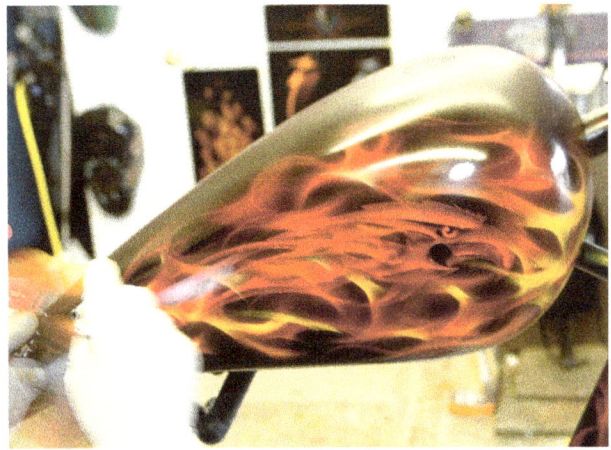

Still working on step 5, chrome yellow (with extra reduction) sprayed on with a stencil.

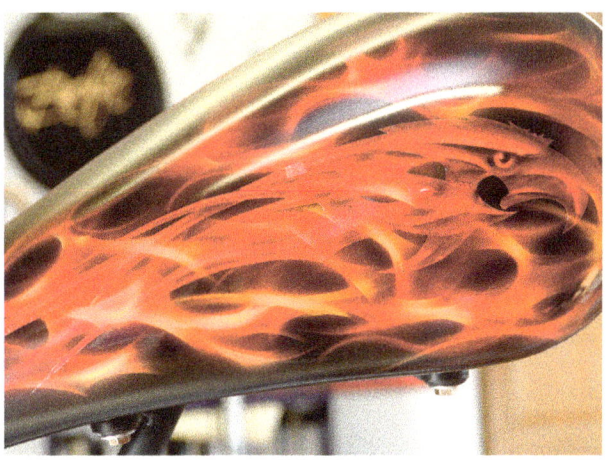

A progress shot, after the candy tangerine. The effect is to mute the yellow and enhance the reds.

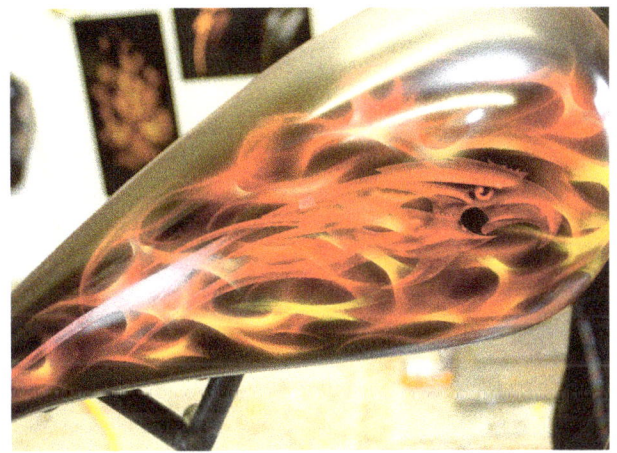

A progress shot at the end of the chrome-yellow phase.

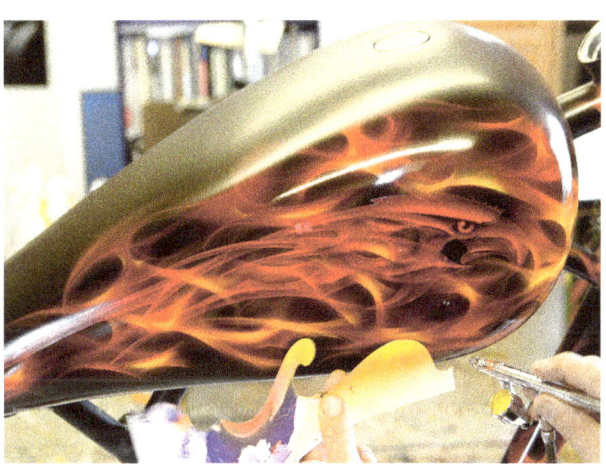

Step number 7, the addition of more chrome yellow.

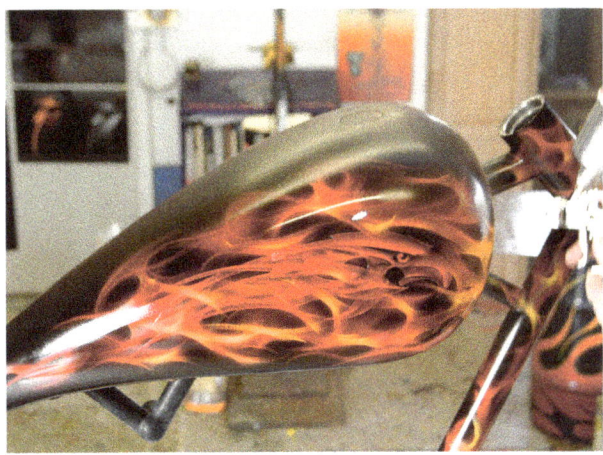

Step 6, a mist of candy tangerine over the whole thing, done with a small touch-up gun.

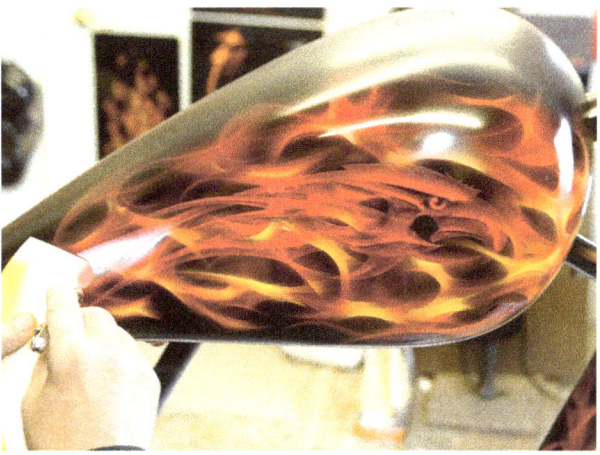

By doing the flames in layers the whole thing takes on the semi-transparent look of a real fire.

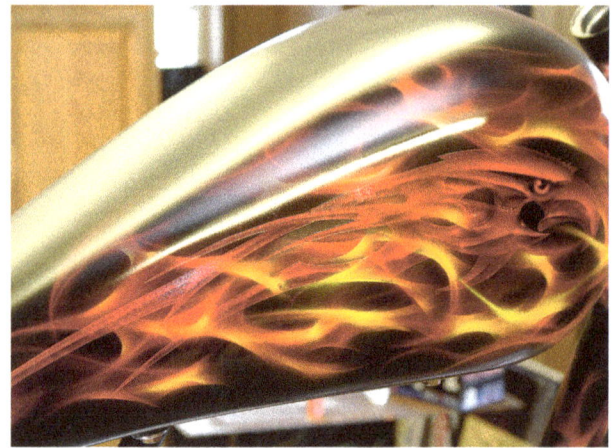

Another progress shot at the end of step number 7.

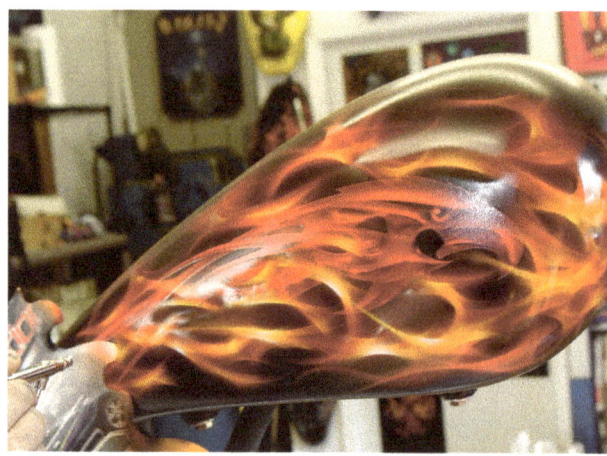

Step 9, a few white highlights on the edges of the flames.

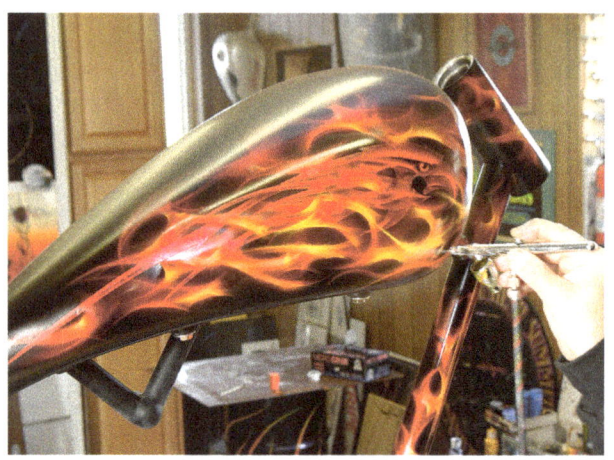

Step 8 is the addition of candy yellow...

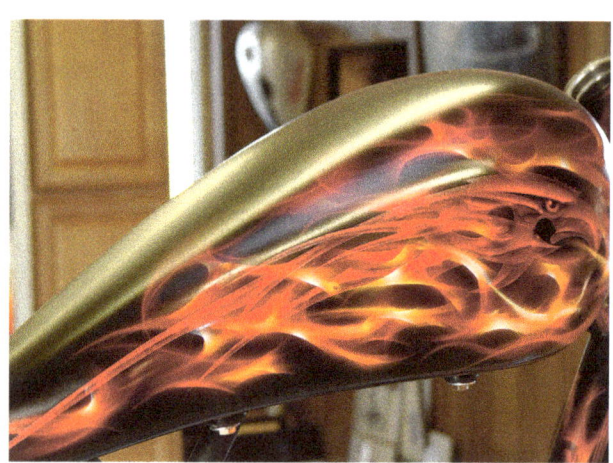

After step 10, a light mist of pagan gold.

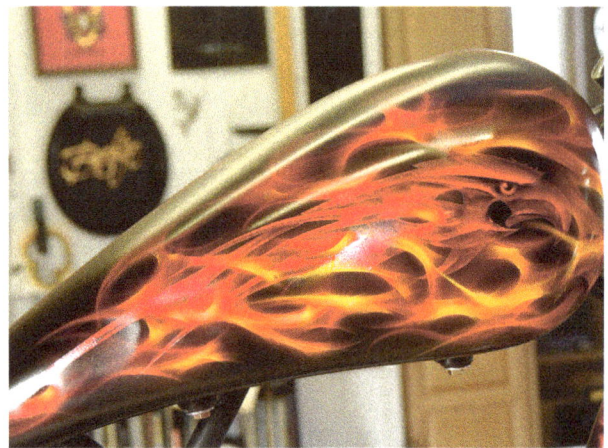

...which brightens the chrome yellow already applied.

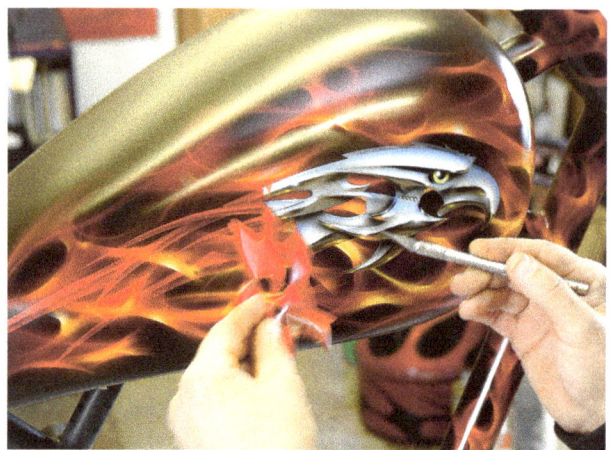

Now Steve can pull the mask to see the full effects of this multi-step project.

Each step, each layer, takes time. The template gives the flames edges. "If you don't use the template the flames have a soft, out-of-focus look."

Step 6: Steve applies a mist of candy tangerine (KK 08) on everything.

Step 7: More chrome yellow basecoat, reinforcing the heat of the fire, "You have to constantly cut new stencils," says Steve. "Because they get a paint buildup at the edge and if you aren't careful it will transfer to the tank. Yellow reality flames only look good on orange, if you make a new flame shape on the black, with yellow, it doesn't look right."

Step 8: Kandy yellow. (KK 02). "Some painters use pagan gold. This will brighten the yellow."

Step 9: White basecoat (BC 26 White Q 01), applied sparingly with a stencil to create small highlights on the yellow edges and points.

Step 10: Steve mists on a little bit of pagan gold.

Now it's time to pull the mask. The only thing left is highlighting (shown on this page), done with white paint and a "slotted template."

Steve explains that there is one more step (one that isn't shown). "You can take black or your base color, and emphasize the hollows, but you have to be real selective as you do this."

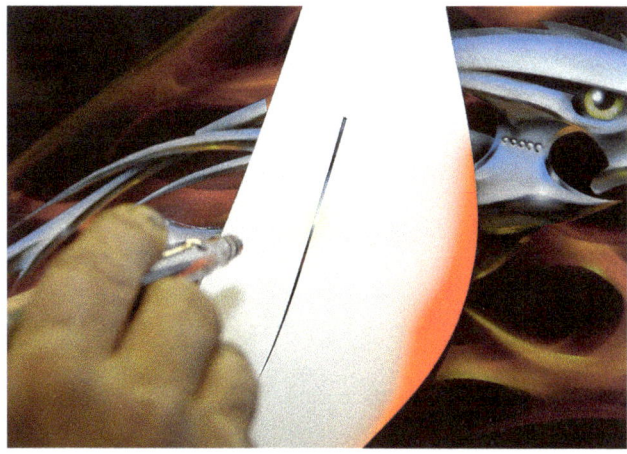

What Steve calls a "gleam" or highlight is done with this homemade stencil.

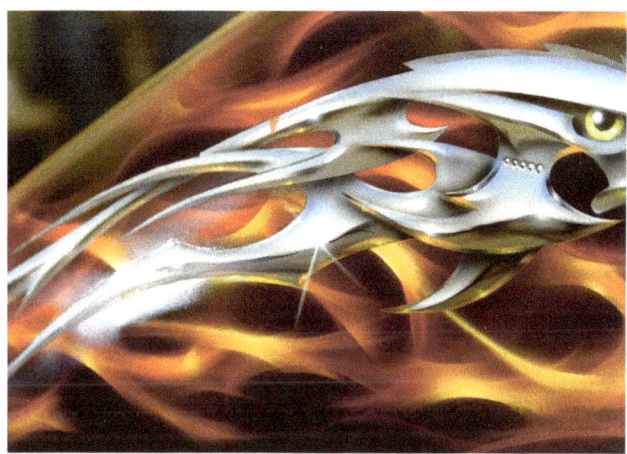

The effect enhances the feel of chrome, but needs to be used with discretion.

The finished machine. Though we only covered the tank, Steve painted both fenders, the oil tank and even the frame's neck.

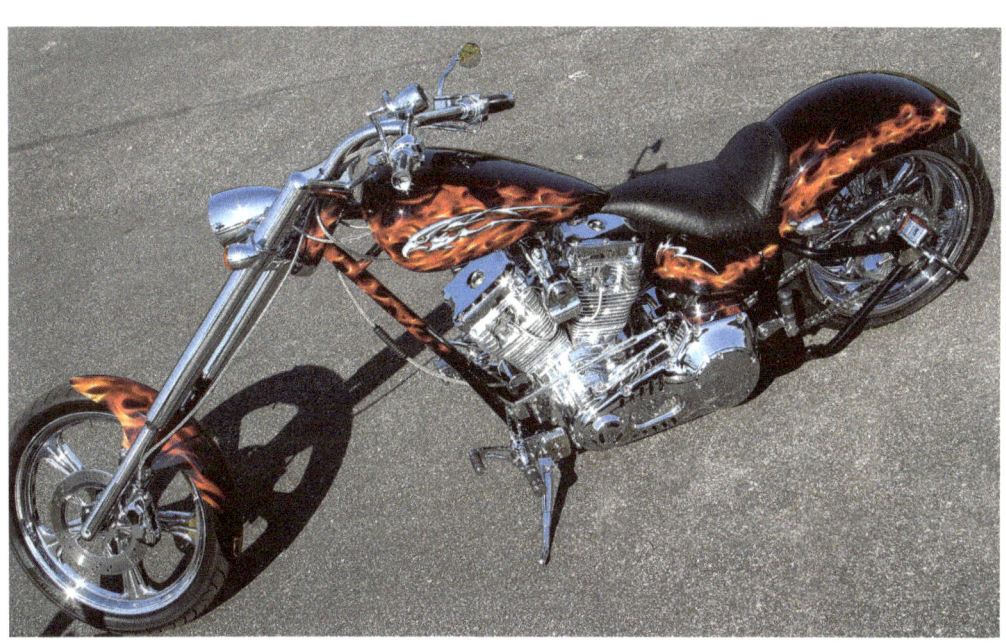

Chapter Six

Ken Simonsen

The Blonde Butterfly

Ken may be a newcomer to the body painting world, but he has been toiling in the airbrush field for decades. His background includes published work on major billiard magazine covers and countless applications within their pages. His art often blends his talents with an airbrush, and the bristled variety, for added depth and texture. As good as he is with an airbrush there are simply some lines that are best left to a brush.

An early exposure to art through his mother's

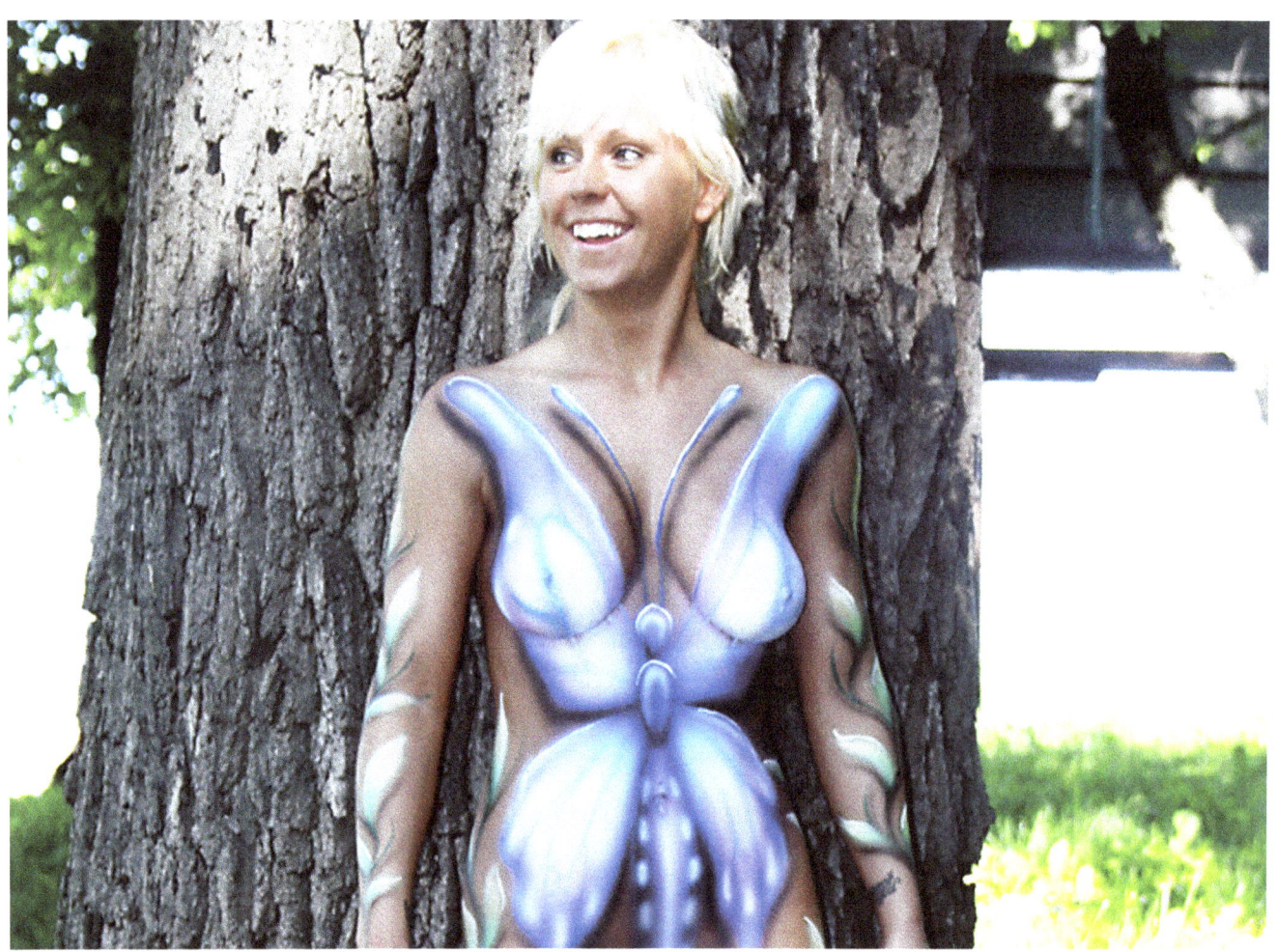

The finished butterfly resting against a tree across the street from Ken's shop.

efforts in the oil painting arena gave Ken his first taste of what could be created from nothing. Changing a blank canvas into a thing of beauty caught his eye when he was only 6 and he began his own artistic endeavors at that tender age. Pen and ink led to watercolors, which took him down entirely new avenues. His talents also led him into a magazine art director position for many years, exposing him to even more styles and mediums. His day to day responsibilities gave him plenty of chances to delve into new areas of the craft, thus expanding his already capacious talents.

His work has been showcased on everything from magazine covers to full-sized aircraft. It doesn't seem to matter what Ken is painting, the results are always amazing and almost endless in their imaginative expressions. While some clients dictate fairly strict outlines of what they want, others set Ken free to do what he does best. No matter which course is followed, happy clients keep coming back for more.

The body painting arena may be fairly new for Ken, but he hopes to have the opportunity to do more in the coming days. The added challenge of painting on a living, breathing canvas adds another level to the practice and he always enjoys trying new things. The materials he uses for most of his paint work were also chosen for this body painting project, and should prove to be durable enough to last many hours. The water based colors from Createx make clean-up fairly easy and don't require any special lotions of devices.

The ever changing world of art will bring many forms of new adventure Ken's way and he welcomes them with open arms.

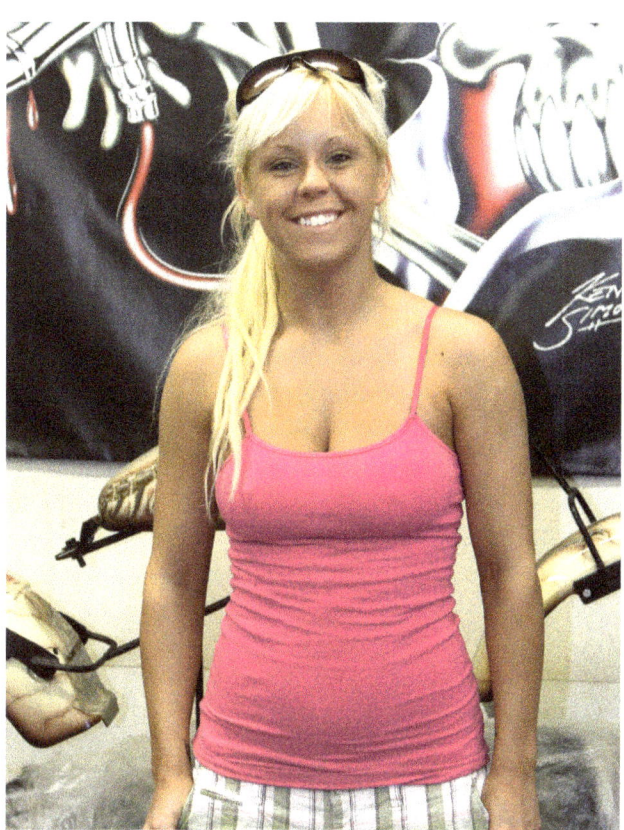

The lovely Mary before the paint gets applied. It was her first body paint experience but she had been hoping to get involved in a project for awhile.

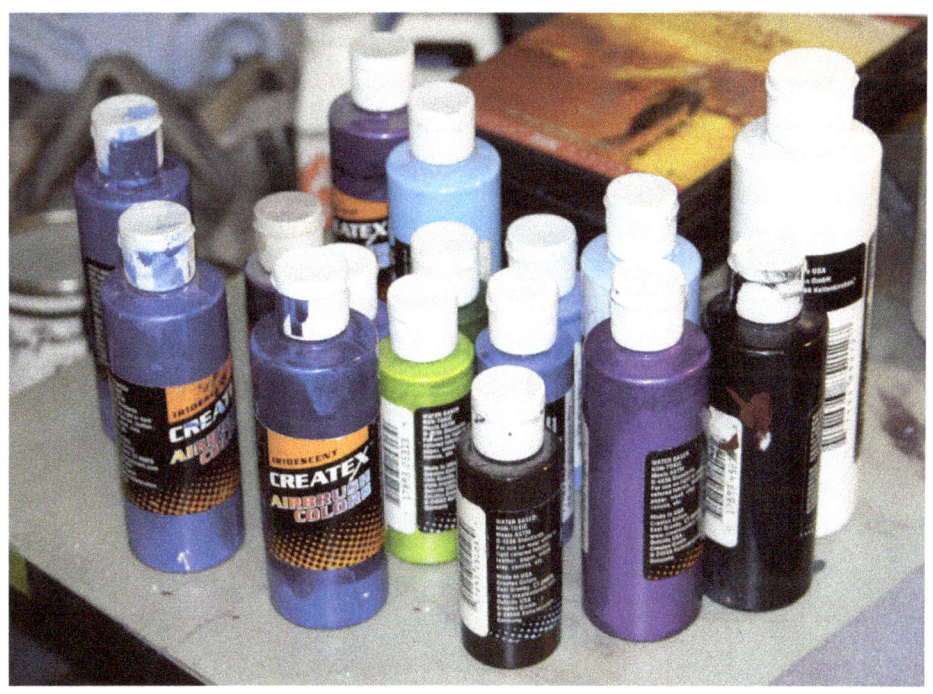

Createx paints will be used for this piece, Ken almost always uses this brand for his work. Distilled water is also used to reduce bacteria on the skin when the painting process takes place.

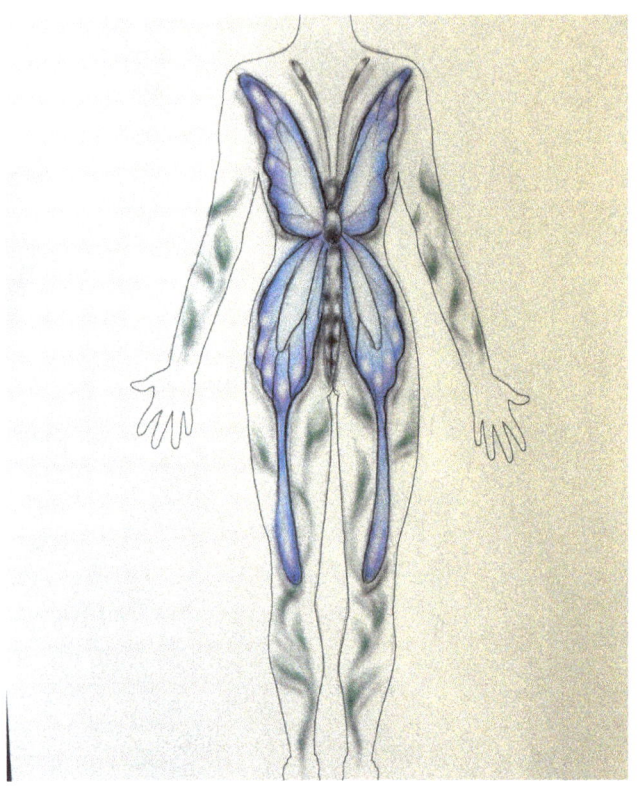

Ken has drawn up a detailed sketch of the piece prior to getting started and will refer to it often as he sets up the rest of the art.

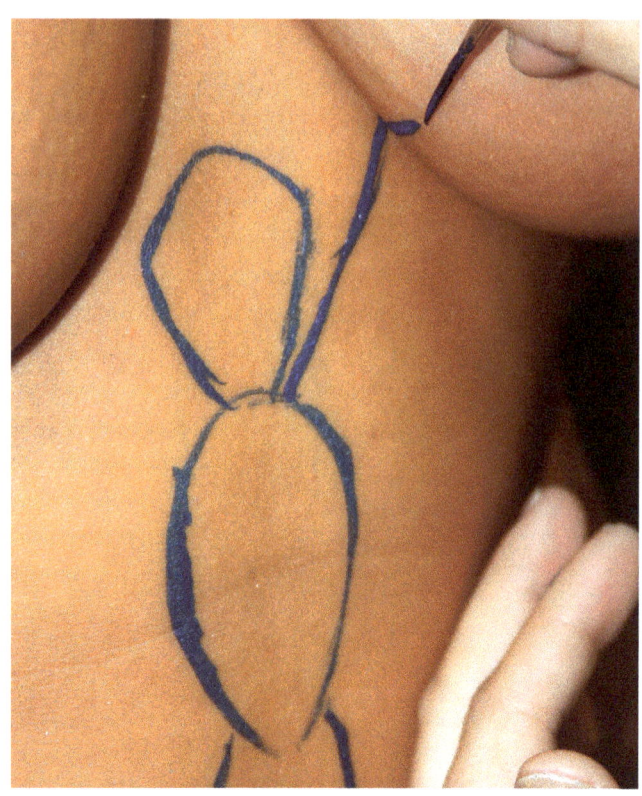

Although the first lines of paint appear crude, the application of additional paint will correct the art to achieve the proper result.

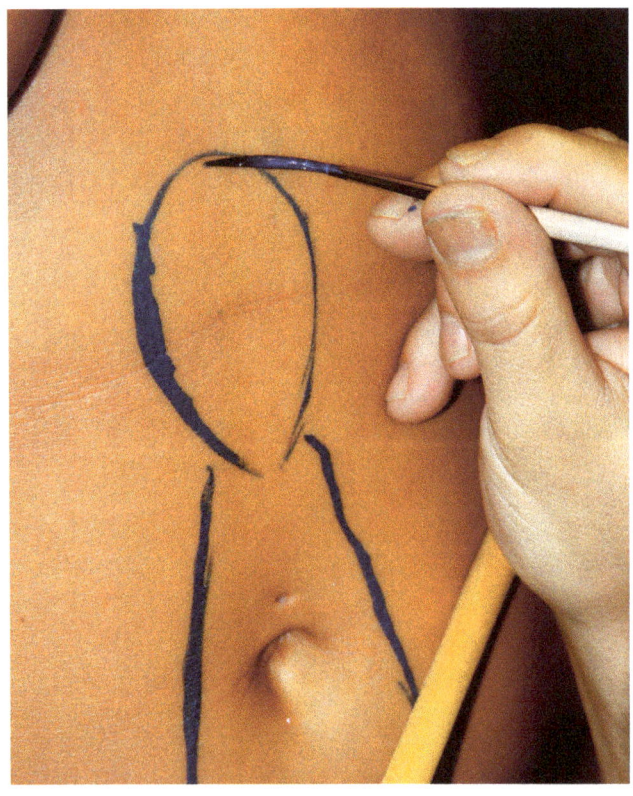

The long bristles of the #4 liner brush allow for smooth application of color.

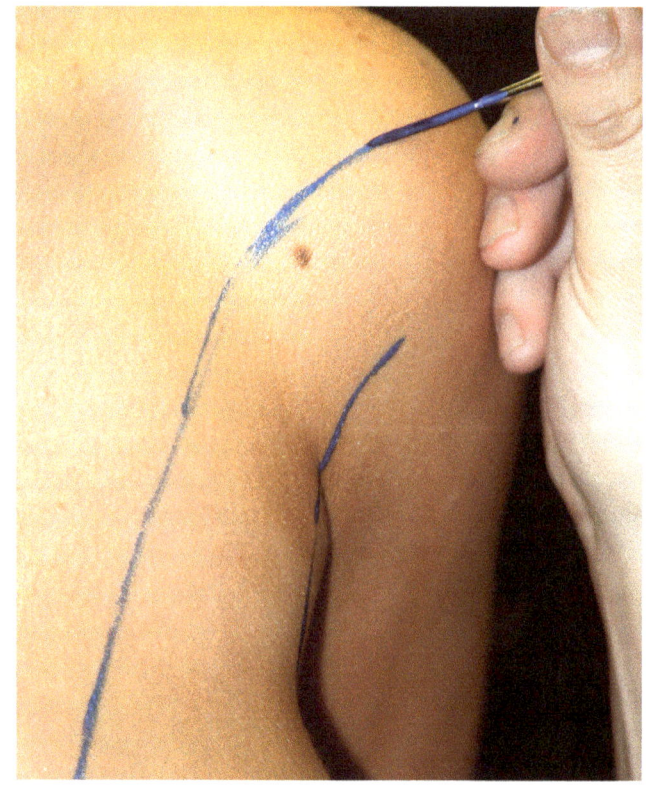

The butterfly Ken is creating will extend from Mary's shoulder down to her thighs.

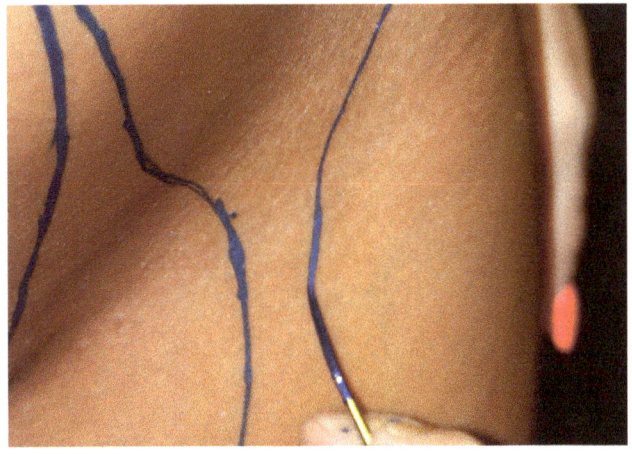

Outlines of the art are now drawn onto Mary's upper legs, and the work moves quickly.

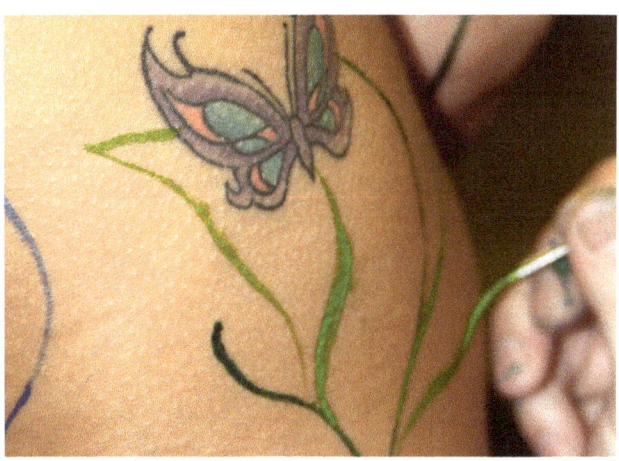

A lighter shade of Leaf Green is now employed to accent the darker green already in place.

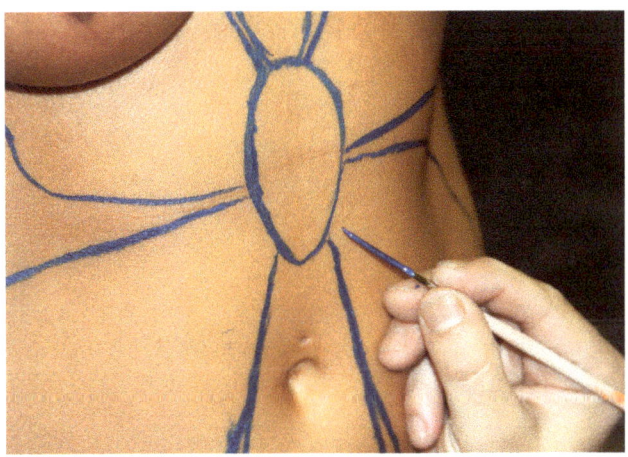

The Iridescent Electric blue color of the guidelines will blend nicely into the airbrushed sections that will follow.

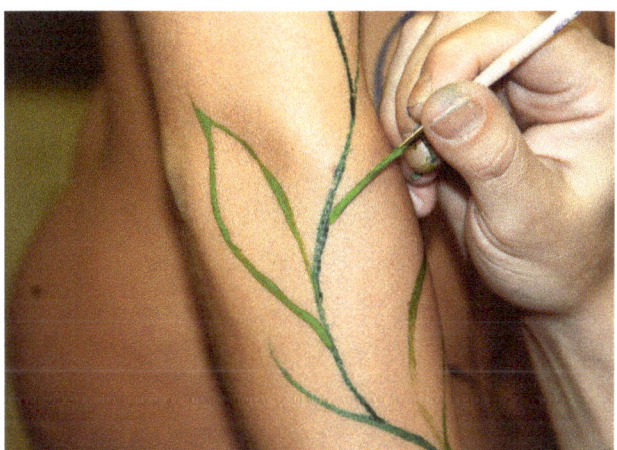

As the name suggests, Leaf Green is used to draw in the outlines of the leaves that will grow from the vines.

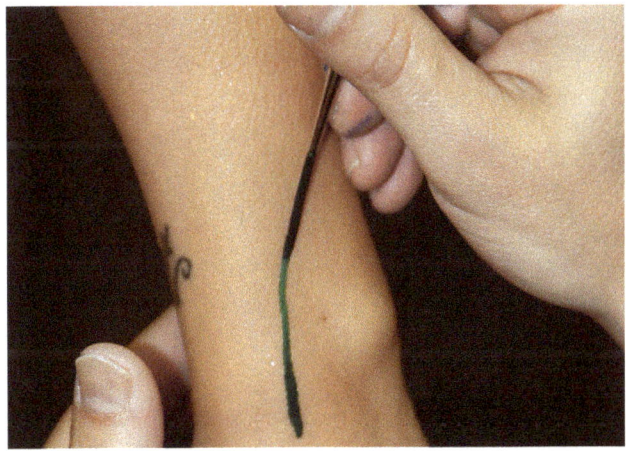

Changing to Forest Green, Ken adds the first of the vines that will appear on Mary's arms and legs.

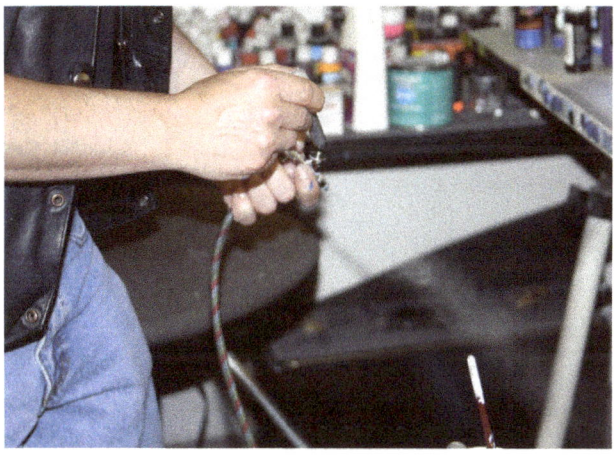

Before loading the airbrush with color, Ken sprays a small amount of clean water through it to cleanse any remains left over from his last job.

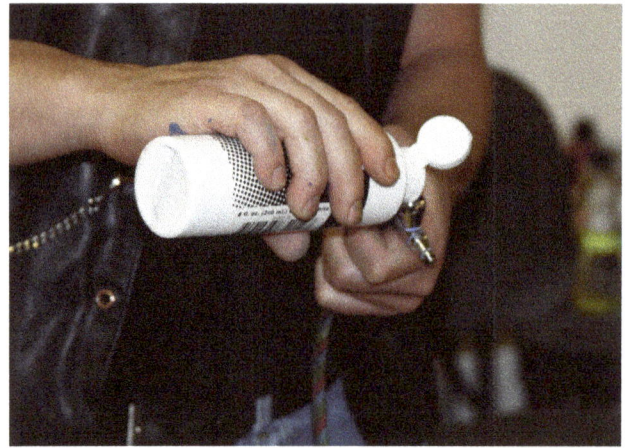

White is now added to the cup of the airbrush and will allow Ken to get the first bits of sprayed color in place.

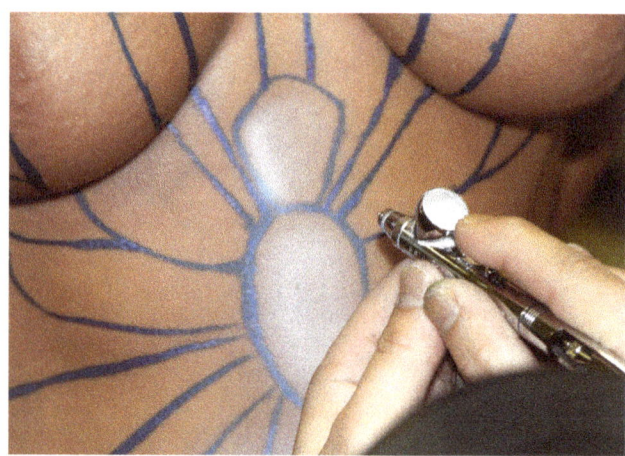

Staying within the lines already in place is achieved with quick hand motions that are still heavily guarded.

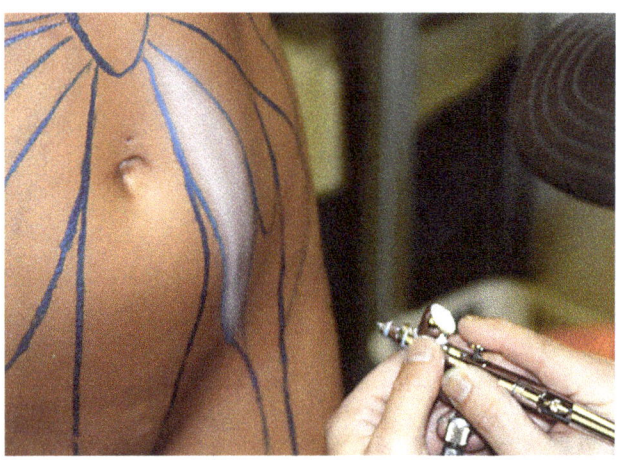

The initial airbrush color is applied to the wing of the butterfly and is done in layers to avoid blocking in the wings.

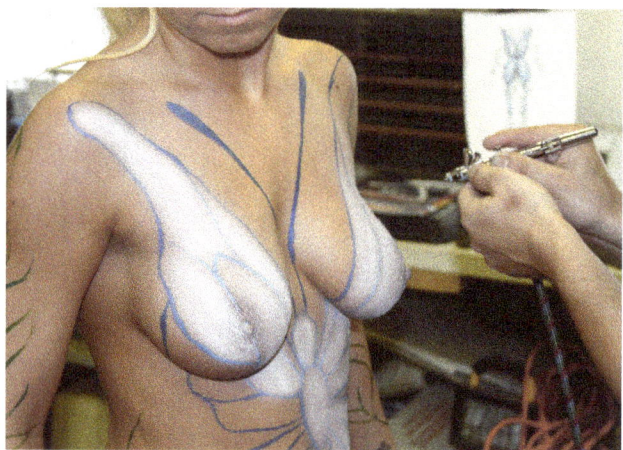

The upper portions of the butterfly are now sprayed in place as the base coat of white will cover nearly the entire piece.

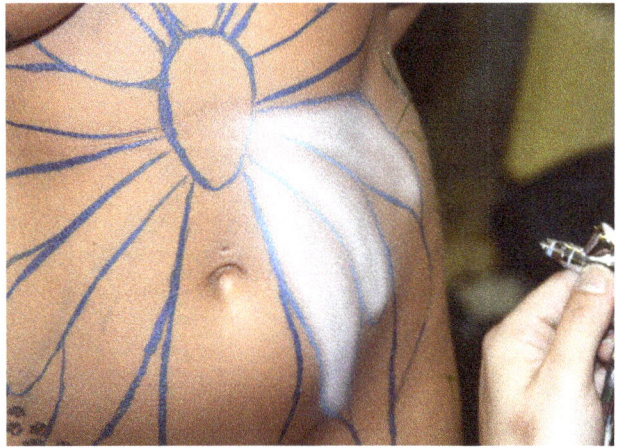

Careful hand and airbrush control keeps the paint only where Ken wants it to go, and goes down quickly.

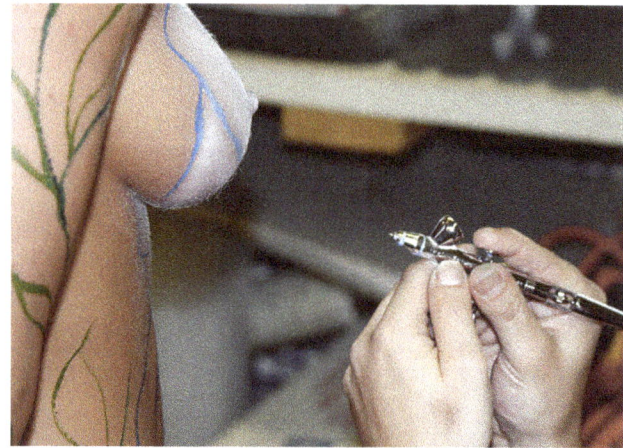

By using two hands Ken gains the control he needs working with the airbrush.

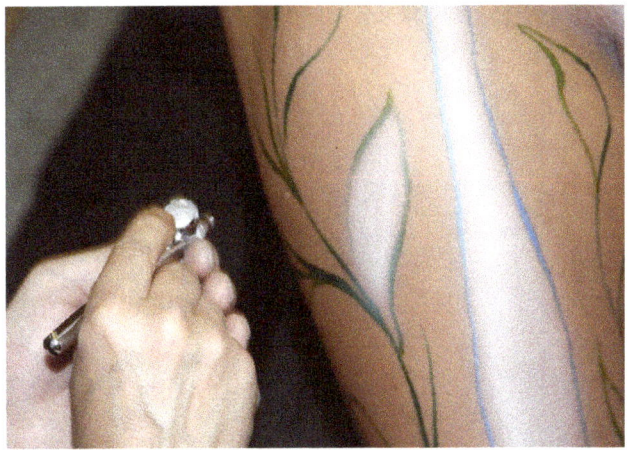

Each leaf will be filled in with a base coat of white before any color is added.

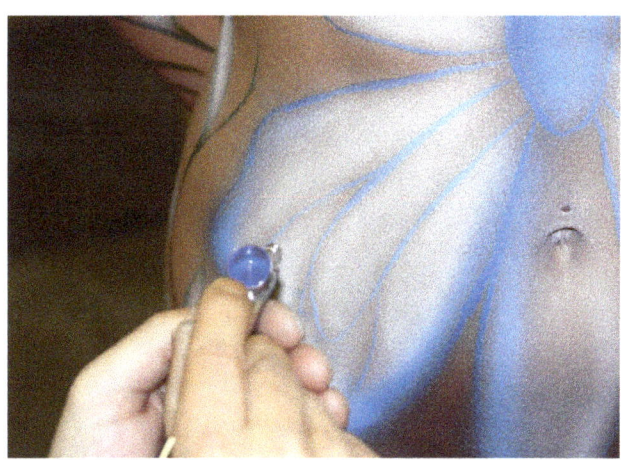

The guidelines are still visible, but are now softened by the next airbrush application.

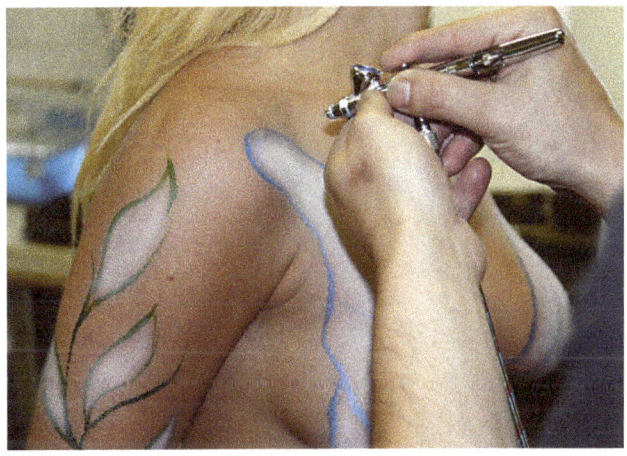

Having loaded the airbrush with the same Iridescent Electric blue as before, Ken begins to add some softer lines to the white base.

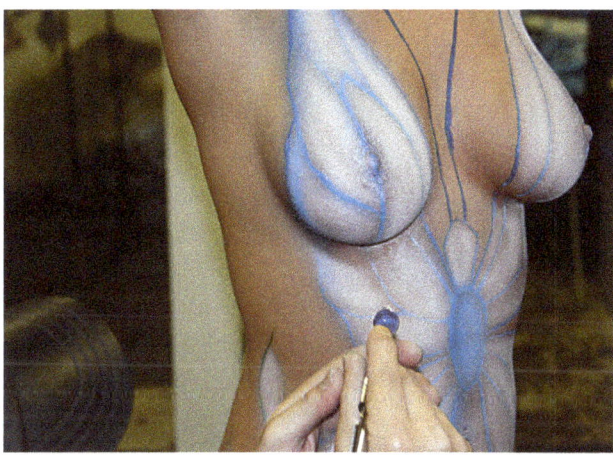

This shade of blue really seems to glow and will help lend realism to the butterfly's wings, even if they are only painted on.

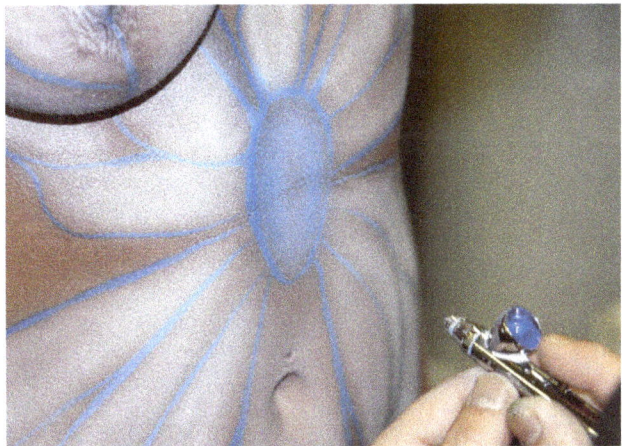

The white base makes for a much brighter blue - when blue is applied over the base color.

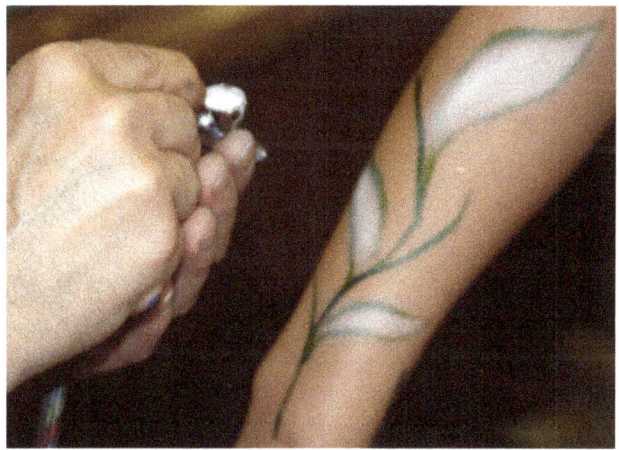

Changing back to white paint, Ken begins to fill in the leaves on Mary's arm

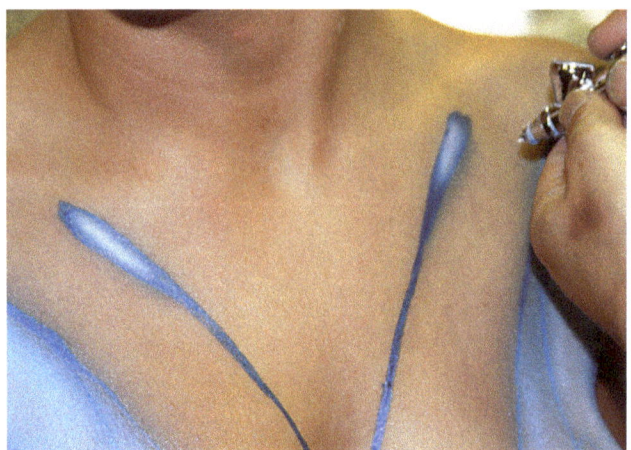

Adding a hot spot to each of the antennae helps to define them a bit more.

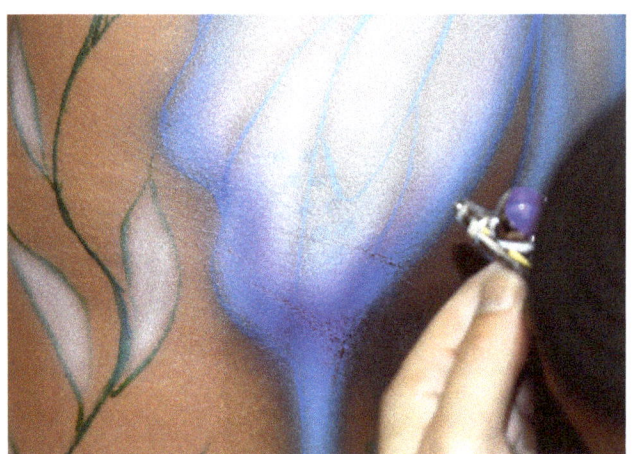

Iridescent Violet is now used to accent and shape the blue and white regions of the design.

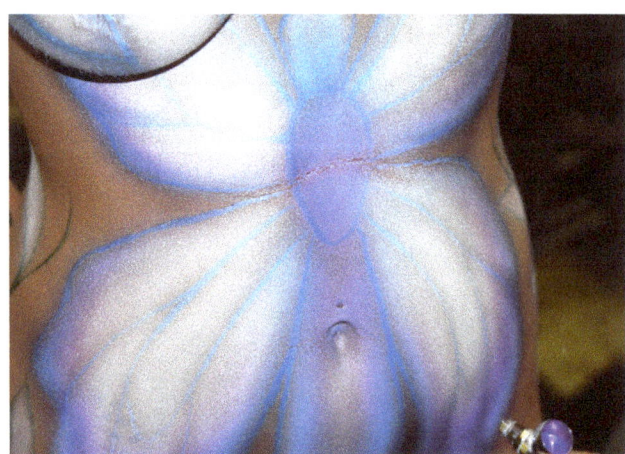

The subtlety of the violet against the white makes a strong statement, when used in careful quantities.

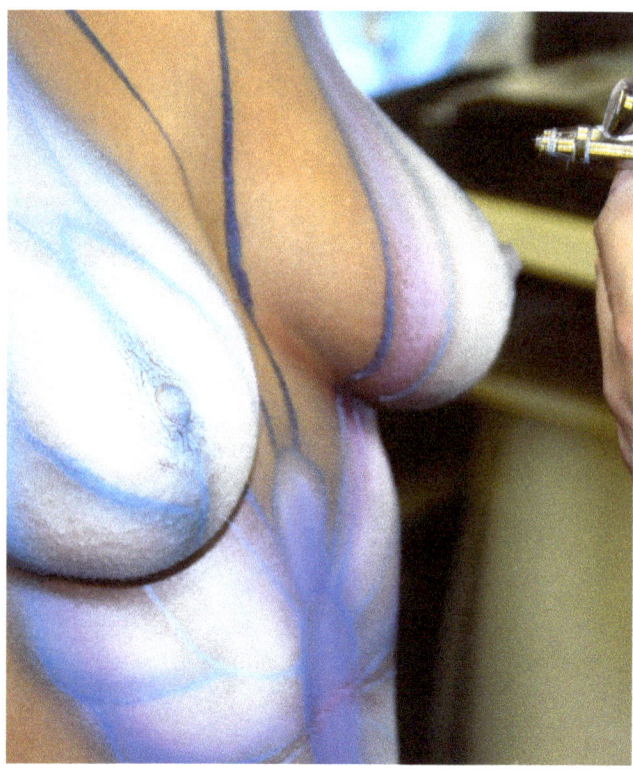

Only the edges of the upper wings are trimmed with the violet hue. This is another task that requires terrific hand control.

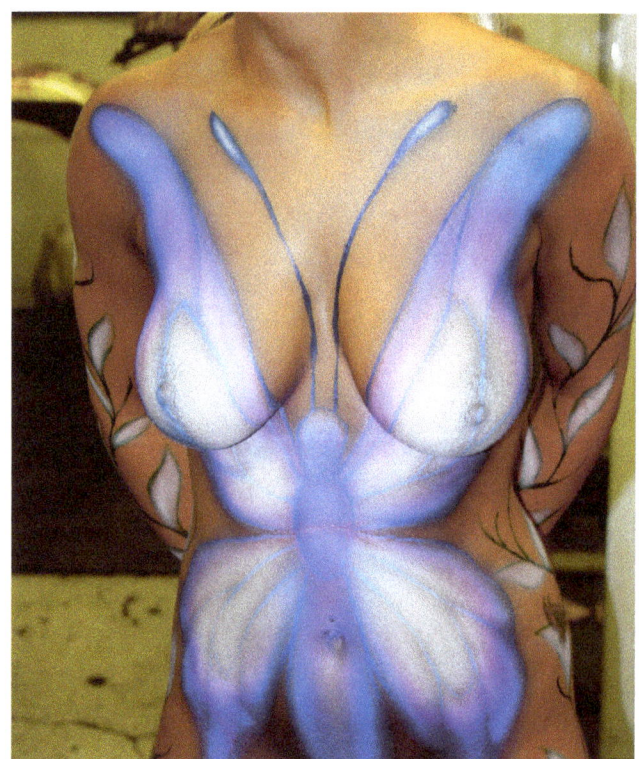

The results of Ken's efforts so far.

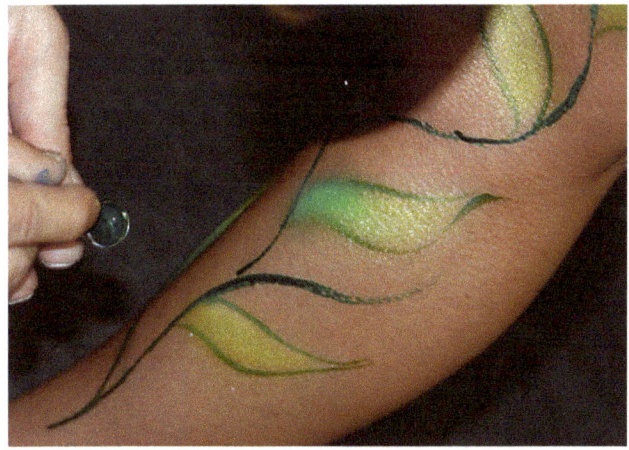

After each leaf has been painted with the lighter shade of green, sections of Forest Green are added to enhance the illusion.

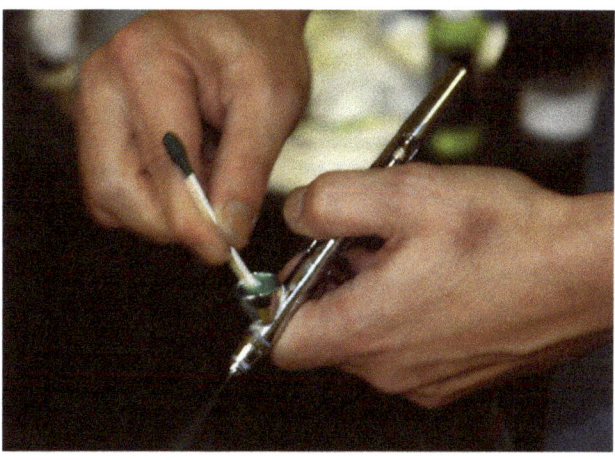

Ken uses a cotton swab to clean the airbrush before reloading with the next color.

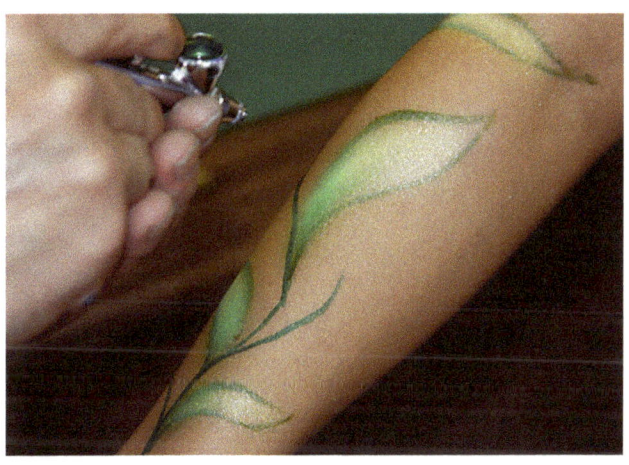

In a single, sweeping motion Ken adds the dark green accent to the lime green leaves.

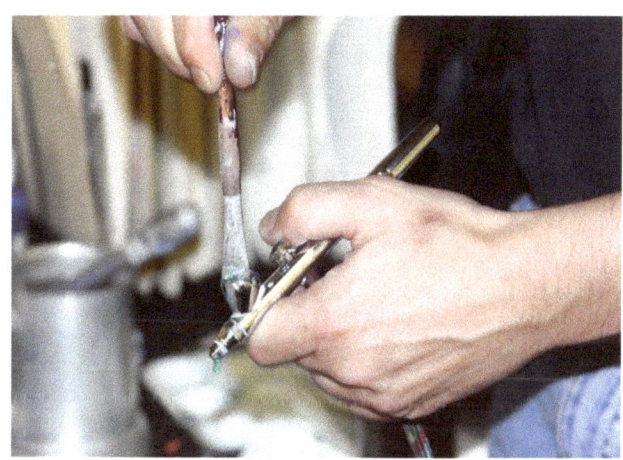

Using a paint brush, and some air pressure through the line, Ken is able to clean the last bits of green from the gun before switching to black.

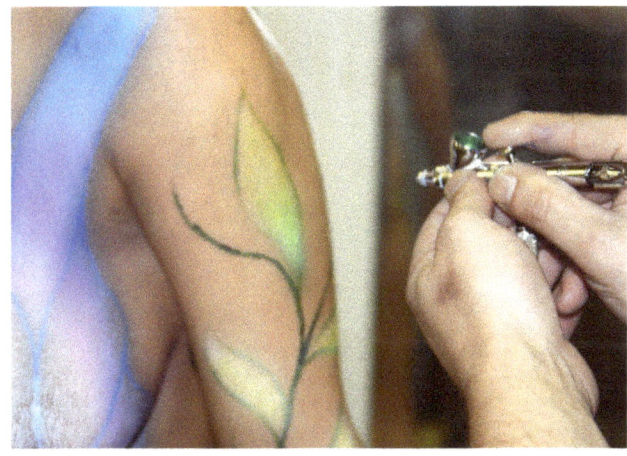

The leaf on Mary's upper arm gets the same bit of Forest Green added to the Pearl Lime.

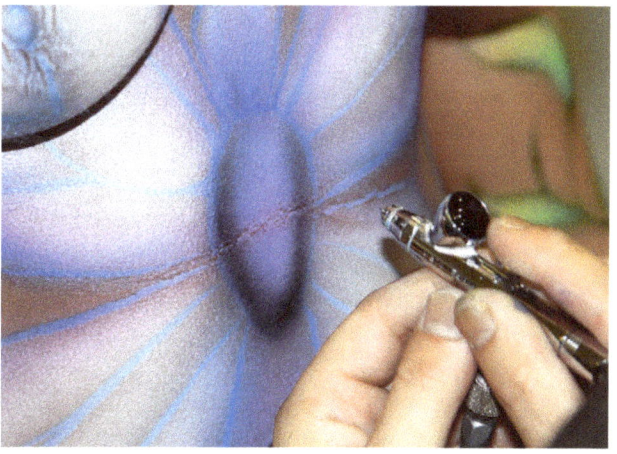

Small and carefully chosen locations now get a hint of black to bring more shape to the area in question.

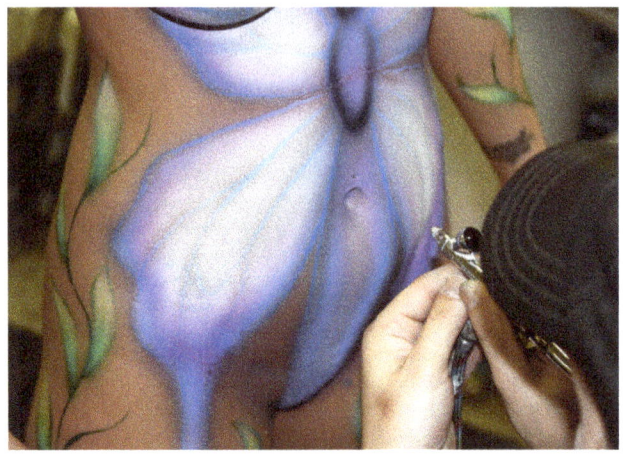

By holding the airbrush farther away from the surface being painted, the effect is more gentle and shades the colors beneath.

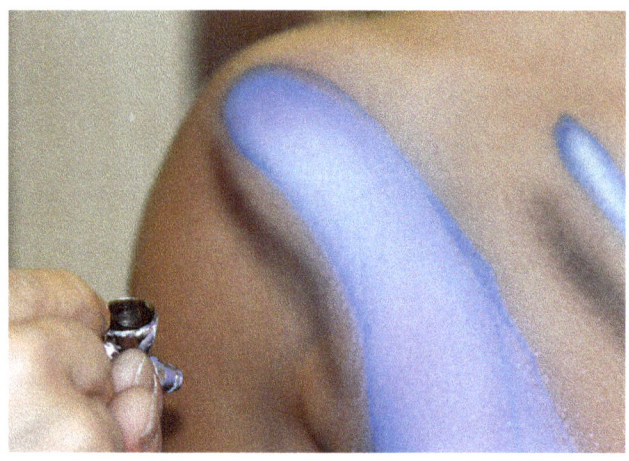

The upper edge of each wing is also given a shadow that will define the piece and add another dimension to the art.

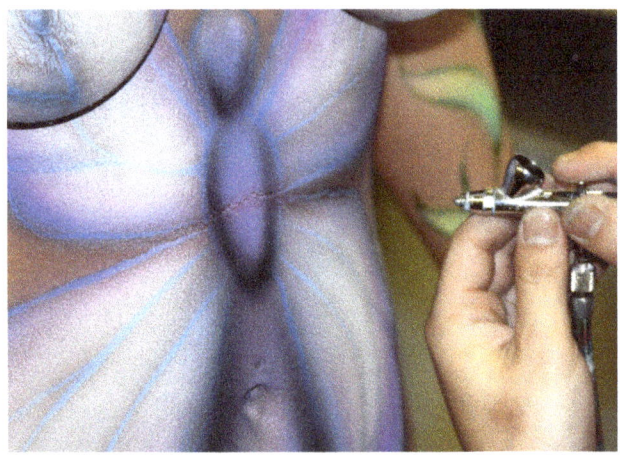

The dual-action trigger of the airbrush allows Ken to moderate the quantity of paint, and air, that flow through the tip.

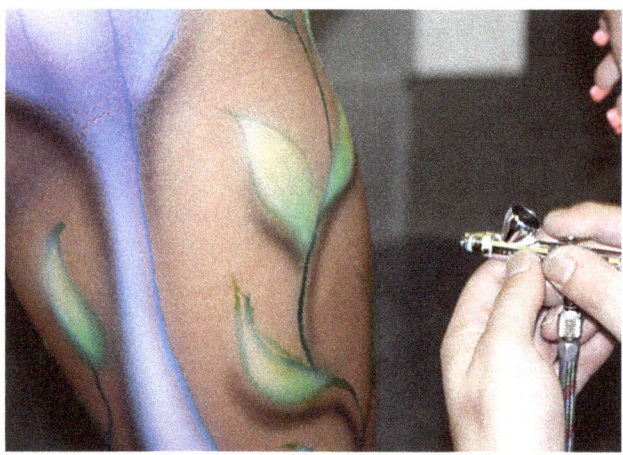

The twisting vines and leaves will also get a shadow which delivers a cohesive theme to the overall design.

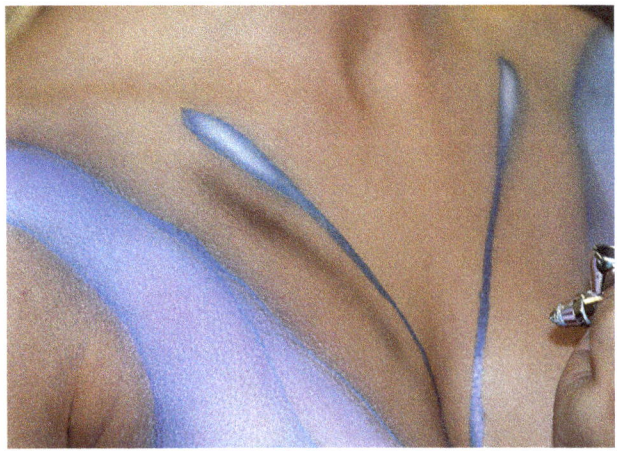

A very subtle shadow is now created behind each of the antennae.

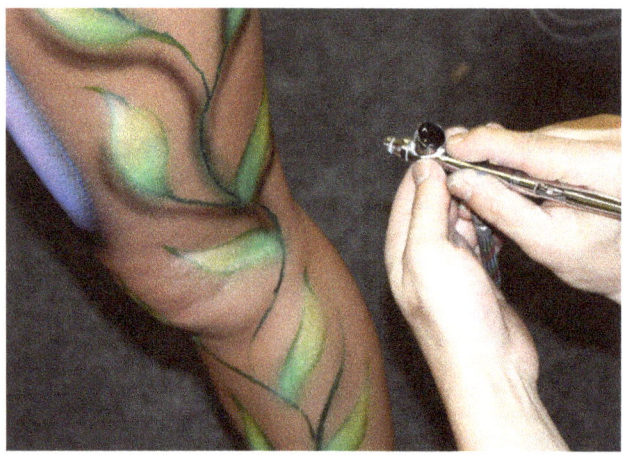

Down each of Mary's legs, the shadows are added to the vinery.

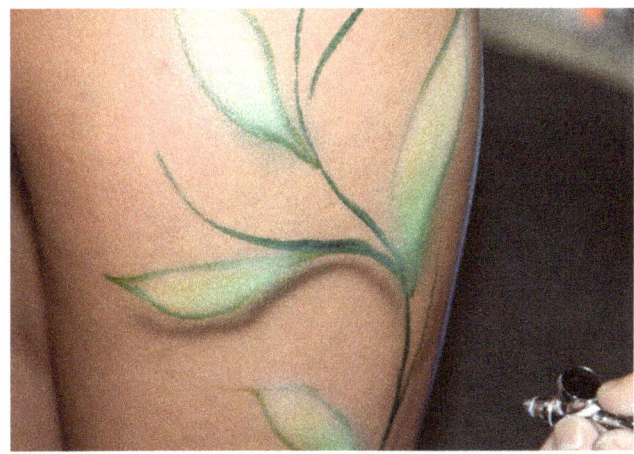

It is amazing to me how a small detail can make such a difference in the completed piece, but Ken is a fool for minutia.

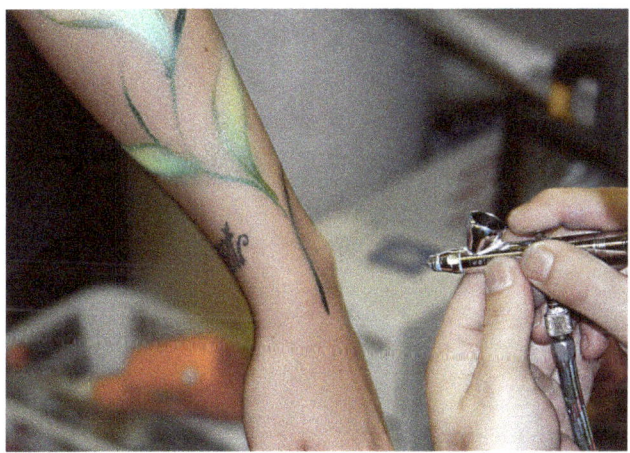

The roots of each vine are augmented with another bit of black to better define their nature.

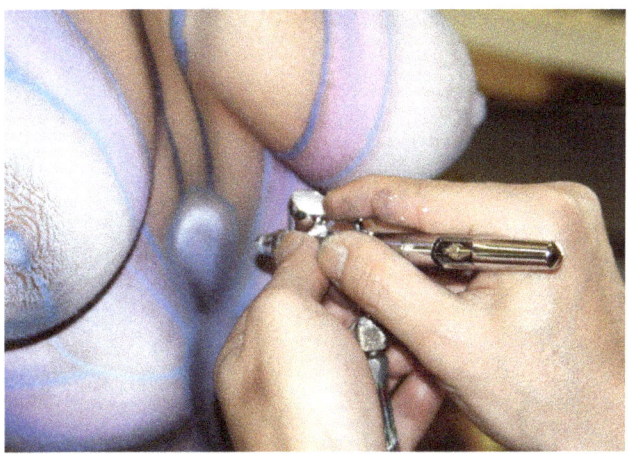

Switching back to white, Ken adds some highlights to the brightly colored areas.

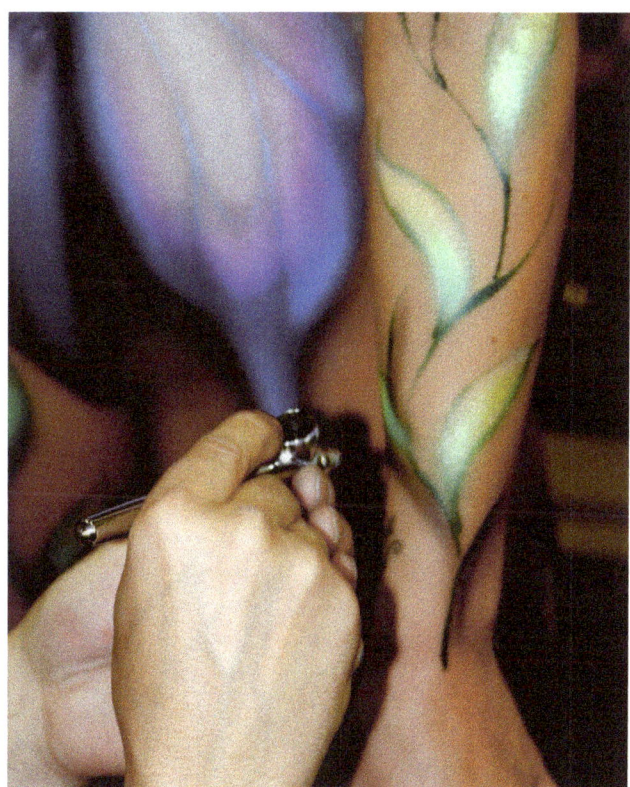

A few more shadows are added to the vines on Mary's arm.

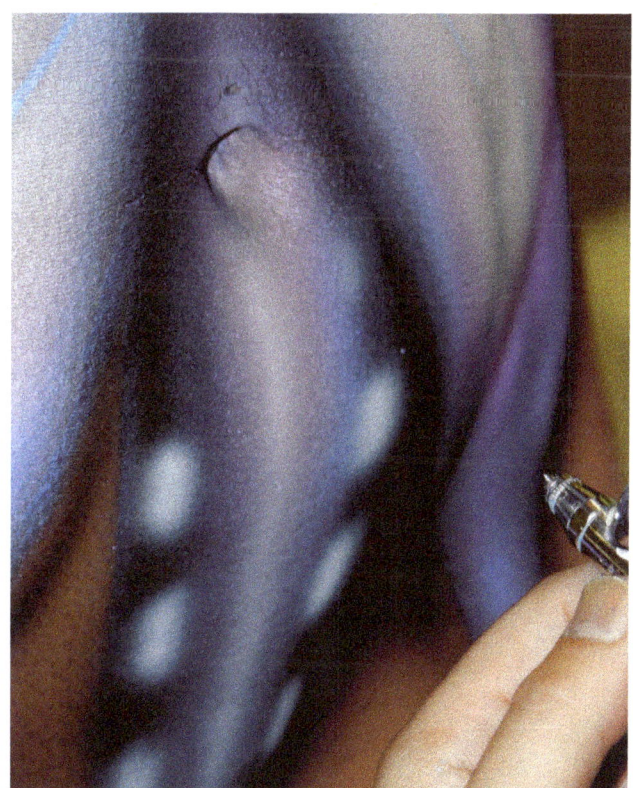

A series of white spots are added to the lower portion of Mary's abdomen to provide detail that was missing.

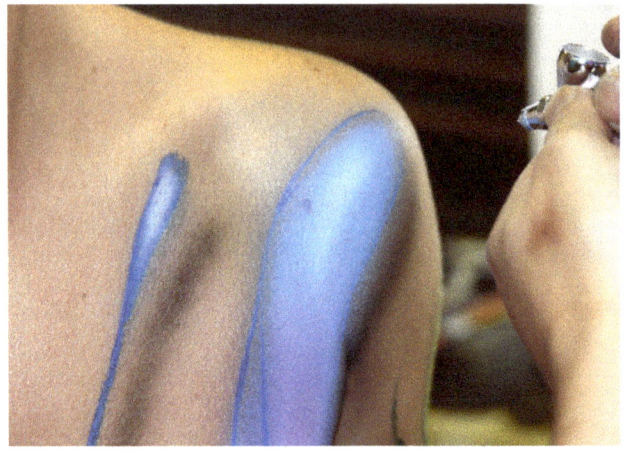

By adding a small bit of white to the wings, they take on a more 3-dimensional look.

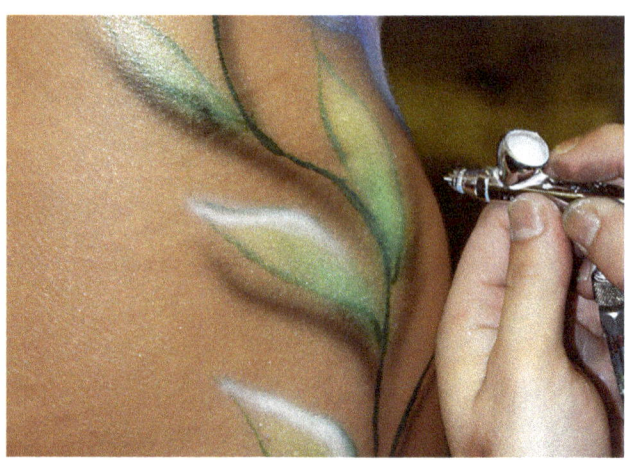

White highlights are added to each leaf on the vine for added depth.

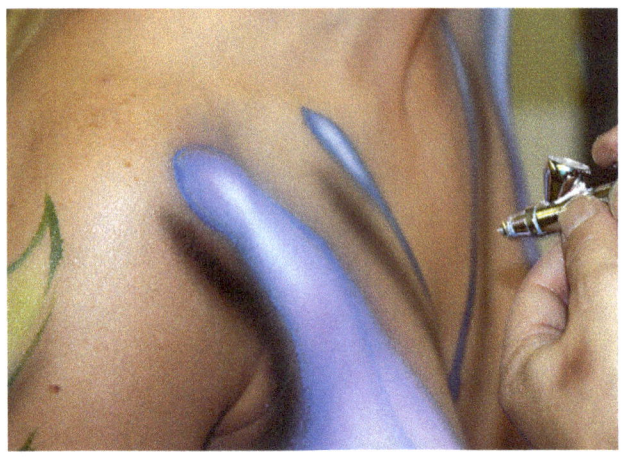

The wings of the butterfly art seem to float above the skin as Ken adds another bit of white shading.

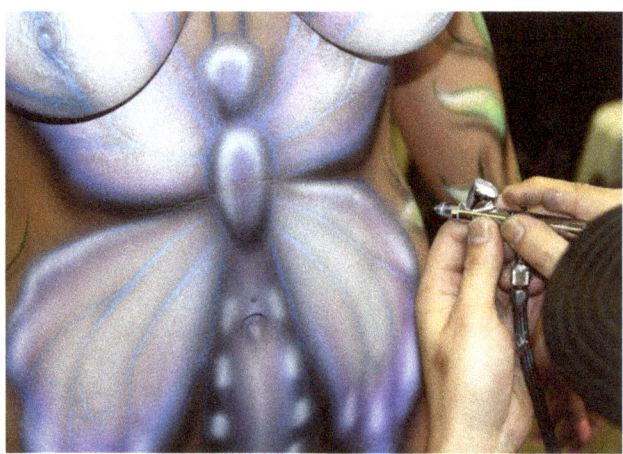

The blue and purple sections of the wing get a few touches of white to heighten the illusion.

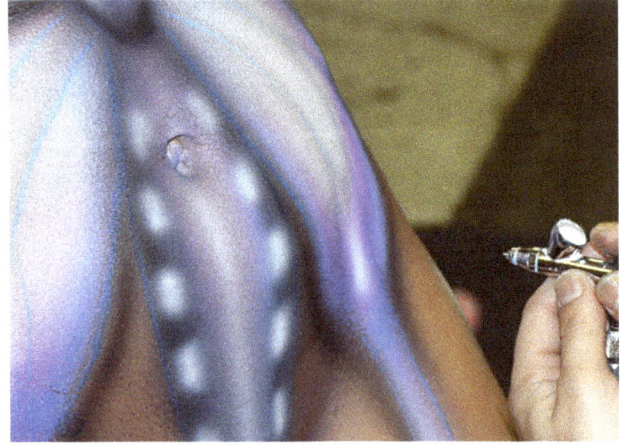

Holding the airbrush a little closer to the skin creates a sharply defined shape versus the more subtle shadows added elsewhere.

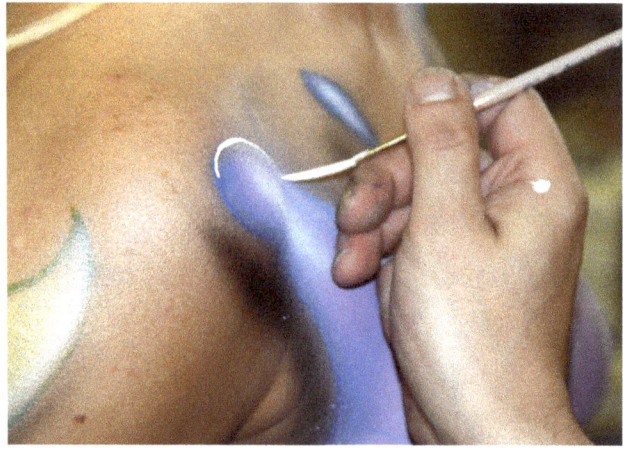

Picking up a brush, Ken begins to add some sharp lines of white for contrast against the airbrushed colors.

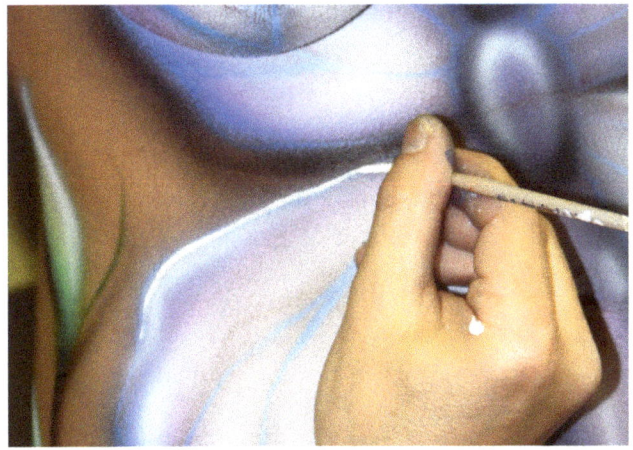

The crisp white lines really help to separate the paint from the flesh, bringing added dimension to the overall look.

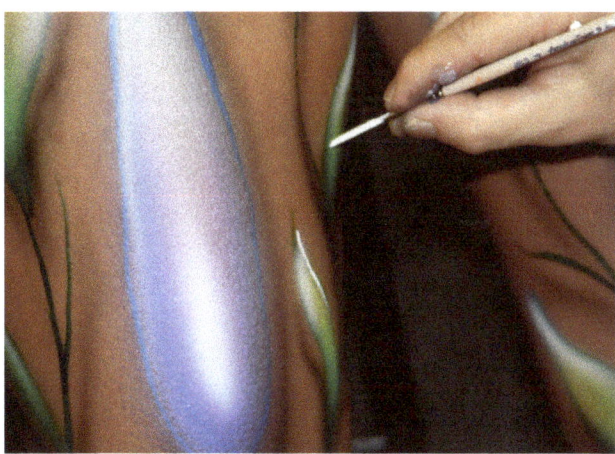

The long bristles of the liner brush allow Ken to add smooth lines of paint in a single motion.

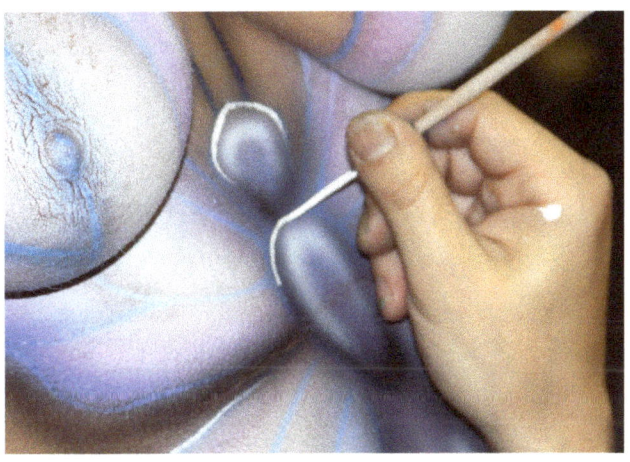

The central section of the butterfly also gets a few white lines, done to increase the realism.

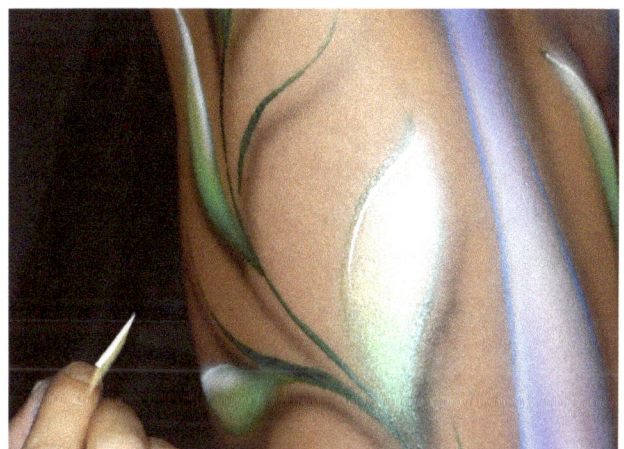

A single, tapered line of white is added to each leaf, which greatly enhances the content.

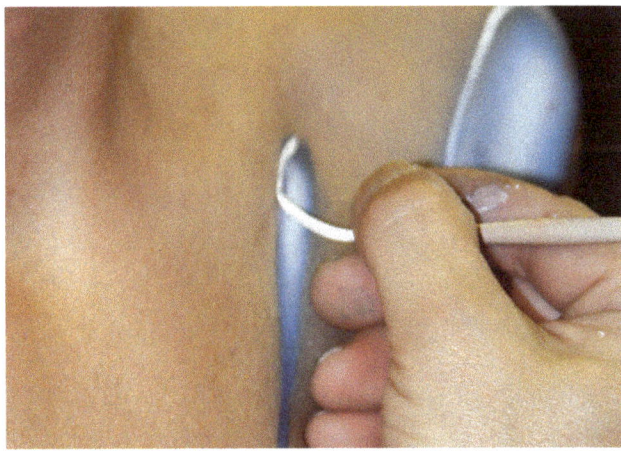

A small dab of white is added to each of the antennae.

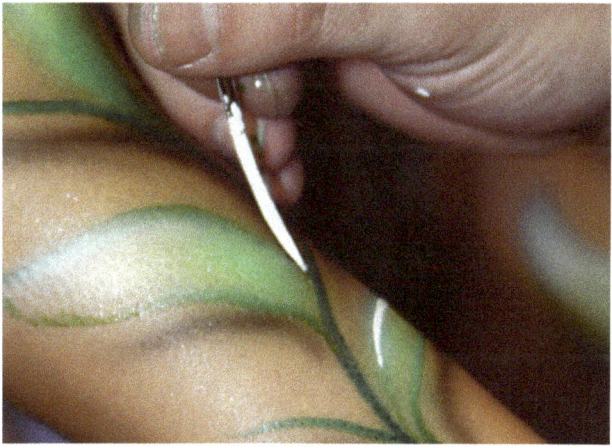

The flexible bristles hold the paint in place, and provide a clean line of white when applied to the skin.

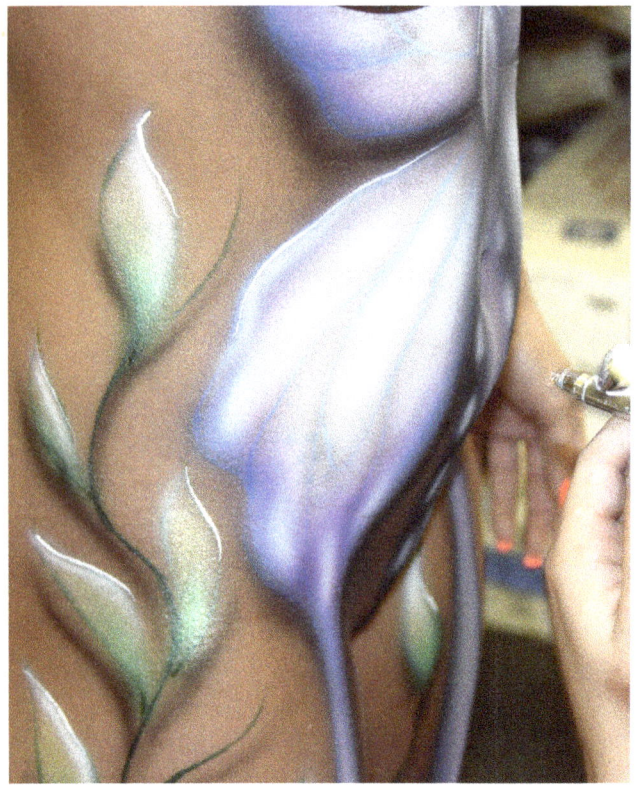

Returning the airbrush, Ken adds a few final touches of white to bring more brightness to the wings.

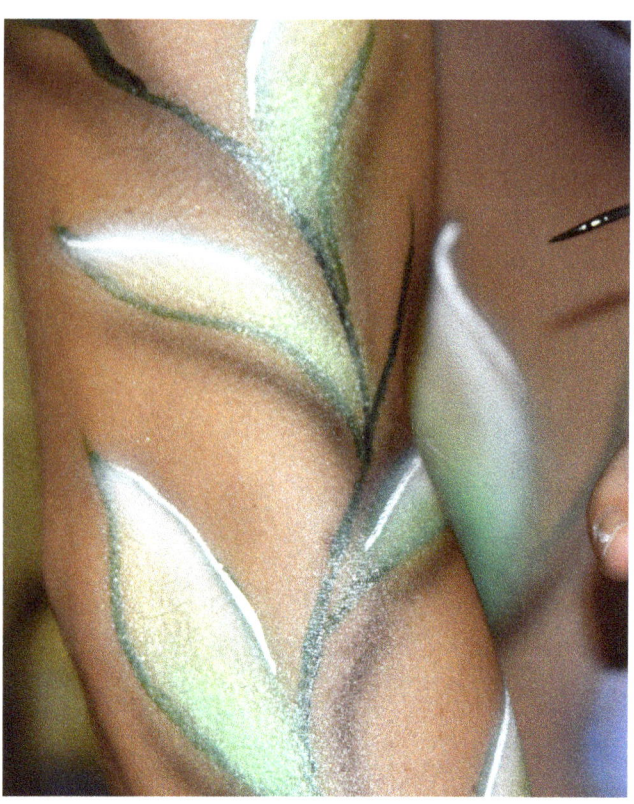

Some final touches are made using a fine brush and black is only used sparingly in a few spots that Ken deemed necessary.

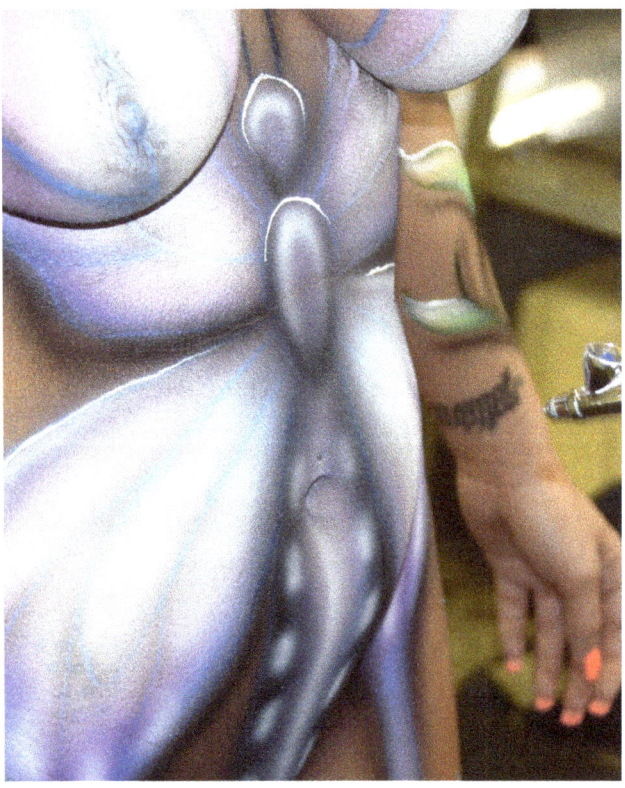

The last application of white brings more depth and clarity to the wings and the results look translucent.

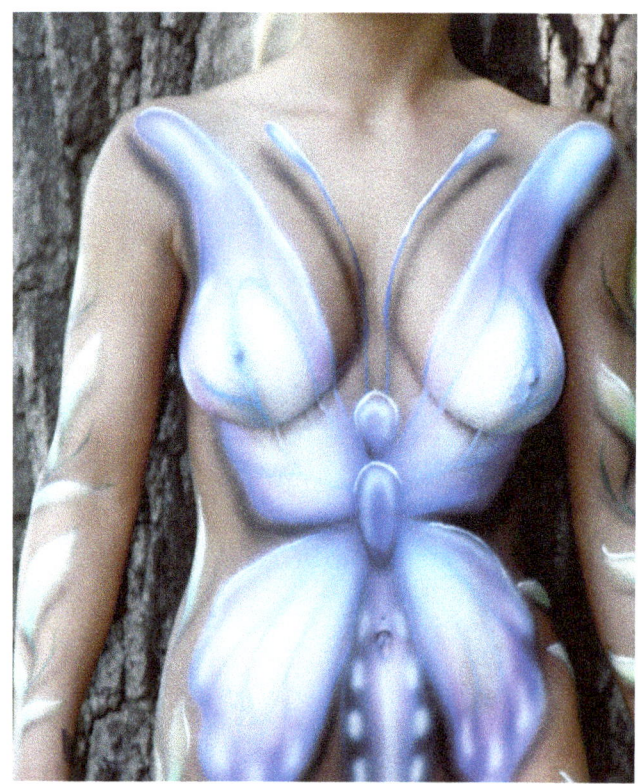

The overall result of Ken's efforts are dazzling in their color and realism.

Q&A: Ken Simonsen

How long has body painting been in your portfolio?

I haven't done too many bodies but created a peacock for a Halloween party a few years back.

What was the first time you noticed body painting?

I suppose the Sports Illustrated feature was probably the most obvious, but it's been floating around on the web for years, too.

What kind of painting experience is in your background?

I've been creating airbrush illustrations since about 1988.

What's your earliest memory of the art world?

I was maybe 6 when I began to draw with pen and ink and even used some watercolors.

What's the best part of body painting?

The variety of human canvas certainly adds another dimension to the art and brings more challenges to the creation.

Any other uses of your body art?

Not really. This is actually maybe only the third time I've painted a human, but I hope it won't be the last.

How much of the art was created in advance?

I typically create most of the piece ahead of time, but always allow for last minute changes as the piece gets rolling.

Any plans for the future?

My friends keep asking me to do tattoos for them, and I've purchased the required gear so that should be happening soon.

What brand(s) of paint did we use today?

I used the same Createx brand that I use for much of my work. It's a water based acrylic that cleans up well and has a great durability.

Airbrush and brush brands?

Iwata is my chosen airbrush and all sorts of brushes are used including natural and synthetic bristles.

Psymonsen Airbrush
Ken Simonsen
966 Villa Street
Elgin, IL 60120
www.psymonsen.com
kensimonsen@earthlink.net
847-741-6632

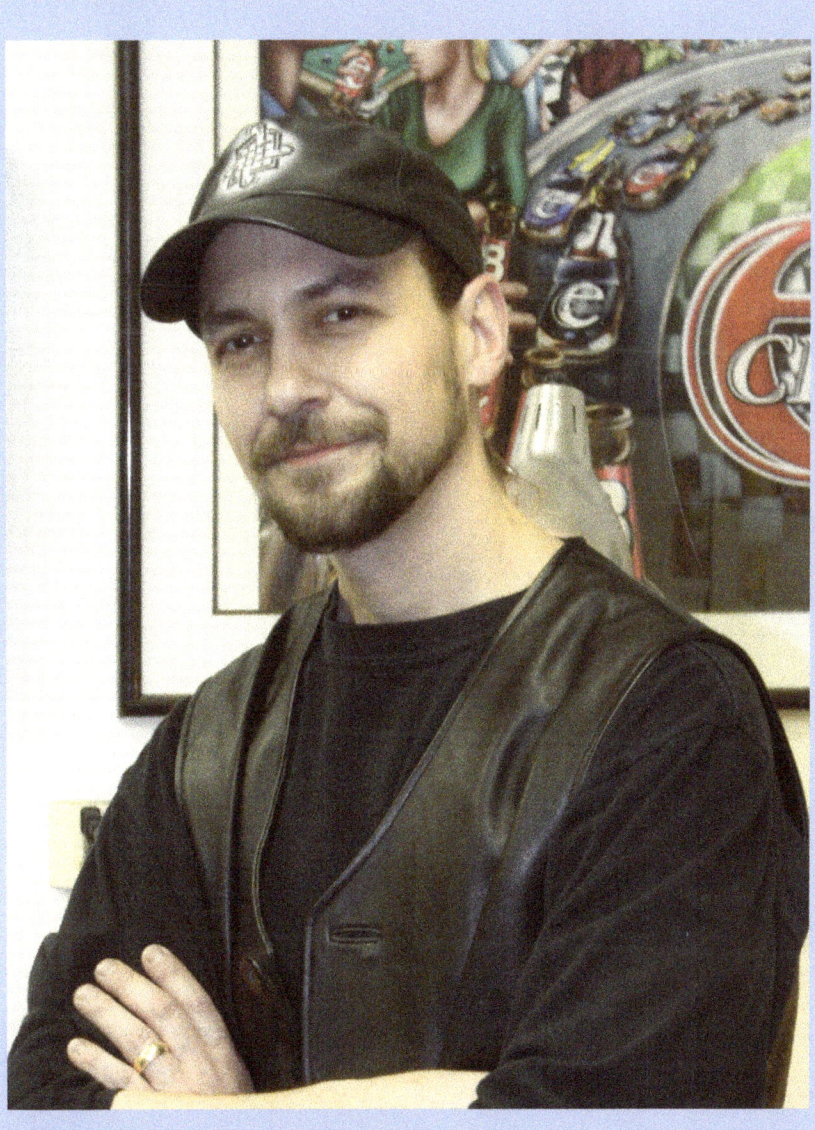

Ken Simonsen

Chapter Seven

Lenni Schwartz

A Particularly Ghoulish Set of Skulls

Skulls are a bit like people, they come in every size and shape imaginable. The skulls seen here are the work of Lenni Schwartz of Krazy Kolors in Oakdale, Minnesota. Perhaps best known as the artist who does the art, graphics and flames for long-time bike builder Donnie Smith, Lenni is equally comfortable with pinstripe brush, or airbrush. The original idea here was to create two skulls, one holding the other, with the flames of hell licking up onto both.

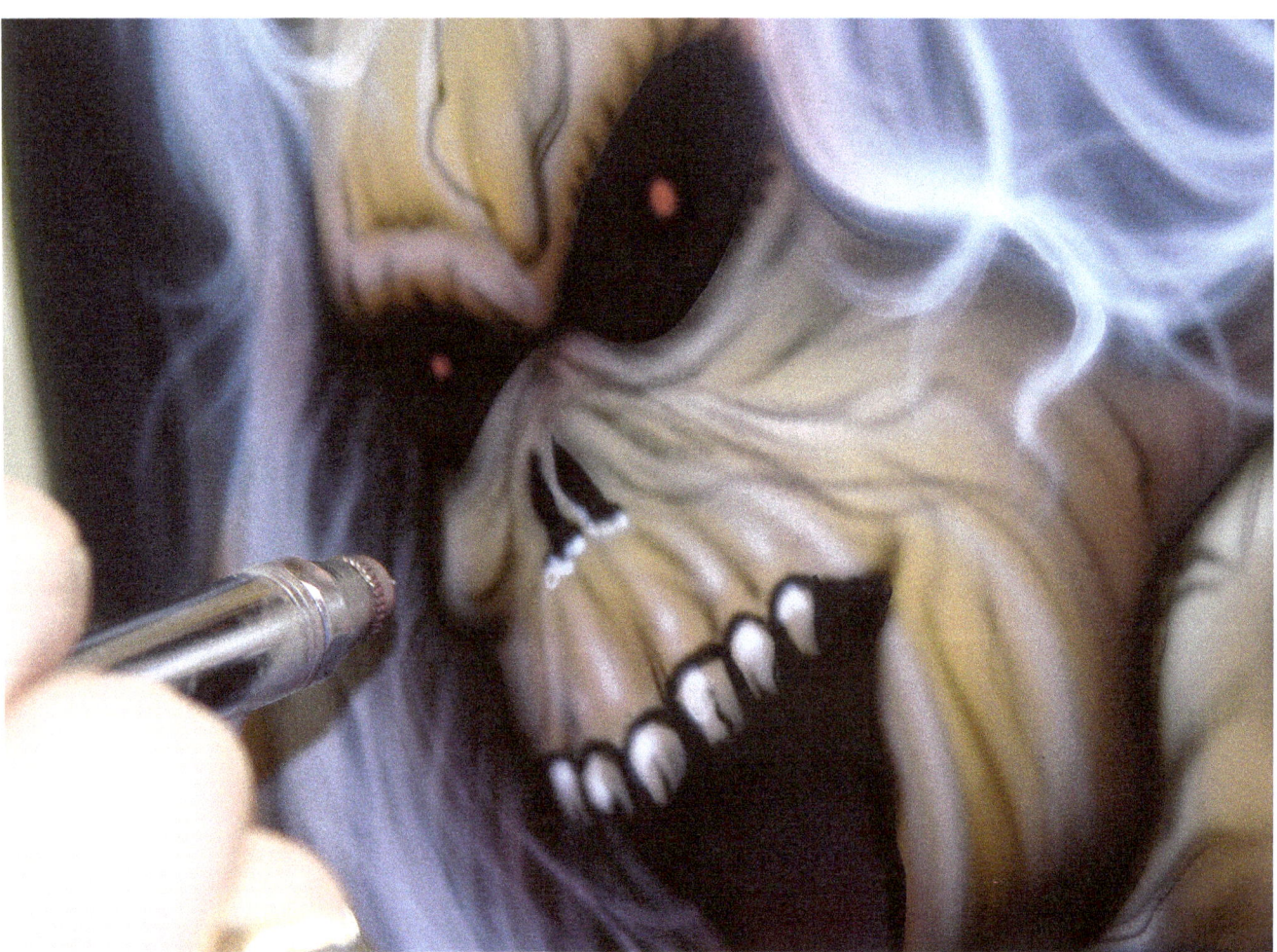

Quality takes time. Creation of this grisly form took time, patience and a very specific set of steps.

No Computers

Lenni doesn't use a computer, so step one is to sketch out the art work in pencil, then trace that image onto a piece of Gerbermask. Transfer paper is then applied to the top of the Gerbermask, the backing removed and the whole thing is positioned on the tank as shown in the nearby photos.

After peeling off the transfer paper Lenni uses a squeegee to eliminate the inevitable bubbles, then physically slits the Gerbermask to eliminate stubborn bubbles.

The mask is cut into sections, according to the original sketch, before being applied to the tank. As Lenni explains, "I hate cutting on the tank, though sometimes you have to." Lenni can now pull the first section of the mask, which defines much of the face and part of the jaw for the upper skull. Highlights are now sprayed in this area using an Iwata airbrush and House of Kolor basecoat white (BC 26).

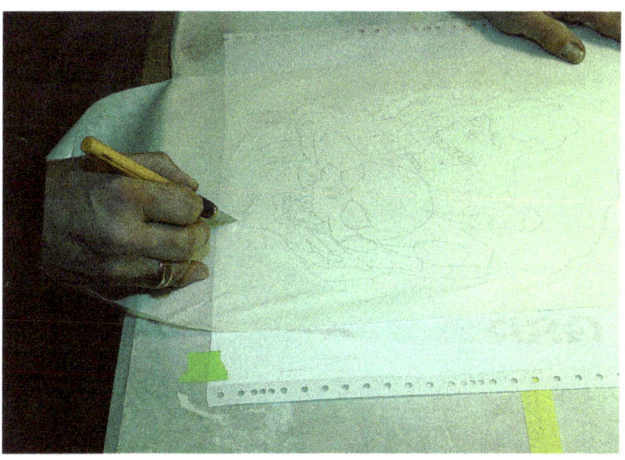

1) After doing the sketch and transferring that to Gerbermask, Lenni applies transfer paper over the top and then cuts out the image.

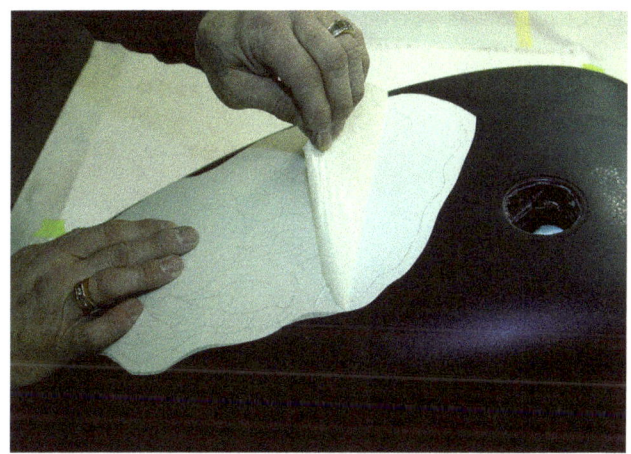

2) Now the skull mask can be positioned on the tank and the transfer paper peeled off.

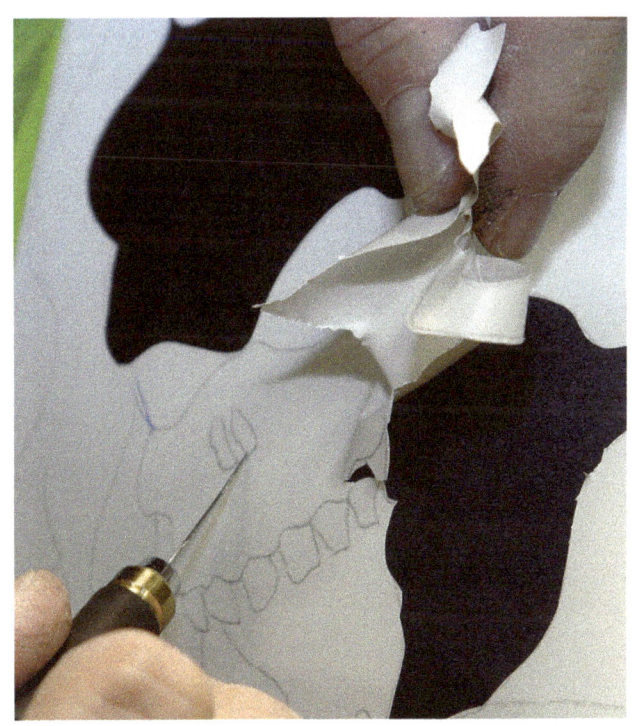

4) And now the area that defines the upper skull can be pulled out.

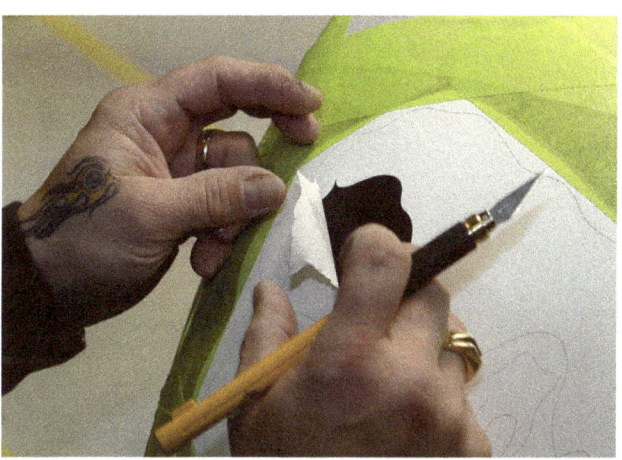

3) The mask was cut into sections before being applied to the tank...

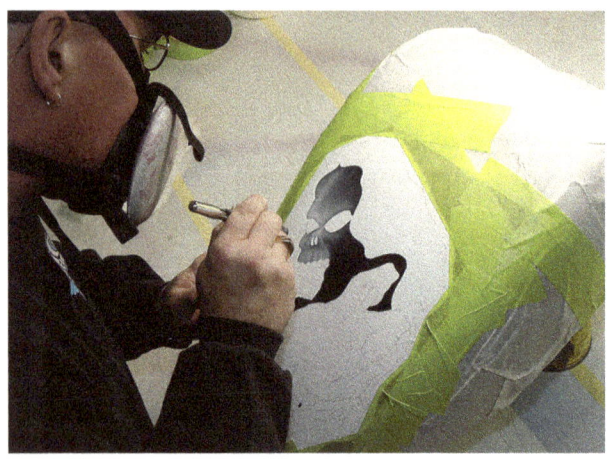

Lenni starts the work with basecoat white, working to establish the brow and cheekbones...

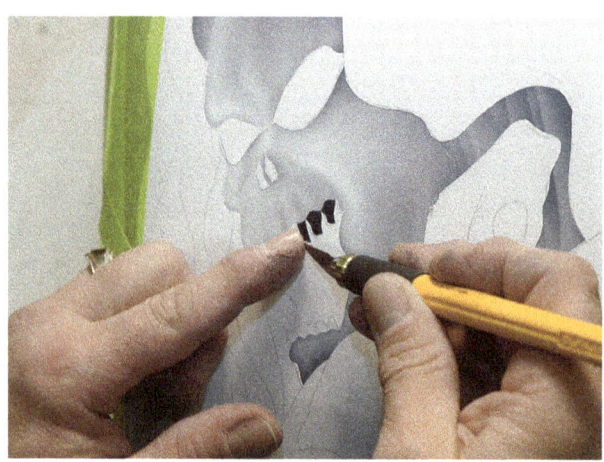

Upper teeth are next...

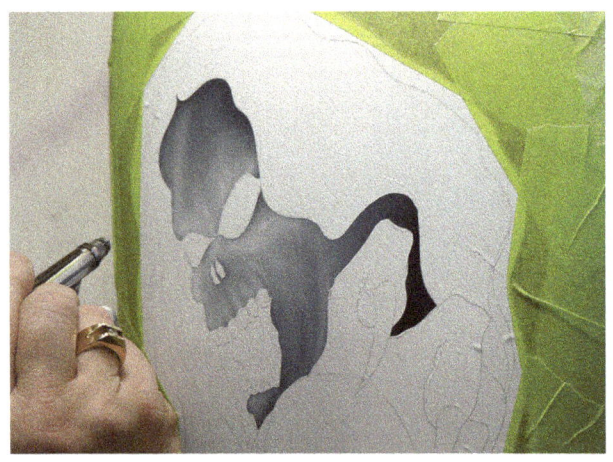

...and quickly an image emerges within the mask.

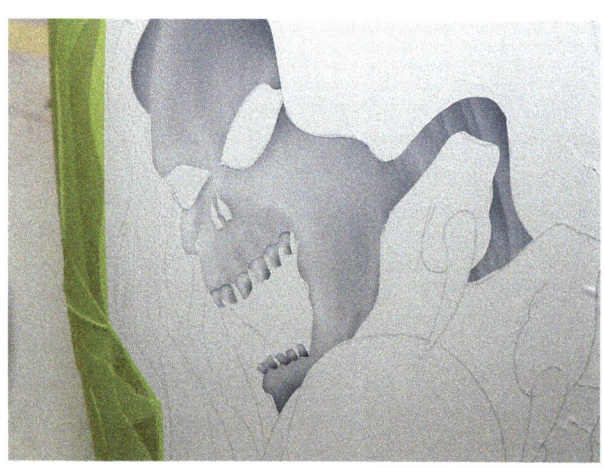

...note how much can be done using only one color of paint.

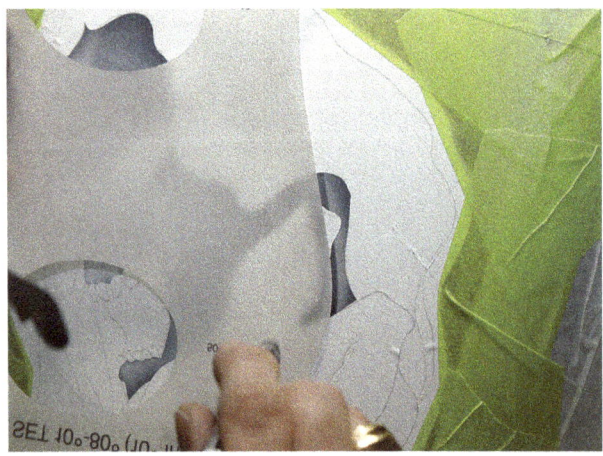

Though it's hard to see, the area being painted with the stencil will be hair, and the lines will work into the overall flow of the skull's mane.

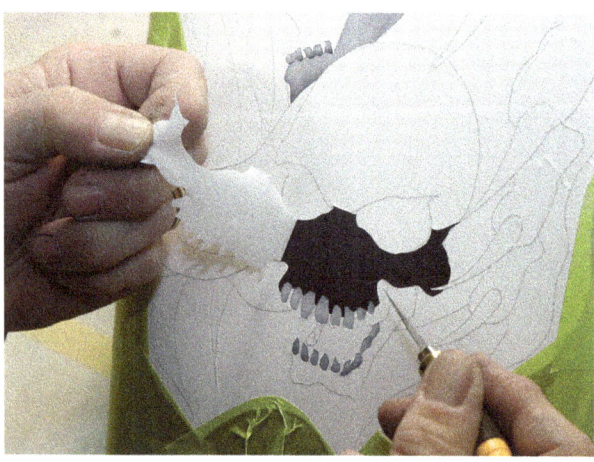

Work on the lower skull now begins.

Start with Highlights

The photos show how highlights done in white begin to define the upper brow, cheek bones and the area above the teeth. With these basic shapes established, Lenni begins to "pull the upper teeth," prior to painting these in the same basecoat white. Because he's working on a dark color, the white works with the underlying dark color to give definition to each feature.

After doing the teeth on the upper skull, Lenni pulls the mask on the teeth belonging to the lower skull and paints in the highlights using the same white used all along. Next, the mask for most of the lower face is pulled and the brow and cheek bones are painted in, much as was done on the upper skull. Once the basic shape of the lower skull is established, Lenni uses more white to provide detail.

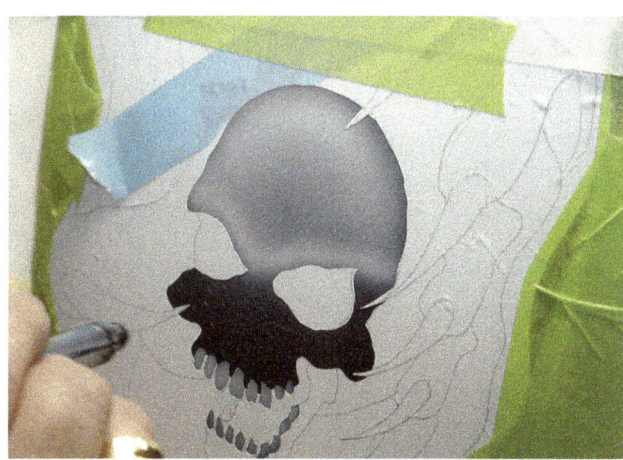

The painting progresses much as it did for the upper skull...

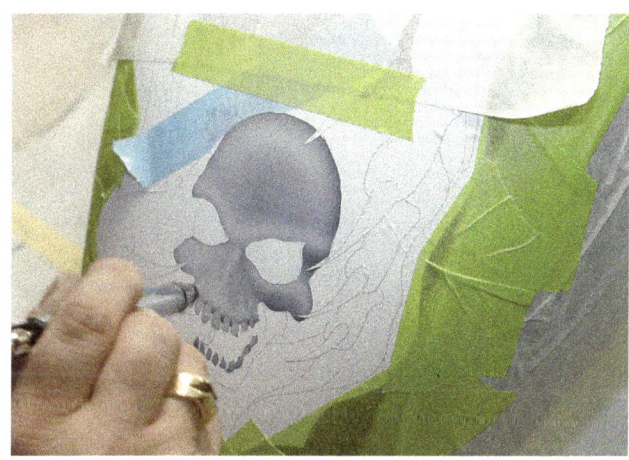

...with the brow line and cheekbones established first...

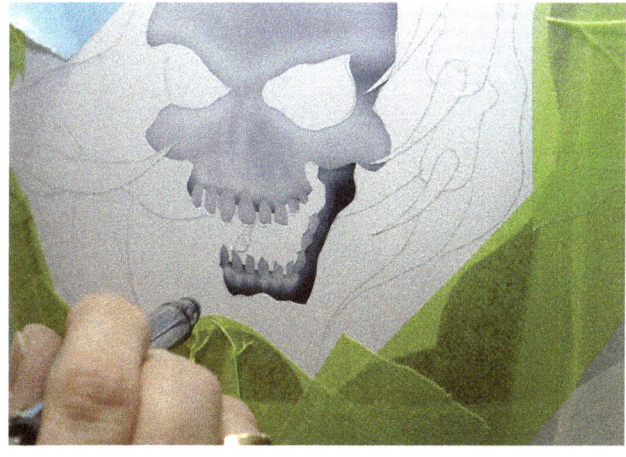

...followed by the teeth and lower jaw.

Q&A: Lenni Schwartz

Lenni, how about a little background?

I started as sign painter, pictorial artist and pinstriper. Airbrushing came in when I did airbrush letters, and when I wanted to create a chrome effect.

How about your airbrush and paint picks?

I use an Iwata Eclipse because it's light and maneuverable. It does anything I need from fine to large and it's dependable. I like bottles, because they make it easy to change colors and I don't need 12 airbrushes. For paint, I like House of Kolor. It's user friendly, you can mix any color you want. Mostly I use their PBC and KBC lines. Not much candy.

Do you do body work and basecoats or just the art?

I just do the art, no basecoat and no clear, and no body work.

What's the hardest part of what you do?

Getting the depth and dimension I want. I do a pencil drawing first, and I take my time.

Any final words of wisdom?

Be patient, don't try to take the world on in one day. Be persistent and don't be afraid to try it out.

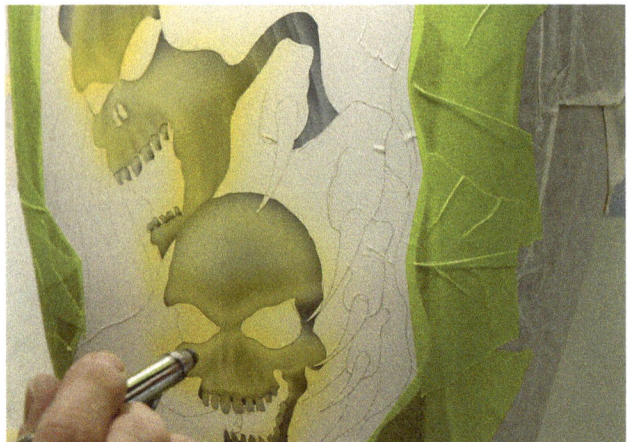

To give the skulls some color Lenni does a mist coat of sunset yellow...

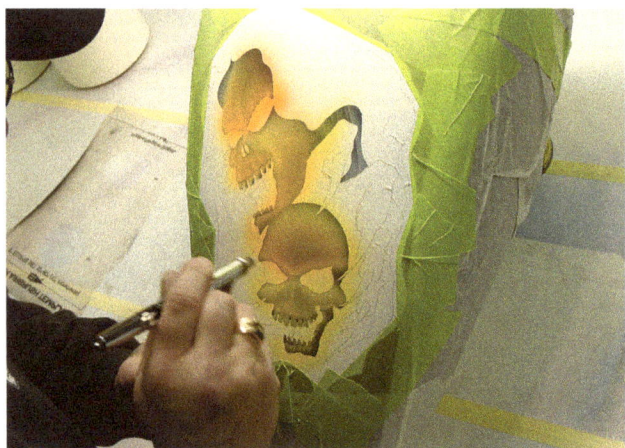

...followed by another of tangelo.

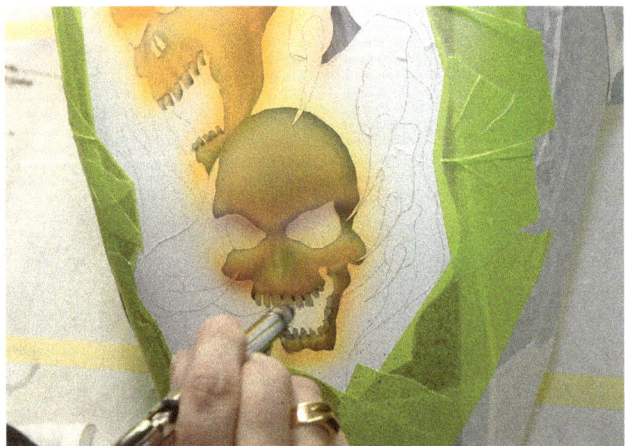

Violet pearl is used more sparingly, to create deeper shadows on select parts of the design.

Now Add Color

Up to this point, Lenni has only used one color, white. It's time now however, to liven things up with a bit of sunset yellow from H of K's PBC line. The yellow (PBC 31) is applied as an overspray, or mist coat over the entire image "just to begin giving it a little color" explains Lenni. The process of adding color continues as Lenni adds a second color, Tangelo (PBC 32), from the same PBC line, in the same way. The third color is violet pearl (PBC 40), applied only to the bottom of the shadows.

Though some airbrush artists change the speed of the reducer depending on the situation and amount of actual paint flowing through the airbrush, Lenni uses number 310, fast reducer, all the time. "I like to be fast," explains Lenni, "I want to tape on top of that paint right away."

After using the violet to darken the shadows, Lenni uses more white to go over all the highlights and the teeth again. He also uses the white to paint in cracks in the skulls.

Big Hairy Deal

With the basic faces and skulls established, Lenni pulls more of the mask covering the hair on the upper skull. As shown in the photos, these areas are painted in a series of passes that follow the basic flow of the hair.

The pattern continues, pull a few mask areas, paint them carefully in white, then pull another series of small masks and paint those areas. It's interesting to see how much more detail Lenni achieves in this way, rather than just pulling all the masks for the "hair" and painting the entire area at once.

To darken certain parts of the face, including the chin of the upper skull, and better define some of the edges, Lenni uses basecoat black. For some of this work, like the chin, Lenni masks off nearby areas before applying any paint (see page 106).

The Hand

At this point much of the image is still covered by the original mask, in particular the claw (or hand) and the eye, both of which are now unmasked. Parts of the image, like the upper jaw and the lower skull, are back-masked before any

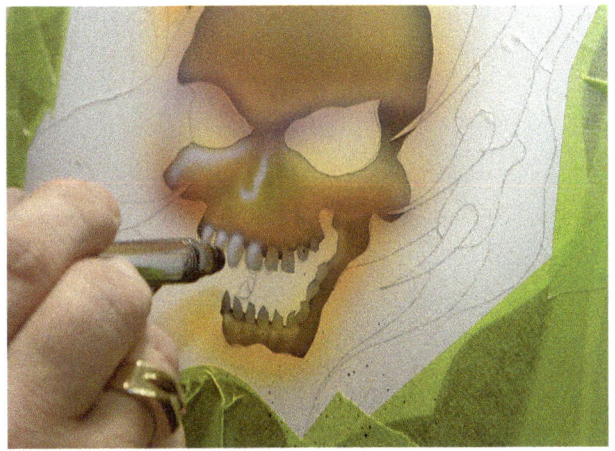

Back to white basecoat, used to create highlights on the teeth and certain raised parts of the skull.

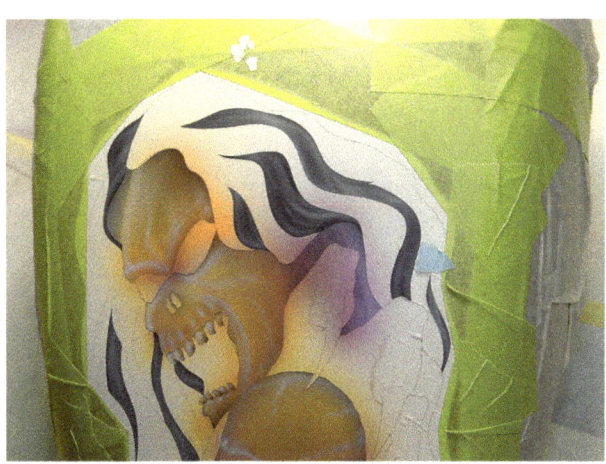

The hair is painted in stages. After pulling a section of mask and painting the area with white streaks...

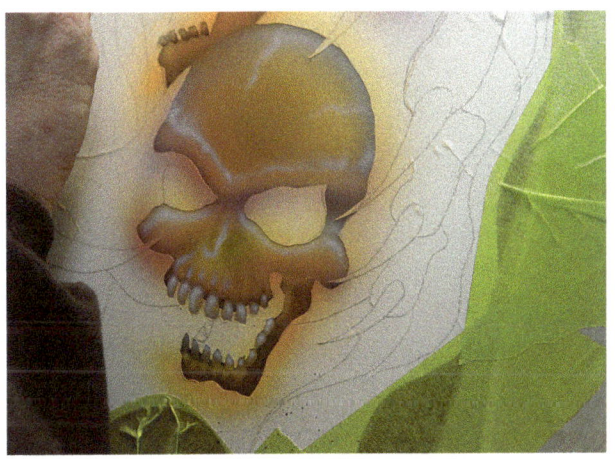

Progress shot shows the lower skull so far, with most of the prominent features established.

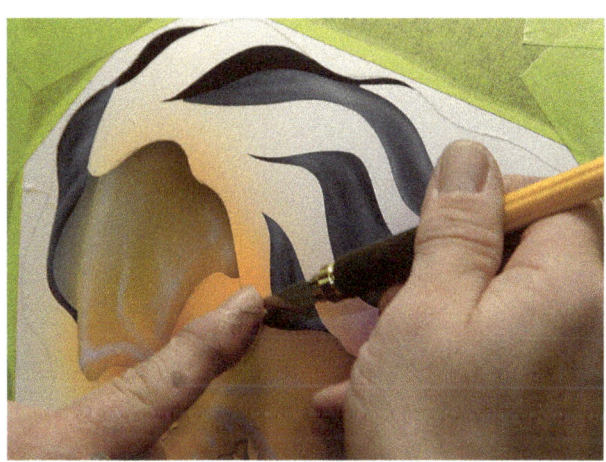

...another section of mask is pulled...

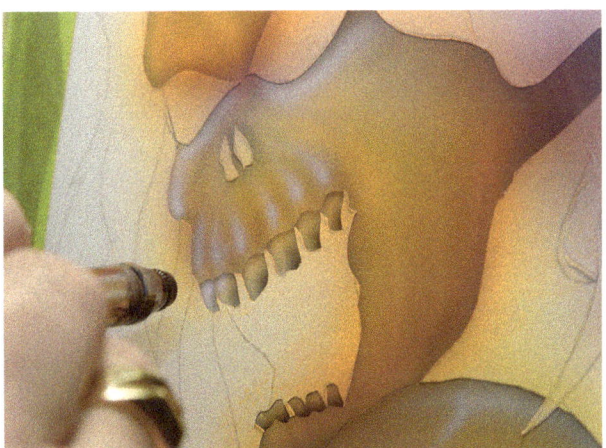

Before starting on the hair, Lenni uses more white to further brighten the teeth and raise the area above each tooth.

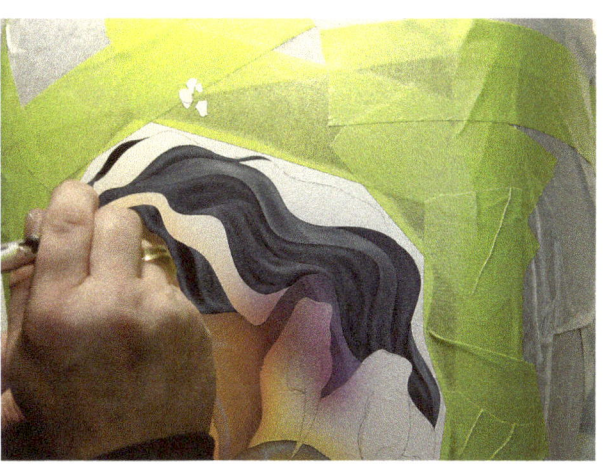

...and painted in the same fashion.

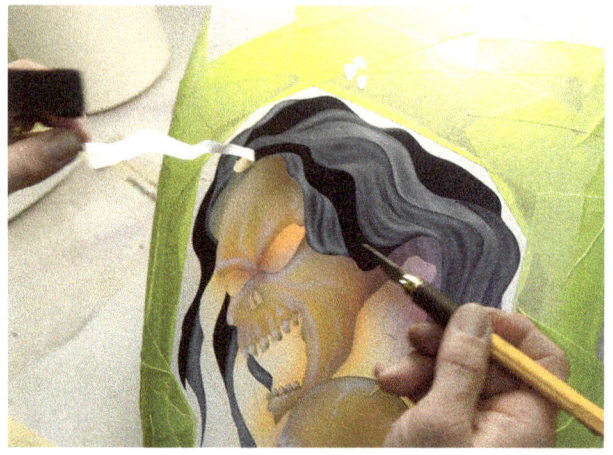

One section at a time, Lenni creates a wild head of hair, flowing and layered.

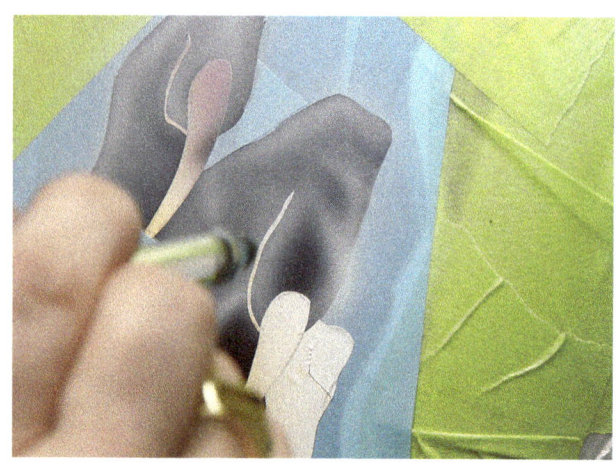

...which is used to establish the basic outline and highlights.

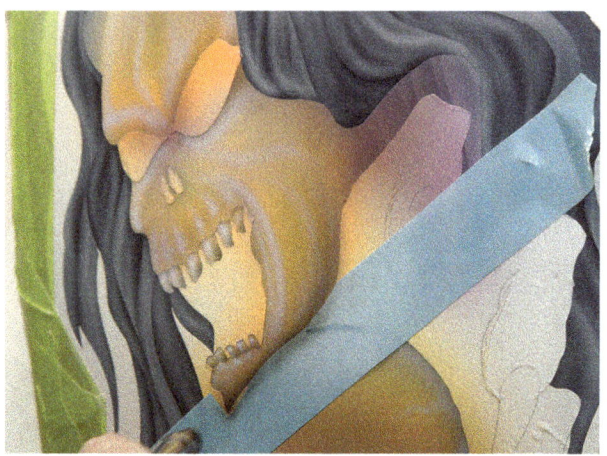

A temporary mask and light coats of basecoat black are used to darken and define the jaw line.

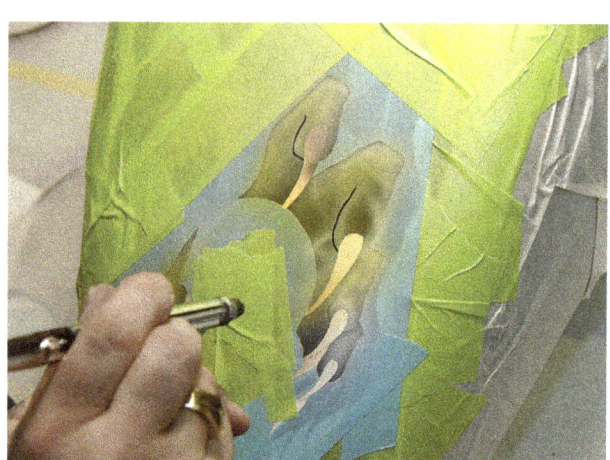

Everything needs to match, so the same color sequence used on the skulls is used on the hand as well...

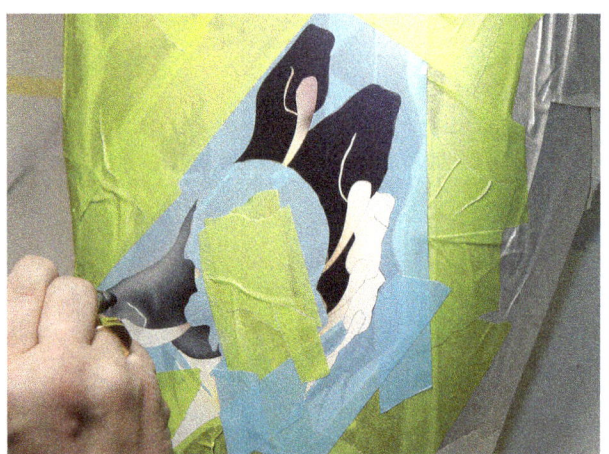

Painting the hand starts with basecoat white...

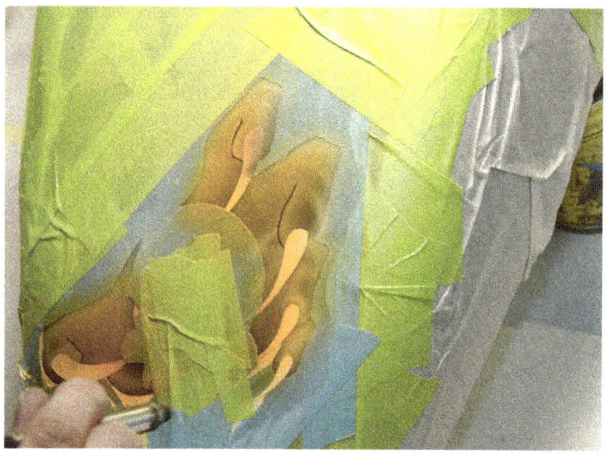

...sunset yellow, tangelo and then...

painting can begin. Once the painting can commence, it's more basecoat white. As was done with the skulls earlier, light coats of white are used to establish the basic contours of the hand, including the knuckles.

To help the hand match the "flesh tone" of the skulls, Lenni applies a series of mist coats, starting with sunset yellow, followed by tangelo and ending with violet pearl. Now the claws themselves are unmasked. The area nearby is masked off and the process starts over with basecoat white used, initially, to establish the highlights. For a little of the ghoulish factor, the tips of each claw are painted with ultra orange (PBC 64) followed by hot pink (PBC 39). Next, black is used to provide detail to the fleshy part of the hand around the claws

Because of the multiple layers of masking, when Lenni pulls the tape he has to be careful not to pull the masking paper underneath.

THE EYES HAVE IT

A good airbrush artist needs to think ahead. In the case of the eyes for the lower skull, Lenni paints these in flames because the lower part of the tank will be flamed later, and this way the flames will appear to reach right up into the lower skull. The colors are sunset yellow, tangelo, ultra orange and a little black along the bottom.

The same basecoat black is used to outline areas like the eyes, teeth and claws, and to detail the upper and lower skull. The photos do a better job of explaining how the detail work done at this point really brings the skulls to life.

FLAMES

After pulling all the remaining masking, Lenni starts his flames with white, applied in a series of passes to the area below the lower skull.

Yellow (PBC 31) is next, applied right on top of the white. Color number three is tangelo, sprayed (again) right on top of the white and yellow that are already there.

Continued on page 111

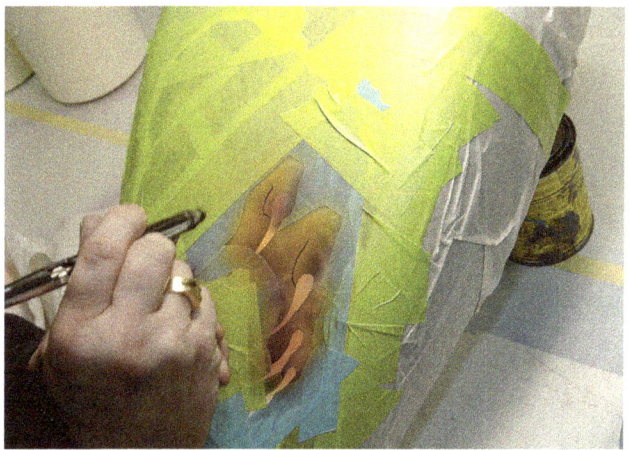

...violet pearl for dark, rich shadows.

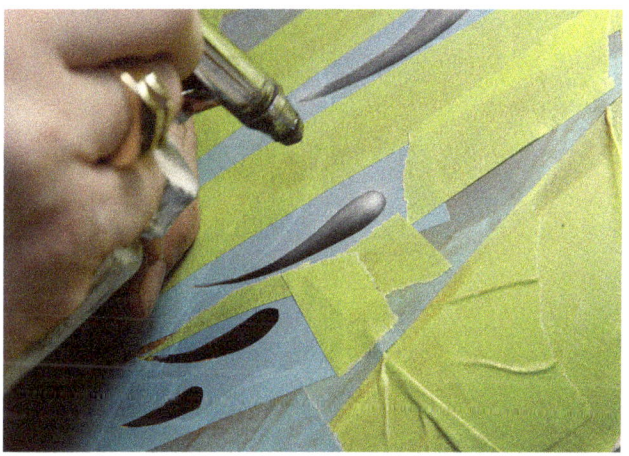

The claws are painted in white, after pulling the mask and back-masking the surrounding area.

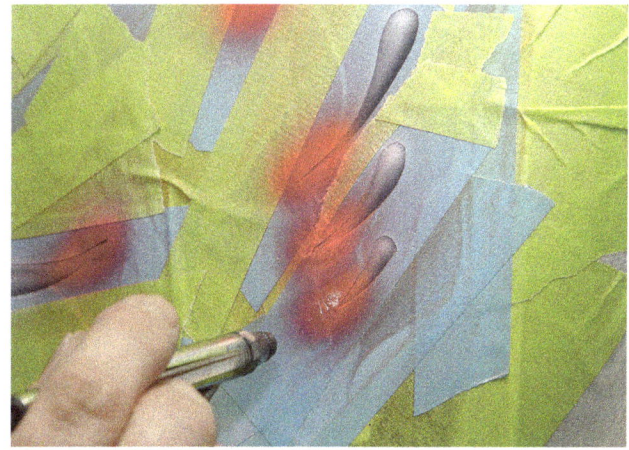

Ultra orange and hot pink create a nice red on the tip of each claw.

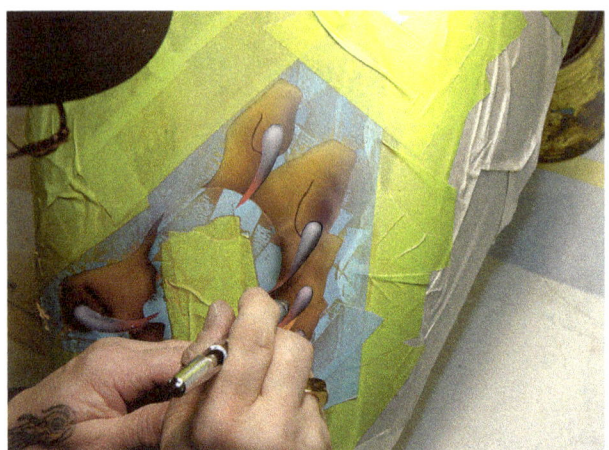

The final step in the creation of the claws is a little basecoat black.

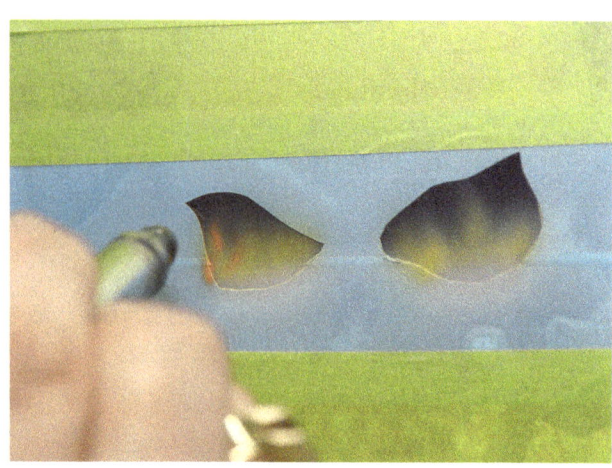

...next comes sunset yellow,...

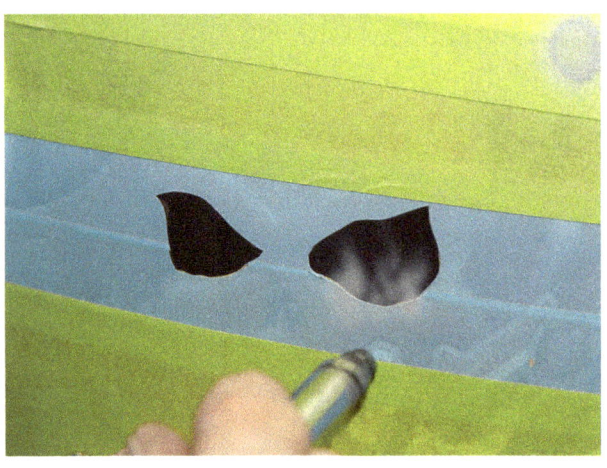

After pulling the mask for the lower set of eyes and back-masking the area nearby, Lenni starts a subtle set of reality flames.

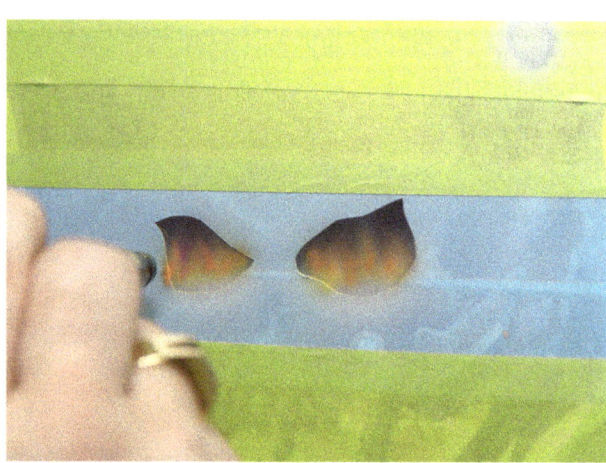

...followed by tangelo and ultra orange.

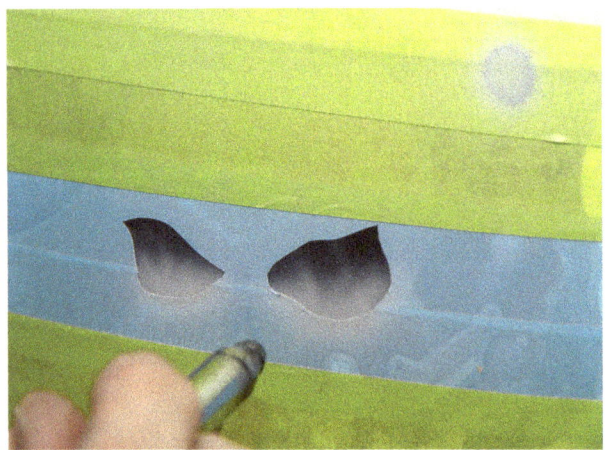

White is used first as a basecoat that will give the flames brilliance...

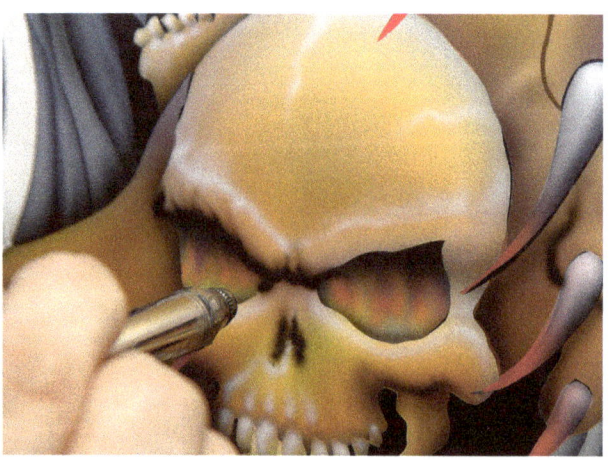

Outlined with black as the final step.

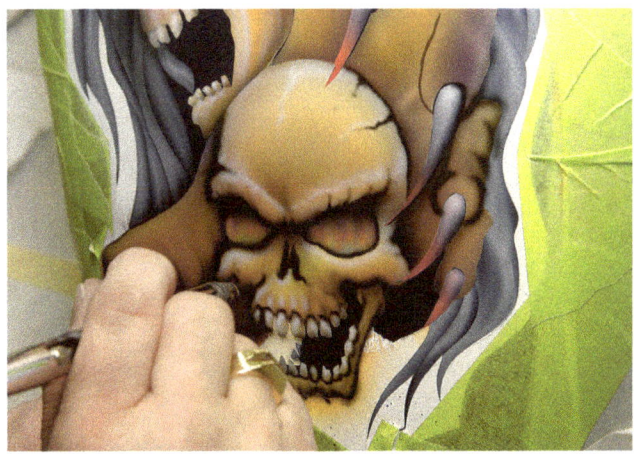

More black is used to detail the nose and eye sockets...

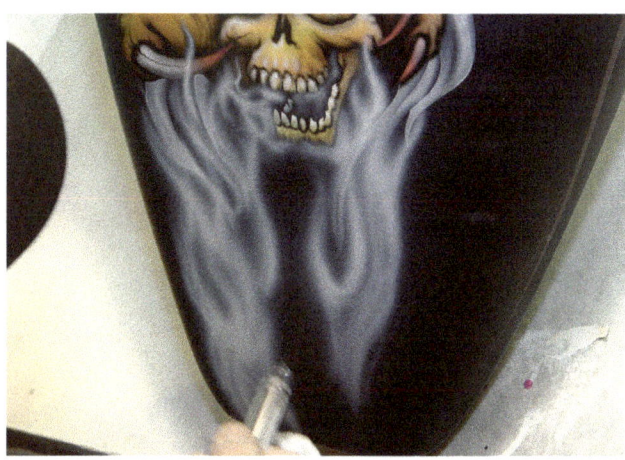

You can see the flame-shapes emerging from the white, the paint isn't put down all at once but in multiple light passes.

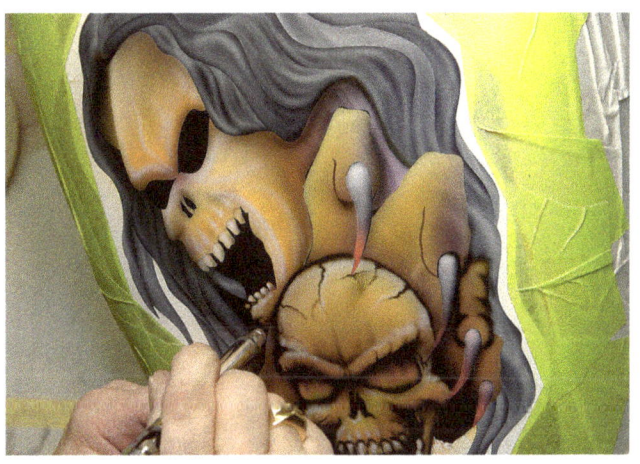

...and separate the two skulls from each other.

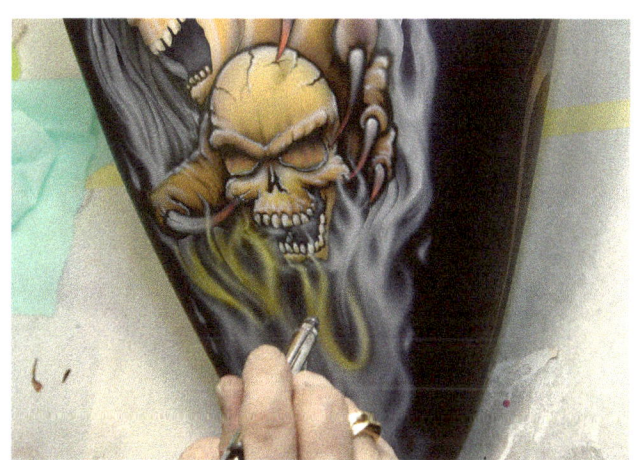

Sunset yellow is next...

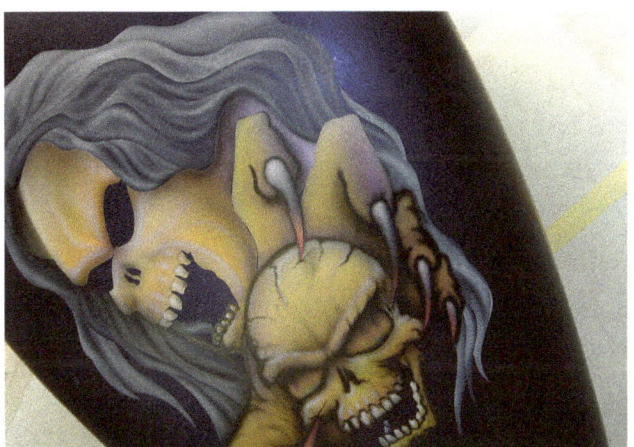

A progress shot shows the two skulls nearly finished and ready for the next step.

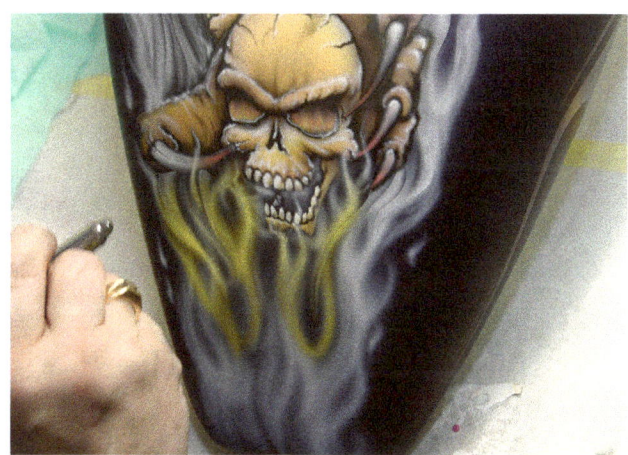

...laid down on top of the licks already there.

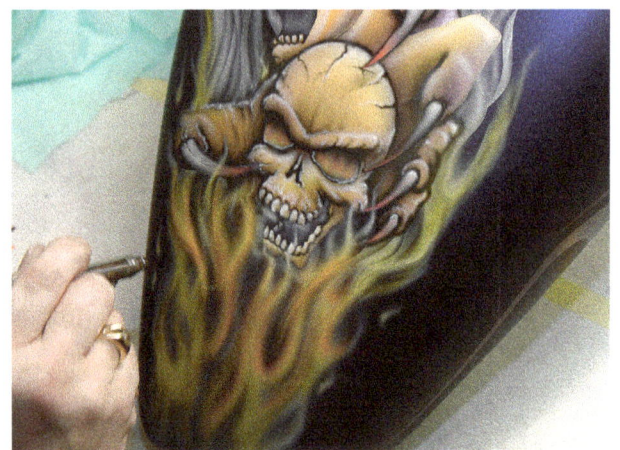

The yellow is followed by tangelo...

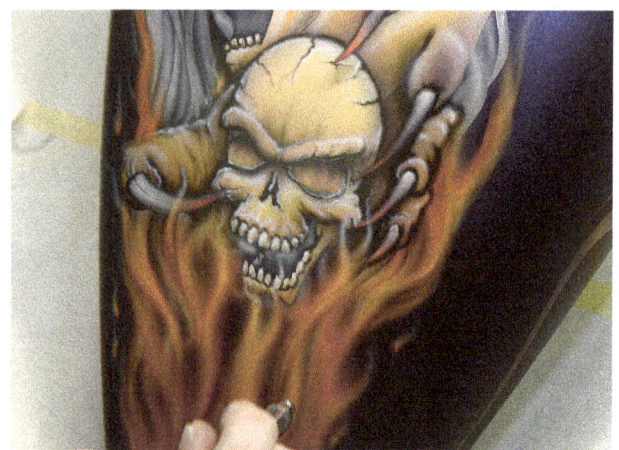

You can see the transition, how the flames are built step by step until all they need...

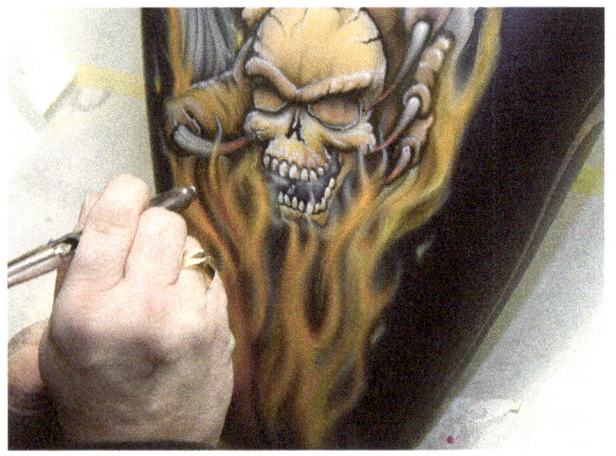

Which is laid down on top of the other two colors.

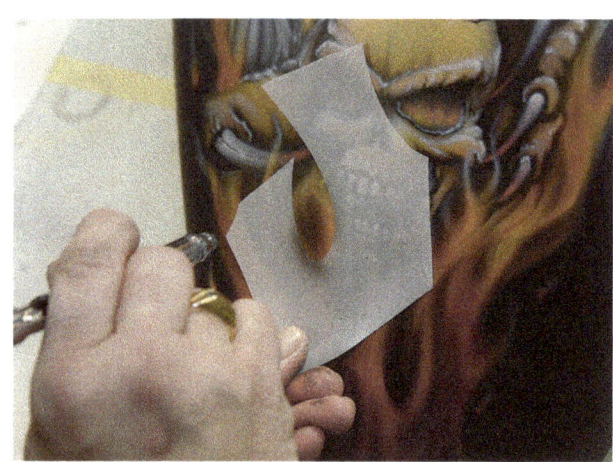

...is a little black to create hard edges.

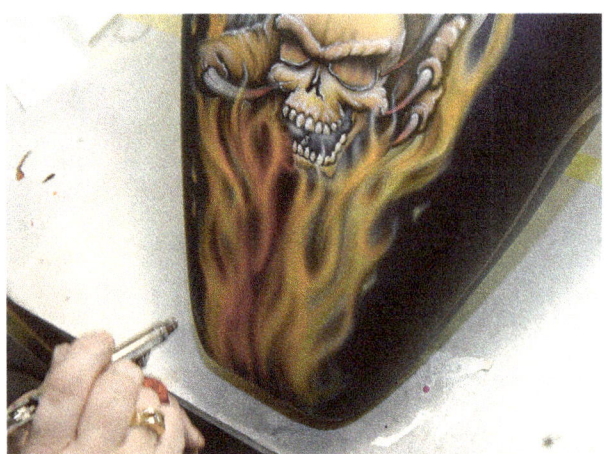

Candy apple red is used to make the fire really red...

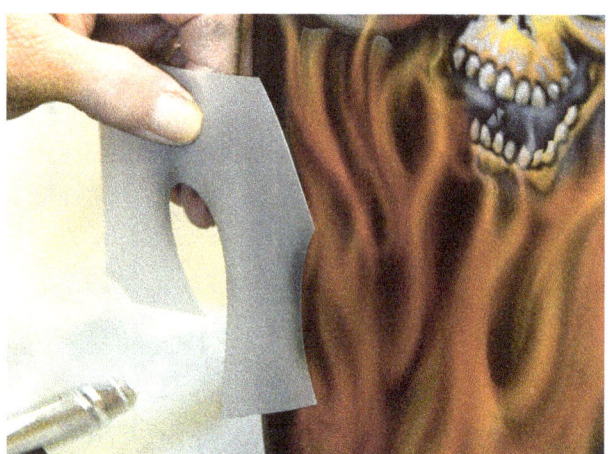

Which is why Lenni uses a stencil at this point.

Next comes candy apple red basecoat (KBC 11). Some of the passes with candy apple are tight and follow the flame shape closely, others are light mist coats designed to tint the whole area. Though black wouldn't seem like a flame color, Lenni uses a little basecoat black and a stencil (check the images on the facing page) to give the flames more definition. At the same time he adds more detail around the teeth and outer edge of the lower skull.

Final Details

The little things do make a huge difference. With the flames finished, it's time to add shadings and outlines that help give the image definition. Cracks around the eye sockets are done with basecoat black. And just a minute later the same color is used to add details to the upper jaw, on the upper skull, as well as to add deep lines in the skull's face.

Though not shown in any of the photos, Lenni stops often during the painting to clean the airbrush.

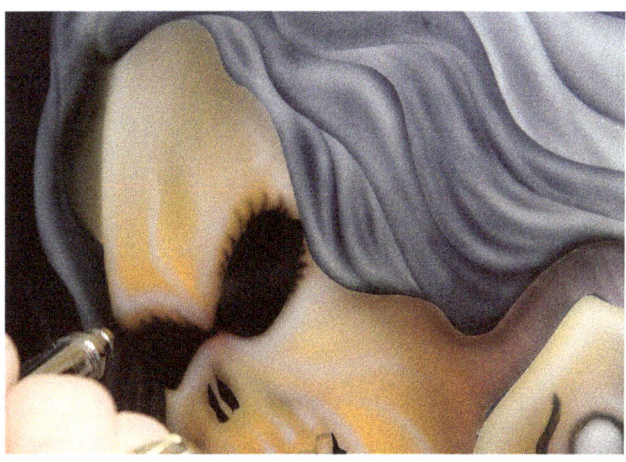

1) The same black is used to detail the eye sockets...

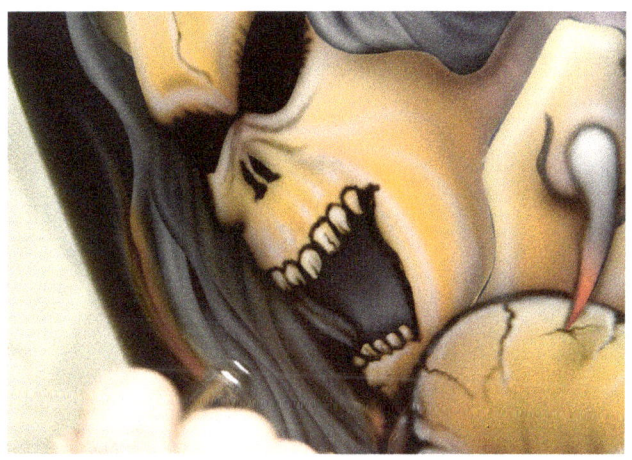

2) ...and teeth.

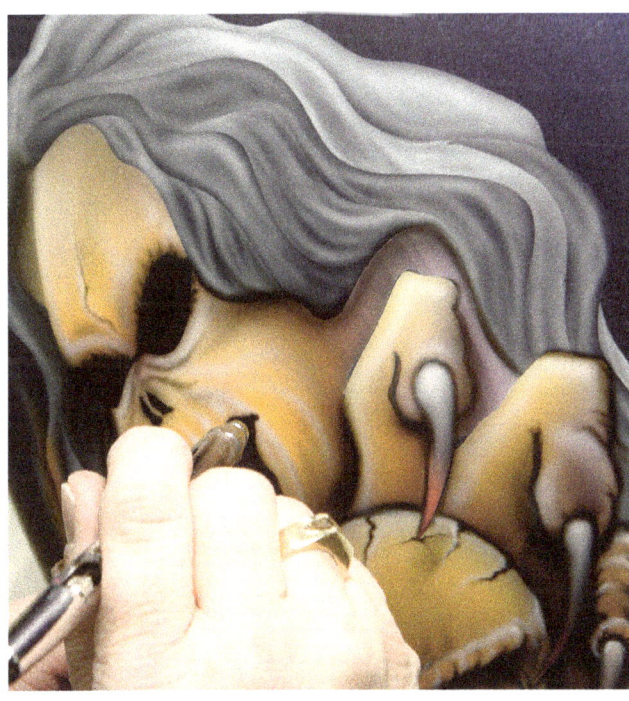

3) Black is likewise used to to create the deep wrinkles in the face...

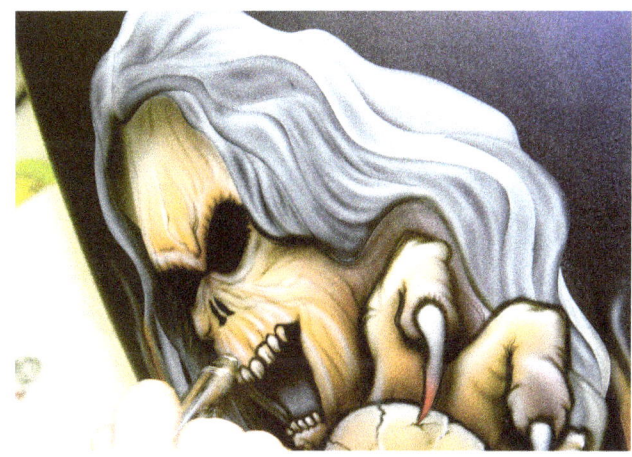

4) ...and upper jaw that help make the skull look really aged and evil.

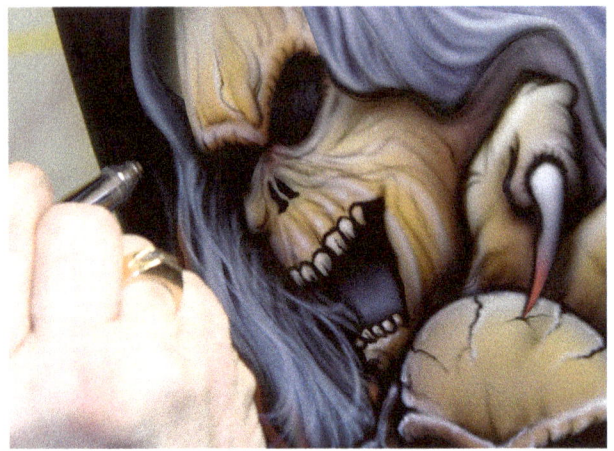

Lenni switches to white, to highlight the facial fissures and change the color of the hair.

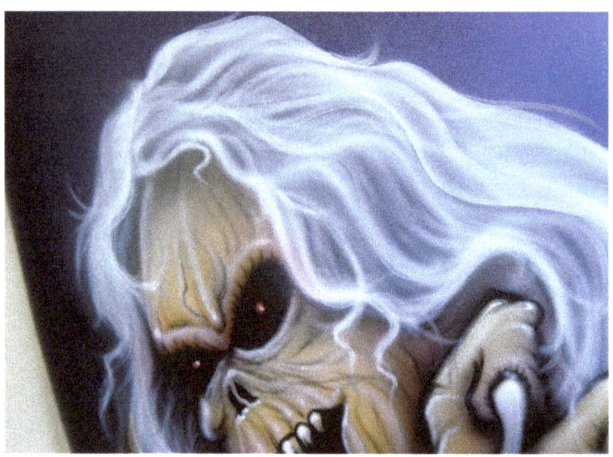

The additional white changes the hair from soft and flowing to crazy and weird.

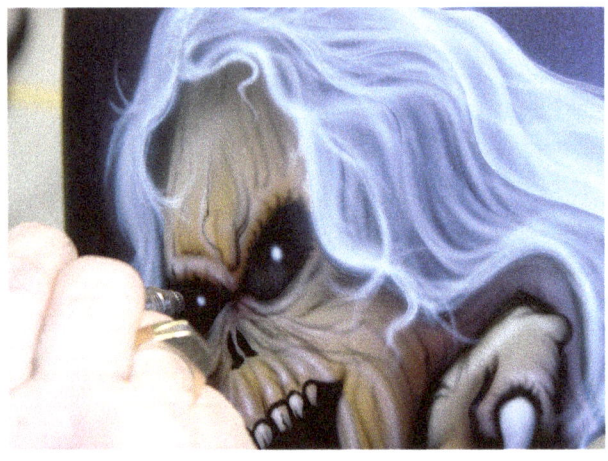

The evil-eye glimmer is done in two steps, first a pinpoint of white, followed by a little candy apple red (for an evil gleam) seen in the next image.

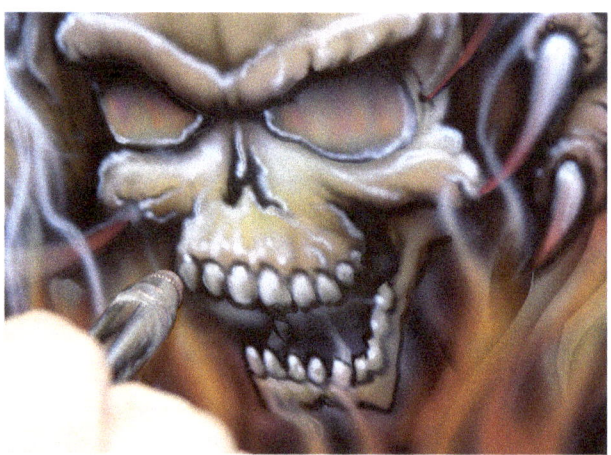

Note the highlights on each tooth, a good example of the detail required for truly good airbrush work.

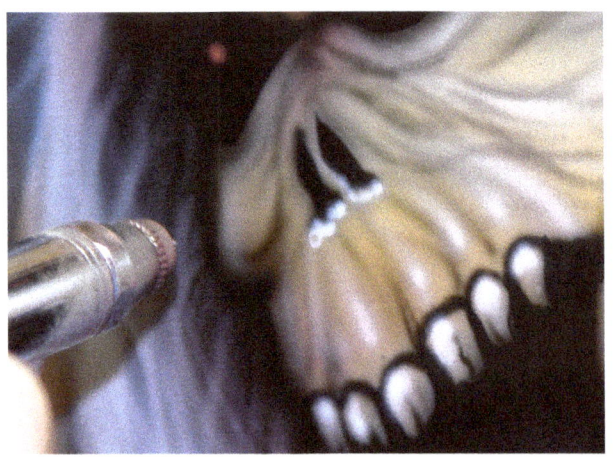

Additional white is used to highlight the "nose"

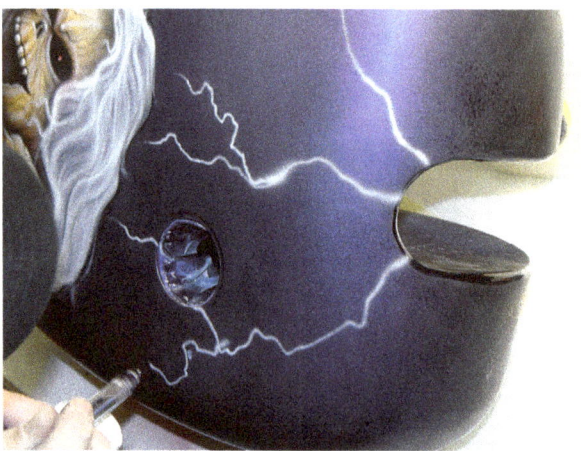

White is used freehand to form the jagged lightening.

Before declaring the piece finished more white is used to add another layer, another dimension, to the hair on the upper skull. As Lenni says, "the hair really finishes him off." A spot of white is added to the eyes at the same time. A mist of candy apple red is then added to warm up the "skin tones" just a little, and to give the eyes in the upper skull a truly evil glow.

White is next, used in multiple steps to provide details to the teeth and parts of the face. Additional details, like more wisps of hair and more highlights on the teeth, are done before Lenni puts away the basecoat white (see the facing page).

Lightening Strikes

Like Frankenstein, these twin ghouls need a little electrical energy to give them life. Lenni starts the bolts of lightening as jagged lines of basecoat white, painted freehand and tinted with a little purple (PBC 65). Next comes more purple to give each bolt of lightening a stronger glow.

The final step is the addition of a little more yellow - used to brighten the flames before the piece is officially declared finished.

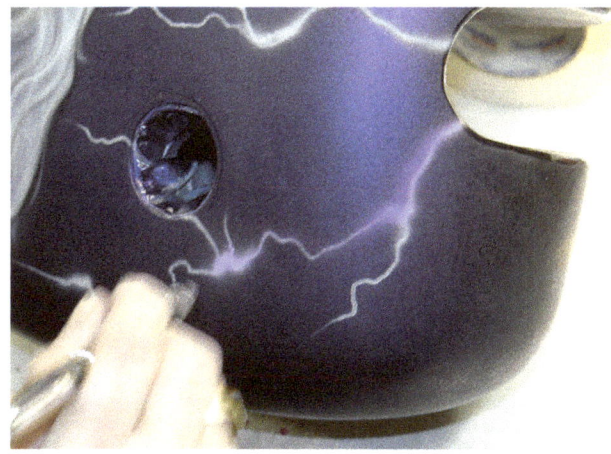

Then the bolts of lightening and the junctions are tinted with purple to very good effect.

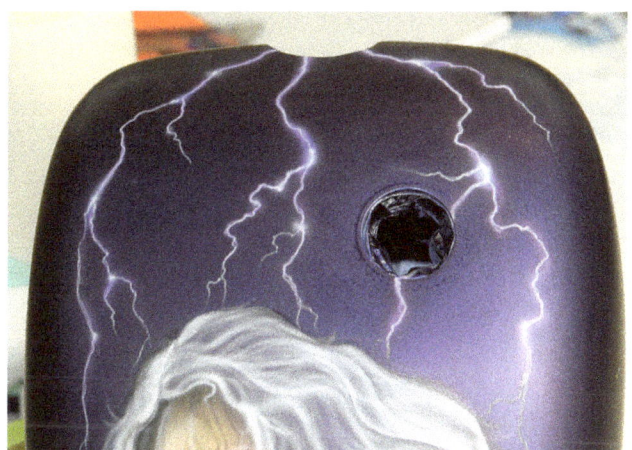

A progress shot shows the lightening raining down on the evil monster.

The best images are often a mixture of effects. Not just a set of flames or a skull, but an image that combines two skulls of slightly different styles with a set of flames licking up from underneath.

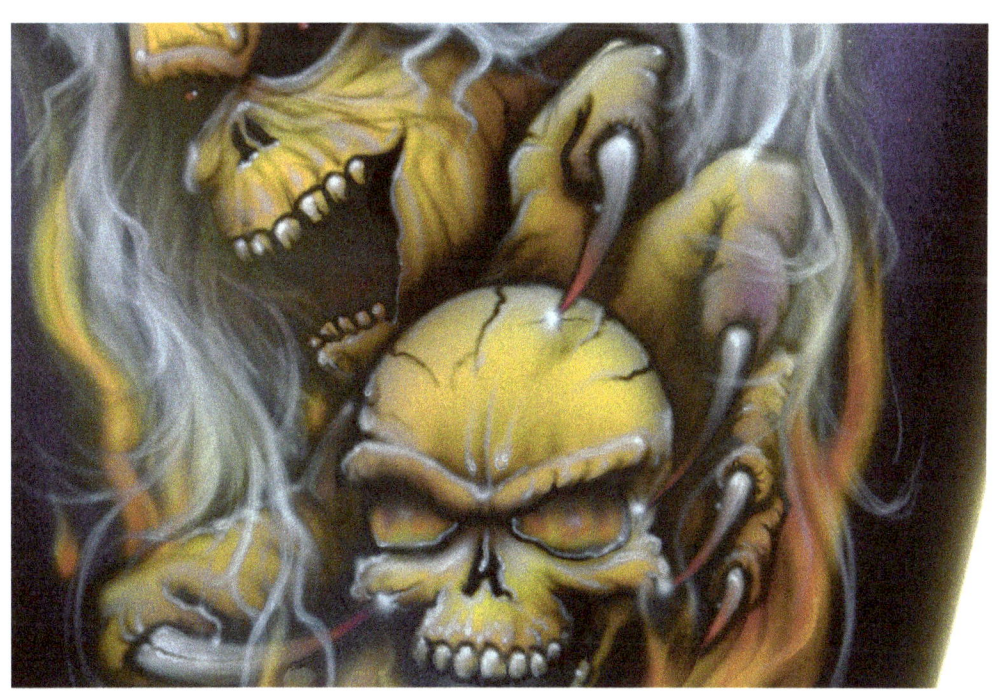

Chapter Eight
Susan Heidi
Quality Takes Time

They say engineers think only linear thoughts. That their brains are logical and orderly to the point of boredom. Pretty much the opposite of what you expect from an artist in other words. So it might come as a surprise to learn that Susan Heidi's training, and her first career, was in engineering.

In Susan's case, engineering was the vocation, art the avocation. "I always did portraits as a hobby," recalls Susan. "Eventually I began coloring in the portraits, and then I became intrigued with pin-ups."

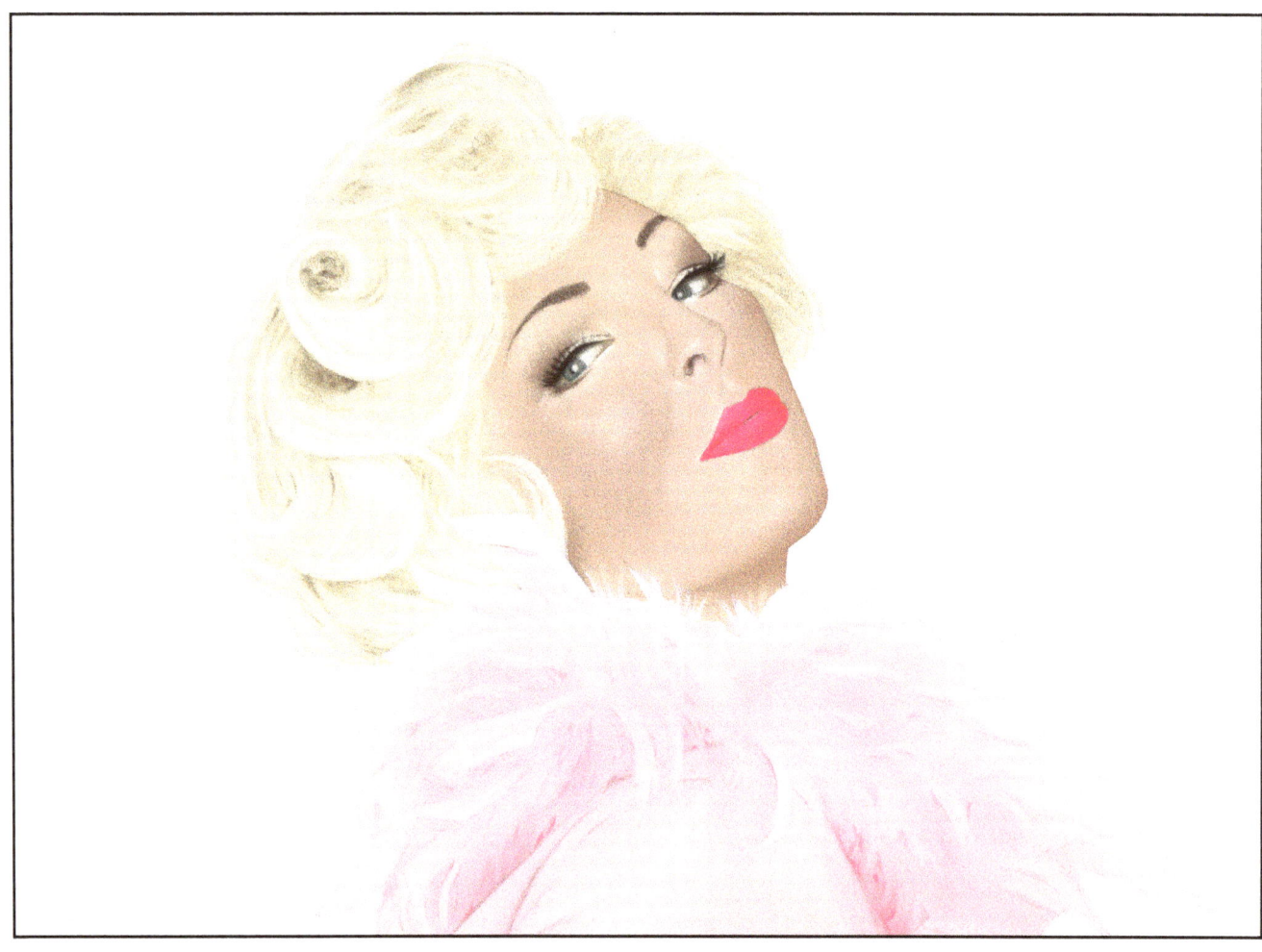

This painting is based on a photo of retro pin-up model Kay O'Hara. Working with retro style pin-ups gives me an opportunity to render lots of fun (and challenging) clothing and accessories. For me, the focus of any pin-up is the expression, which for this painting is an archetypical come-hither look.

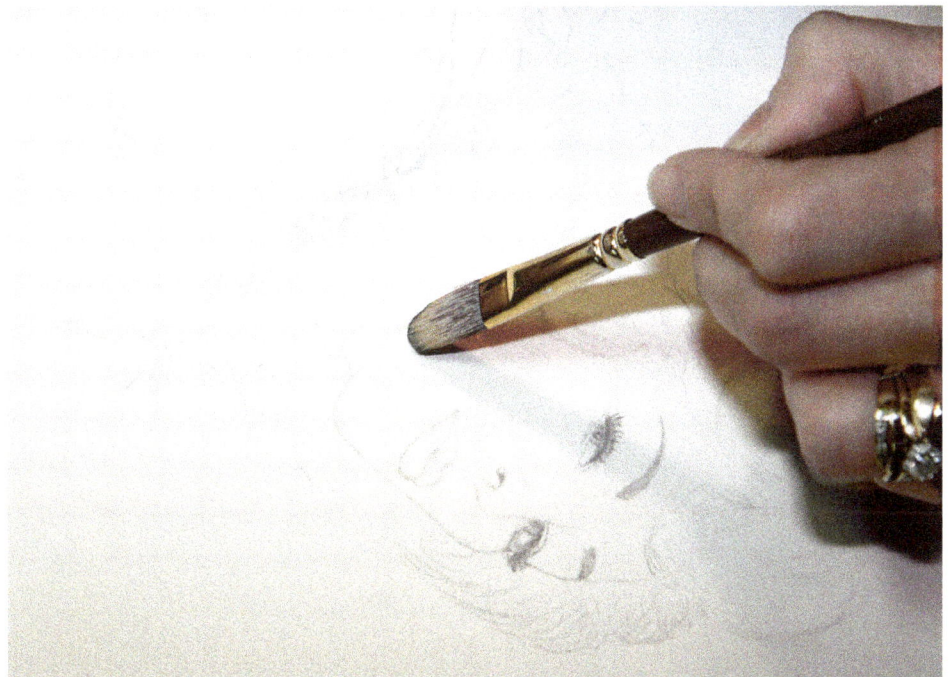

A completely rendered graphite drawing on Strathmore illustration board is sealed with Myston workable fixatif and then dilute gesso. After drying overnight, this under drawing can be painted over with dilute acrylic washes using sable brushes.

If you look at one of Susan's pin-ups, it's not hard to believe that she started out doing portraits. What grabs most viewers are her faces, and in particular, her eyes. Inanimate eyes with the ability to bore right through you, the most beautiful eyes you've ever seen.

Though it took Susan years to make the conversion from engineer to pin-up artist, she's making up for it now. Once she decided to make the move, it took Susan less than five years to go from total unknown with her first pin-up image to a well-respected and well-known pin-up artist. Which makes for interesting speculation as to what the next five years hold for Susan Heidi.

Patience might be the one word that can be used to describe Susan at work. No detail is too small to warrant intense concentration as Susan works slowly to get each one just right. In Susan's art-world, good work takes as long as it takes – you can't rush the process.

Susan is of the subtractive school, creating her images with transparent paint, erasing her way to highlights. Her skin tones glow, the eyes sparkle. Though she doesn't display very often at pin-up conventions, she reports that when she does, print sales are good. In the case of Susan Heidi's art, seeing truly is believing.

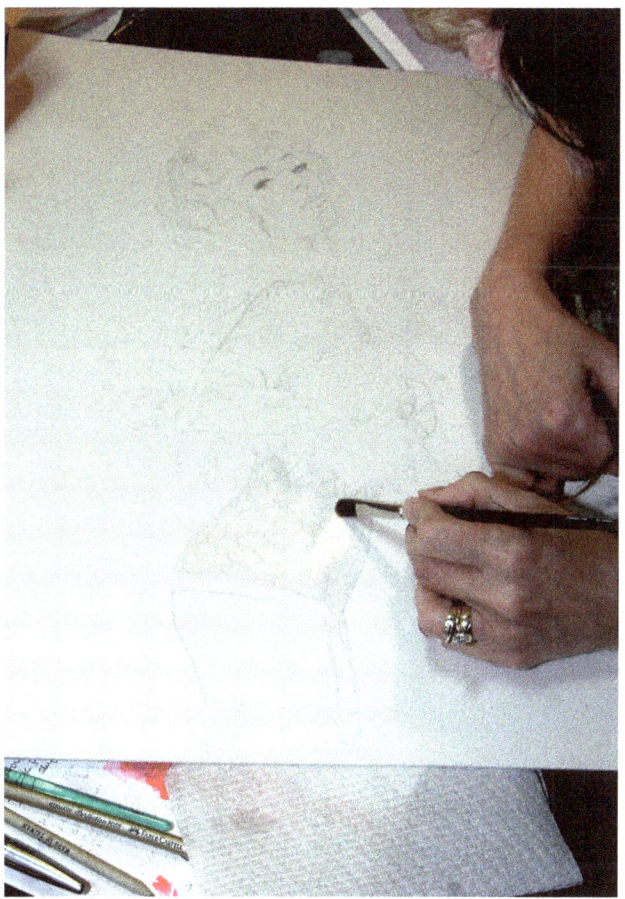

Before laying down the washes, Susan wets the board thoroughly using a sable brush that will be used for water only. All areas of the painting are painted lightly with pre-mixed color washes that will be used throughout the painting process.

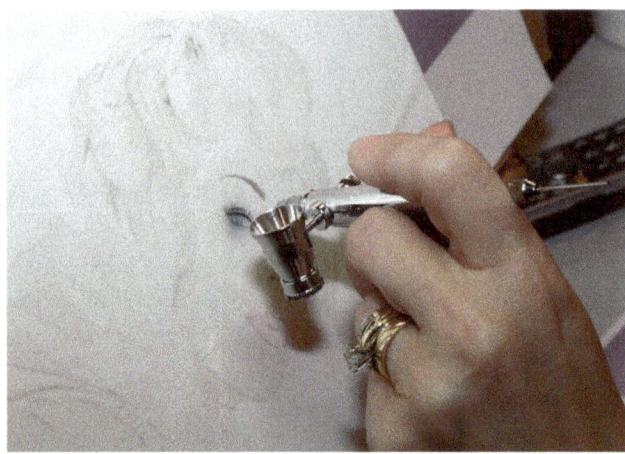

The darkest areas of the painting - in this case the eyes and lips - are painted first to set a value comparison.

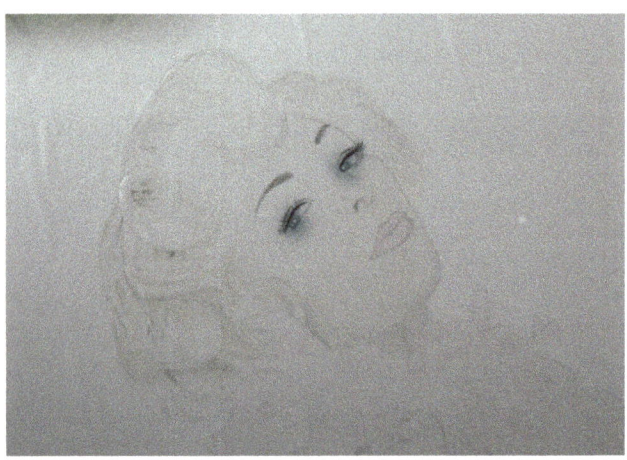

This painting is all about the model's expression, so a great deal of time is spent building up the tiny details of the iris.

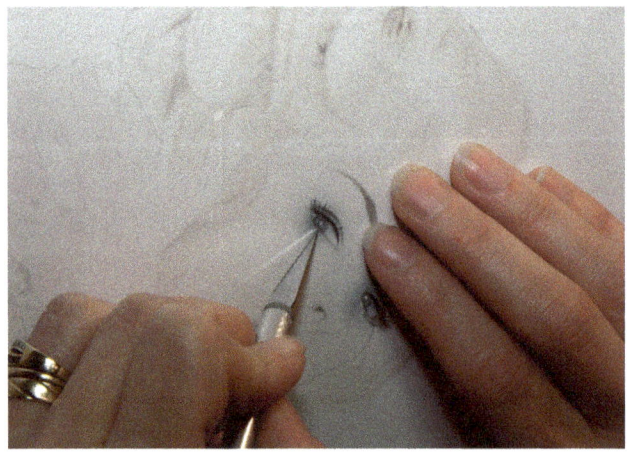

Erasing or scraping the highlights in the iris, layering paint, and repeating the process creates depth and texture.

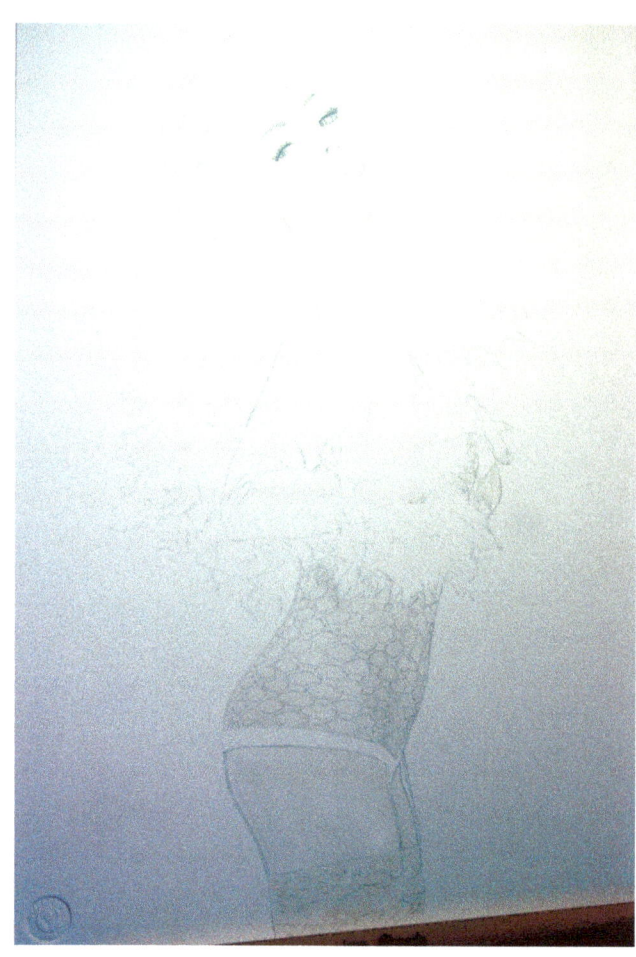

After the under painting dries overnight, the entire piece is covered with frisket. The outer edges of areas that will be painted are cut with a very sharp Xacto blade, changing the blade often. Care is taken to "cut into" the hairline to create a natural transition.

Though most of the details are created with the airbrush, positioned so close it almost touches the board, Susan also uses hand brushes to create details or hard lines difficult to achieve in any other way. Fisket is her friend as well, though she more commonly uses plastic masks and templates to achieve the necessary separation without a hard line.

If you ask Susan what makes a good pin-up, she talks about the sexual ambiguity. Susan is an artist who understands the notion that what you can't see may be more important than what you can.

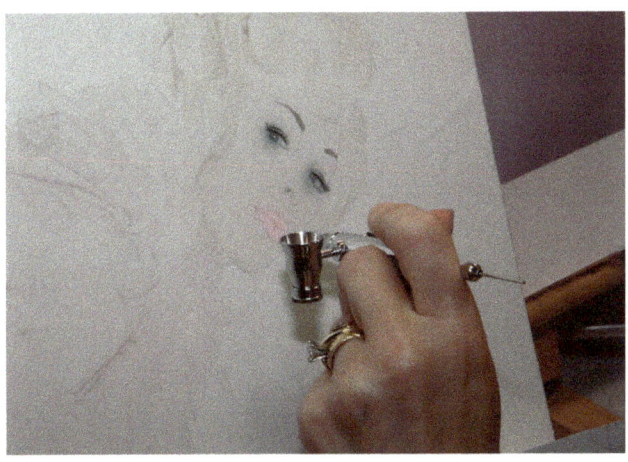

The lips are painted using much the same technique as the iris. A small amount of liquid frisket covers the white area where the lips are parted.

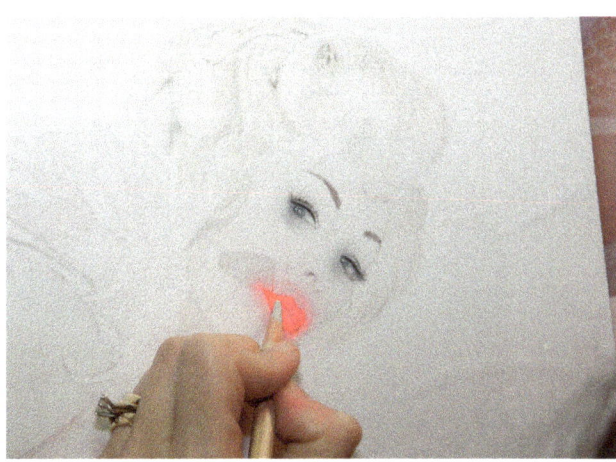

By concentrating the paint in the center and erasing highlights on the outer area, I create the line that separates the two lips.

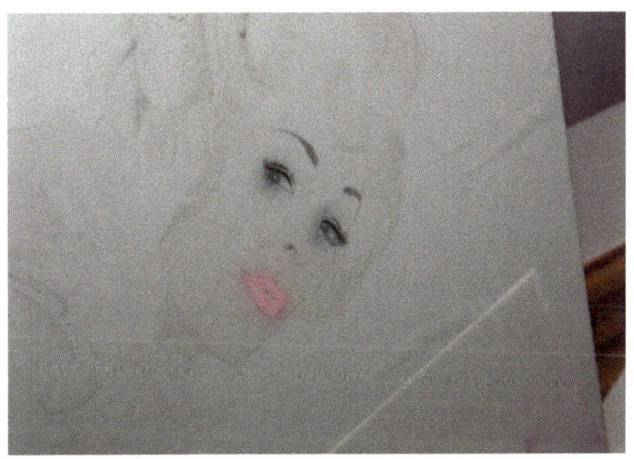

By layering thin layers of paint, erasing highlights, then adding more paint, I get a more realistic, subtle look.

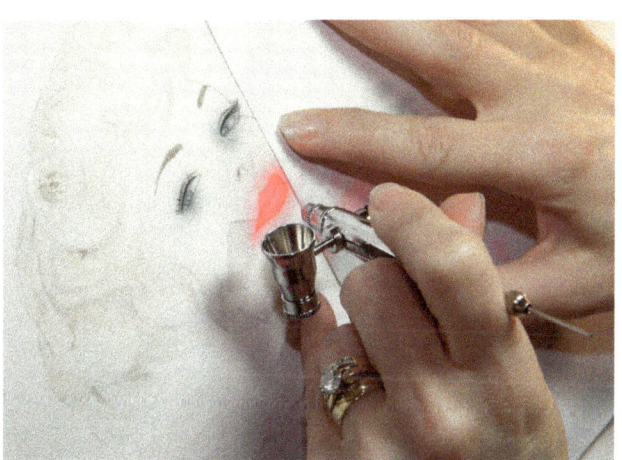

At this point you can start to see the fullness of the lips, like she's pursing her lips.

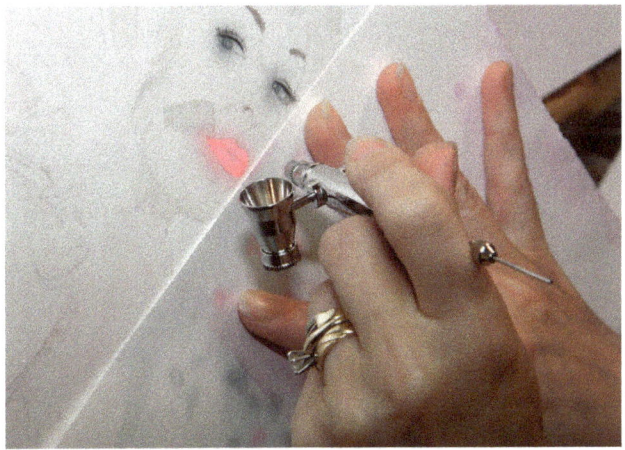

I'm careful to not create too harsh a line where the lips meet the face, softening that edge with an eraser while painting the lips.

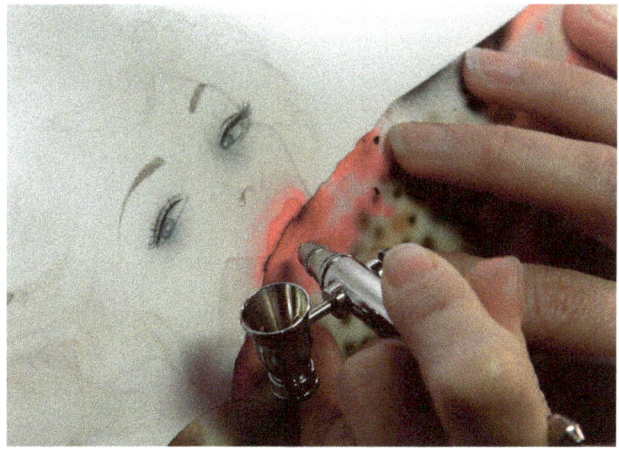

Using a handheld mask, I darken the line between the lips and sharpen that edge.

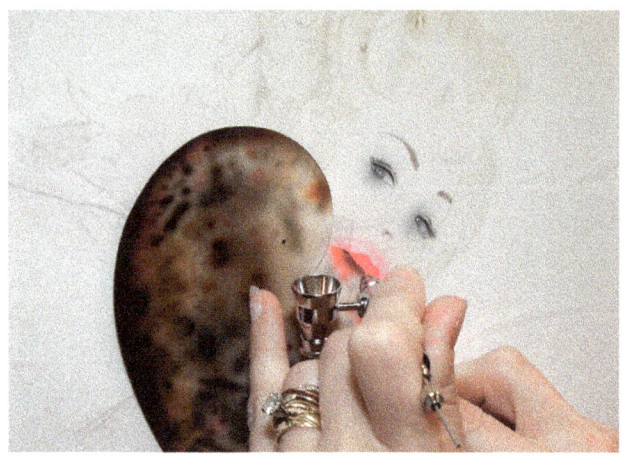

I'm working very close to the board when creating these details.

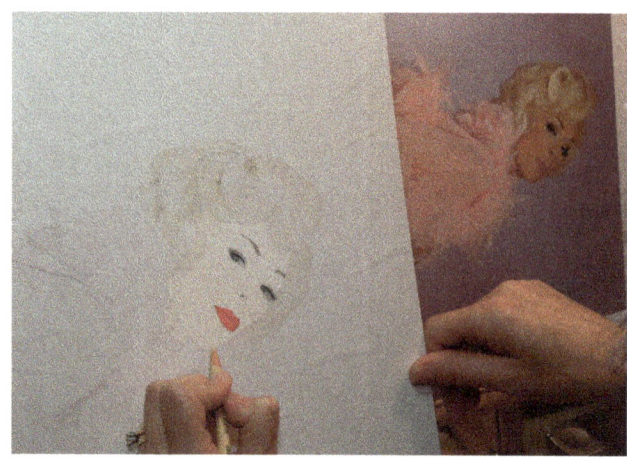

To begin rendering bone structure, lighter areas are broadly erased.

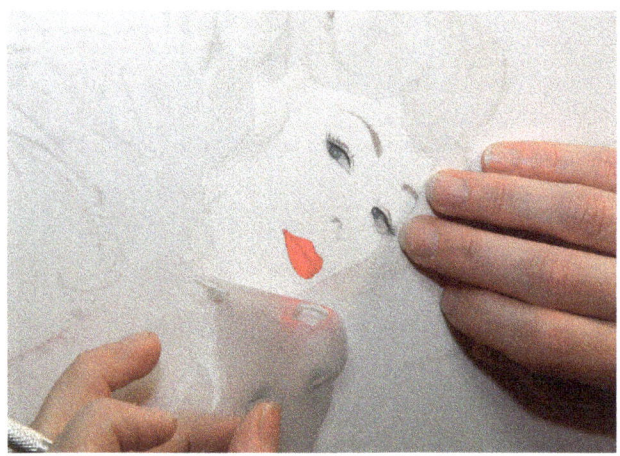

The frisket is removed from all the flesh areas. For this painting they will all be painted at once, but that's not always the case.

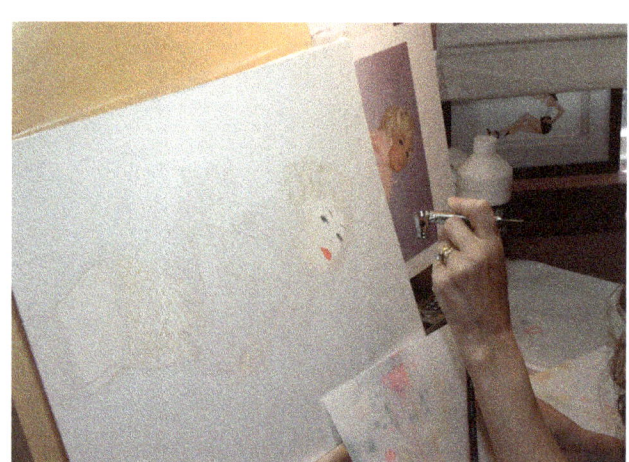

Another layer of light skin tone is added.

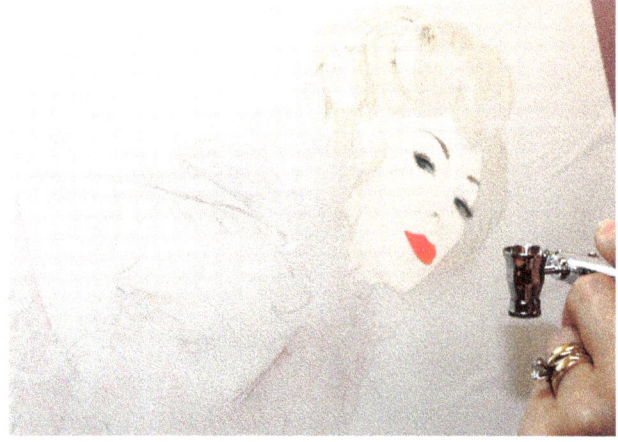

A premixed light flesh tone is used first, dusting it over the flesh area.

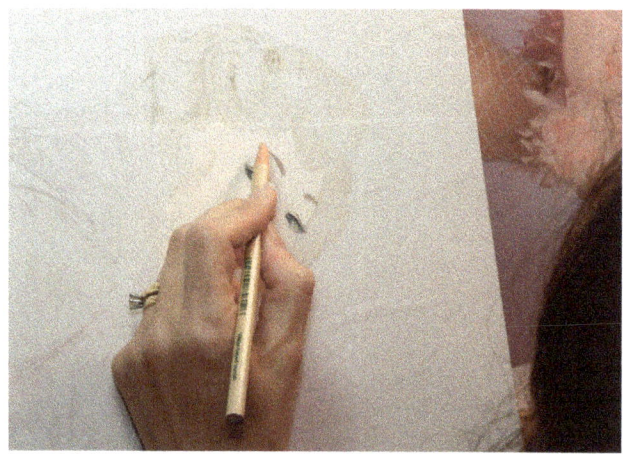

Erasing over the light areas early on creates a more subtle effect than if I went back at the end to remove the highlights.

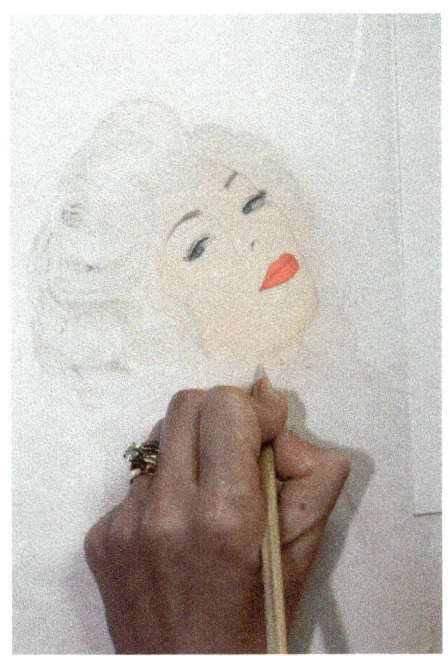
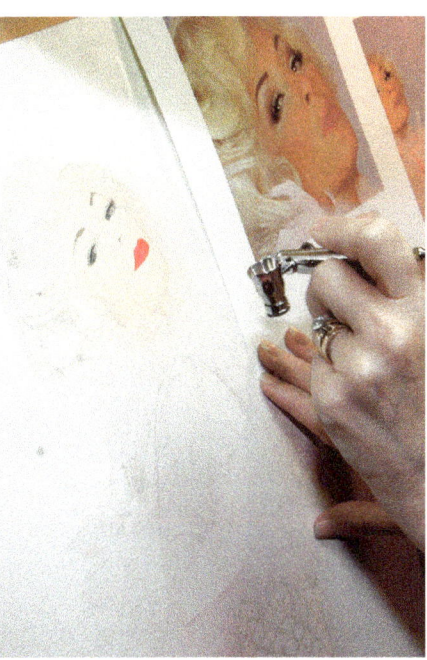
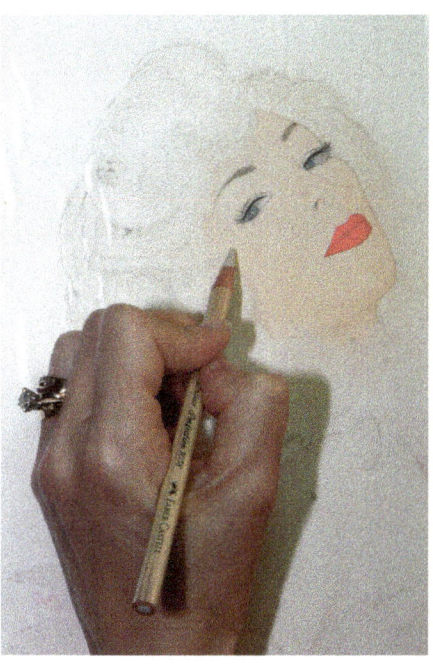

Time is spent using an eraser to soften the line where the hair and feathers meet the skin.

Layers of skin tone can be painted more broadly at this stage, working farther away from the surface of the board.

The process of erasing out the bone structure continues.

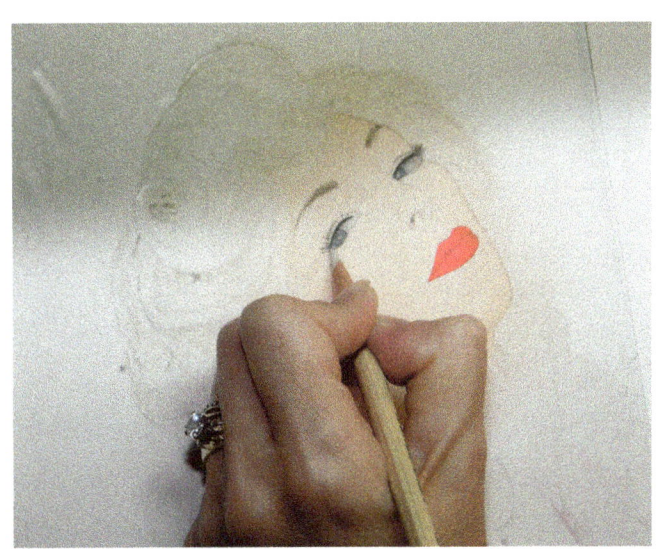
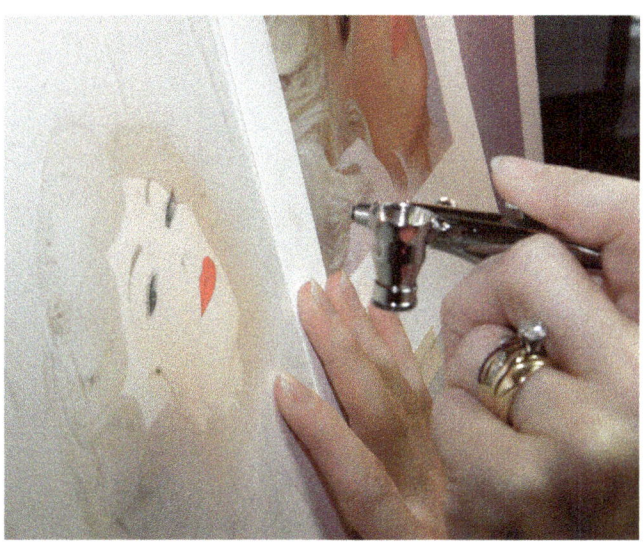

Attention is paid to even the smallest areas, like the lower lids of the eyes.

Additional application of light skin tone.

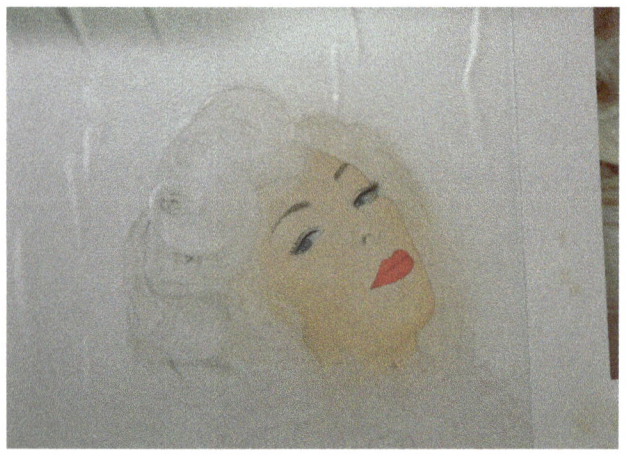

At this point you can see the structure of the face quite clearly. The shadows and highlights are subtle but there.

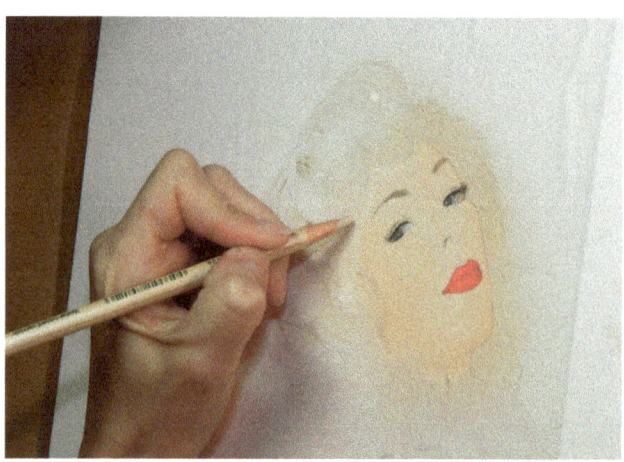

The hairline is kept soft by erasing the edges where the hair meets the face.

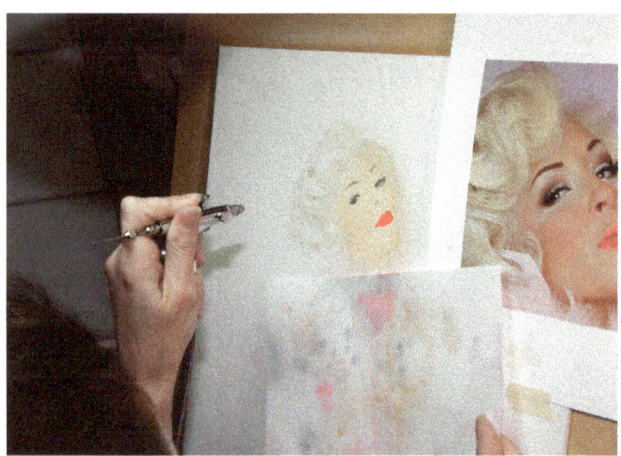

A light dusting of skin tone darkens the face.

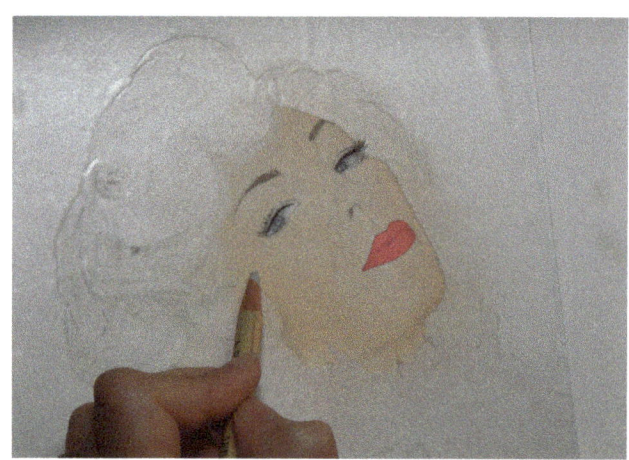

Some small stray hairs can be created by carefully erasing fine lines.

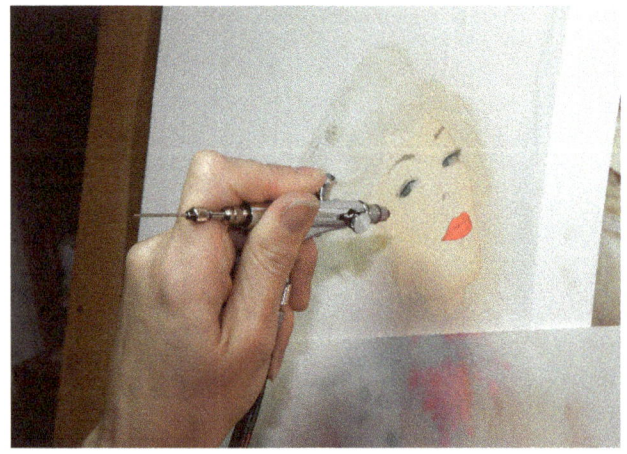

Working closer to the board gives more control. At this stage shadows are being created by controlling the application of the skin tone.

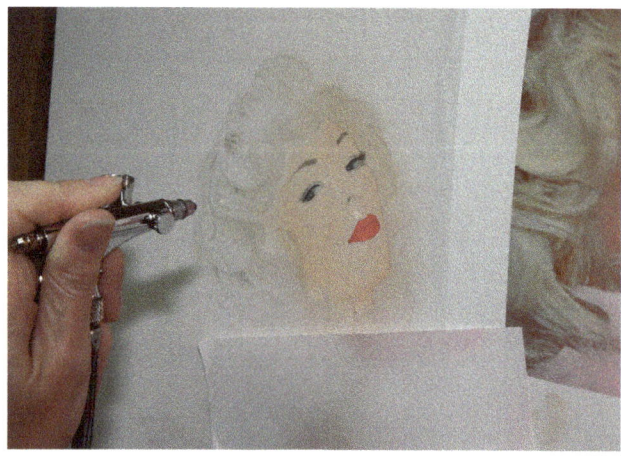

A thin wash of violet is lightly sprayed over the flesh areas to add more depth to the color.

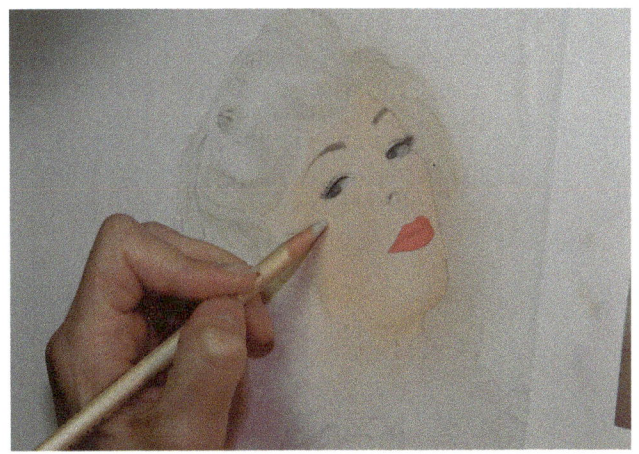

It's important to retain the highlights after every application of color.

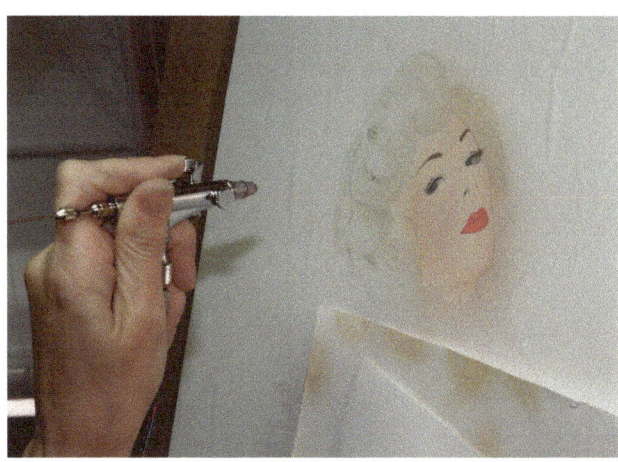

A scrap piece of paper is kept close at hand for testing the paint before adding it to the painting.

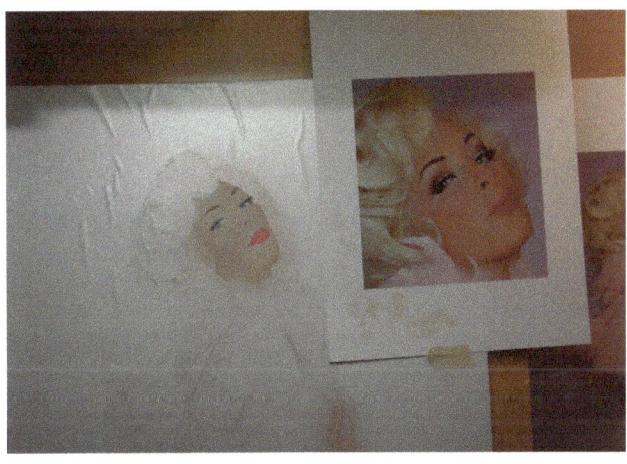

To create a likeness, the reference photo I'm working from is kept close.

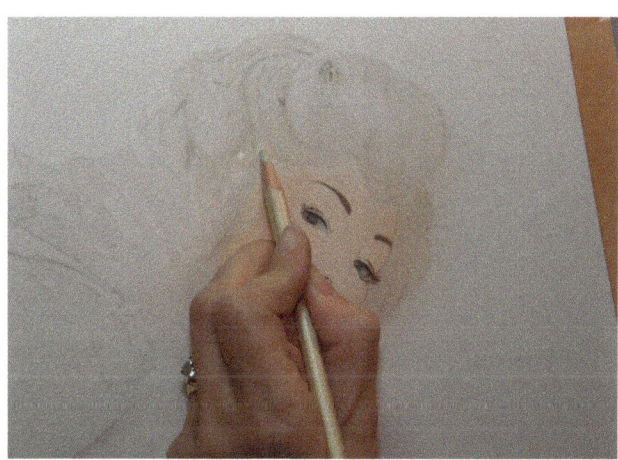

Care has to be taken throughout the painting process to keep edges soft.

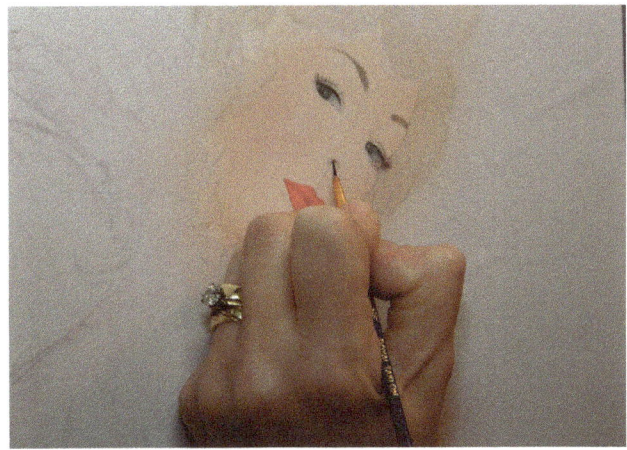

The tiny details of the nostril are done with a fine brush. Here the shadow in the nostril is darkened using diluted sepia.

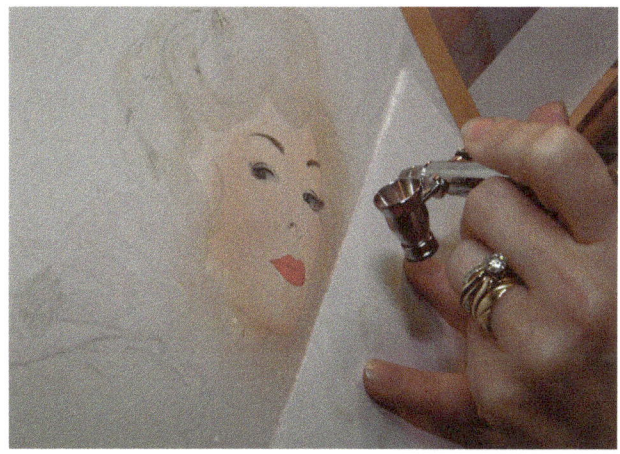

Turning the painting sideways helps me look at it differently, to see a shape as a shape and not a body part.

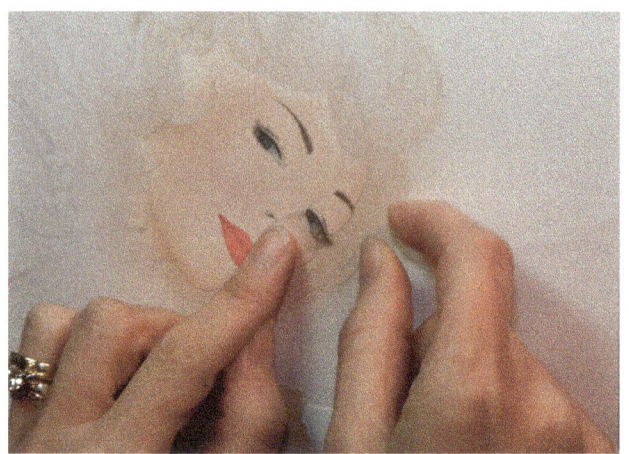

Once the painting has progressed to this point, it's important to keep more control of where the paint is going by working closer to the board.

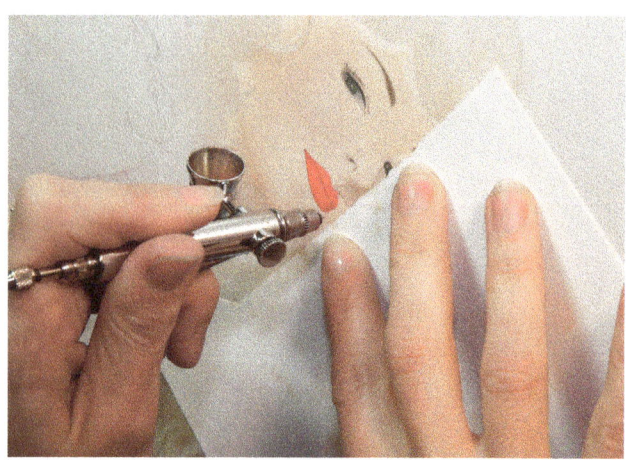

The shadow under the edge of the nose is created in the same way.

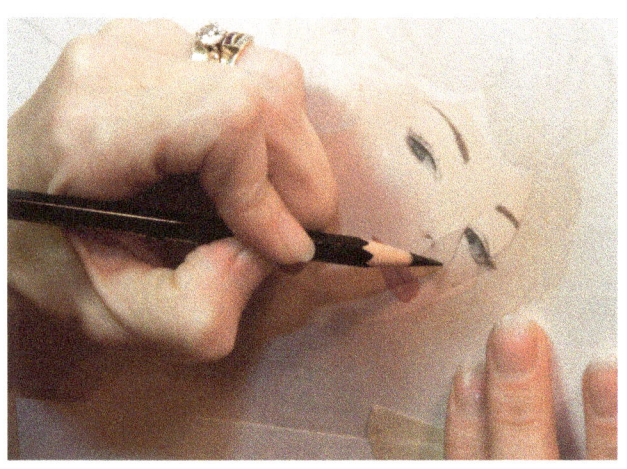

Hard edges like the bridge of the nose can be created by making a mask with frisket. I've switched to using a darker pre-mixed skin tone for these shadows.

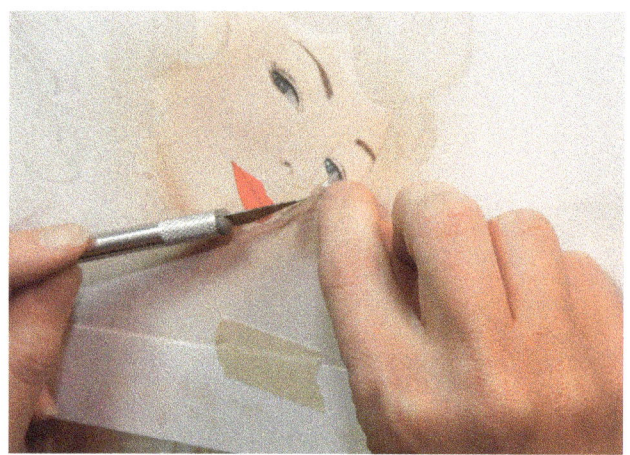

The point of an Xacto can be used with care to help pull the frisket off the painting.

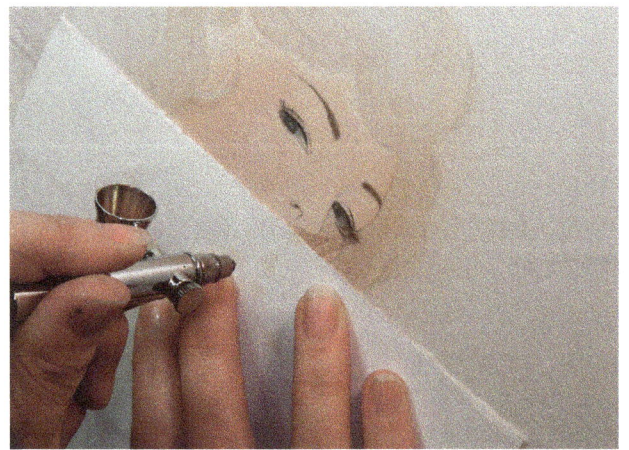

First, a piece of frisket is laid on the area and marked with pencil. The frisket is removed to a work table and the edge is cut with an Xacto blade.

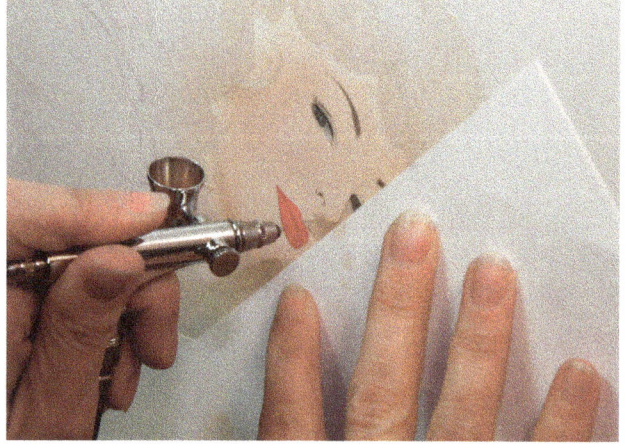

The process can be repeated if the shadow needs to be darkened.

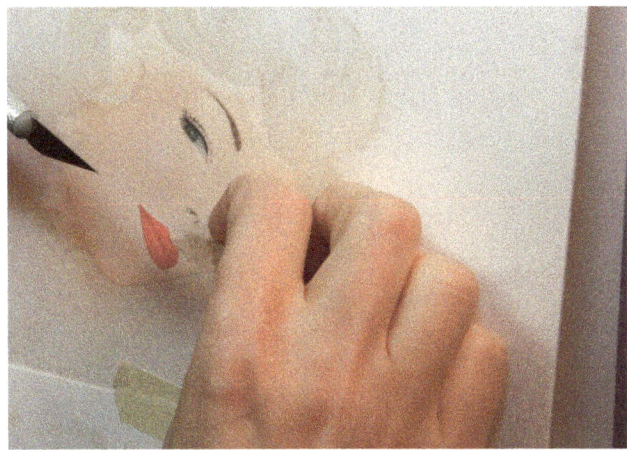

The small frisket mask is removed very carefully from the surface of the board.

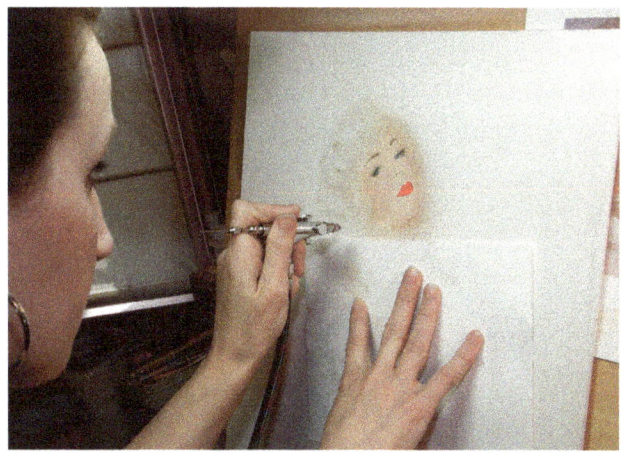

A plain piece of paper can be used to create a straight-lined edge.

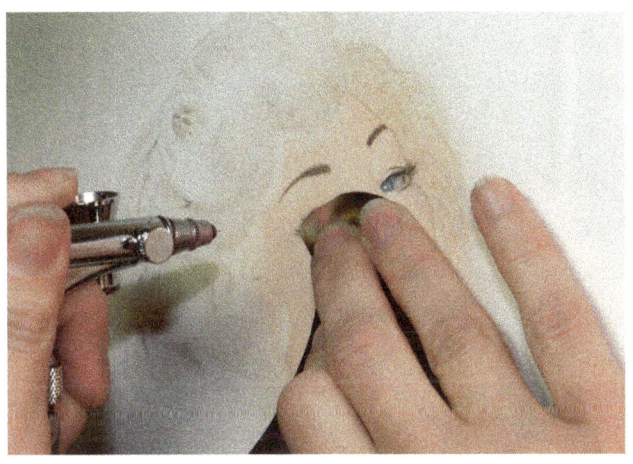

A handheld shield, made using heavyweight bristol and a french curve, helps me create hard edges where I need them. Care needs to be taken not to create hard edges where I don't want them.

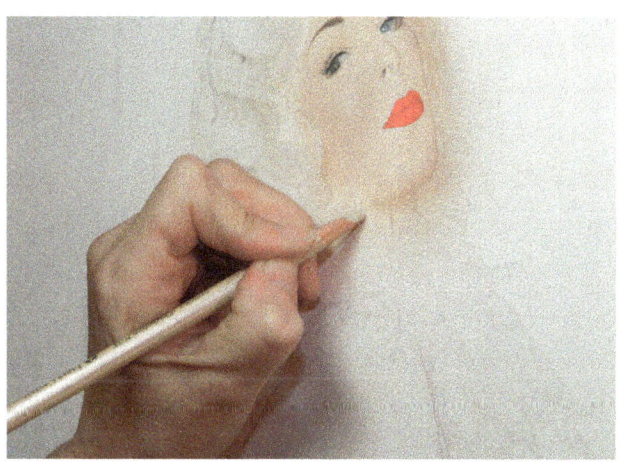

Erasing with a sharpened eraser helps to establish this edge of a feather.

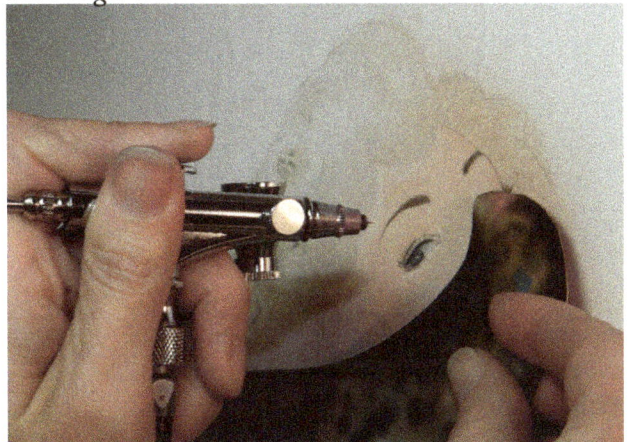

The same shield has mostly all of the angles and curves I need for creating the hard edged shadows around the eyes.

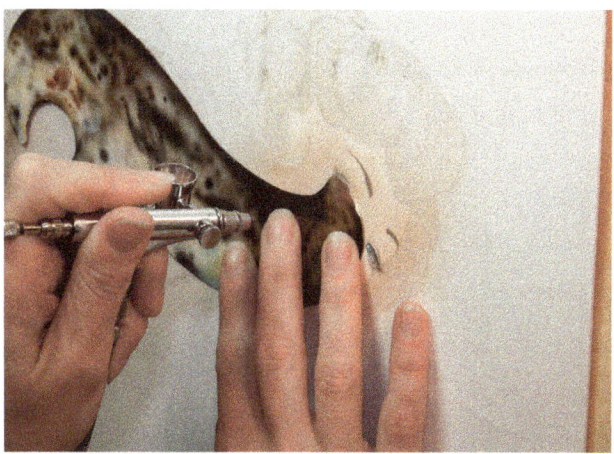

Going back to the eyes, I darken the shadow in the crease of the lid. I like to move around a painting - working on one area and then jumping to another.

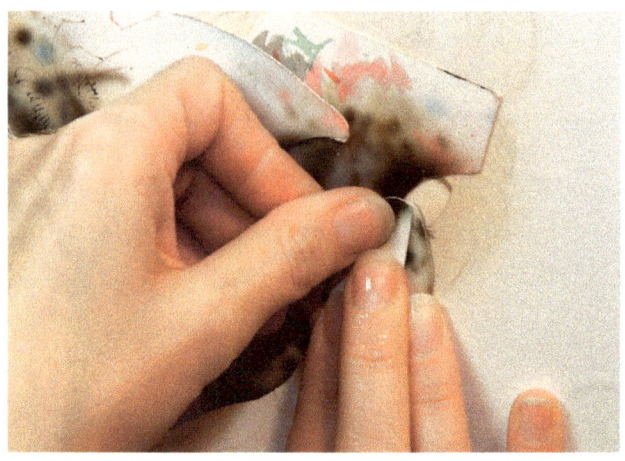

There are times when more than one shield is needed to create just the right shape. That's when dexterity comes into play.

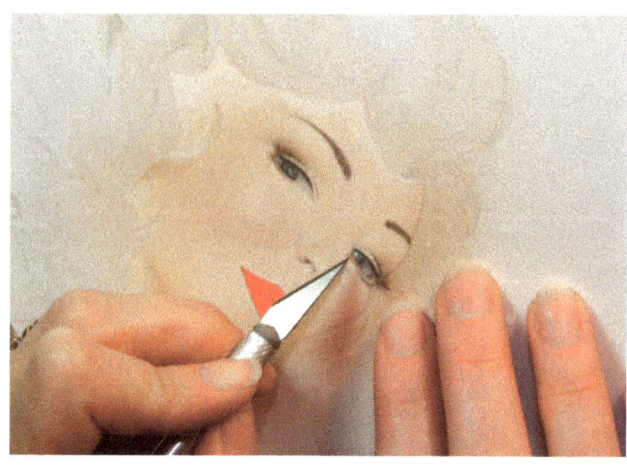

The highlight of the pupil is carefully placed using an Xacto blade. Placement of this highlight is critical to achieving the gaze I want for the model.

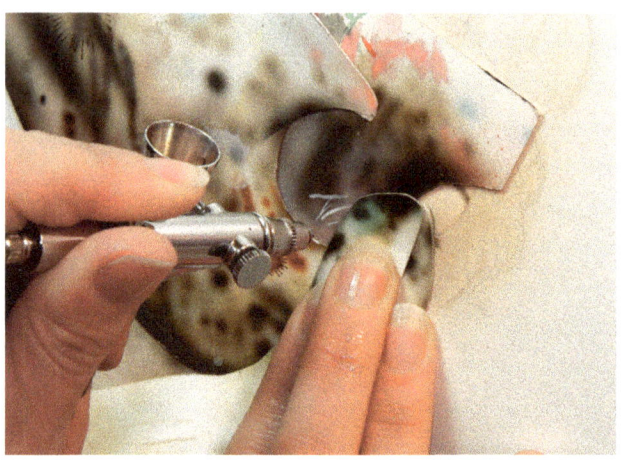

Holding several shields against the board with my right hand, I pick up the airbrush and paint with the left hand.

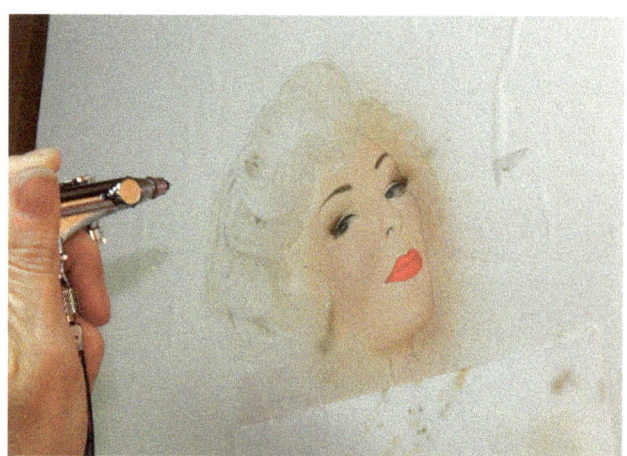

Now that the area around the eyes is darker, it becomes apparent that the skin tone needs to be darkened.

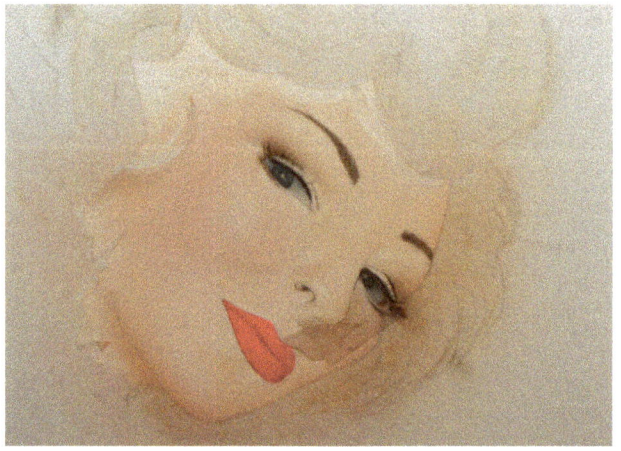

Smoky shadows on the eyelids help create that dreamy effect.

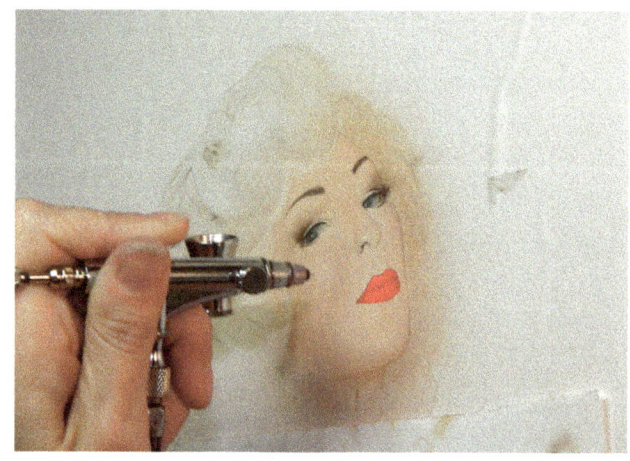

Shadows are added to the face free-hand. At this point, avoid erasing all but the brightest highlights or too much texture will be created.

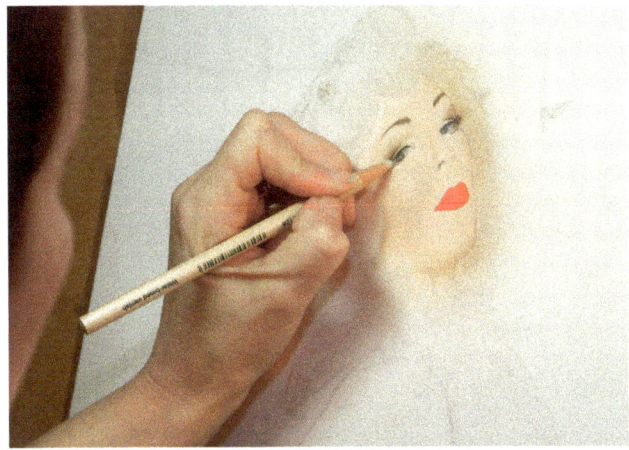

Whenever I see something that needs adjusting, I do it right then to keep the painting unified.

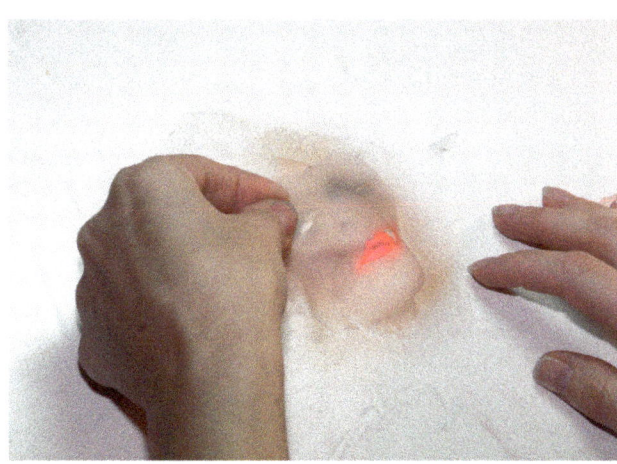

Ready to move on to the feathers, small pieces of frisket that were stored on the original backing paper are placed over the painted face.

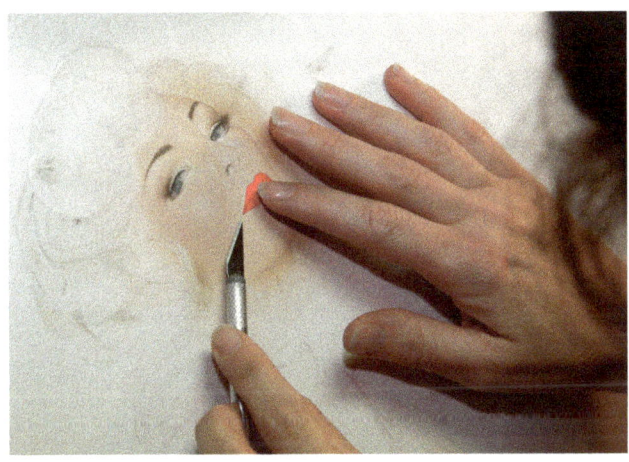

The sharp point of an Xacto blade can be used to help replace small pieces of frisket

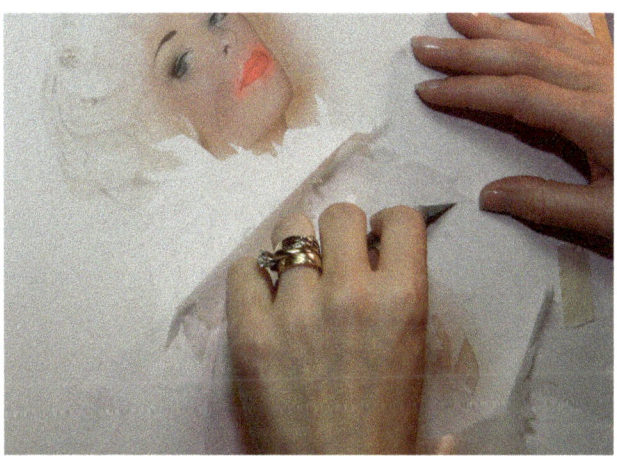

Frisket is carefully removed from over the feather boa wrap, taking care not to tear the surface of the board underneath.

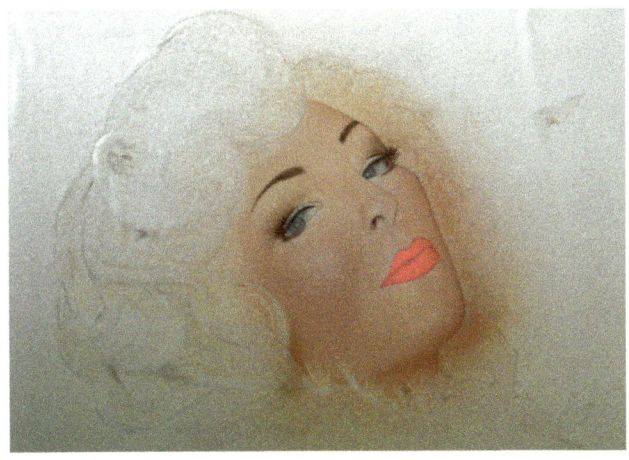

It's a good idea to stop occasionally and assess the progress of the image so far.

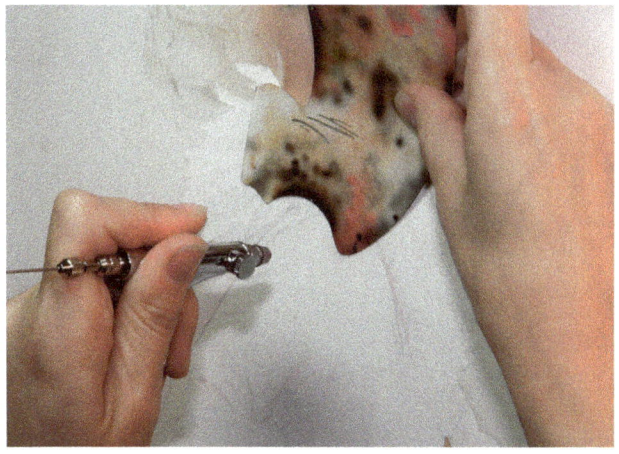

To start painting this area, I first mark in the hard edges using the pre-mixed pink wash and a hand-held shield.

Masking With Liquid Frisket

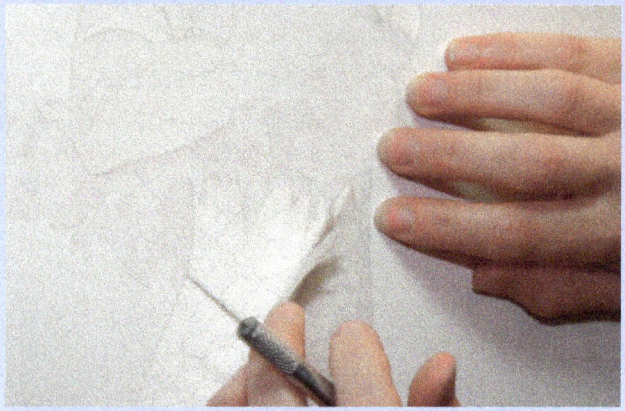

Liquid frisket can be used in situations like this to mask off irregular areas. To start, carefully remove frisket film from the area to be painted.

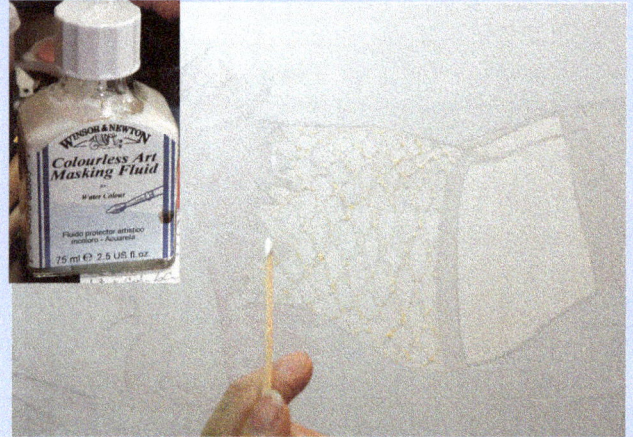

Mix liquid frisket with water, half and half, then "paint" areas that you want to keep unpainted. Use an old brush that you don't care about ruining for this technique.

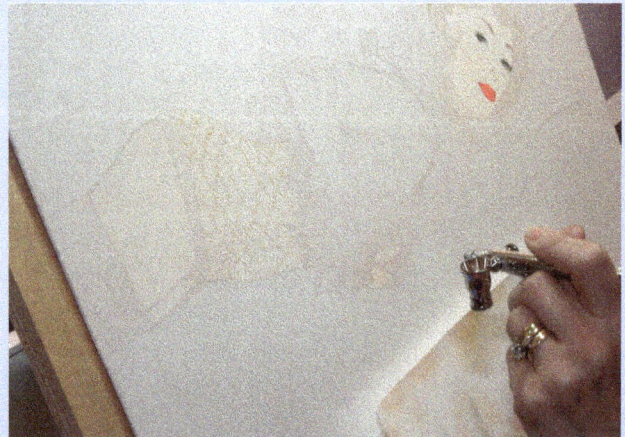

Dust light skin tone over the entire area.

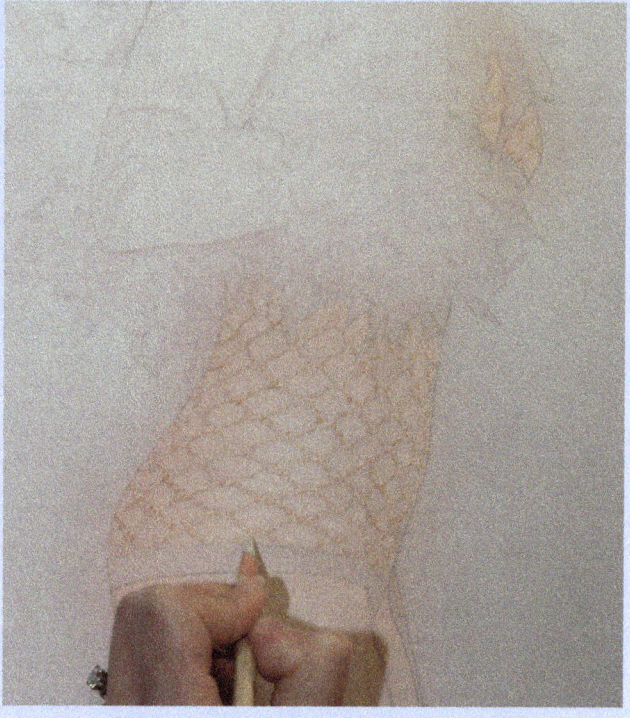

As with the face, start erasing lighter areas early on in the process to keep the highlights subtle.

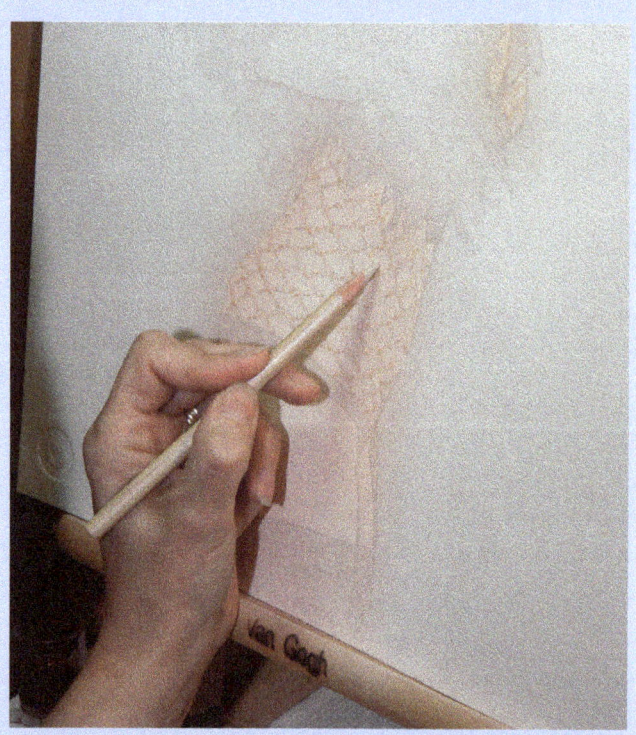

Continue to dust, erase, dust until the bone structure starts to appear.

Masking With Liquid Frisket

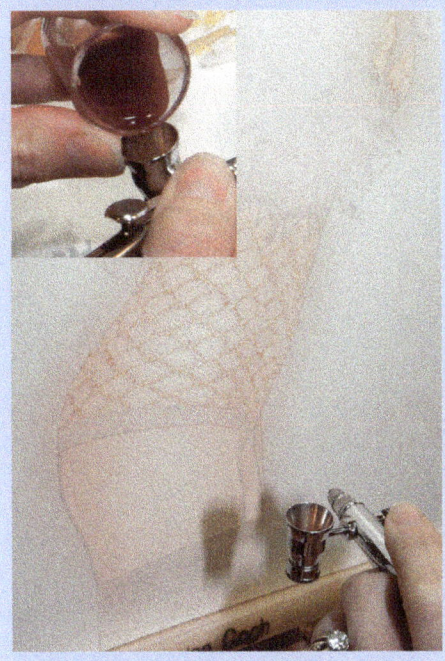

I notice that the color of skin on the body is redder than the face, so violet is added to the light skin color for this area.

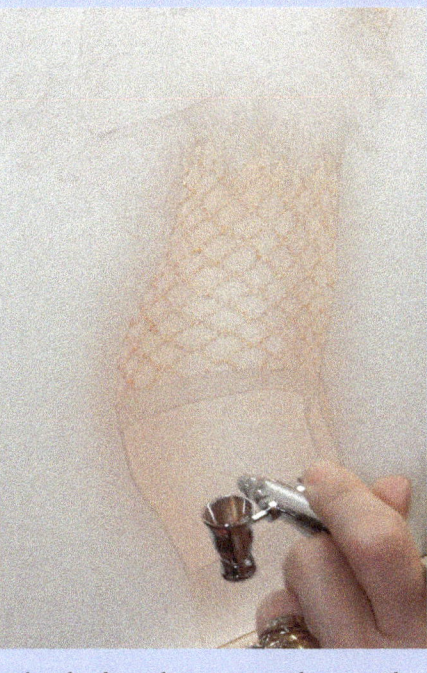

The shadow that creates the roundness of the form is reinforced using the darker skin tone.

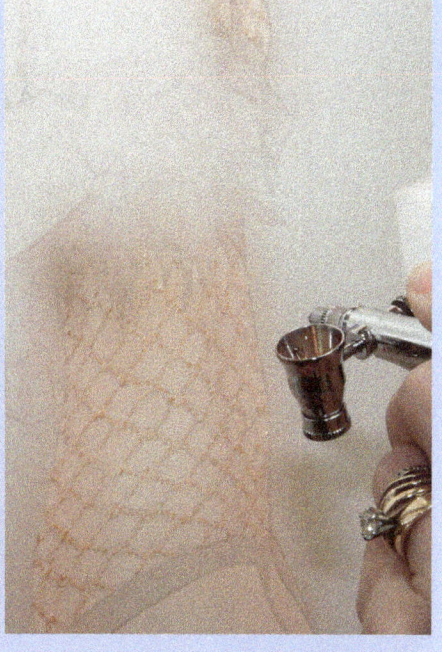

The dark shadows under the feathers are created first using dark skin tone.

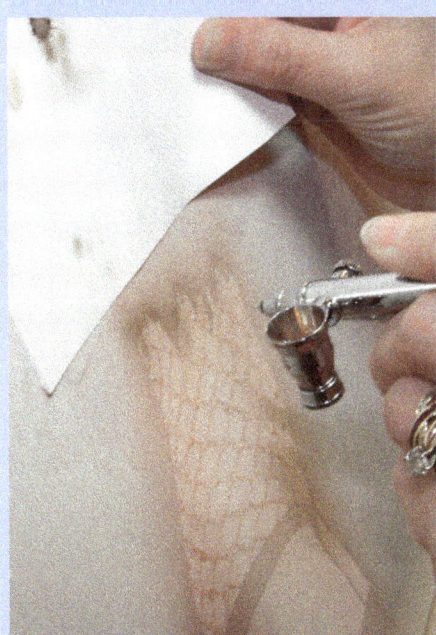

A harder edge and darker core of the shadow are created using diluted sepia.

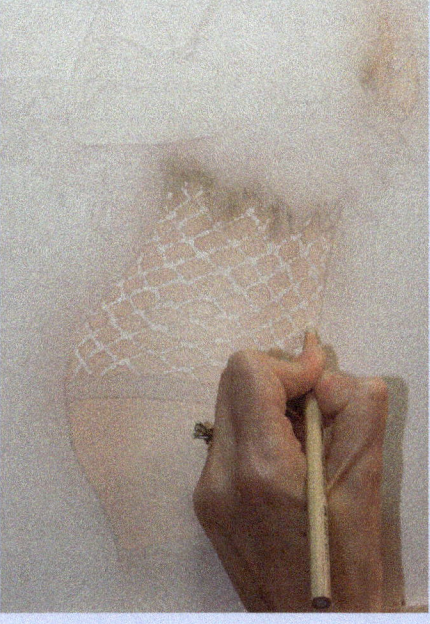

Once the skin areas are done, "erase" off the liquid frisket. The contrast was more than I wanted, so the strands of fishnet...

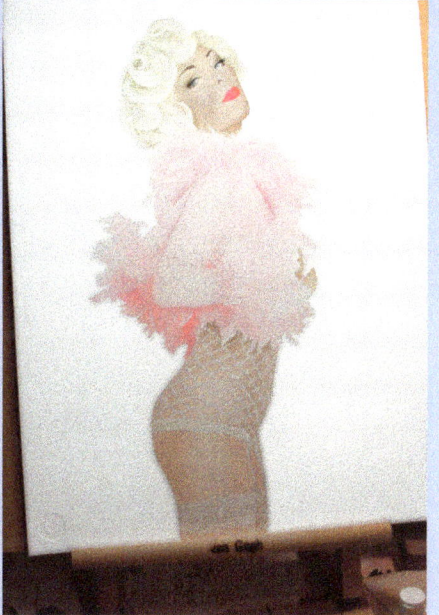

...had to be painted over by hand using dilute sepia and a fine detail brush, leaving the painting with the effect seen here.

127

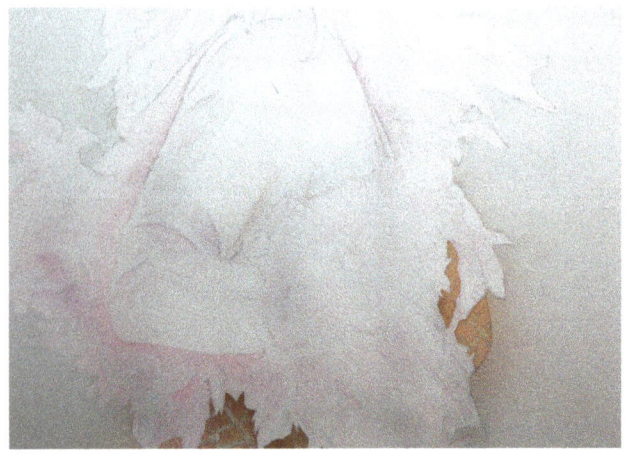

It's easy to see how light this area appears compared to the already painted skin tones.

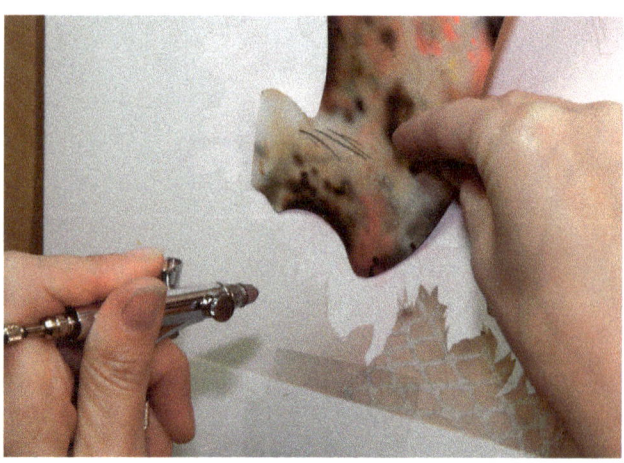

Mark more crisp shadow edges using the handheld shield.

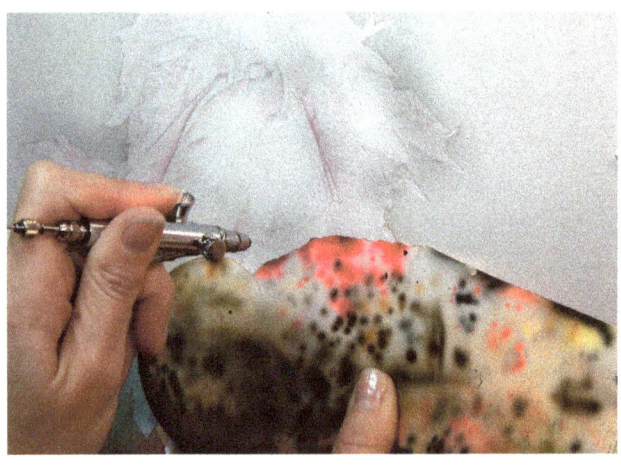

A torn area of the shield can be used to create ragged edges.

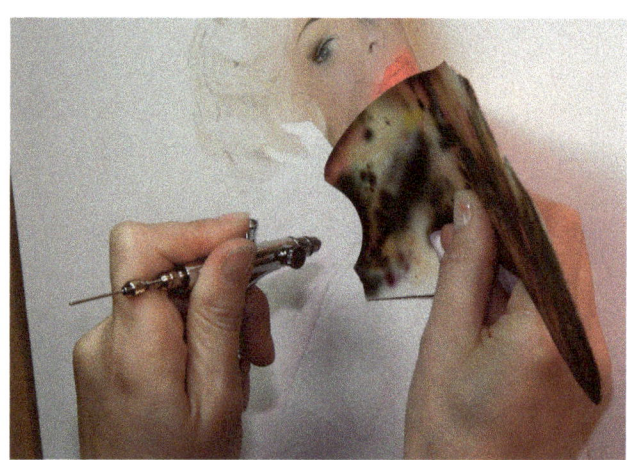

The shadows have to be placed just right so they make sense visually and contrast with the highlights.

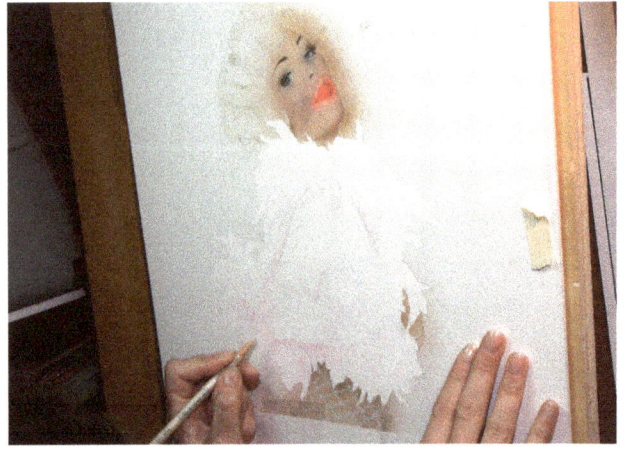

After dusting the entire area with color, highlights can be erased. This area has much more texture than the model's smooth skin.

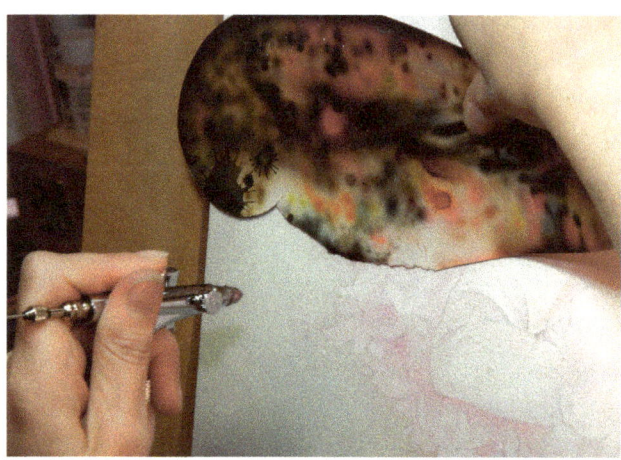

Continuing this way, the "feathers" start to appear to float away from the boa.

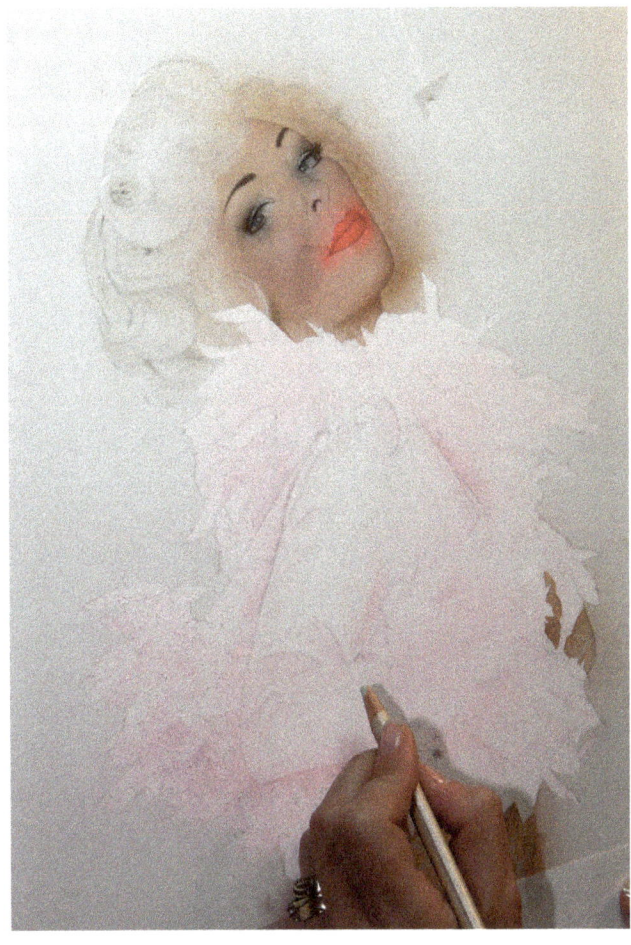

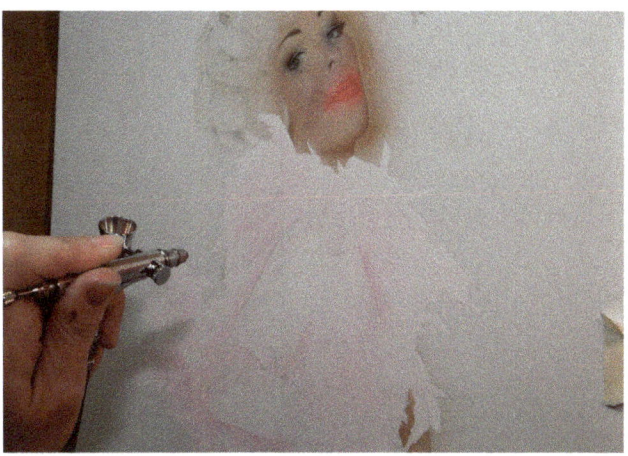

Some shadow areas are "fluffier" than others and don't require the hard edges that the handheld shield will create.

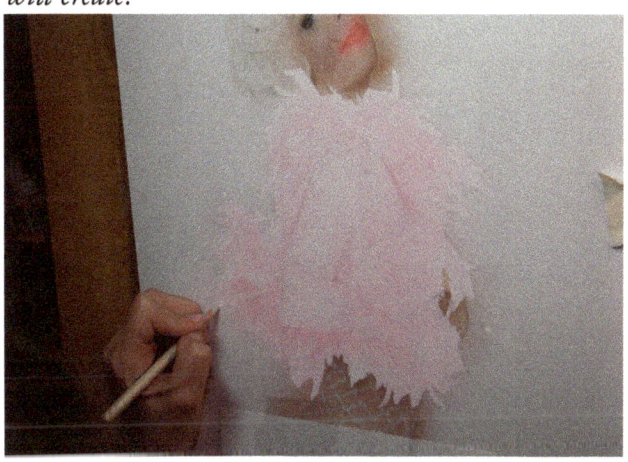

Even these areas have some of the soft downy feathers that stand away from the model and need to be highlighted.

Rendering her arm under the chiffon wrap requires attention to detail. The seam of the garment and soft highlights make the arm look solid under the fabric.

Despite a lot of overspray on the frisket around the figure, it's apparent that the feather boa wrap is beginning to take shape.

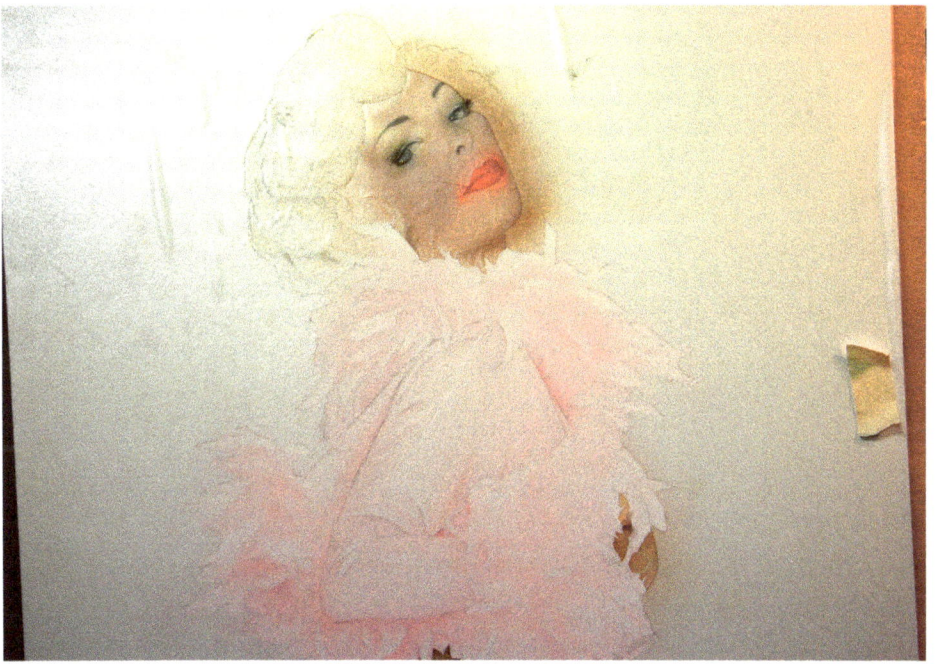

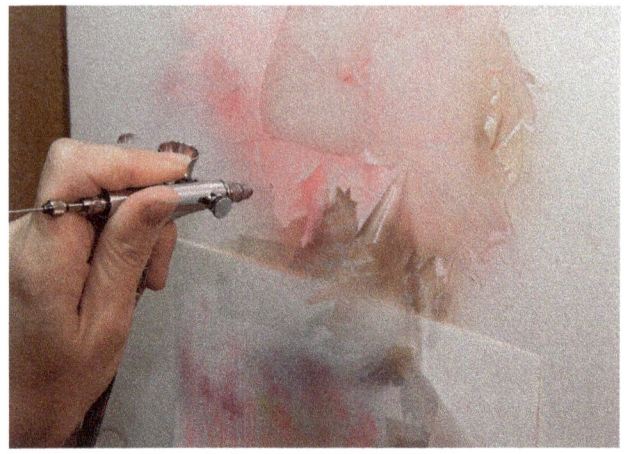

Some areas stand out as being much darker than others, but to get depth in these areas it's important to build the color slowly with layers of diluted paint.

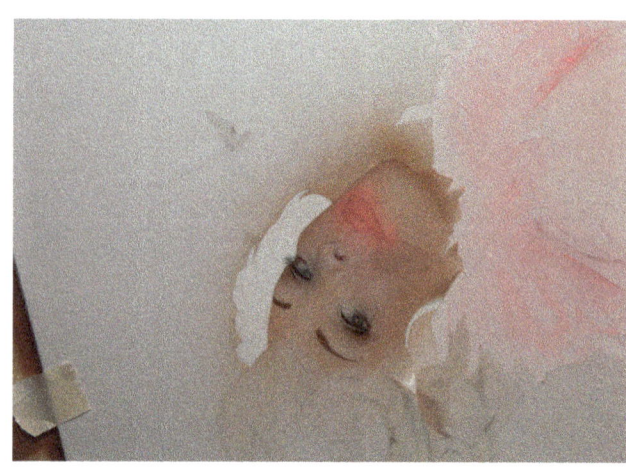

It's obvious how much painting has gone on next to this area once the frisket is removed.

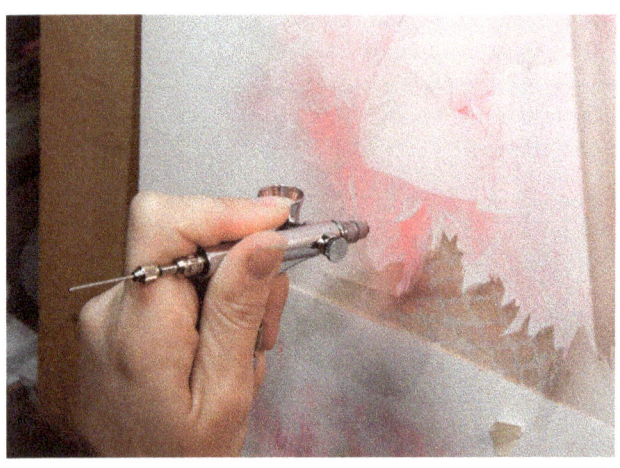

The shadow edge under the arm takes on more form by keeping the edge soft with a freehand application of paint.

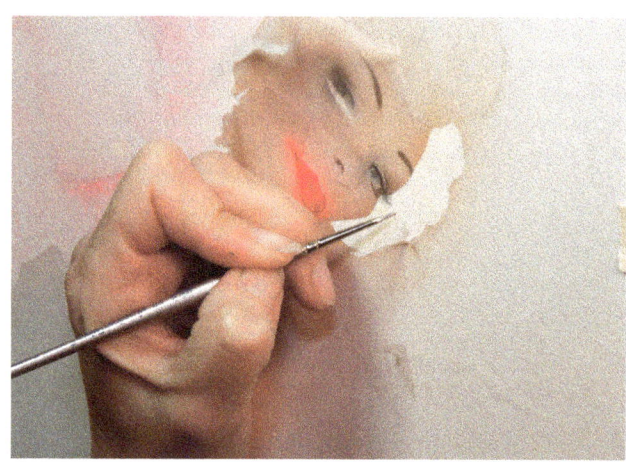

Painting the hair begins by applying diluted liquid frisket with an old brush on the lightest strands.

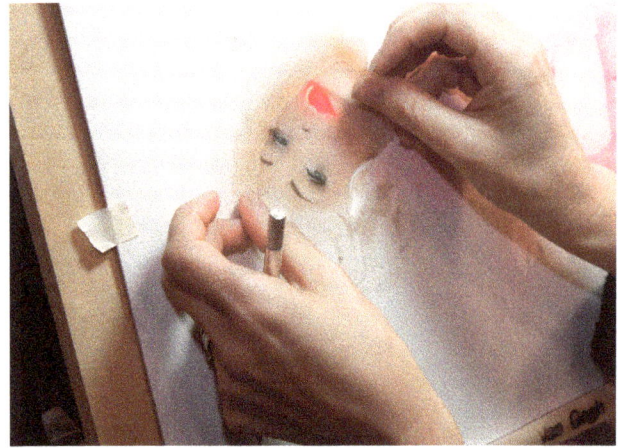

The hair is the last to be painted. Frisket is removed from the hair on the right side of the painting first, because it is darkened by the cast shadow of the face.

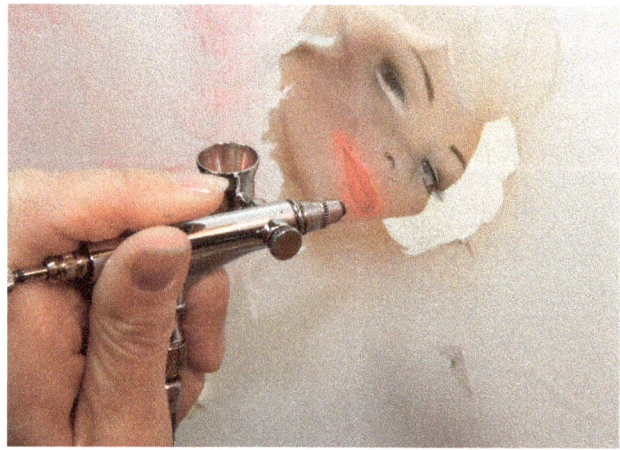

The pre-mixed hair color is dusted over the entire area.

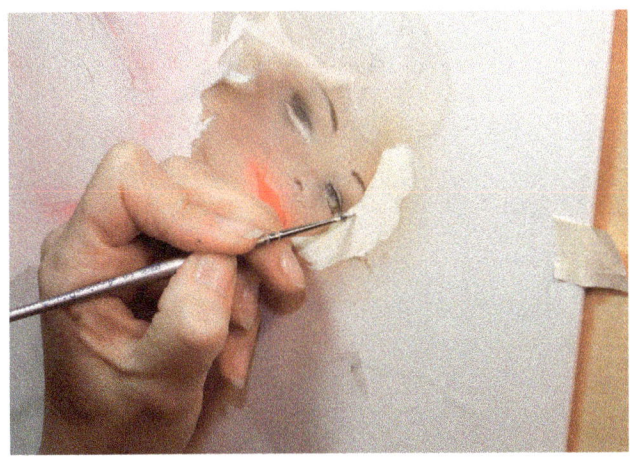

Repeat the process of applying liquid frisket, overlapping some highlighted areas and keeping other areas covered with liquid frisket and dust with paint.

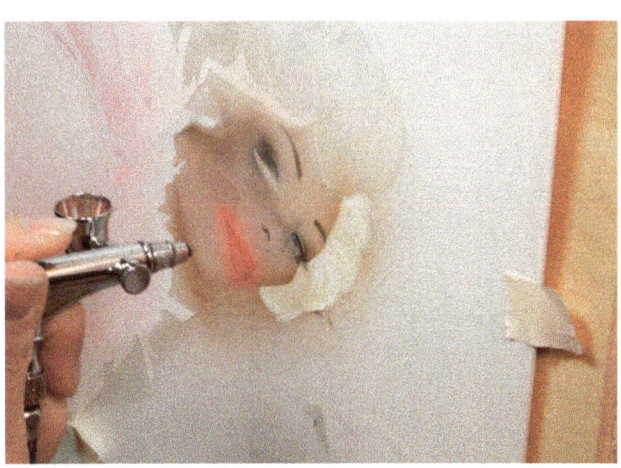

Continue to build the hair color slowly.

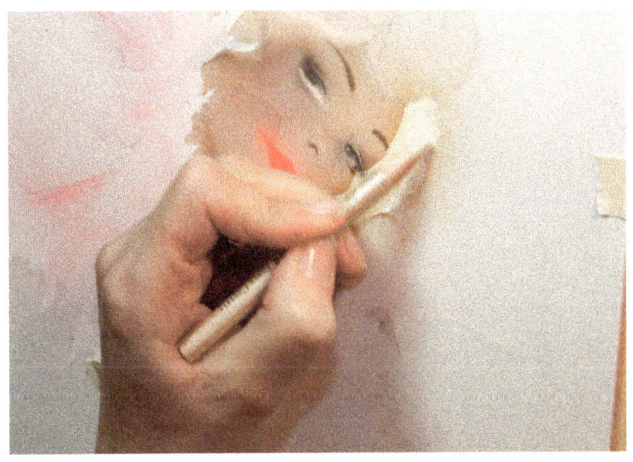

After repeating a few times, "erase" off the liquid frisket to see how it is going.

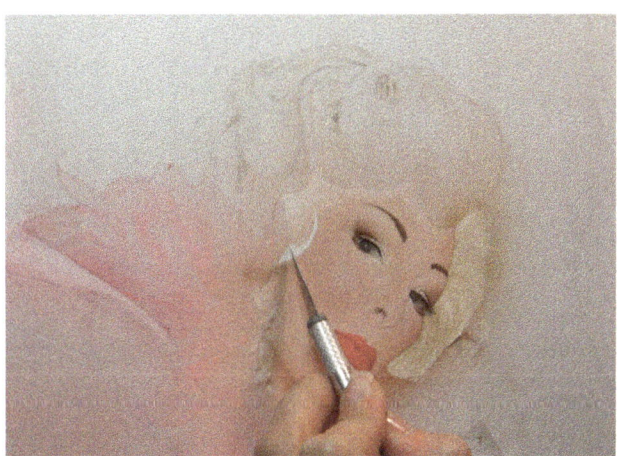

The hair on the left side of the painting overlaps the face, so the frisket is removed from the face to render this area. An Xacto is used to sharpen the contrast of an overlapping curl of hair.

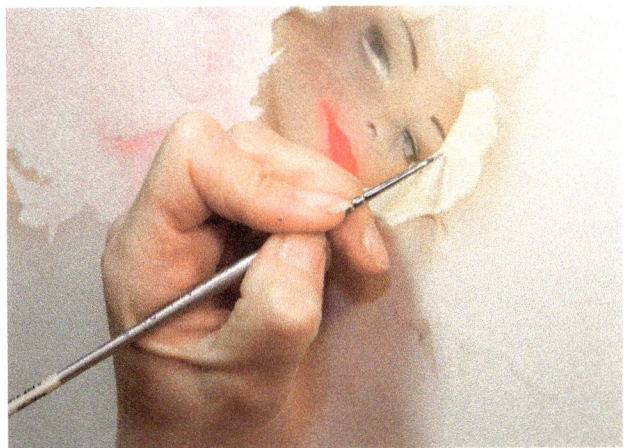

Paint the liquid frisket on again to increase the light-dark contrast. Be precise with some highlights and random with others. Don't have all the strands lined up in a row.

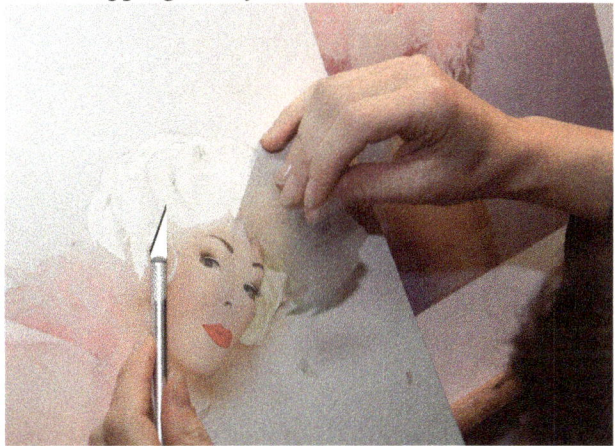

Removing the frisket from the hair on this side makes it apparent why these edges were kept soft to blend the hairline into the face.

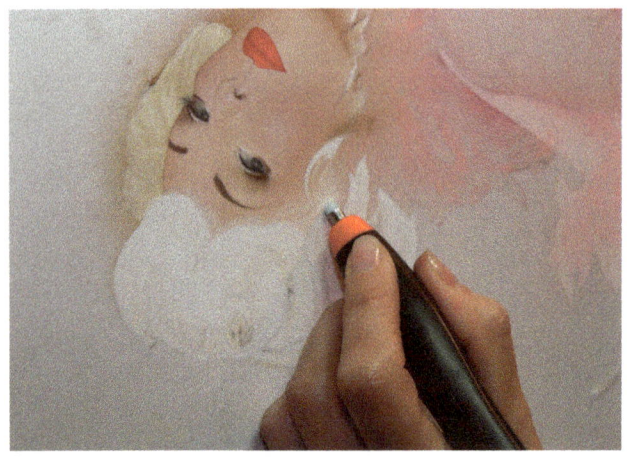

An electric eraser is used to create larger, softer areas of highlights.

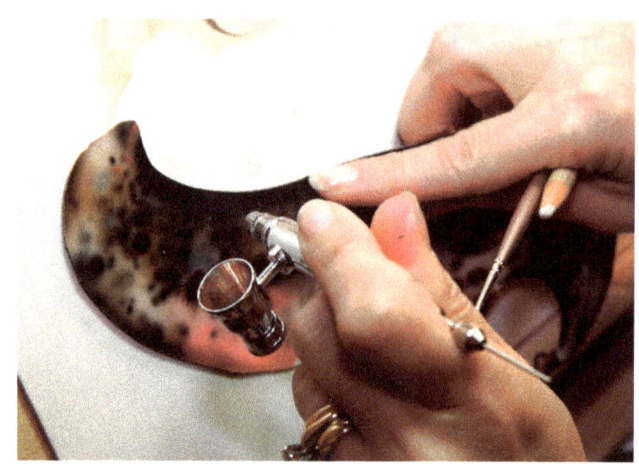

The handheld shield is used to mark out darker shadows with sharp edges.

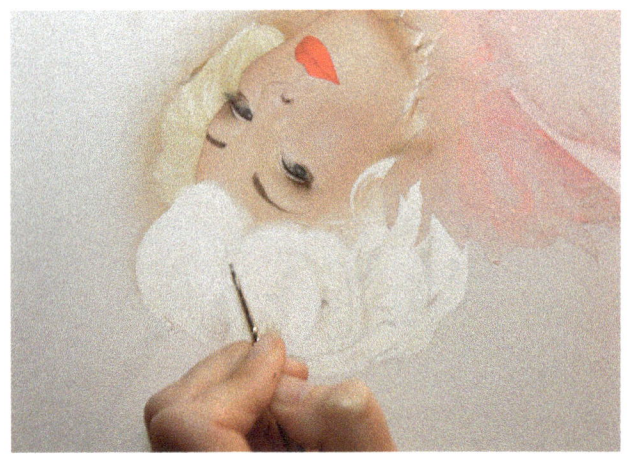

Once again, liquid frisket is "painted" on to retain lighter strands of hair.

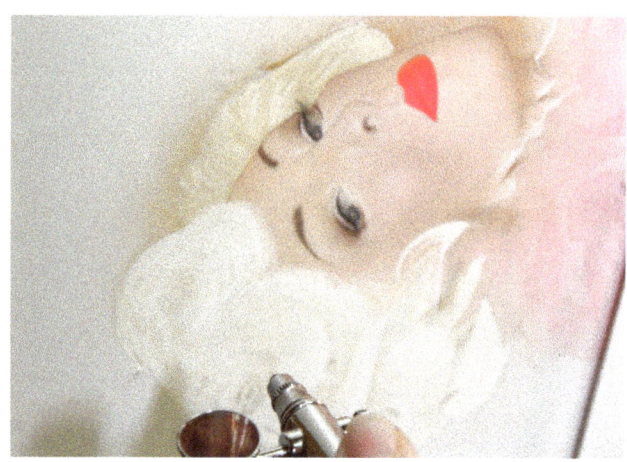

More hair color is applied over the entire area.

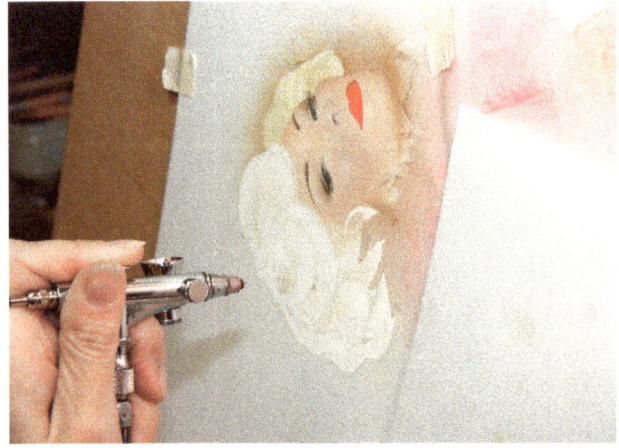

Hair color is sprayed broadly over the area.

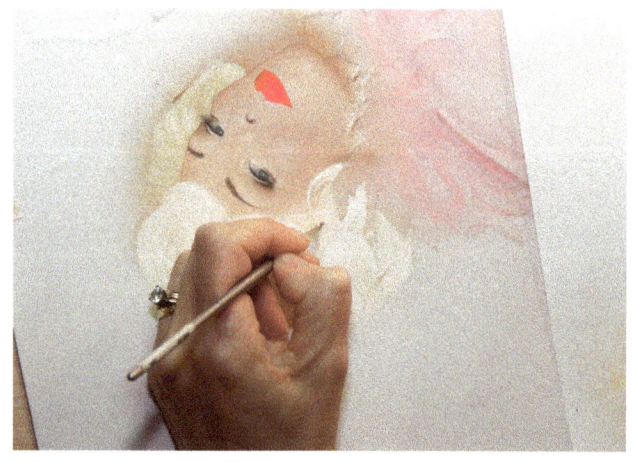

Areas are erased to sharpen the highlights.

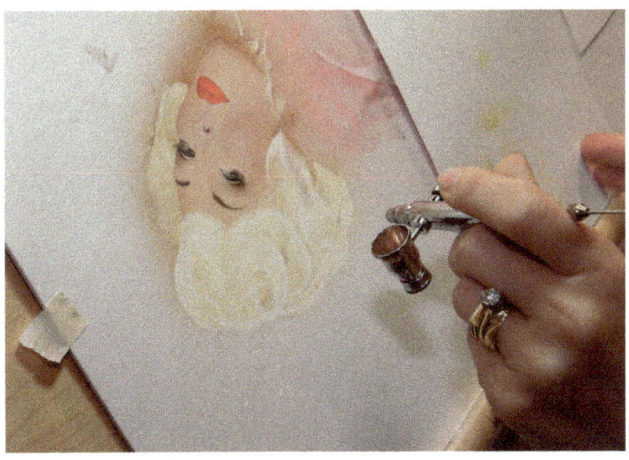

The hair color is built up some more with heavier applications of paint on the darker areas.

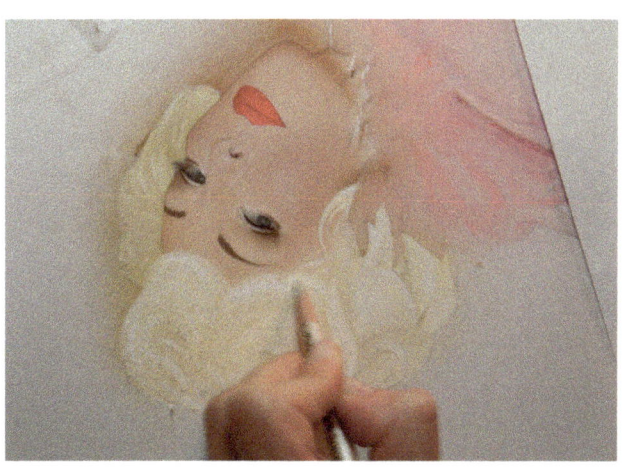

Highlights are reinforced with an eraser.

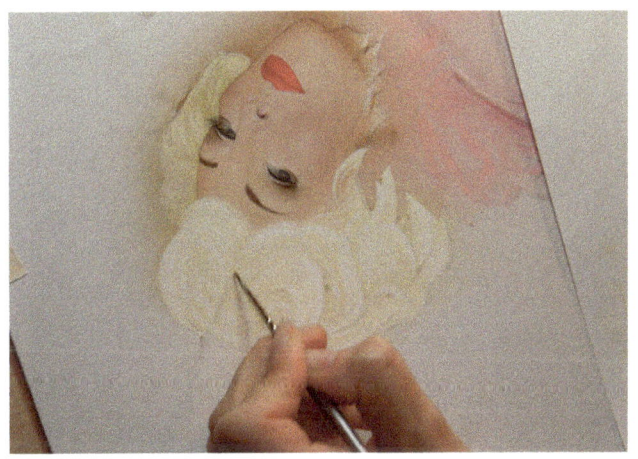

More liquid frisket is "painted" directly over the previous layers of frisket and paint to build depth.

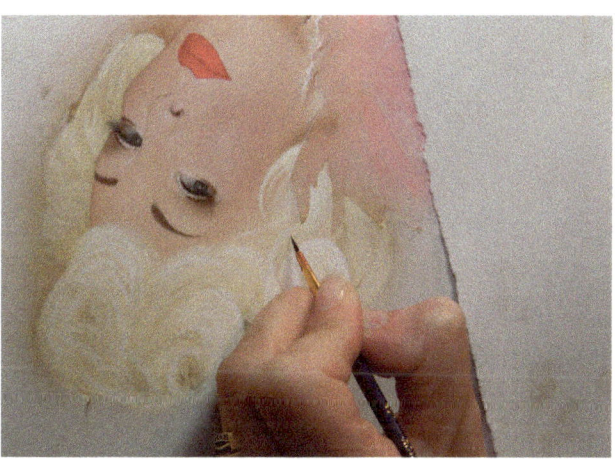

Some of the hardest edged areas of shadow in the hair are created by hand using a fine detail brush and diluted sepia.

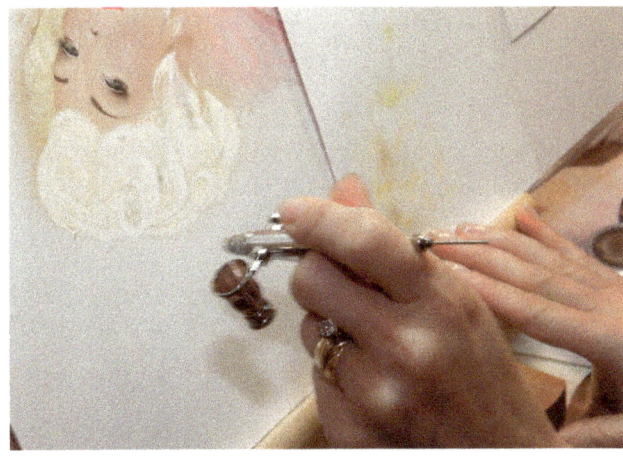

The hair color is sprayed again.

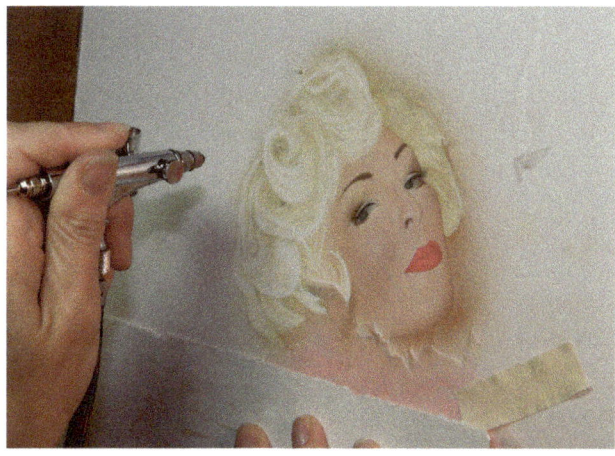

The same diluted sepia is sprayed to create the darker areas at the center of a curl.

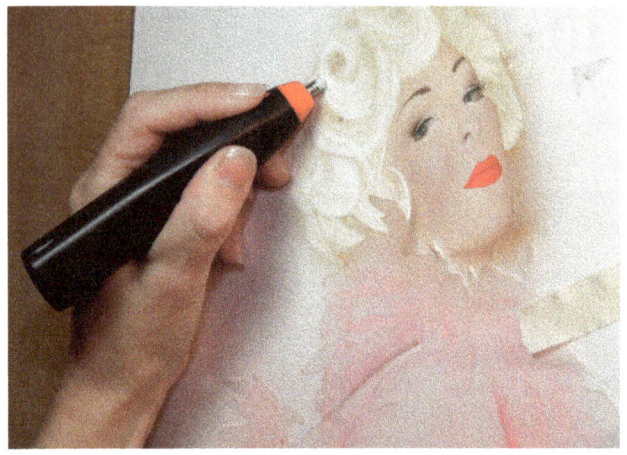

The shape of the curl can now be emphasized by erasing highlights on the outer most strands of hair.

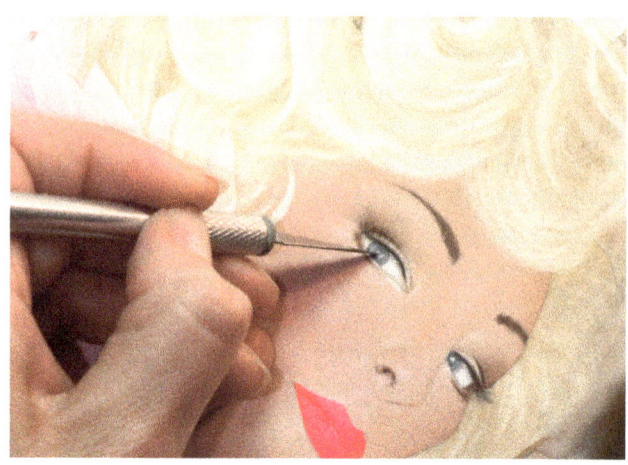

Using an Xacto to define the catch lights of the eyes.

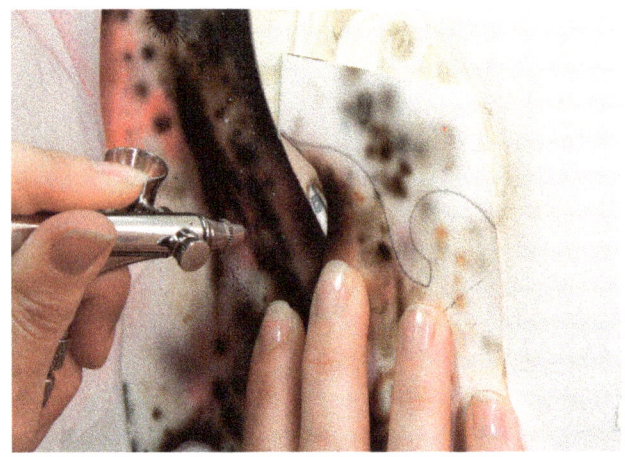

Once the hair is done, I want to go back over some details of the eyes. Two handheld shields are used when darkening the inside corner of the eye.

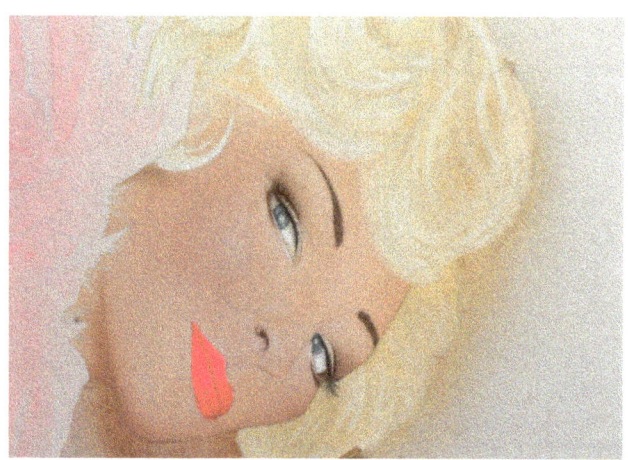

Placing the pupil and highlights just right creates a smoldering eye focused on the viewer.

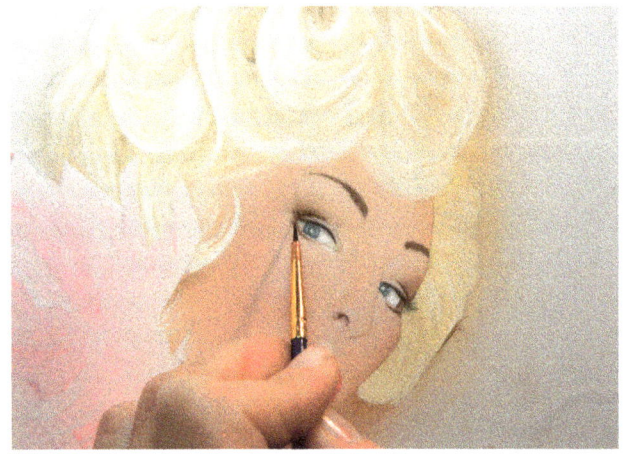

A small detail brush is used to darken the dramatic black eyelashes.

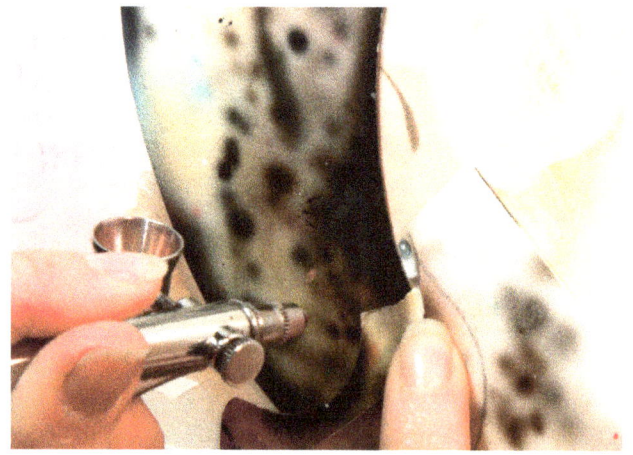

Two shields are used again when darkening the outer corner of the model's left eye.

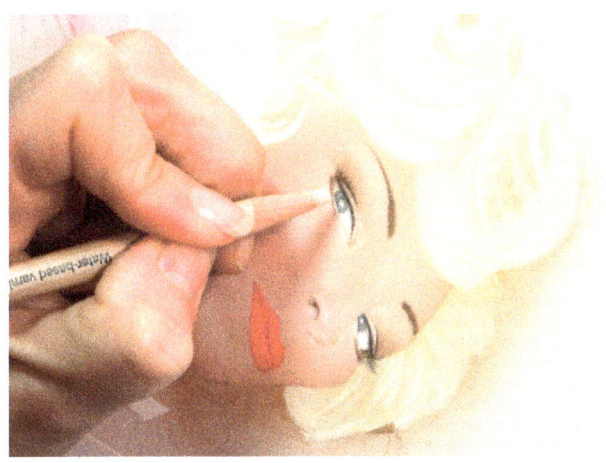

More erasing is needed to emphasize the catch light in the iris. Making this highlight stand out creates the illusion of sparkling moist eyes.

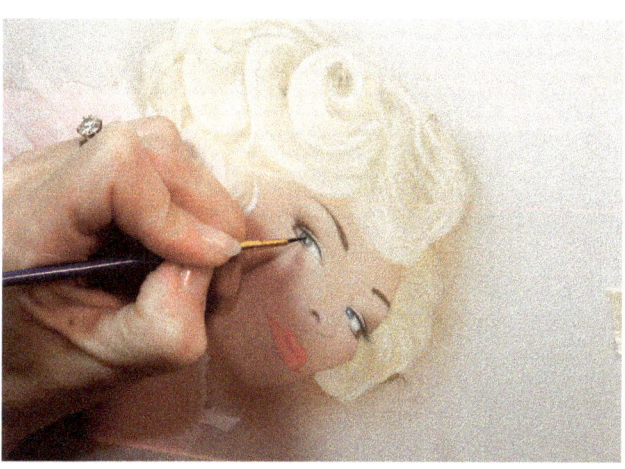

The pupil is painted by hand. Placement is critical to getting her sideways gaze just right.

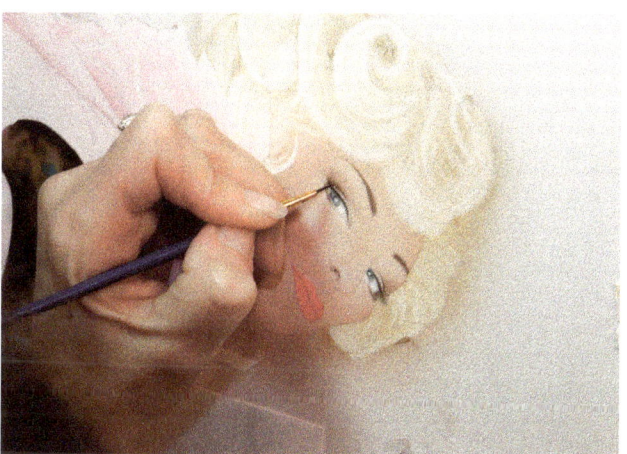

Using a small brush to hand paint the eyelashes, be mindful that some areas appear to clump together as they would naturally. Don't paint them all lined up like the teeth on a comb.

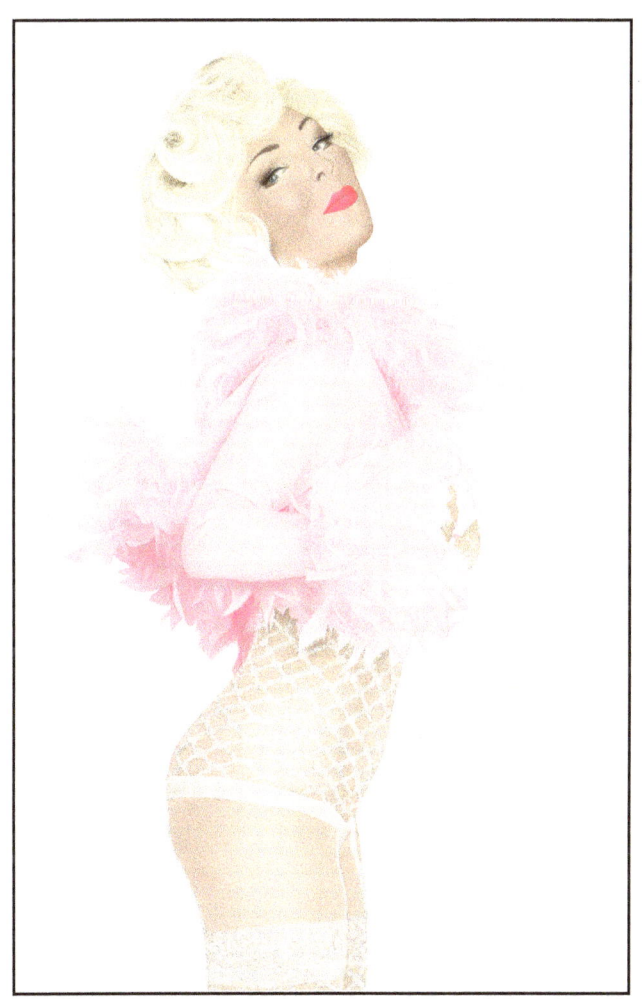

Once the frisket is removed from around the figure, the outer edges need to be "feathered" into the background. Some edges are kept hard while others are lost into the background.

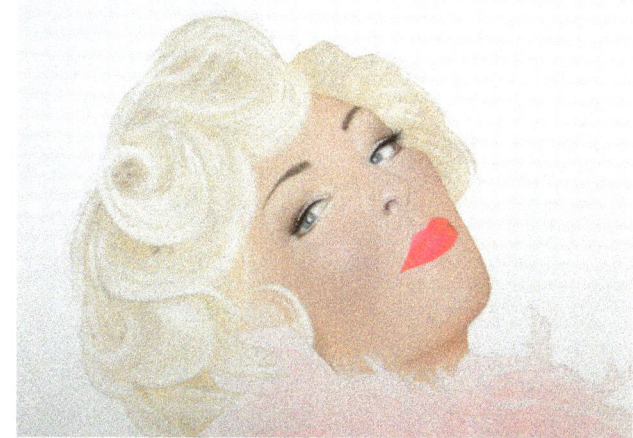

The last few minor adjustments make a huge difference in the final piece. At this point I like to let the painting sit for a few days to see if any other adjustments are needed.

Susan Heidi Q&A

Give us a little background on you, how did you get started in art, and are pin-ups the main focus of the work you do?

I've been doing pin-ups for three years. In 2006 I did my first full pin-up. I have always liked portraiture. Before doing my first pin-up, I did black and white portraits with charcoal or pencil as a hobby. Then I started coloring in those sketches with watercolors. I've always been fond of the glamour era of the 1940's and 1950's…. so pretty soon I wanted to do full-figure paintings like the artists did back then. I took Dru Blair's portrait class to learn how to use the airbrush and create photorealistic images. I highly recommend his classes.

Currently I sell prints through my website (www.susanheidi.com) and at trade shows and galleries. I usually keep the original paintings, but original studies and sketches are sold at the shows. I do commissions working from photographs. Sometimes a client wants an image of his wife or girlfriend, or a company wants a pin-up for their logo.

My work also lends itself really well to the hot rod, pin-up, and kustom kulture shows.

Who inspires you, who are some of the artists you look up to?

When I started to study pin-ups, the work of Alberto Vargas stood out to me. His style is different from Elvgren's - there's a sensitivity in his use of watercolors that I relate to. I started studying his work and found a book that had a how-to section written by Vargas. I like the way he used washes of color and built up layers of paint. He typically used an airbrush to finish off paintings, but when he went to Esquire he used the airbrush more, to speed up production.

How do you find the models, typically who does the photographs that you use for reference?

I work with professional pin-up models as reference for my paintings. They are all very much into the retro lifestyle and have studied the hair, make-up, clothing, and poses that make a classic pin-up. Either I take the photos or I have their photographer take the pictures, usually to my specifications.

Novice artists sometimes have trouble rendering believable skin tones, how do you achieve life-like skin tones?

Well first, I pre-mix my paints and dilute them with water to create washes. I don't use anything directly out of the bottle. I mix light and dark skin colors first. The light is burnt sienna, with a little alizarin for the red, a little red violet, and cobalt blue (blue is the opposite of orange so it knocks down the saturation and makes it more natural).

Then I'll take some of the light skin tone and grey it down with cobalt blue and a little violet, and use that for shadow areas. I'll usually mix the light and dark skin colors right on the board by over-spraying them for mid-tones.

These are retro pin-ups. They have a rosy soft skin tone that goes with the feel of the era, so I work toward that color to get the vintage look.

Paint, which type of paint do you use and why?

The paints for this demonstration are all transparent acrylics by Winsor & Newton, Liquitex, or Aeroflash. Sometimes I'll use watercolors or oil paints to achieve a different look. I

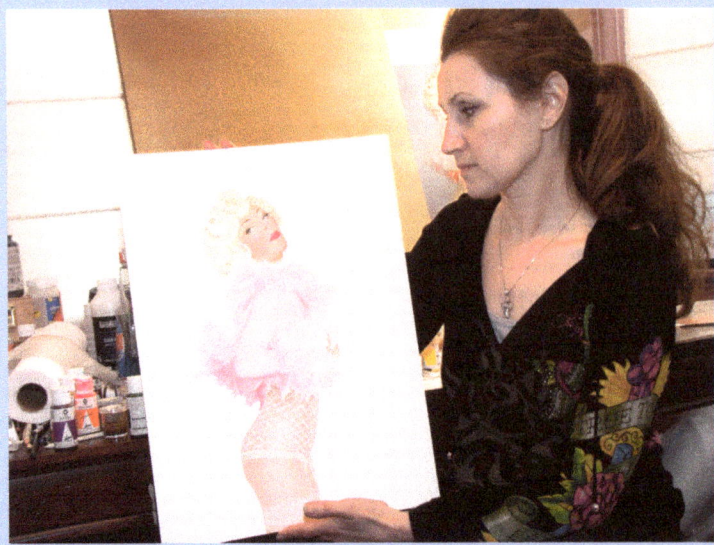

Testimony to the idea that you can make a major career change as an adult, Susan Heidi now makes her living as a full time artist.

Susan Heidi Q&A

like the feel of transparent paints, but they are very unforgiving.

How did you learn to mix your own colors?

It's intuitive for me, but I suppose I understand the color wheel from science class, knowing what you get when you mix colors. I used watercolors first, and mixed those to see what I could get. More formally, I took Dru Blair's class which includes a very thorough treatment of color theory. Chris Saper is a portrait artist whose book on painting portraits was very helpful. It goes into great detail about color theory.

Faces, how do you create such beautiful faces?

I focus on the expression; the eyes, the mouth, and how the model holds her head, all work to bring the image to life. I pay a lot of attention to each of the slightest little curves and angles to get it just right.

Are there some rules or guidelines you follow in terms of your compositions?

I try to pull the viewer through the image. In classic art everything is based on the triangle. I try to keep that in mind when laying out the composition for a painting. I'm also concerned with where the viewer's eye enters the painting.

Why did you pick this image to paint, you talked about the texture of the body stocking, the tension in the pose, the ambiguity?

I usually paint the full figure from head to toe for a pin-up because that was traditional for 1940's and 50's pin-ups. The time constraints for this demonstration limited me to painting only part of the figure. I felt that with all the texture going on in this piece it would demonstrate the techniques that would be used to create a full figure pin-up.

I also like the come hither expression on her face and the tension in her arms as they hold the feather boa. The composition flows because your eye has different things to look at. Her face draws you in first, then the feathers draw your eye down through the rest of the painting.

What equipment do you use?

My airbrush is an Iwata hp sb with a side feed cup that I can switch around because I'm left handed. The The paints I use are acrylic Windsor and Newton, Liquitex, or Aeroflash. I like acrylics because I can use them like watercolors, but they make it a little easier to build up to brighter colors.

Do you use other media like hand brushes to add detail or achieve effects that are hard to do with an airbrush?

An airbrush can be used to achieve just about any effect when used freehand or with frisket and shields, but I'm not a purist when it comes to using the airbrush. I enjoy doing the under painting by hand and some little details are quicker to do with a small paint brush. As long as the edges are controlled properly (soft, hard, or lost), it doesn't really matter which technique is used to achieve the effect.

What makes a good pin-up painting?

For my focus, which is the retro pin-up, it's important to have the right expression and pose. You need that soft vintage look, and that is what I try to achieve

Ten words of advice for someone starting out?

With aspiring artists in any area, the big thing is to slow down and take your time during each phase of painting. You'll end up moving quicker with your skill level. Essentially, you can speed up by slowing down, and then getting things just the way you want them. Think before you put anything on the paper.

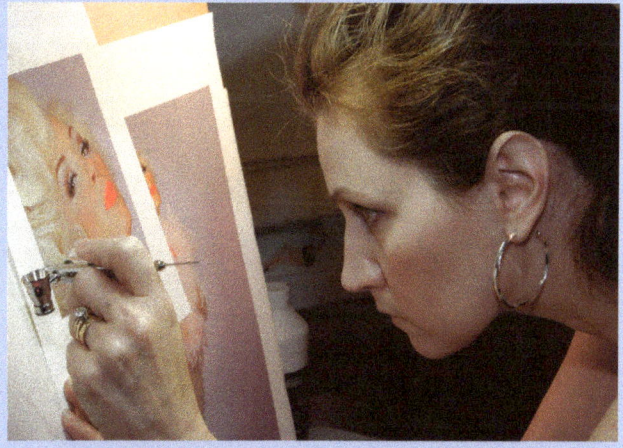

The word intense does not begin to describe Susan at work.

Chapter Nine

Vince Goodeve

Devil's Playground

For this project I flew to Idaho where my friend, and client, Steve lives. I left home with nothing more than a pencil, which was promptly confiscated at customs. With no computer, vinyl cutter or other luxuries, I proceeded to embark on an adventure of hunter-gatherer. Securing equipment and product indigenous to the area became my first task. Next came the sketches and layouts of the complex graphics that would cover Steve's Big Truck from one end to the other.

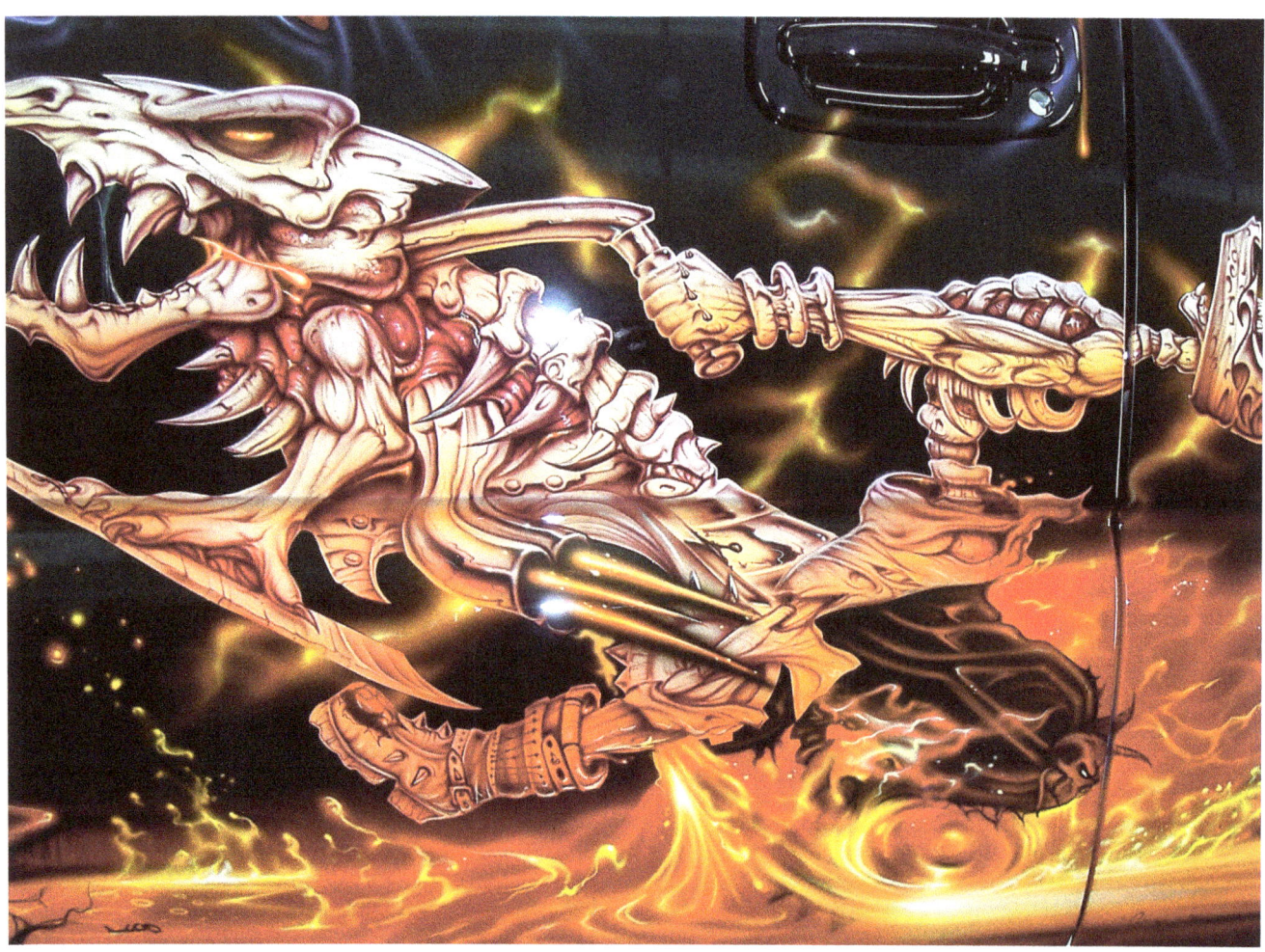

Here's a finished shot of the driver's side door with our boney gleeful jockey riding his hellish creation. The piece is approximately ten feet long, and I think it should make a great visual statement just sitting at a stop light.

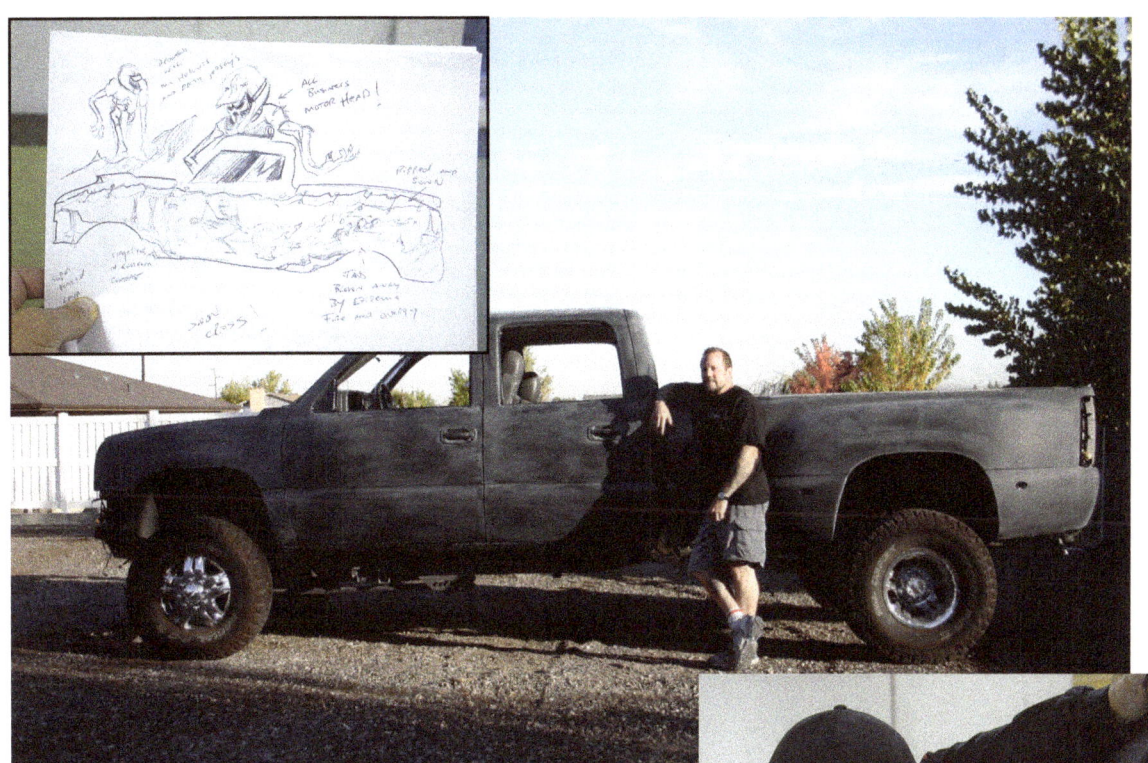

Say hello to my little friend. This is how the vehicle came to me, ready to paint thanks to Todd and his buds. At first the square footage of the project overwhelmed me, but I got over it. I start with the preliminary sketches and layouts, keeping them loose and basic as usual.

Next, I lay down application tape, being sure to remove any loose spots or bubbles with a squeegee. Now, I sketch my first element on the truck.

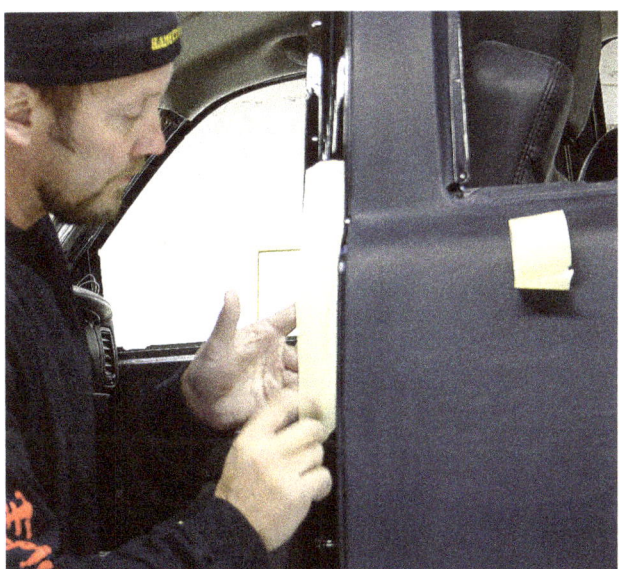

I start by taping the door jams and fender wells to avoid creeping overspray that could enter the clean black interior.

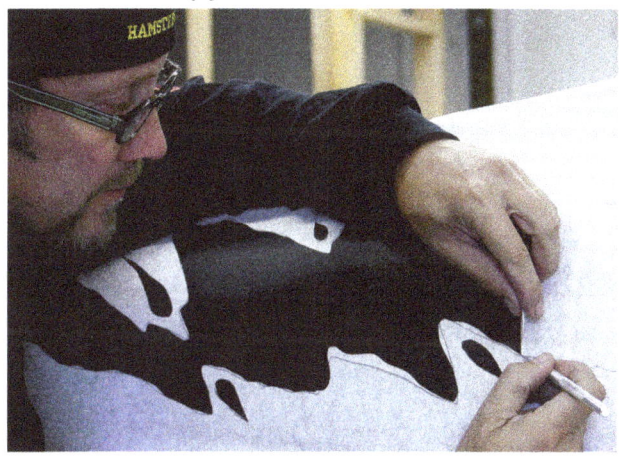

With a # 11 x-acto knife I carefully cut out the areas to be exposed. Don't hulk out and cut deep...

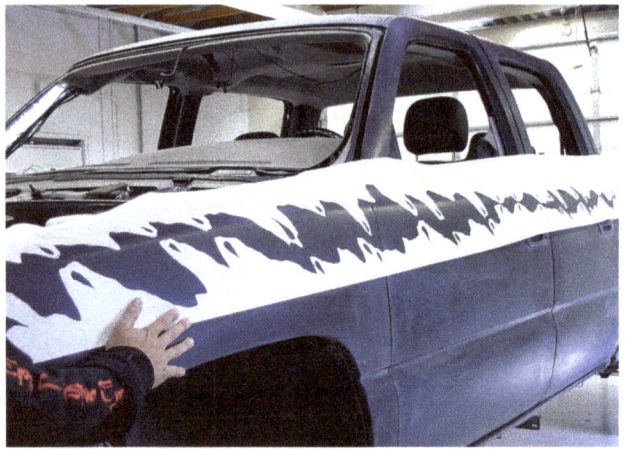

...be sure to use new blades and just cut the tape. The sharp blades give you more control.

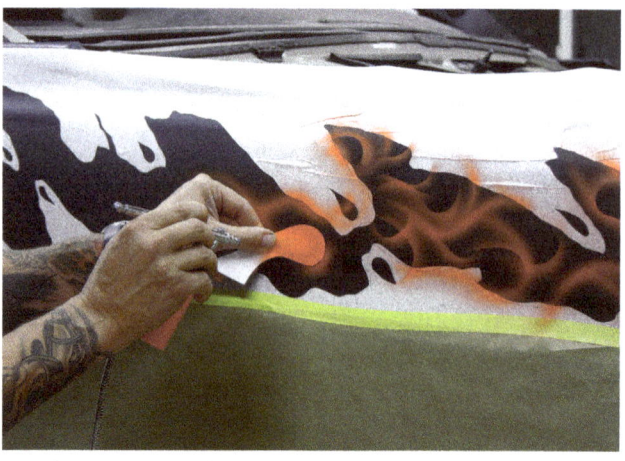

In this step I use bright orange from my mixing bank. It's opaque and builds color without the need for white under-painting. Using a French curve ellipse, I create random background texture.

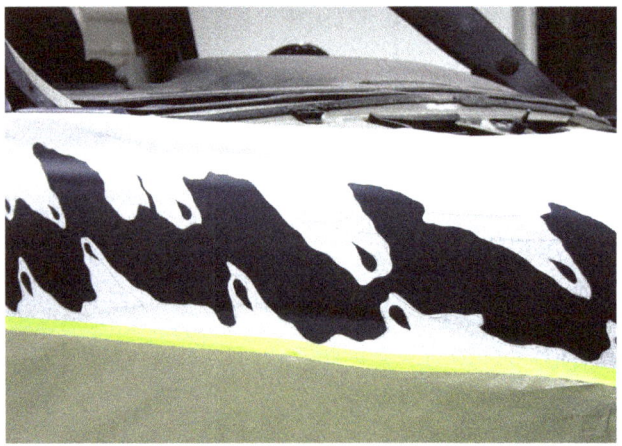

Here is a close-up of the cut-out application tape and masking, this will give us a nice crisp edge to work off of later.

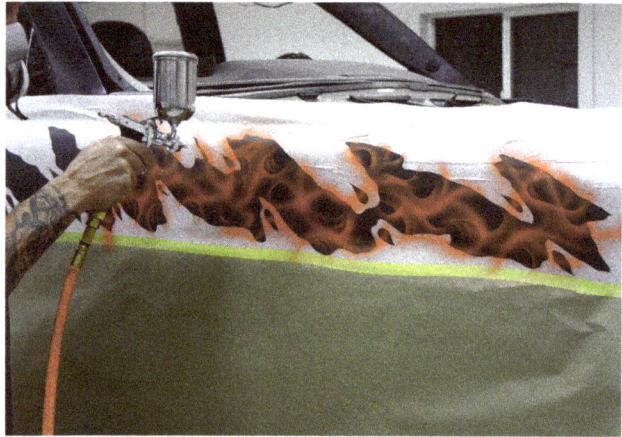

Next, I create a candy mixture and reduce it to a sprayable viscosity of about 2:1. Next, I mist a light coat of the red candy on top of my orange shape, using a detail gun, to knock it back in intensity.

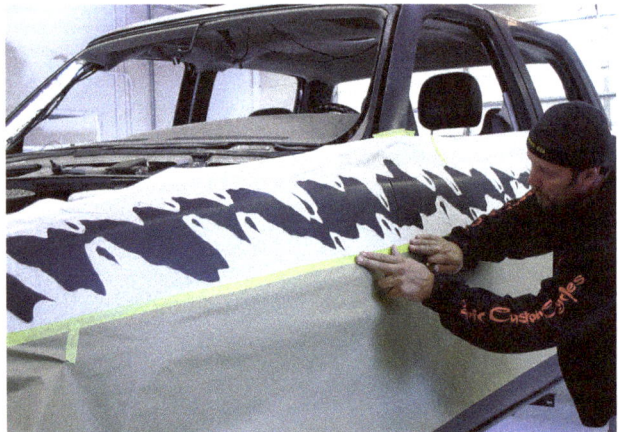

Using 24 inch body shop paper, I mask the outside edges to avoid overspray. Don't underestimate the creeping ability of overspray.

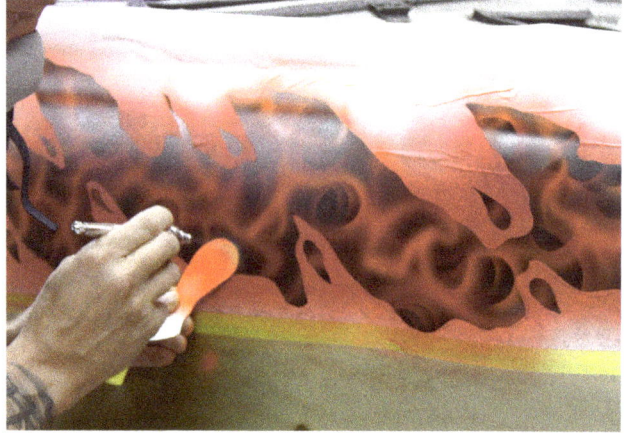

I repeat the process seen at the top of the page with the curve template and the same orange. The orange I applied earlier is darker now due to the candy red topcoat applied in the last step.

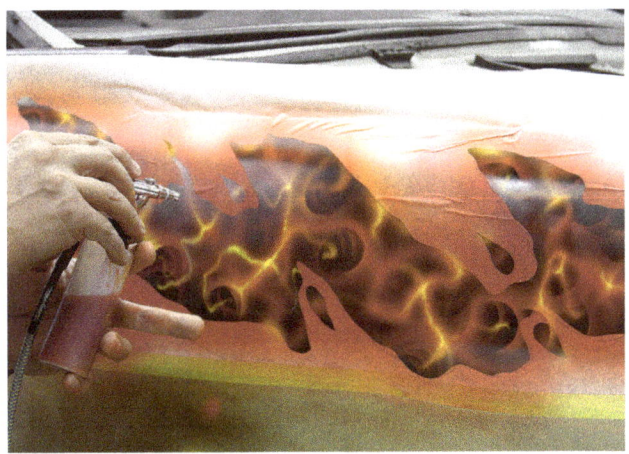

Using opaque yellow I add light-energy, winding the bright color into the tunnels I've created earlier with my template.

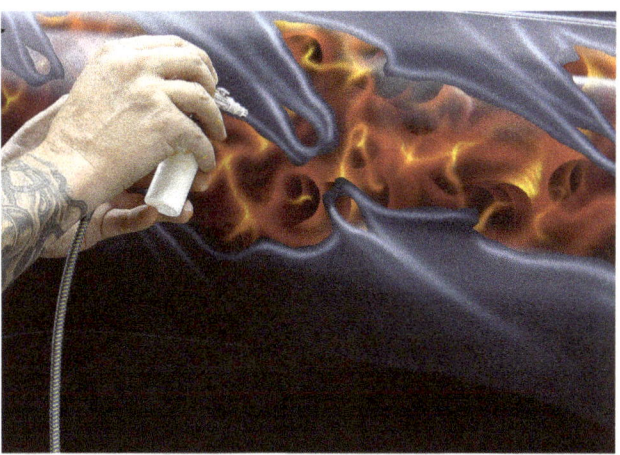

Using pure white basecoat, I then airbrush the outer texture, to create the "stretching" sheet metal, bearing in mind a constant light source.

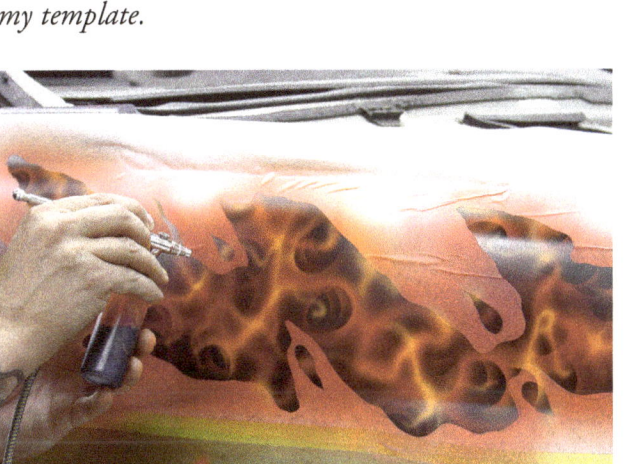

Another coat of DMX, but this time I use an orange mixture, reduced exactly like our earlier application of orange.

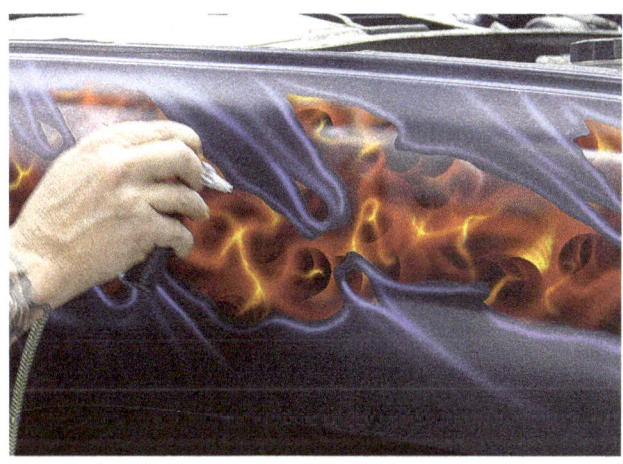

A transparent purple wash over the white is a good compliment to the reds and oranges within the tear. I give all the white a nice even mist coat.

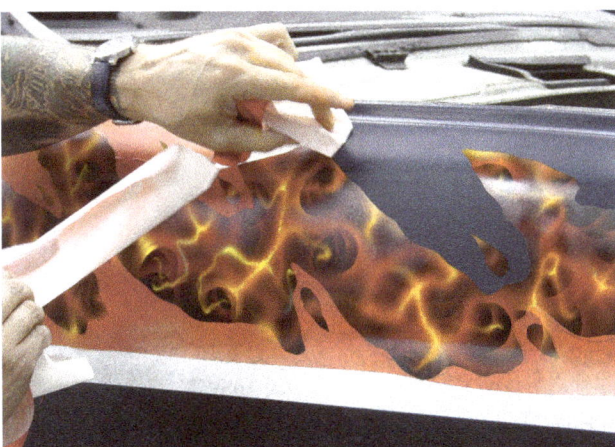

Now, I remove the masking system. Always be sure to get any adhesive off the black basecoat by using PPG's DX 320 wipe.

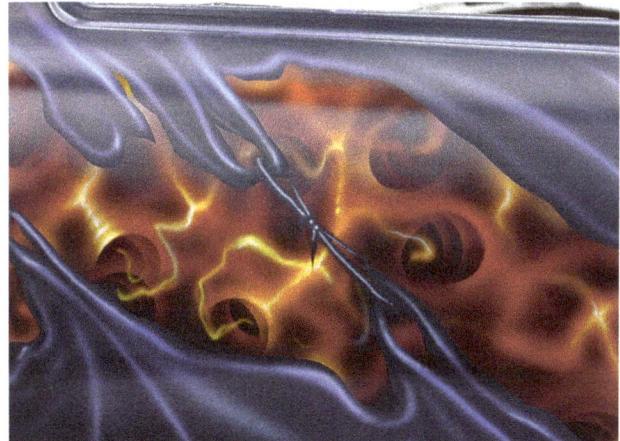

Using pure black for extreme contrast against the graphic, I create the stitching that holds the tear together. Going back in with white, I pop a few highlights onto the appropriate parts of the ripples in the sheet metal.

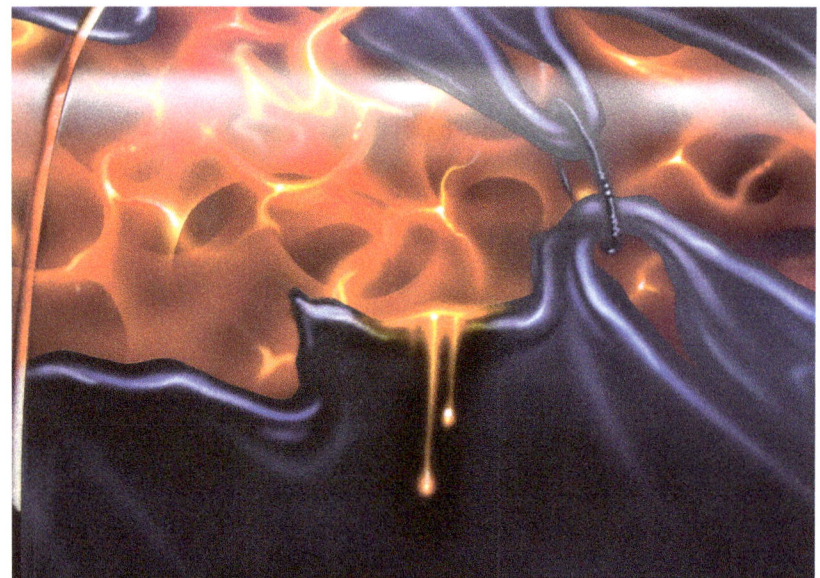

Here is a close-up of some of the eye candy, namely the dripping lava and "stitching" that holds the tear together.

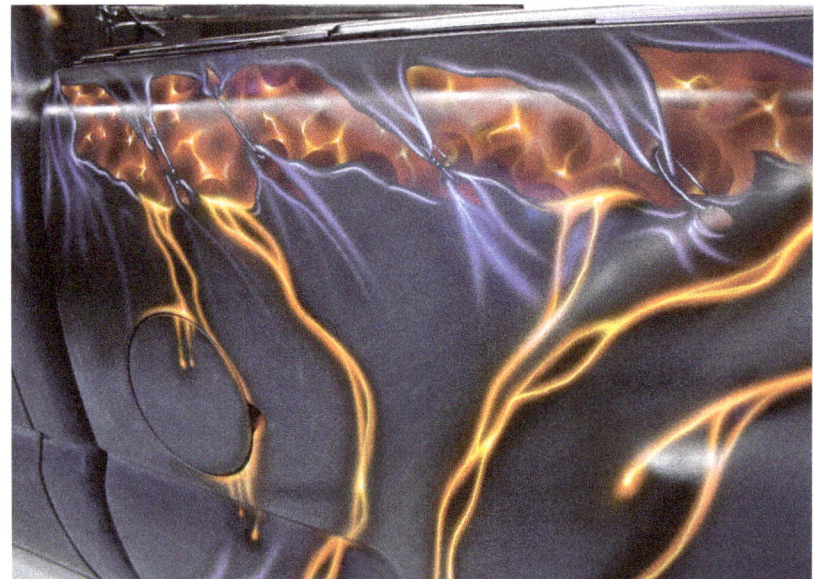

These are the lava flows that run down the quarter panels, I try to follow the contours of the vehicle just like liquid would flow naturally.

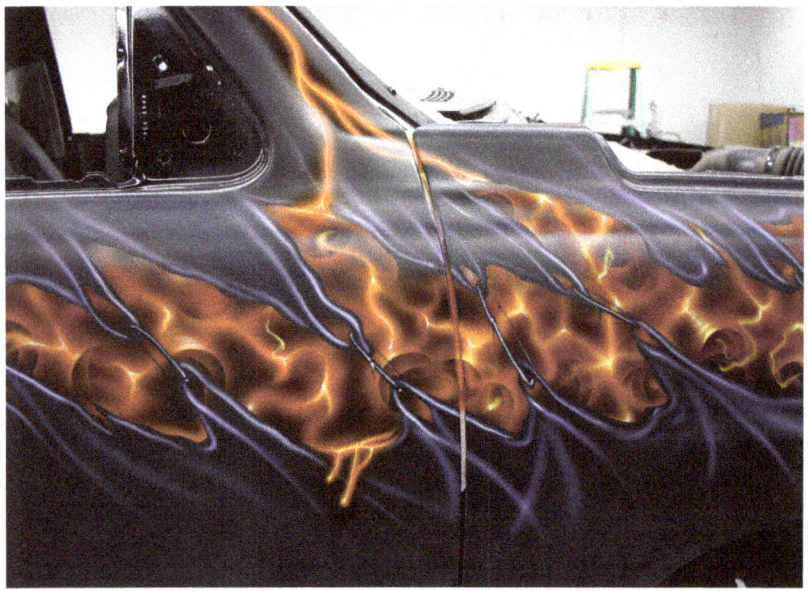

I also run the lava down the door pillars to sort of add some light and color to the top of the truck.

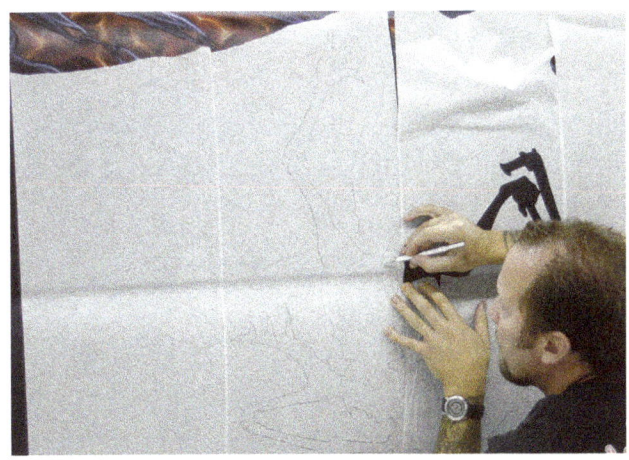

For composition sake I want to project my original sketch on the side of the truck in order to get a feel for placement and size. I use a 24 inch application tape to mask the vicinity of my first image.

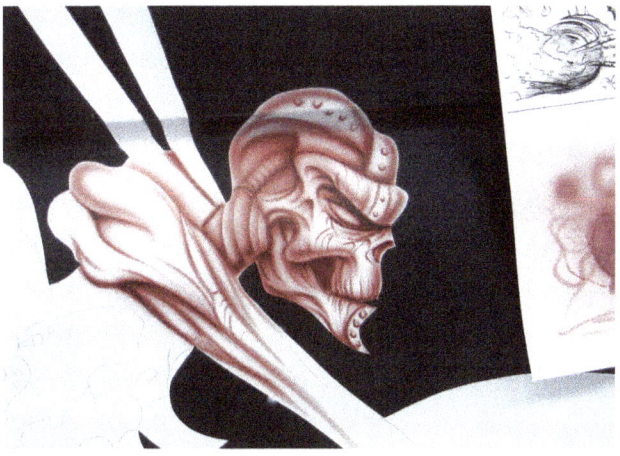

I start cutting out my malevolent friend with a transparent maroon mix (trans red 75%, purple 20% and green 5%). Working off my original design, I begin at the headlight.

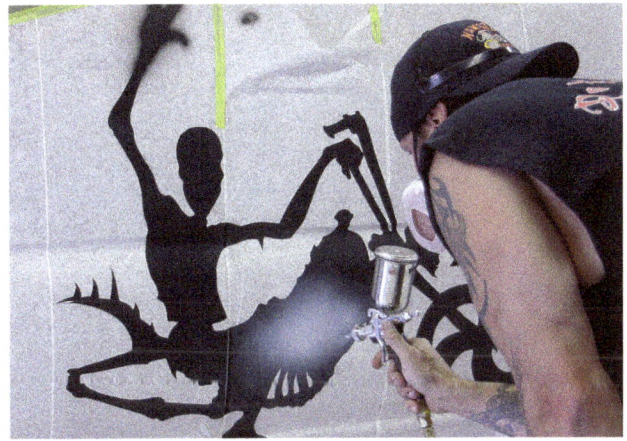

I then use a large format spray gun and apply a medium dry coat of white to the area I've exposed in the application tape mask system.

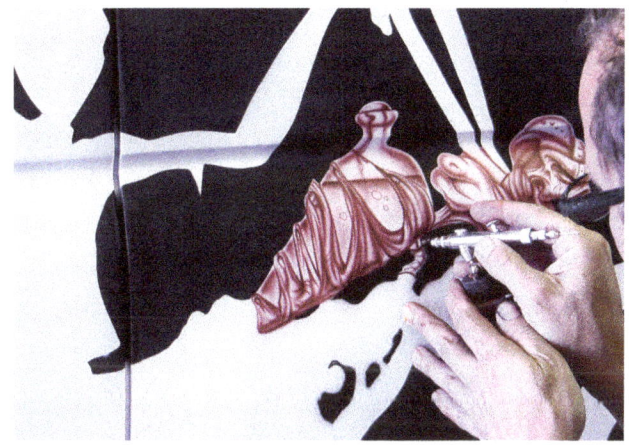

Here I am developing the texture of the sinew that holds the fuel tank. The beauty of not having a ton of reference lines is that you can create on the fly, sort of designing as you go.

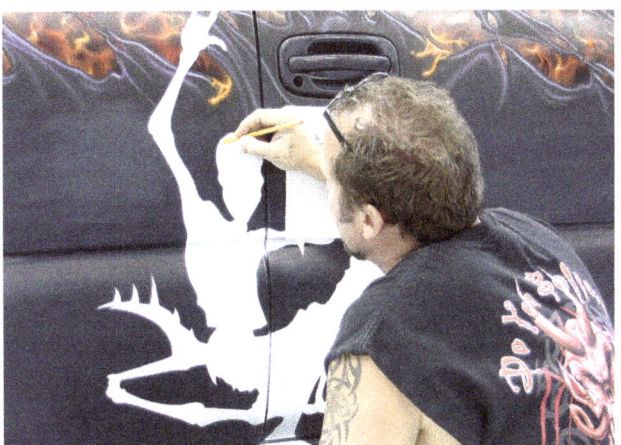

Using a light lead pencil (HB) I draw in the major components of my sketch, leaving the fine detail to be created when I'm actually airbrushing.

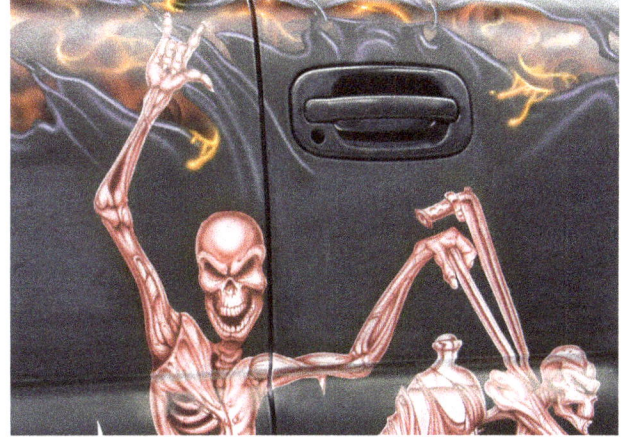

Our demonic daredevil emerges complete with fashion-conscious vest. I like the way his high five hand works in front of the other graphic elements.

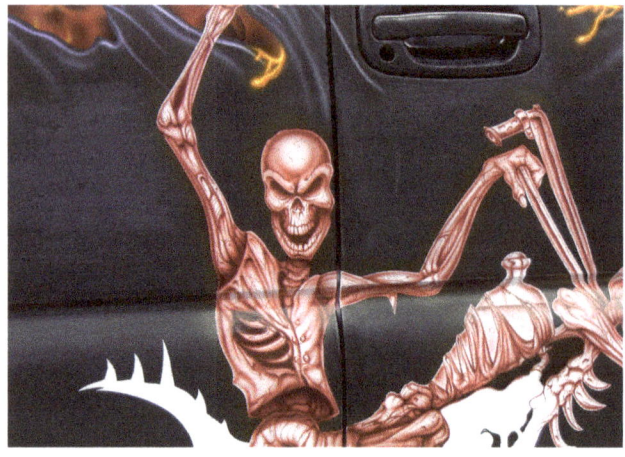

A progression shot carrying on into the legs. I'm constantly flicking my concentration over the other areas I've worked, making adjustments for balance in the shadow areas.

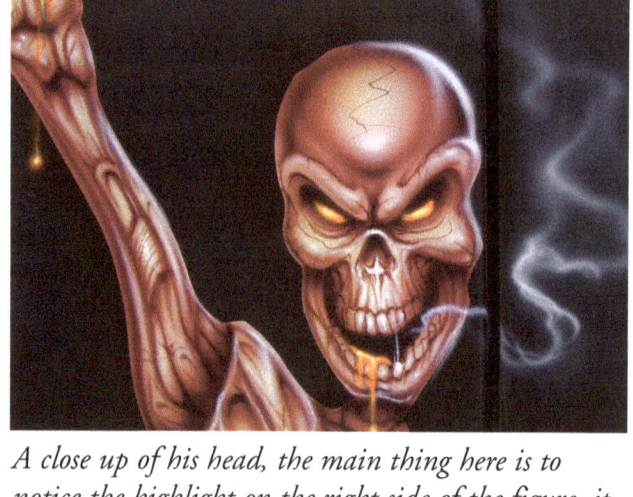

A close up of his head, the main thing here is to notice the highlight on the right side of the figure, it helps lose the cut out look, or masked white underpainting.

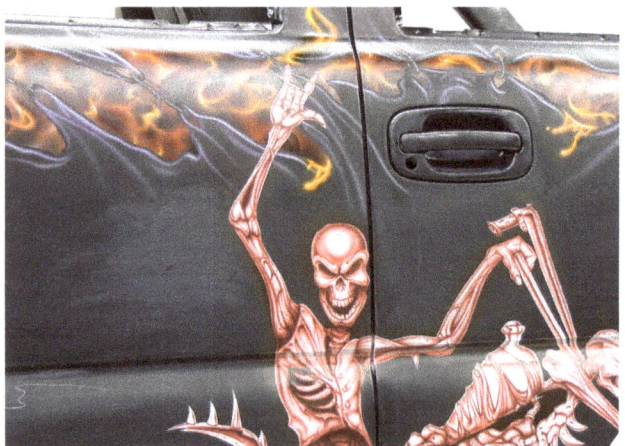

This shows a progression into the rest of the image. Just remember, be sure to make up enough of your color to last through the whole project.

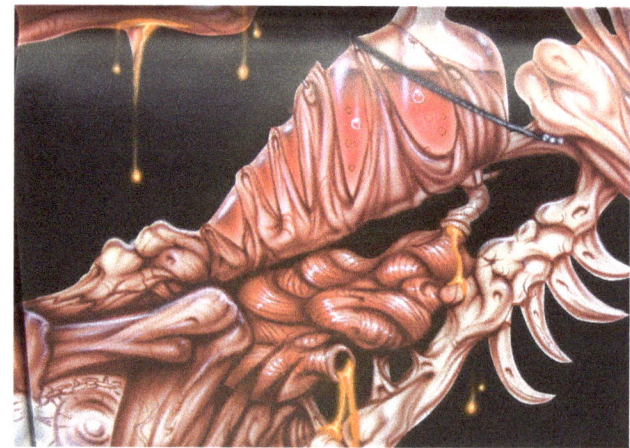

I use the lava to give a little life to the heart of the motor.

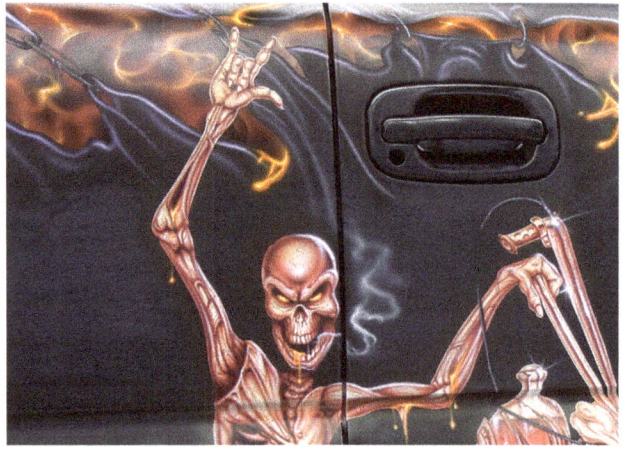

Using white, I under-paint the burnout and the cigar smoke. I then give the "Bike Thing" and the sinewy specter a case of heartburn by adding heat and lava in the key areas.

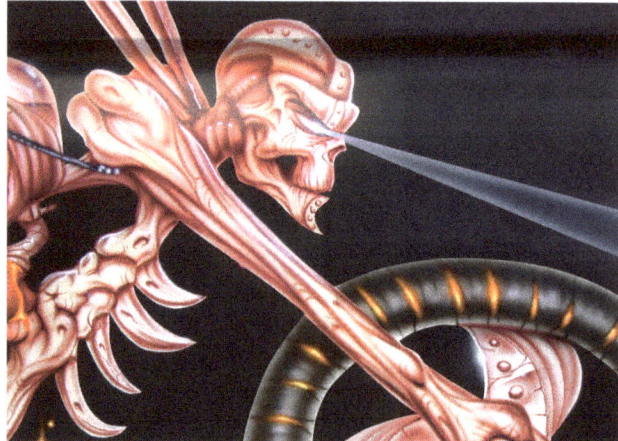

Slashed tires reveal a molten center. Just another point of interest that strays from the norm.

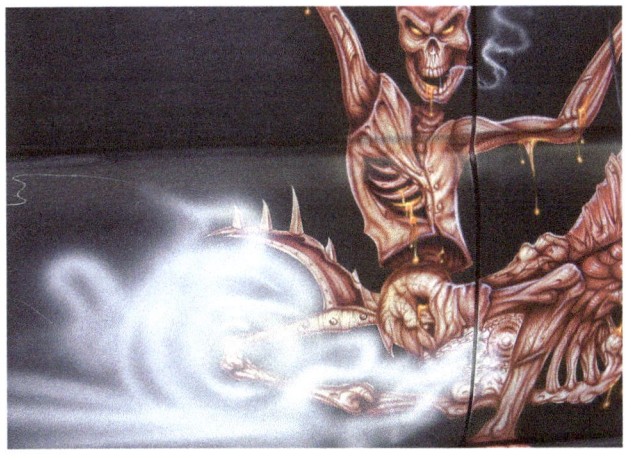
Using white basecoat, I suggest motion in the drive line and the rear tire.

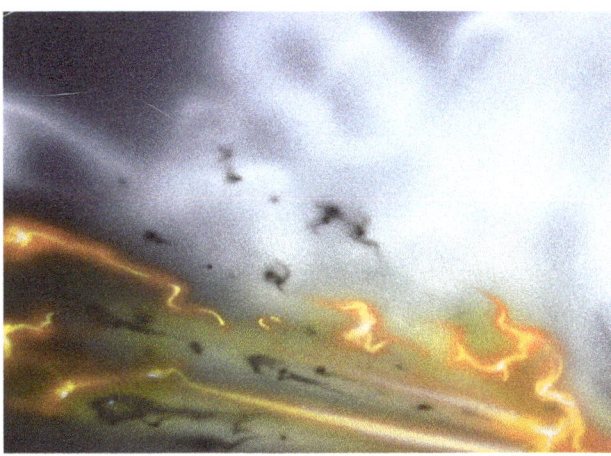
Details are extremely important, note the little things like the flying, frying rubber.

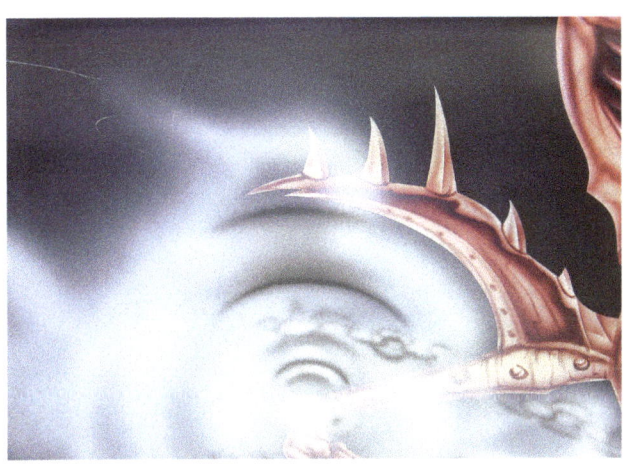
Dark grey is used to create the illusion that the misshapen tire and chain are in motion.

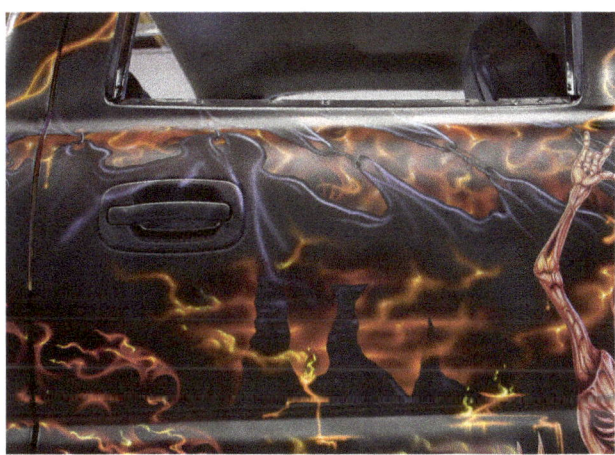
Using darks and lights in silhouette, I create a hellish panorama. The strange rock formations contain personal hidden requests from the client.

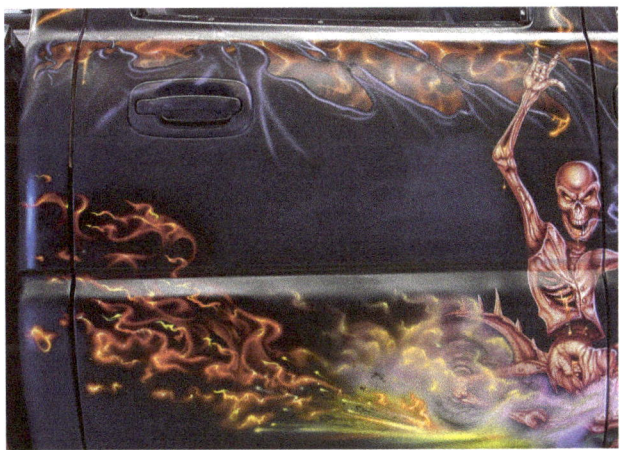
I then heat up the burnout using the same principles mentioned at the beginning of the chapter.

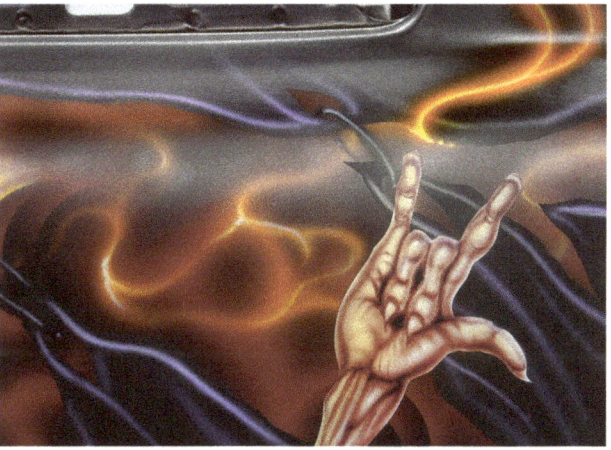
Hang Ten, a close-up of the creatures hand against the torn or ripped graphic.

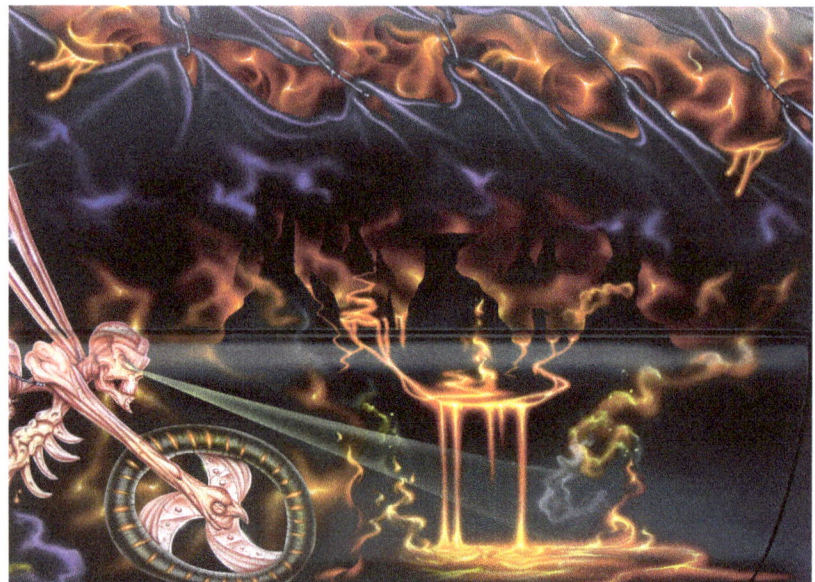

I use a series of loose templates, cut from Bristol board, to create the mountains in the background - along with the lava (which forms pools and rivers), as well as a sense of heat.

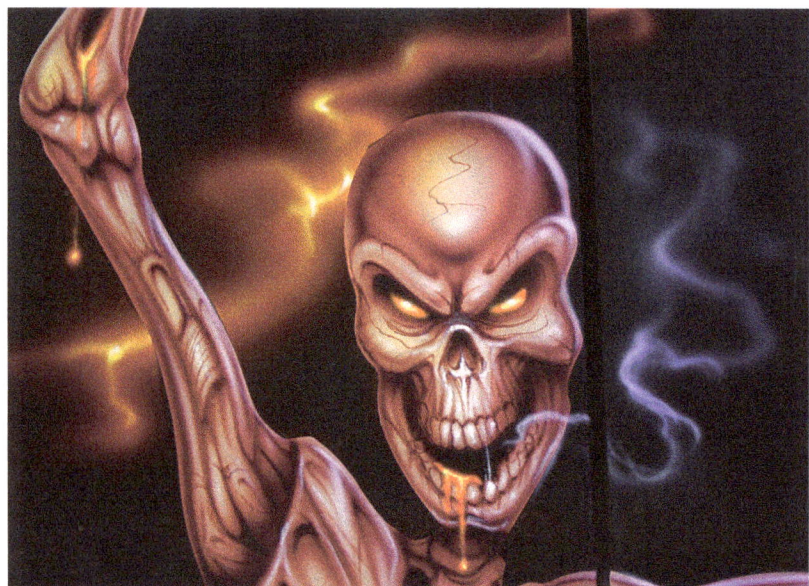

By adding darks against lights and lights against darks behind my figure, I lose the pasted look.

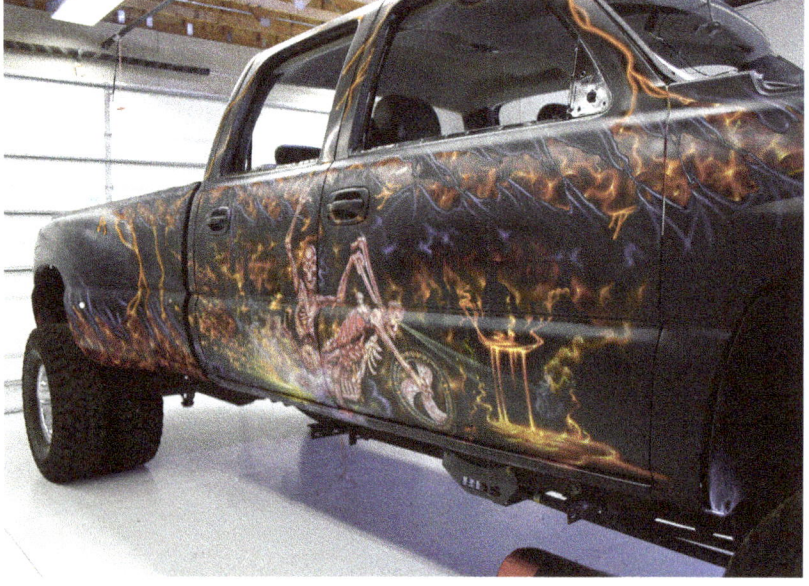

This is an overall shot of the passenger side. It's a lot of real estate to cover with an airbrush.

The next sequence reflects the client's fascination with flying up extremely steep mountains at high velocity on snow machines. Generally speaking, the color sequences are similar to the burnout, but with a few twists. So I begin by taping off with application tape.

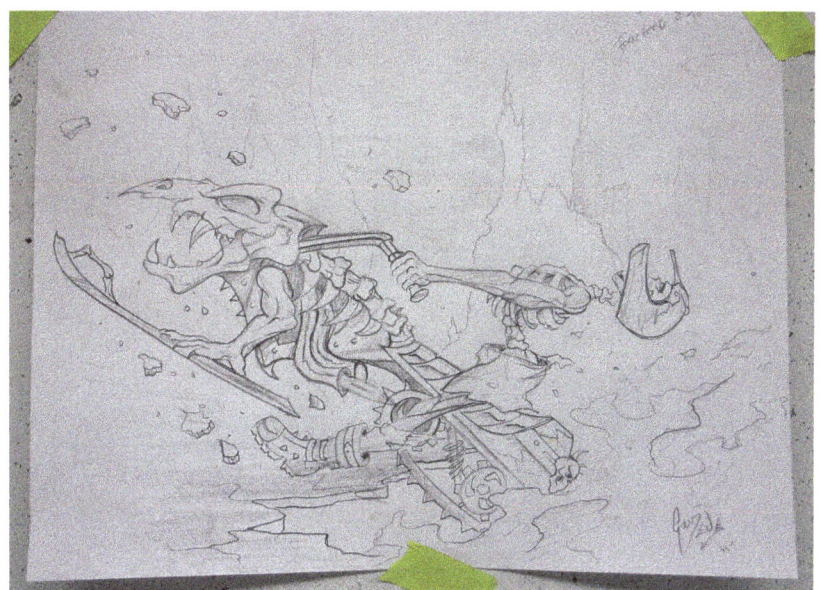

Using the # 11 X-acto I cut out the outer edge of my design. Just be cautious not to press too hard and damage the underlying basecoat. Sharp blades are a must.

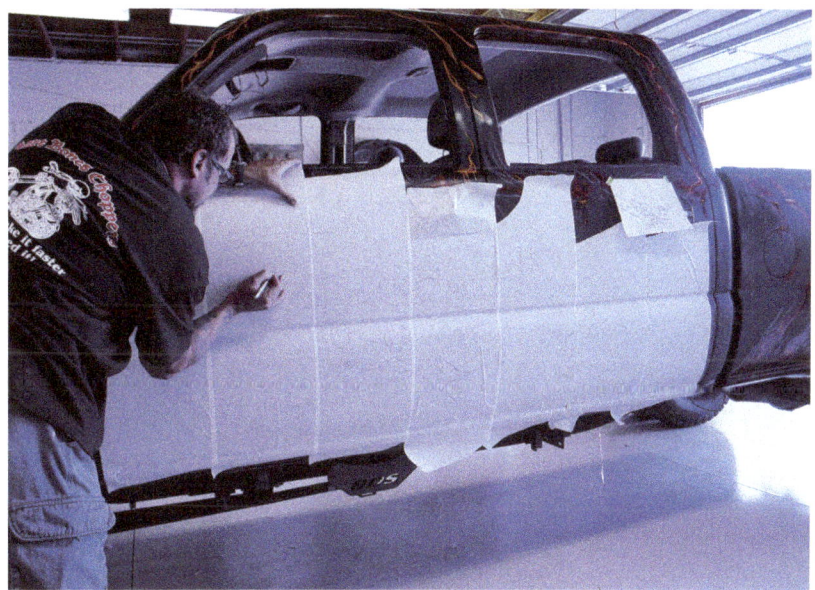

A medium-light basecoat of white will do the trick. I use a large format gun for this process. Be sure to pay attention to safety by wearing your respirator.

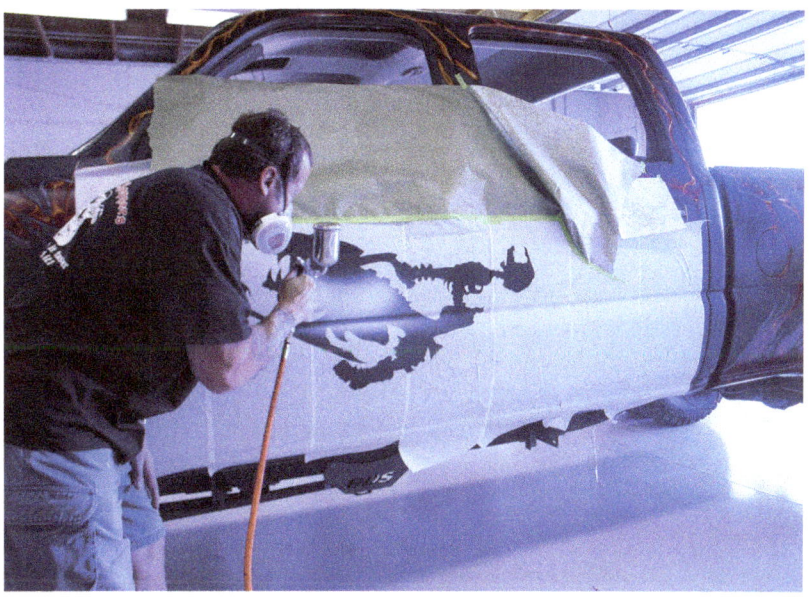

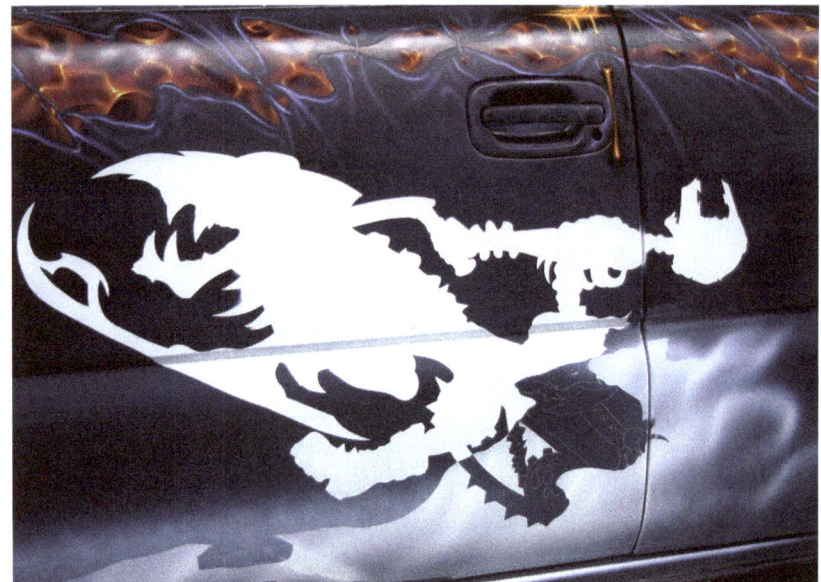

I remove the application tape revealing the silhouette of the image. Notice that I've left the back of the sled dark against a light background, this will really help with the illusion of heat later on in the project.

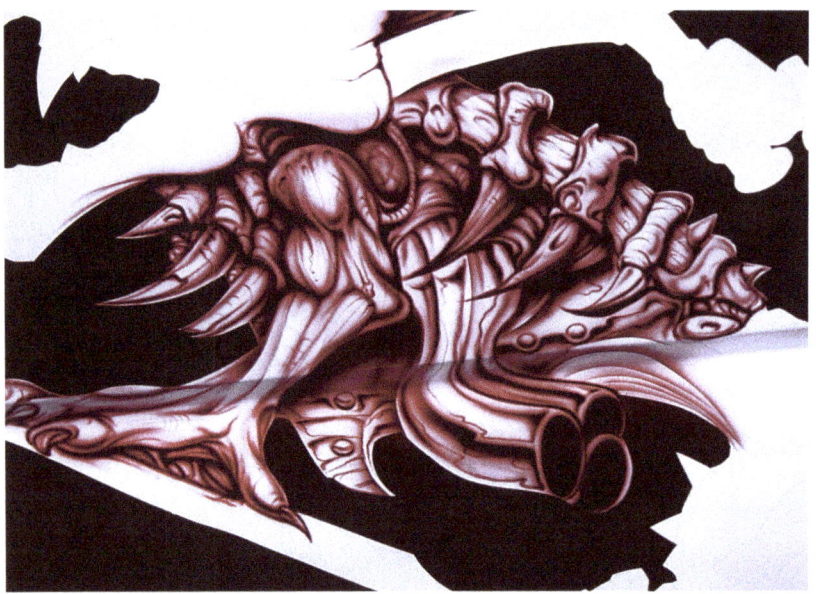

I develop the details in the same manner as the chopper in the previous steps, using a mix (75% red 20% purple 5% green).

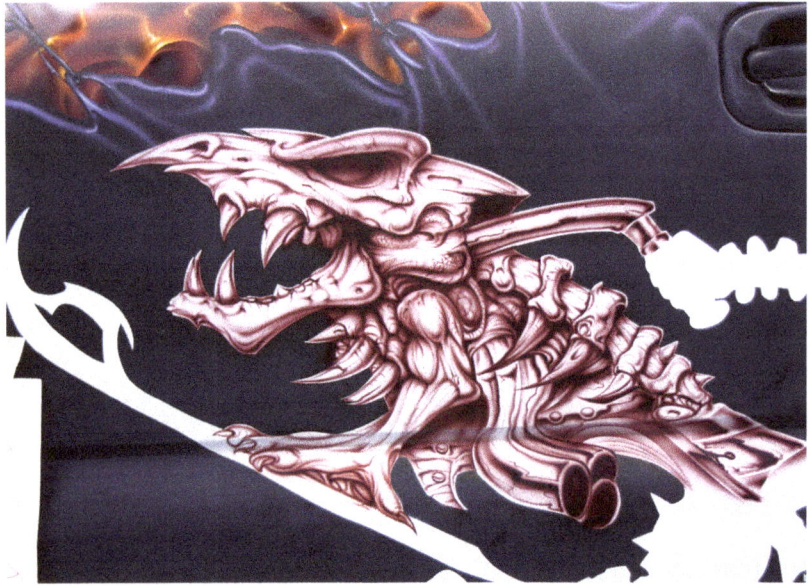

I continue airbrushing in all the details as I go, just letting my imagination run wild.

I add some more elements like guts and flesh to the sled, as well as heat in the exhaust pipes.

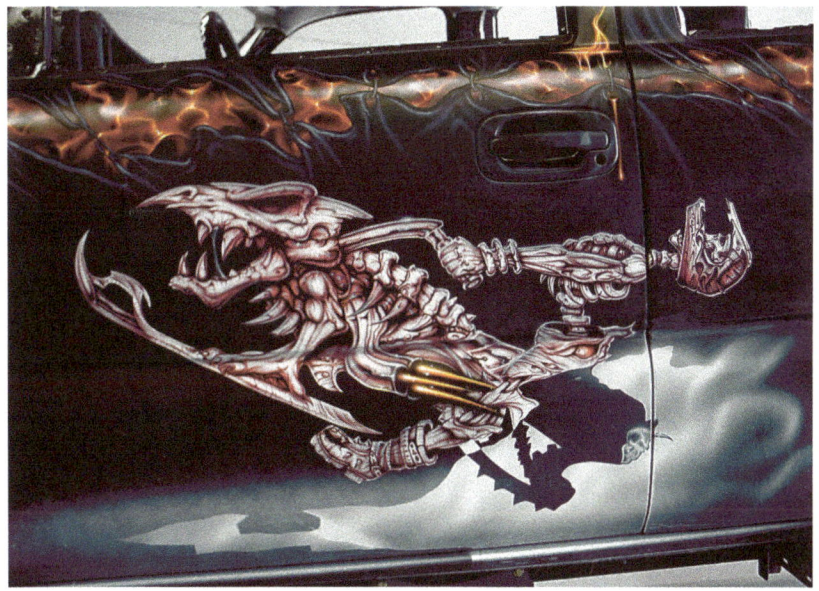

Using the transparent colors and sequences for heat seen in the previous segment, I create a wicked rooster tail to suggest horse power and movement.

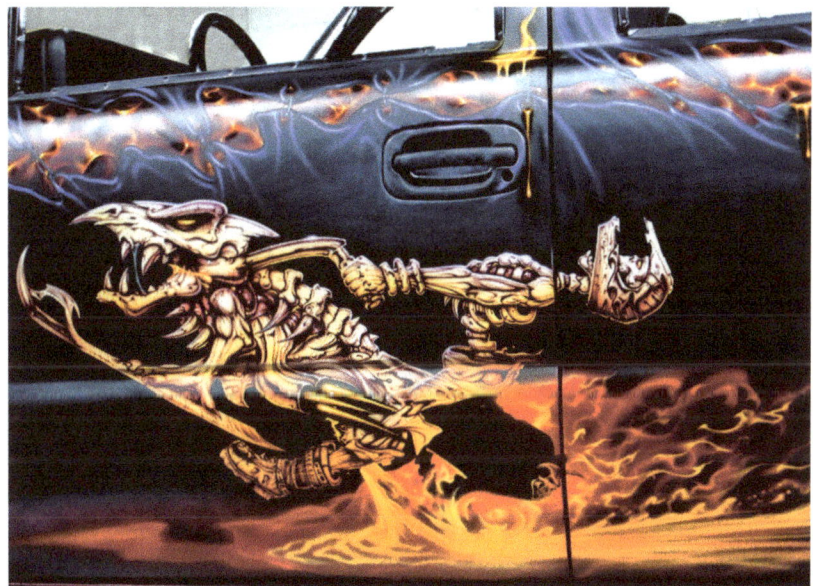

To emphasize the heat from below, I create a secondary light source from above. I choose purple because it's a perfect compliment to the oranges and reds. To do this I spray a trans-purple wash to the top side of my design. I simply reduce trans-purple basecoat and spray a light mist coat from about 8-12 inches, watching for even coverage.

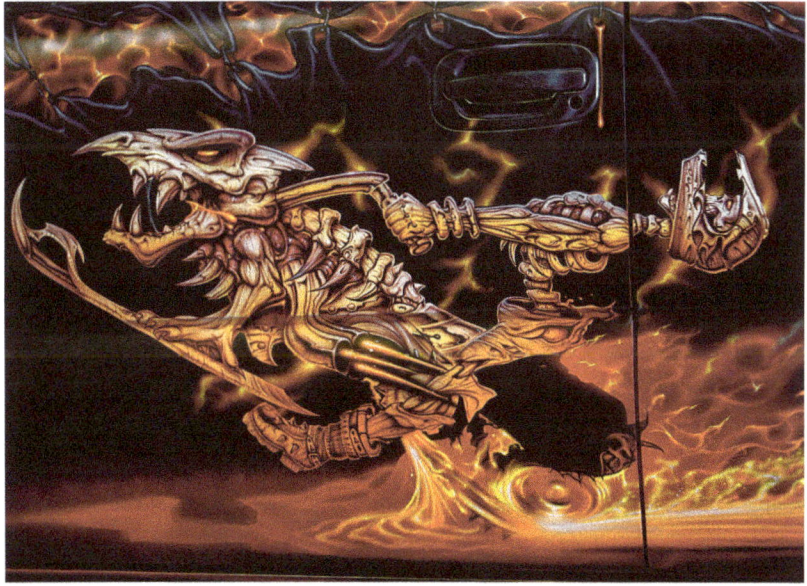

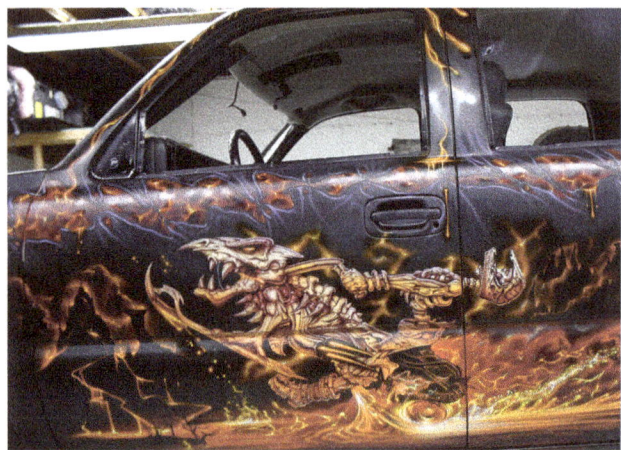

Next, I complete the background in the same manner as the other side of the truck with lava flows and strange scenery.

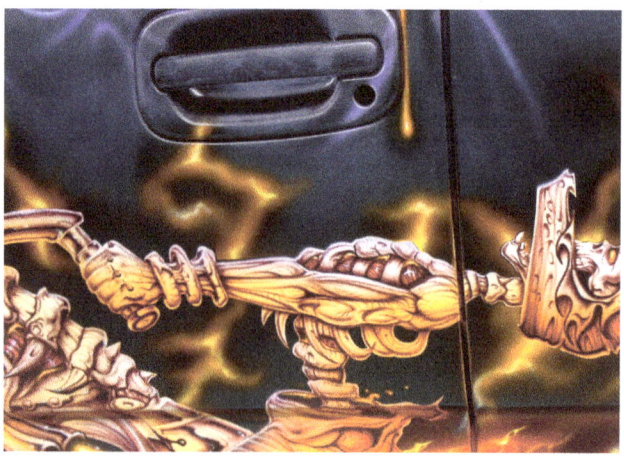

The look of glee is evident on our boney buddy as he hurtles forward from his fiery platform. Even though the figure is made of bone and sinew, you can still capture emotion through body language and position.

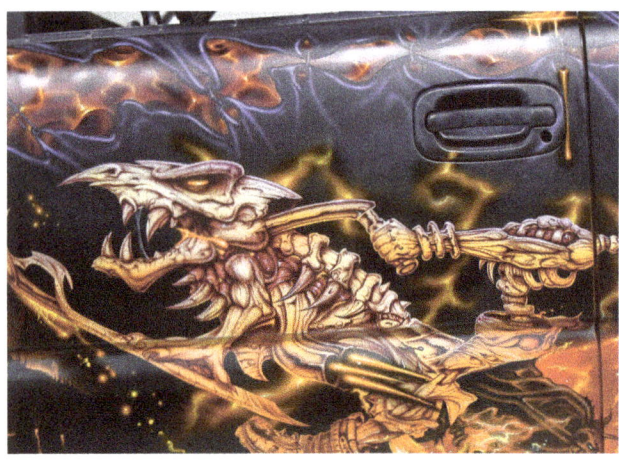

I then go in with white in my airbrush and enhance the highlighted areas throughout the image.

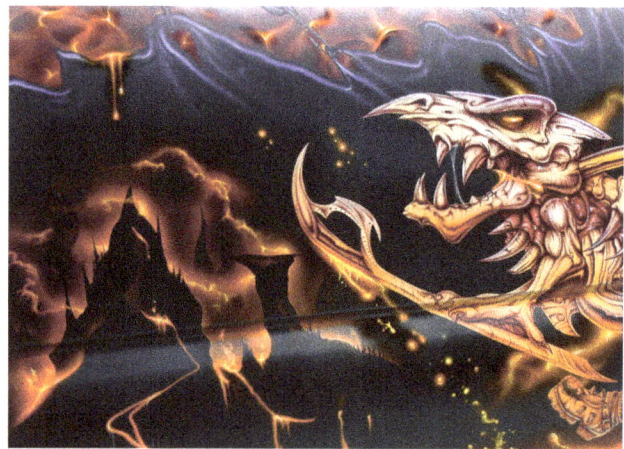

Here is a close up of our mobile monster showing the action captured as the beast rears out of the lava pool. Streaming liquid and other details help add to the effect.

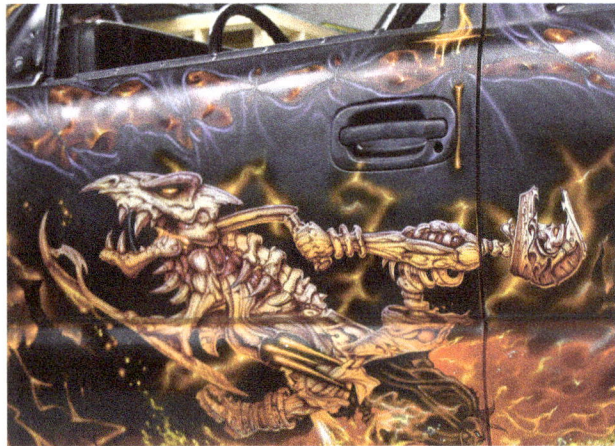

Next, it is a simple matter of adding more eye candy such as lava drips, smoke and all the rest. I'm just kind of rounding everything out.

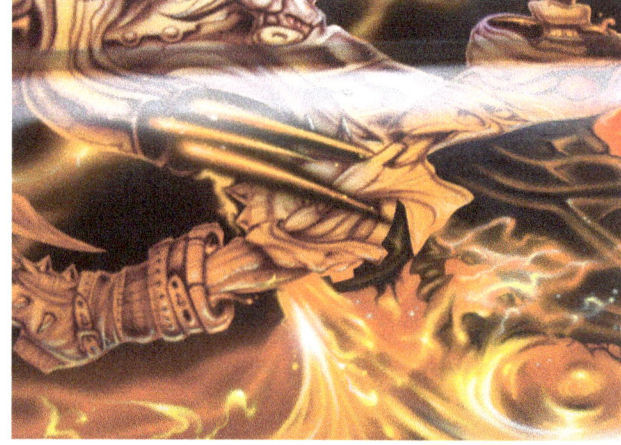

Little details like the crazy laced up motocross boots, as well as the torn pants, all add points of interest.

A bizarre 4x4 truck seemed to fit the bill. The iron-cage wheels filled with molten lava are a neat touch.

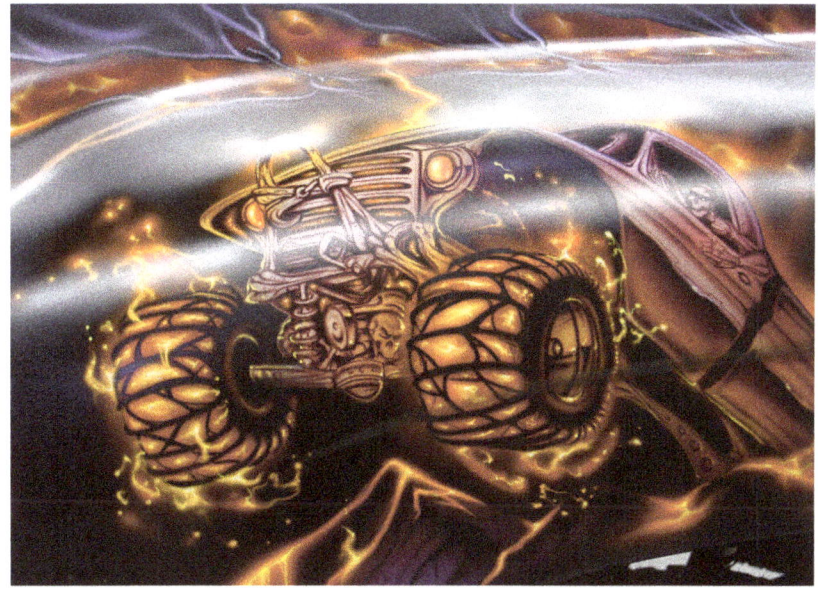

A custom built moto-cross bike doing a tail whip is always cool, especially when the frame is made of bones and the wheels are on fire.

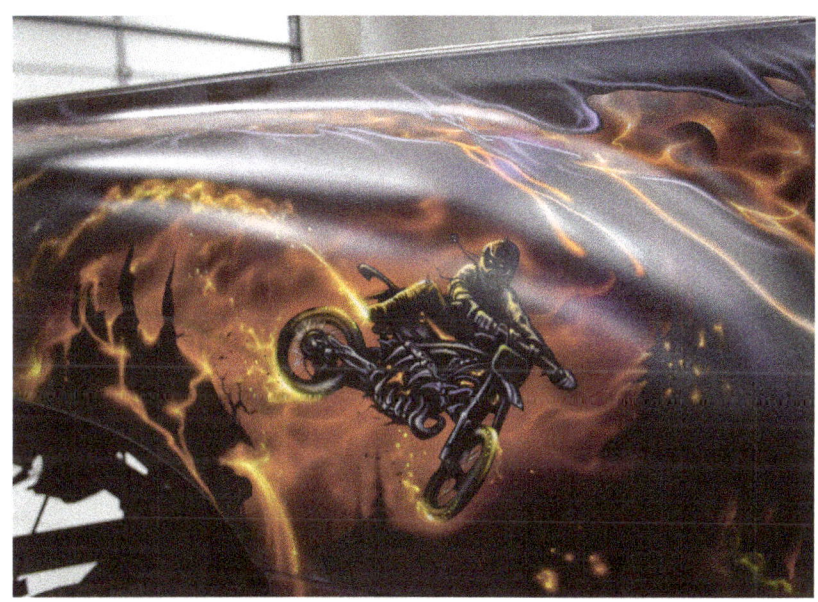

Here is a shot of the tailgate prior to clear coat. Somehow scantily clad ladies appear on the list of things to do in a lot of our commissions.

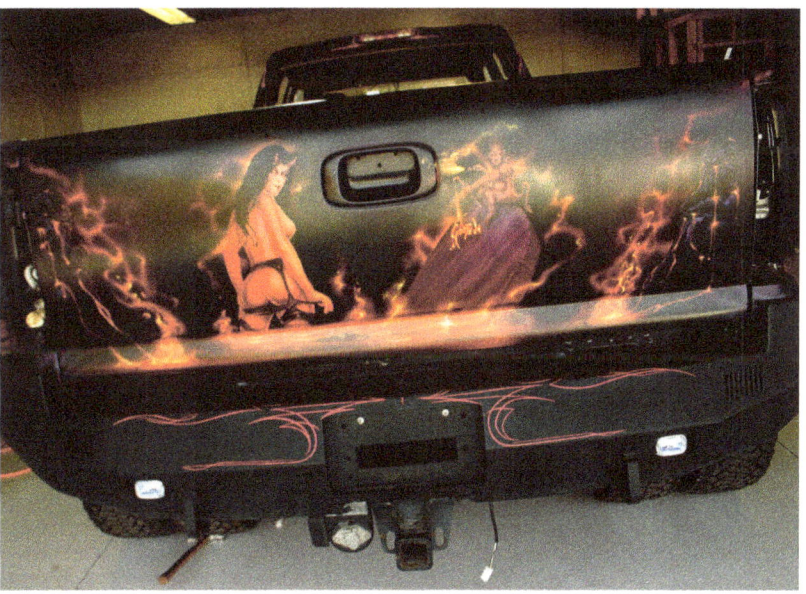

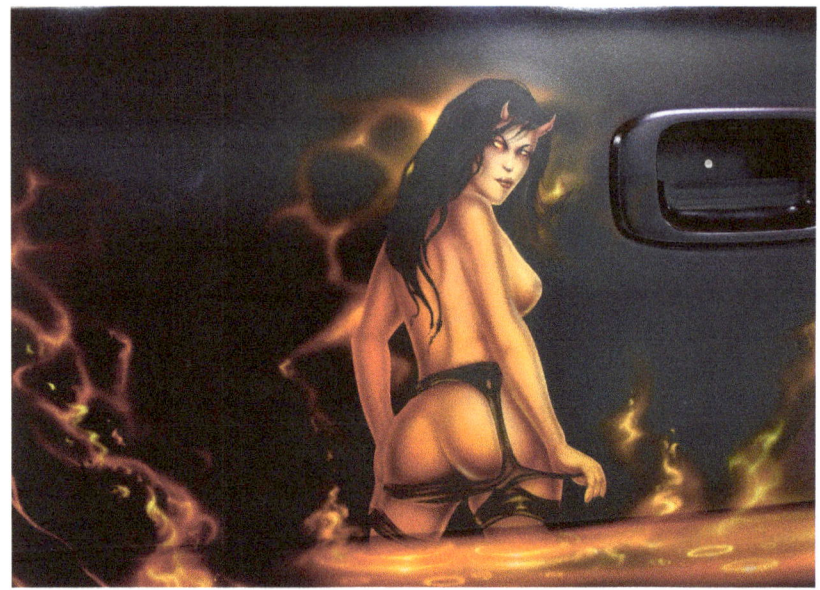

Speaking of which, I try to show some skin but try not to be too revealing. I guess you could say she's "HOT".

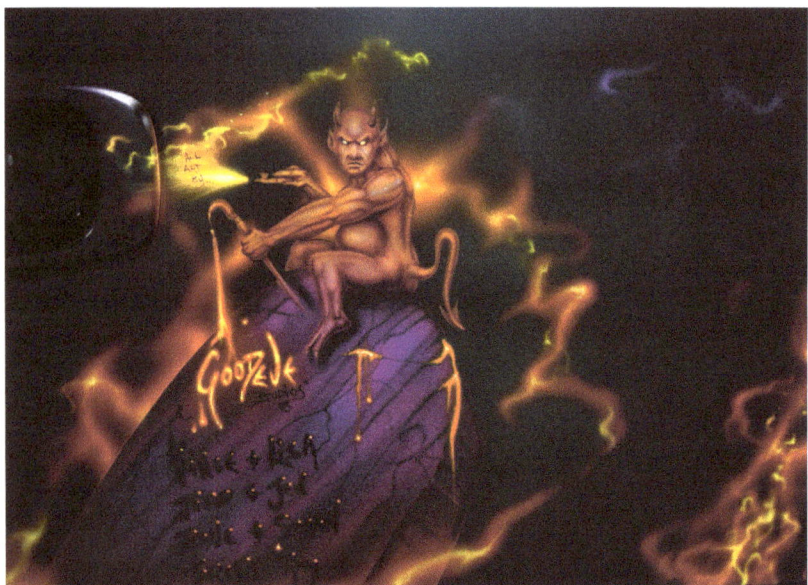

A sort of self portrait, as well as thanks to all the folks involved in the project.

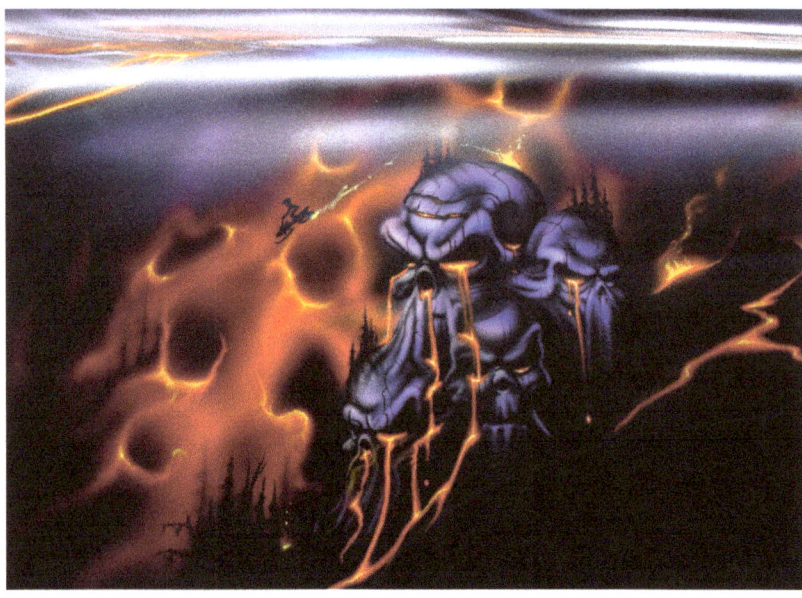

Another part of the painting, a series of mountainous faces, each one dripping with hot lava.

The last thing I do is pinstripe the bumpers so they're not so bald. The rest of the stuff, like the hood and the tonneau cover, are shipped to my shop to be completed there. In fact, the airbrushing of the tonneau cover became the subject of a new Vince Goodeve DVD, now available through our web site or by calling our shop.

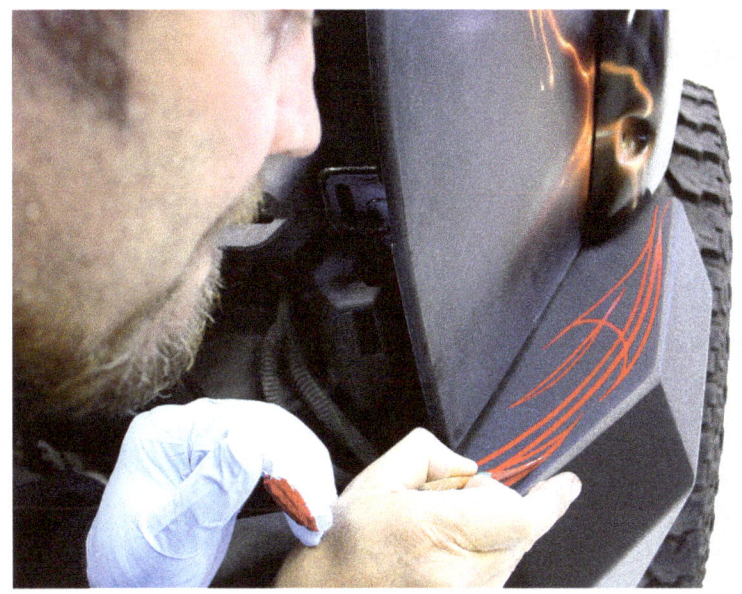

Running the striping brush over the slightly textured bumpers was initially weird, but once I found the groove, a matter of the right speed and consistency, it worked well.

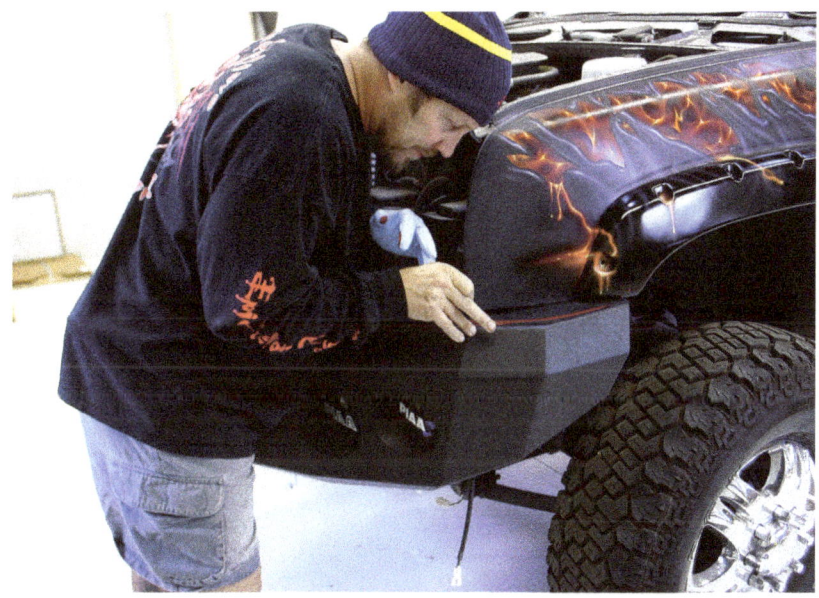

Just a little color or striping on the bumpers ties them into the rest of the truck. We also wanted to give it the moto-cross look that's showing up lately on some of the super cross bikes.

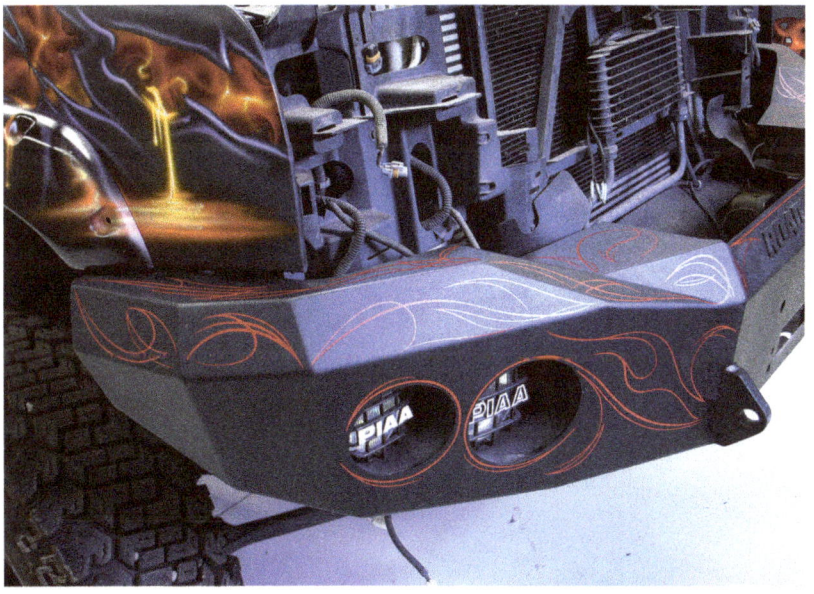

Chapter Ten
John Nicholas
Beauty and the Beast

The airbrush creation seen here is as complex as any in the book. Designed and painted by John Nicholas, (employed at the time by KC Creations in Overland Park, Kansas), the painting combines a pinup with a skull, a set of reality flames, a poker hand and an extremely detailed bottle of Whiskey. The starting point is the basecoat of platinum metallic (MBC02, Q01) from House of Kolor, with a clearcoat.

John starts by wet sanding the clearcoat with

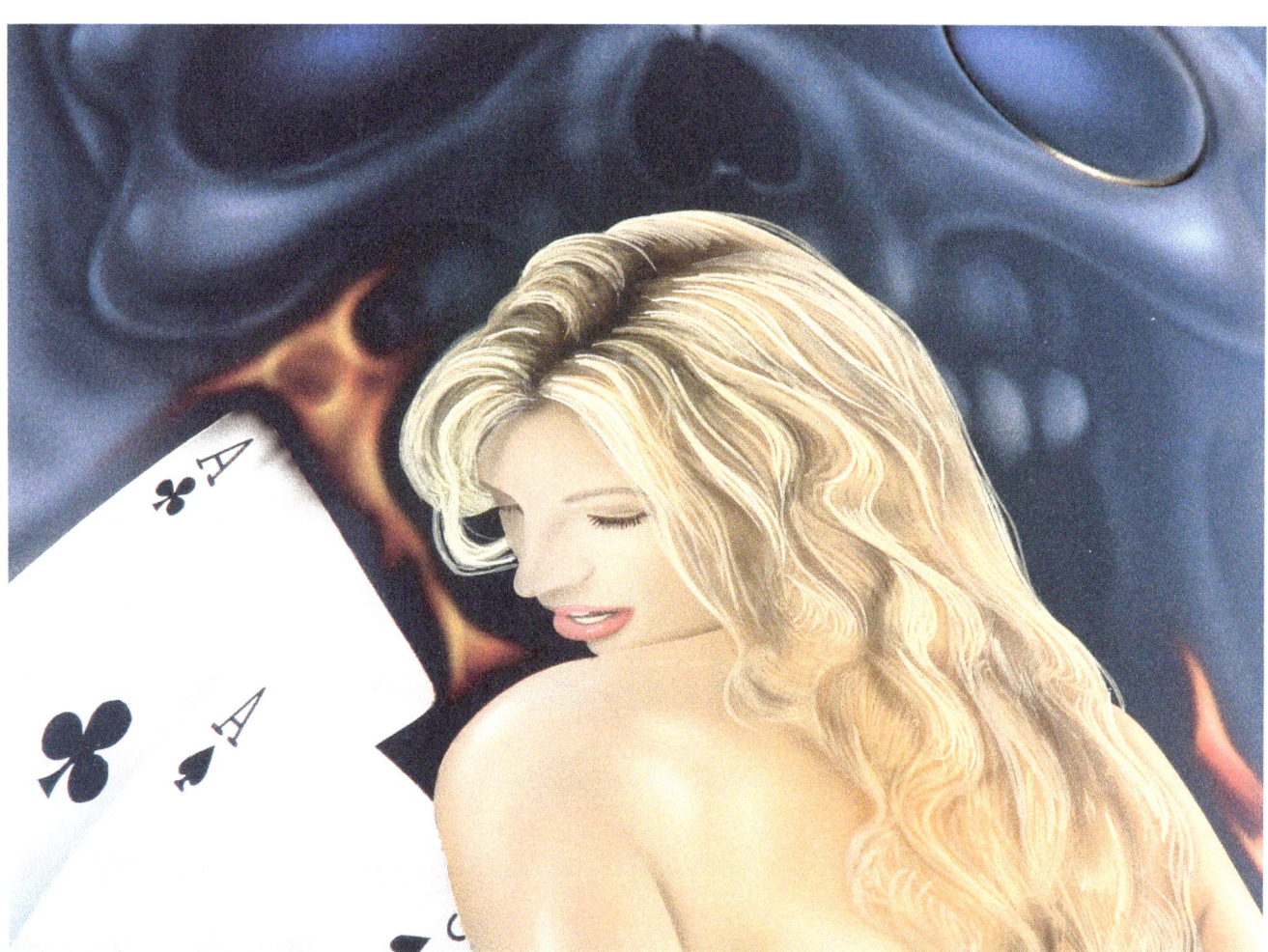

Known as "Man's Ruin," the graphic painted on the tank of this custom bike is actually the melding of five separate images.

800 grit to knock down the shine. Everything is sanded except the seams and high points. Those areas are scuffed with grey scotchbrite because, as John explains, "you don't want to sand those areas with sandpaper because you might sand through.'

To create the main image, John uses transfer paper (Frisket film) to trace an image from a calendar. The transfer paper has a sticky back. John sticks it down onto the tank and works out the bubbles before masking off the rest of the tank. John extends the drawing slightly making the legs longer, explaining as he does, "this is the area where the image will fade out."

The image is cut out now, and pulled off the tank so the actual painting can begin. The first coat of paint is black, "this is so we don't have the metallic effect," explains John, "and it also means we won't show a white line at the very edge when we pull the masking paper. To mix the skin tone paint I use white, red, yellow, and a little green. You can add a little black if you want to tone it down but you don't want to make it muddy. You can also use transparent red oxide (Deltron DMD 623) over white as a skin tone, but you have to add a layer of intercoat clear before adding any highlights or the highlights will blend right into the skin tone and make them brown."

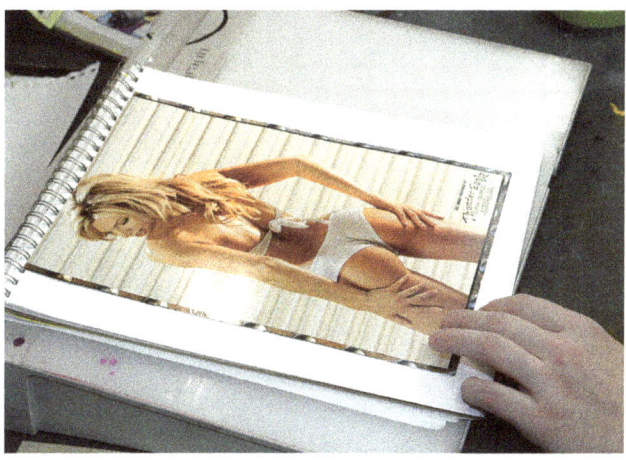

John often uses an existing photograph or illustration as the start of his airbrush design.

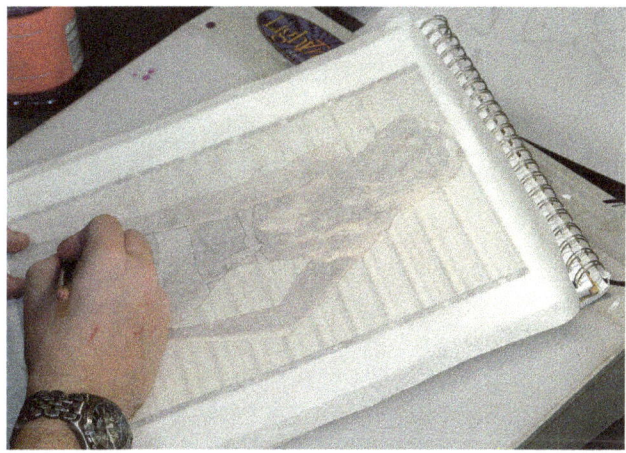

Working on a light table, John does a detailed tracing onto Frisket paper.

After peeling the Frisket from the picture, John sticks it onto the tank and works out the bubbles with a squeegee.

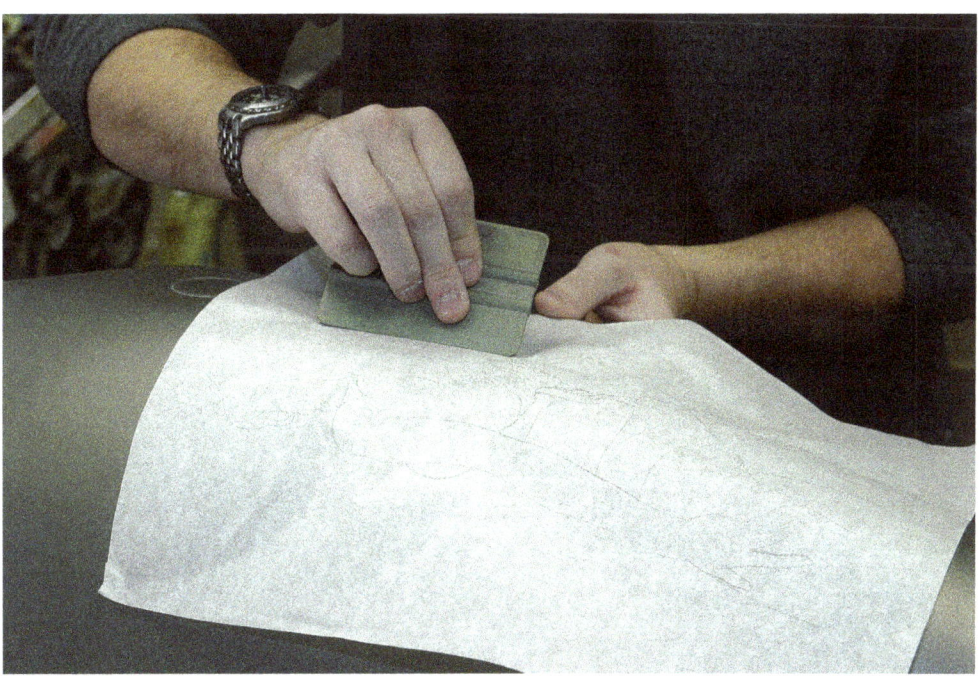

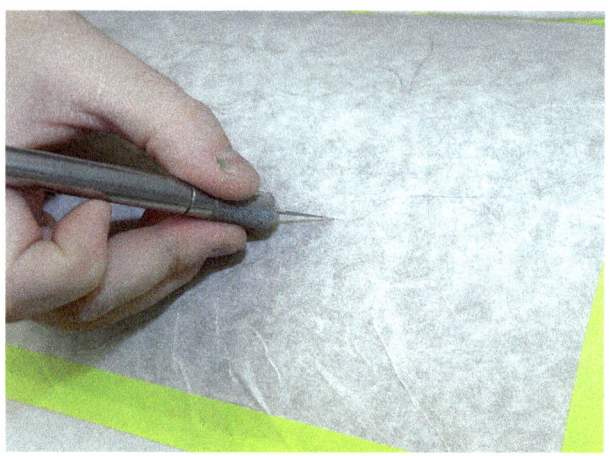

"Cutting out is like pinstriping with a knife, the knife needs to be sharp as the devil or you don't cut all the way through."

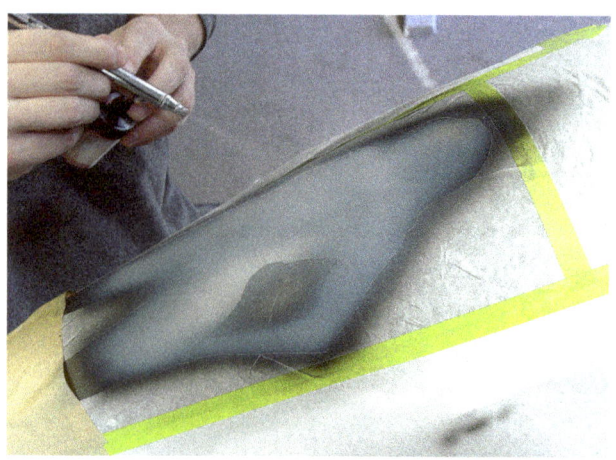

The special-mix skin tone paint is applied to the area uniformly. "Keep in mind you want to start where you imagine the highlights to be."

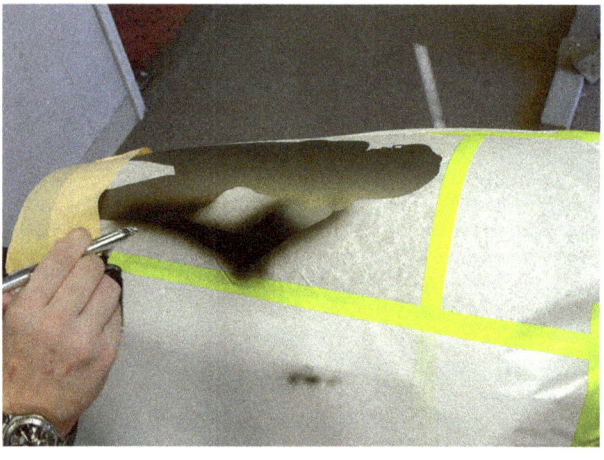

The first coat of paint is basecoat black, applied with one of John's Iwata Eclipse HP-BCS airbrushes.

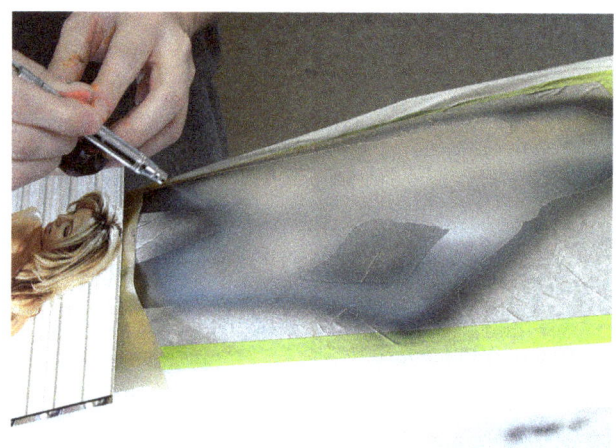

"I often work from dark to light, and then from light to dark."

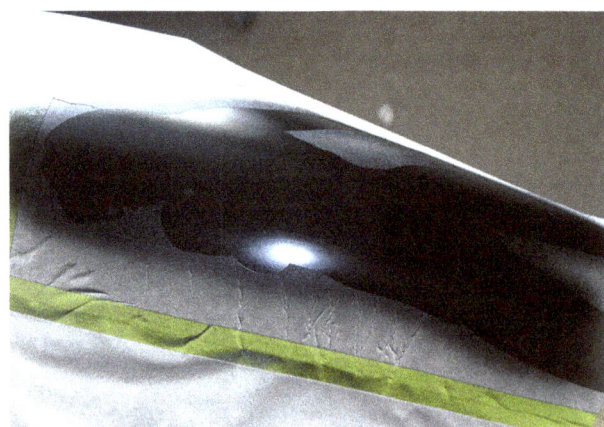

Here you can see the finished basecoat, now the real painting can begin.

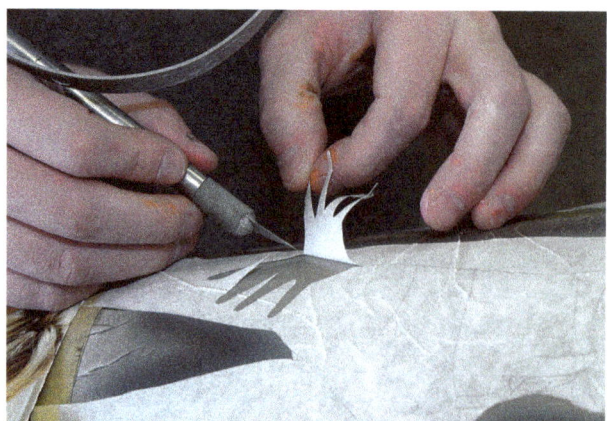

After applying an intercoat clearcoat (DBC 500) and allowing it to dry, John puts the stencil back onto the tank, then pulls back selected areas he wants to paint.

"I always put any new color into a bottle that had a similar color in it when used last, so any residue left in the bottle won't hurt the new color. In this case I put the skin tone mixture in a bottle that had red in it. I don't want to put this color in a bottle that had metallic in it because even a little fleck of metallic will kill my skin tones. I've mixed the paint with PPG 870, medium-speed reducer".

Highlights

Now come the highlights and details, "It's all the same color at this point," says John. "I don't want to kill it all at once. I'm going to put on a heavy coat of intercoat clear because if I put frisket film back on it will pull the paint, but the clear will lock it down." During the work John works hard to minimize film thickness, "I don't like to use the big gun because it puts out so much paint - it creates an edge you'll have to deal with later."

Next, the stencil is put back down and various parts are pulled up so John can do detail painting on those areas with more flesh tone mix.

Heavier applications of flesh tone paint are used to create highlights that define the image. Gradually a hand and arm arise from the cut-out area. Eventually, John sticks the arm back down and pulls the next area. "Sometimes the stencil gets so beat up that you have to hold it in place with extra tape," explains John, "or just make a new piece. This is all a matter of light and dark, I'm always going from one to the other."

"Now I'm going to mix up a special color for toning. I want black, but I want it to be transparent. I mix black and transparent red oxide, reduced a lot so it has a transparent quality. Transparent red oxide (aka trans-red-oxide) is sort of a dye so I have to be careful how much of it I use. PPG and House of Kolor use the same reducer. I use both systems. Sometimes I use Dupont, but then I have to use their reducer."

Shadowing

John explains how he uses the new paint, "First I bring the light up, then I put shadows in with the over-reduced black color I just mixed."

Continued on page 160

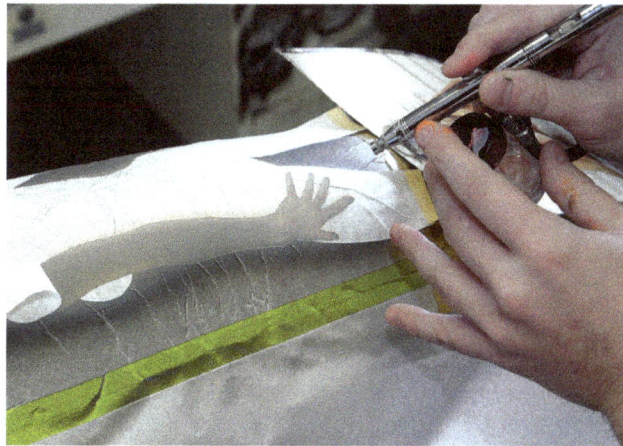

Heavier applications of the skin-tone paint are used to create highlights on the hand and arm.

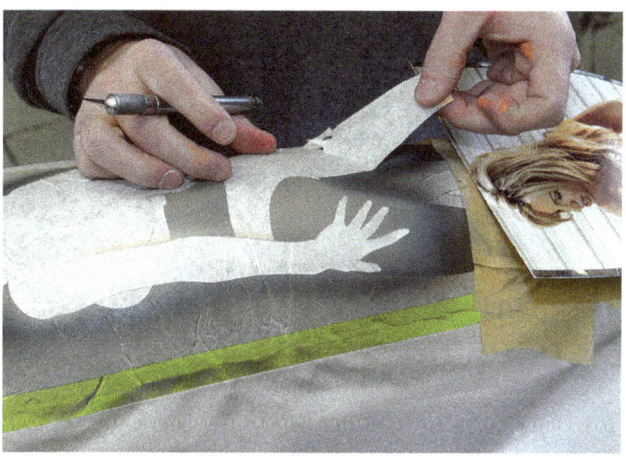

After working on the arm, John puts that part of the stencil back down and pulls the paper off the legs.

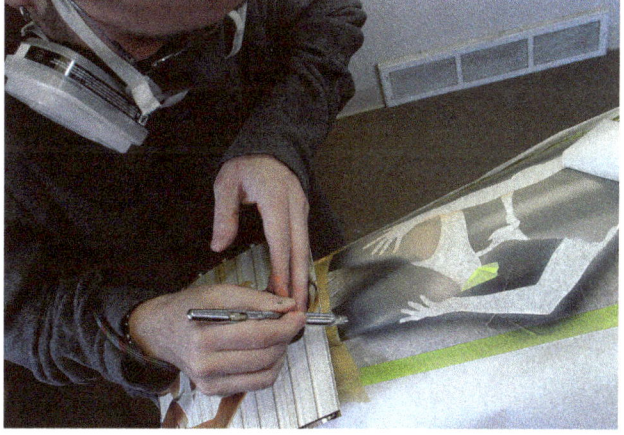

Again, heavier applications of the same skin-tone paint are used to create highlights like the one on the side of her leg.

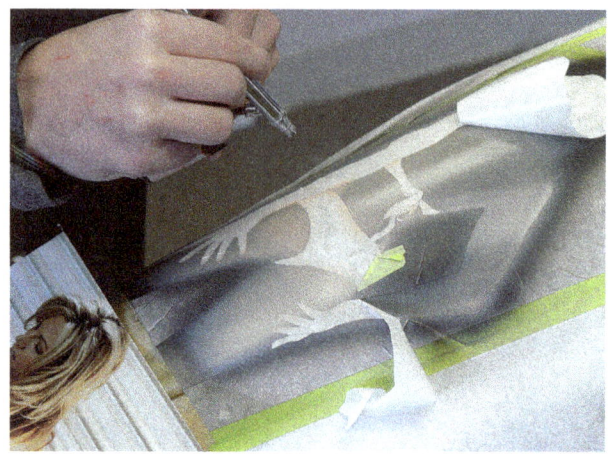

"Some pieces are pulled for shadow lines and some for highlights, I do the highlights freehand first."

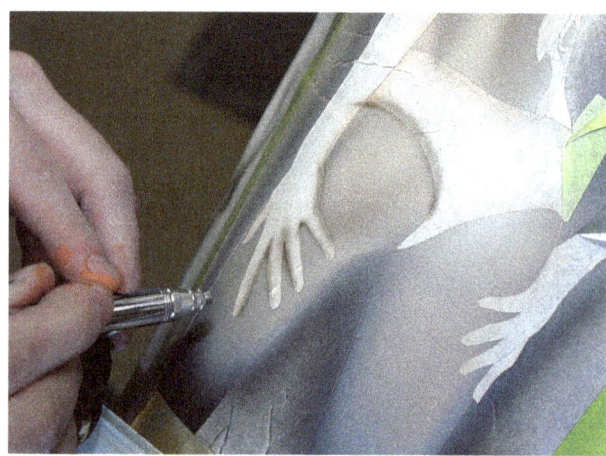

More shadows define the line where the fingers meet the legs.

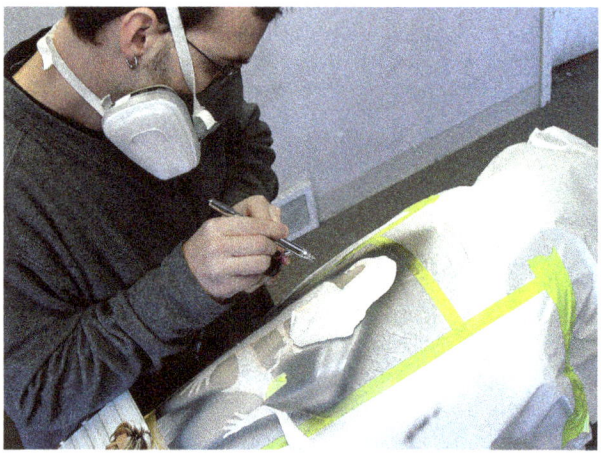

After mixing the "toning" color John starts to create shadows, explaining as he does, "First you have to know where your light source is."

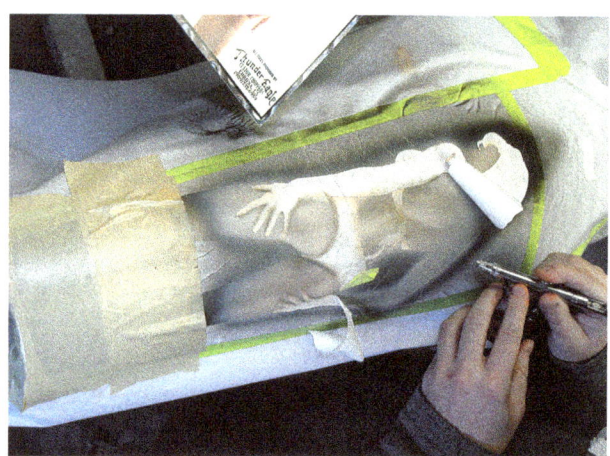

Careful application of the nearly transparent toning paint creates a very life-like shadow on the back of her right arm.

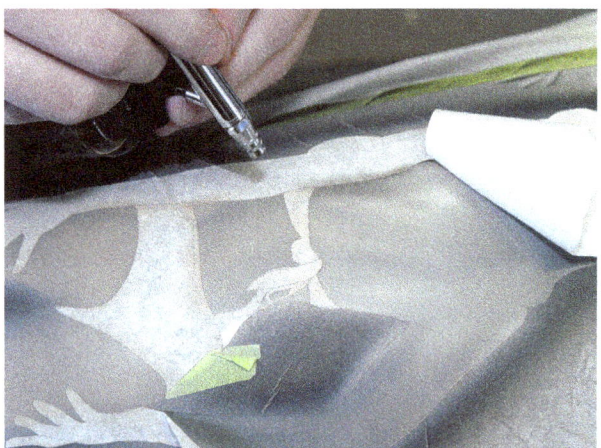

More of the same darker tone is used to create shadows on the pinup's back. "The black is thinned way down with DT 870, but don't get it too thin."

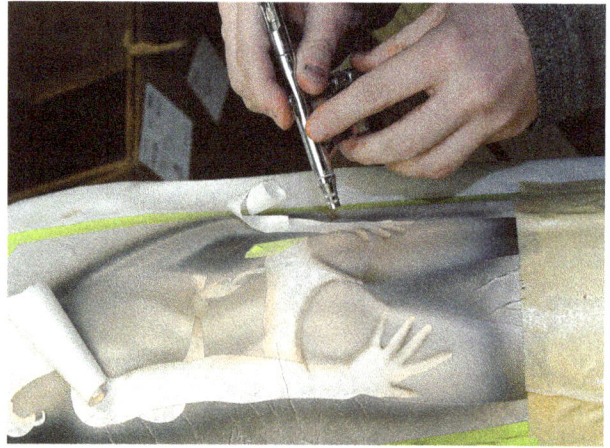

By pulling up only small areas of the mask, John is able to keep a particular effect confined to one precise area.

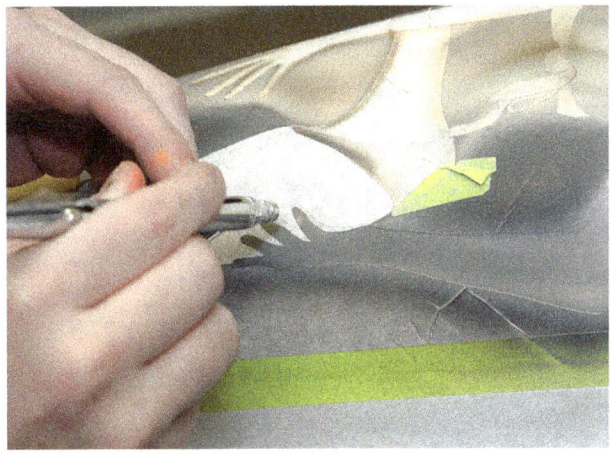

More skin-tone paint is used to create highlights on each individual finger.

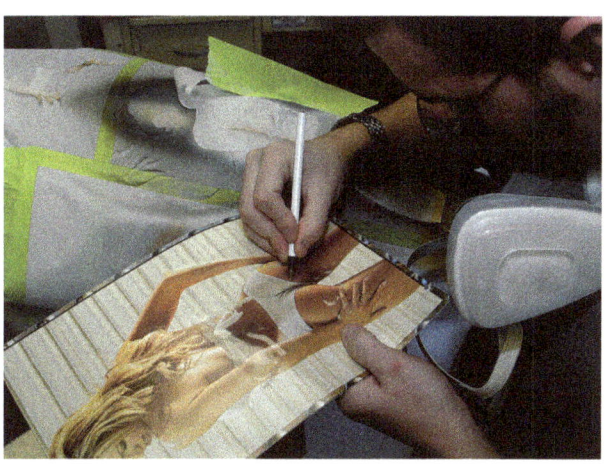

For detail areas John makes another mask from clear material.

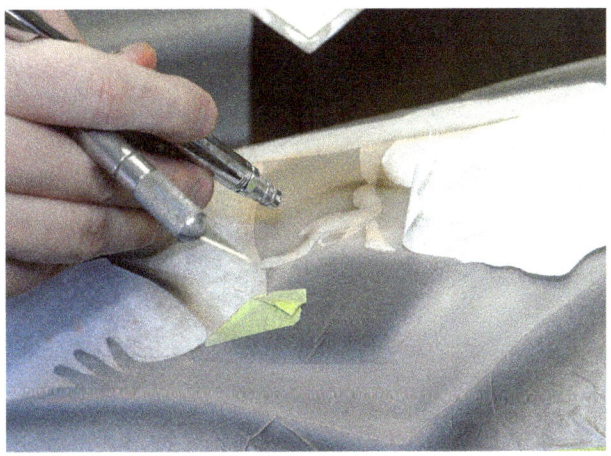

The image evolves slowly, much of it a matter of highlight and shadow, like that being sprayed onto her back.

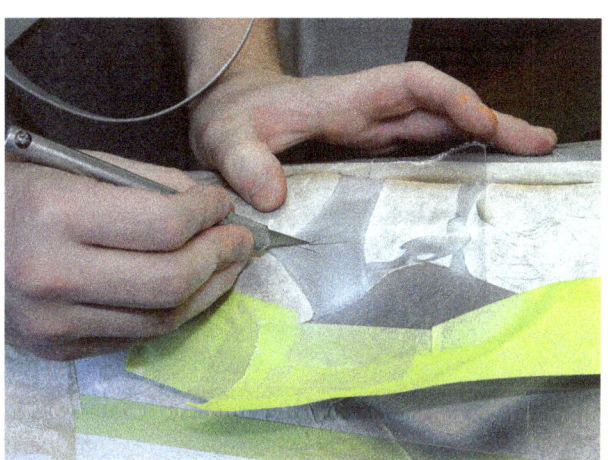

Now the mask is transferred to the painting, then cut and pulled back wherever John needs a shadow…

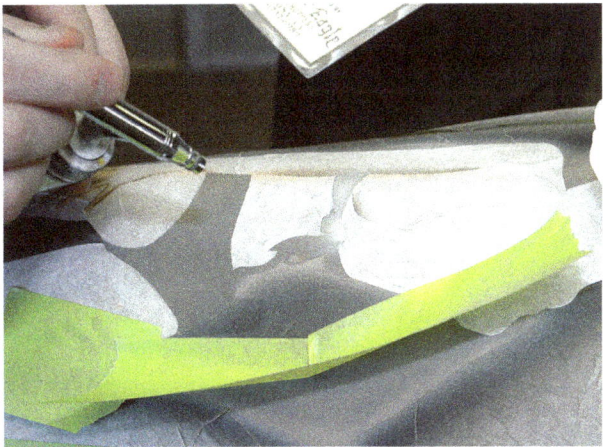

Masks are put in place around the swimsuit. Like the body areas, the swimsuit will be defined by highlights and shadows.

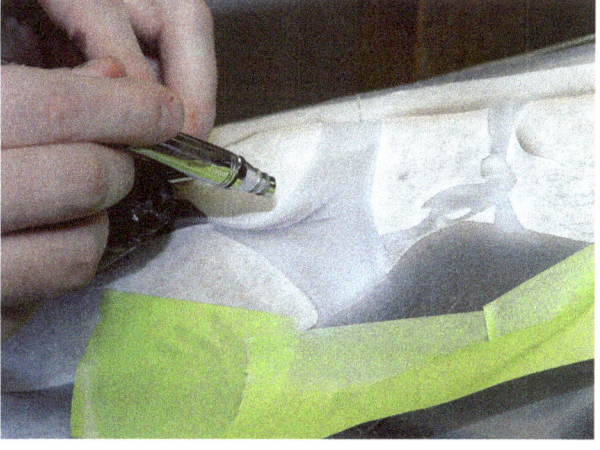

… in this way John is able to put creases in the suit that perfectly match the photograph. For detail work like this John uses 15 psi instead of 20.

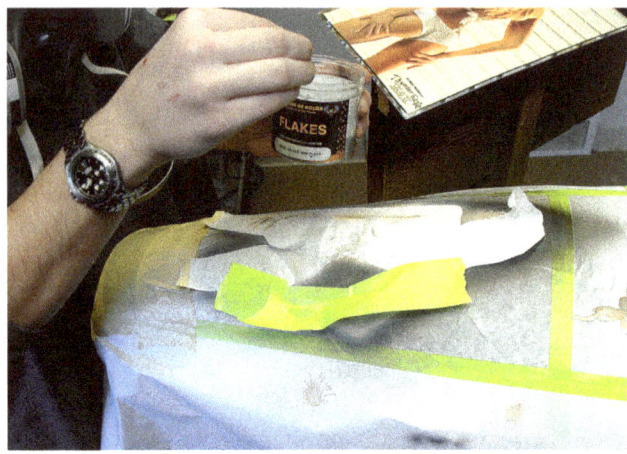

While the DBC intercoat clear is still wet, John sprinkles House of Kolor flake material on to mimic the sequins in the photograph.

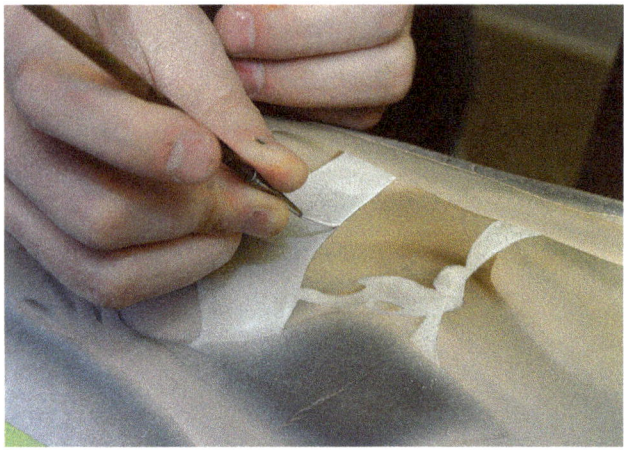

Details, like the seam on the edge of the swimsuit, are best created with a Painters Touch 2050 Script fine line multimedia brush using water-based paint.

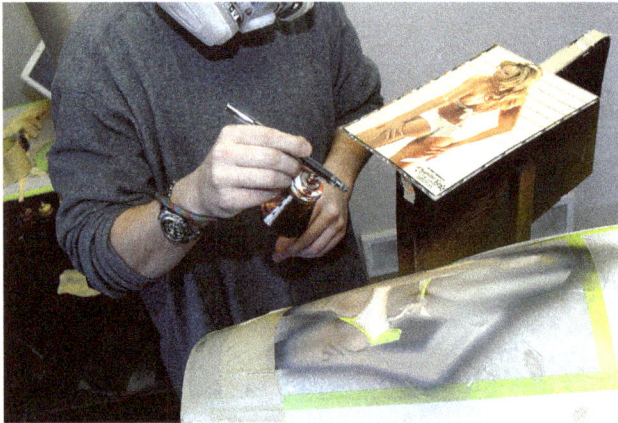

Using transparent red oxide (see text), John tints all the skin tones in a few light passes. "This mixture needs to be on the thin side so it's not so grainy and you have more control. Thin with DT 870."

On the next page you can see how John creates shadows and darker areas on her back with the light, semi-transparent toner. If one of the shadows goes too dark, John just comes back over it with a little of the original flesh tone color.

As was done before, John pulls various parts of the main mask so the effect he's after is contained to one small area. To paint the swim suit he puts the masks back down on either side of the suit. Working on the suit is, again, a matter of developing light and dark areas. To get the shadow details just right, John makes a second temporary mask from clear material, and then pulls part of this new mask out of the way to paint in the dark areas (see the preceding page).

John often uses water-based paints, applied with a brush, in conjunction with the airbrush work (the paint typically comes from Com-Art or Createx). "But if you use water-based paint," explains John, "then you have to clear it with inter-coat clear before proceeding or the paint will be wiped off when they wipe the job down with wax and grease remover. Water-based paint is nice for that reason though, because you *can* wipe if off if you don't like the effect, without wiping off anything else."

Now, with many of the masks back in place, John tints all the skin tones with a light mist of transparent red oxide. And, in the familiar pattern - the highlights come next. These are done in white, though it doesn't stay bright white - the paint will darken a little as it blends and melts into the paint underneath. Some of the shadows are darkened with shading black for the dark shadows while others are darkened with transparent red oxide. At this point John does another coat of intercoat clear to lock it all down,

Time now to create another mask for the face and the hair. This is made from the same clear transfer material used earlier. The dark areas like eyelashes and eyebrows are cut out from the mask after it is placed on the tank (see the next page).

"For eyebrows, I use hardly any paint, otherwise it turns into a dark brown line. Later I go in and dab on some water-based paint with a brush. When people do faces they put on too much paint, less is more. For lips they want to do red, I

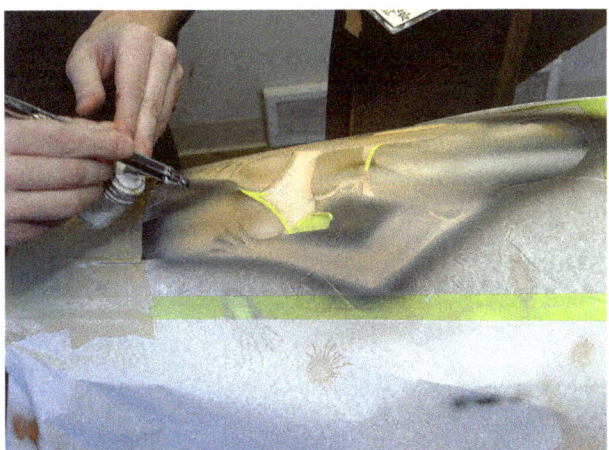

After warming up the skin tones, John works on highlights again, using basecoat white.

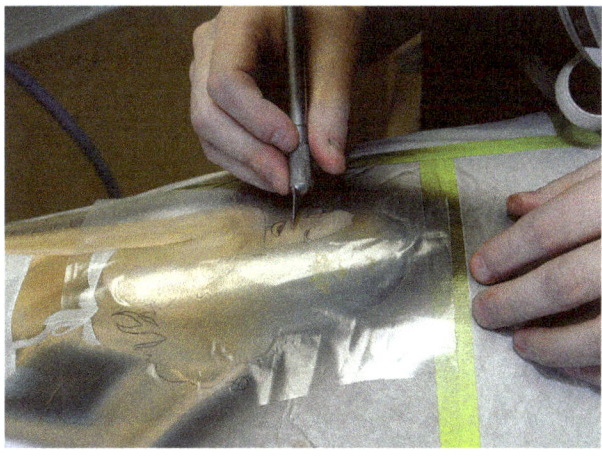

The mask is carefully laid over the dry clearcoat, then small areas like lips and eyelashes are slit and pulled back.

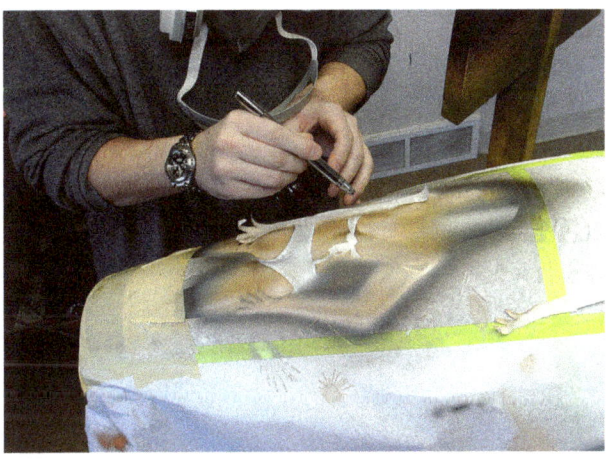

More transparent red oxide is used on specific shadows to tint them brown instead of black.

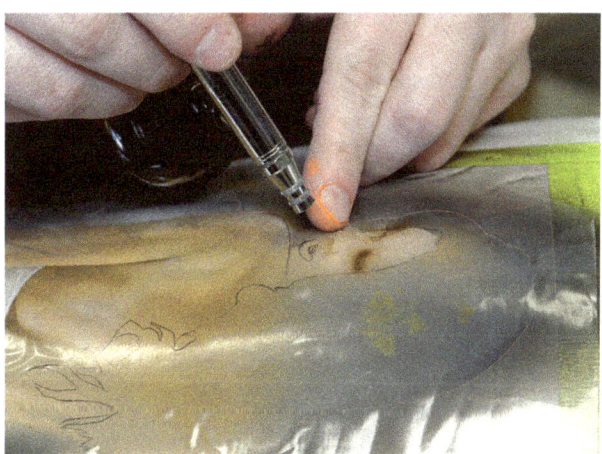

For the lips John applies "oh so thin" magenta paint.

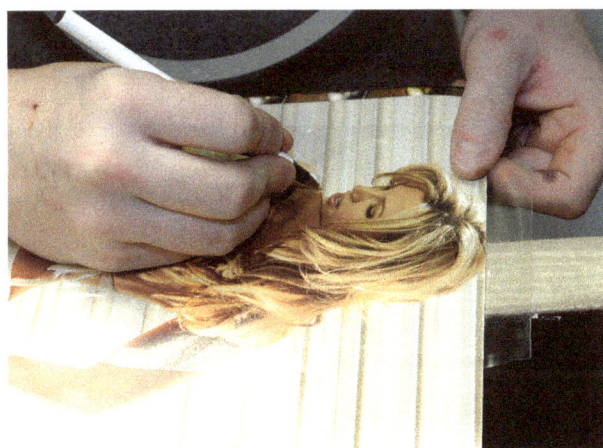

Before airbrushing the facial details, John creates another mask on clear mask material. Before putting this down, John will spray on another clearcoat.

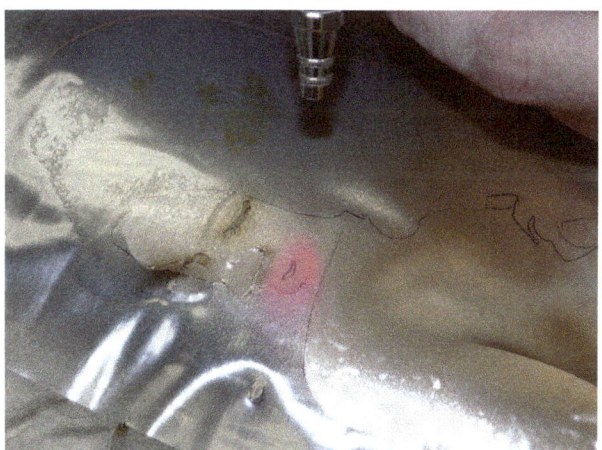

To get the right color on the lips, John applies the magenta in a number of light coats.

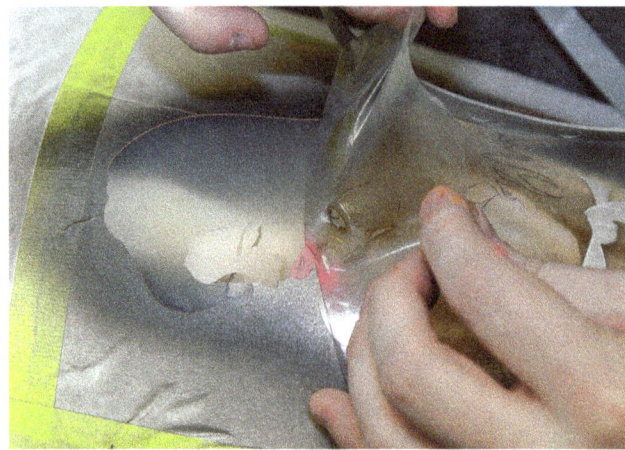

Time now to pull the mask and do some work on the facial details with a small brush.

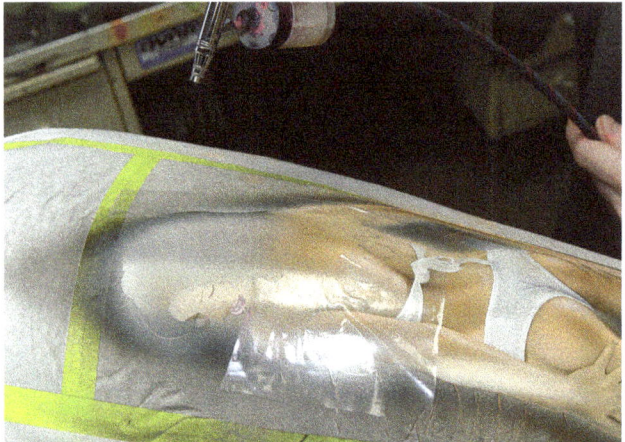

The foundation for the blonde hair is a coat of the same paint used for the skin tones.

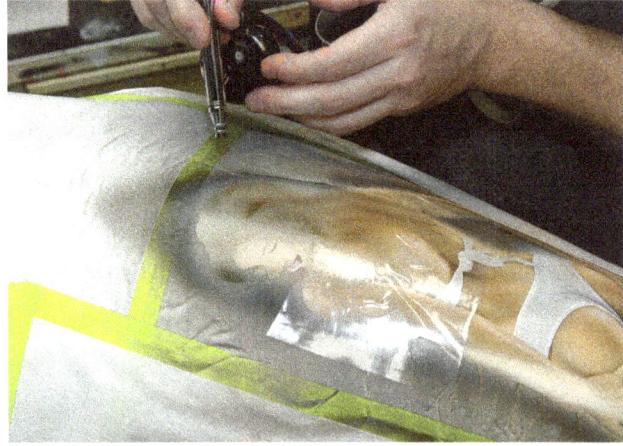

To create the shadows John uses shading black as shown, followed by just a little white. "I stress the word 'little' and the use of quick passes for the white."

use magenta. Magenta, thinned down, is like a pink. It goes on transparent and picks up skin tones underneath." After the multi-step creation on lips, John rolls back the mask and does the left shoulder.

Hair and Facial Details

John starts with more flesh-color for foundation of the hair, explaining, "If you really look, the hair is about the same color as her skin." Then he starts adding shading black, at random. Next, he goes over it with a little white for highlights. The eyeliner is done with shading black. I haven't used any true black here," explains John, "because it's not a real color." Details are done with transparent black and white, water-based, by brush. And finally, John does a clearcoat over the whole thing with the big gun.

Shifting Gears

At this point John masks over the pinup and starts spraying straight black and candy black on the surrounding area, "this will be background, I will have it fade as it gets farther away from the figure." The paint however, is not lying down evenly on the tank, so John stops painting and starts cleaning with wax and grease remover, then water-based cleaner, adding, "the water-based will remove any static electricity.

Next he goes back and fades the black onto the bottom of her legs and sprays in a little transparent red oxide at edges of the body so the black blends better with the flesh tones.

Jim Beam

The first step is to trace the Jim Beam image onto frisket transfer paper and apply that to the tank. Next John masks off the surrounding area and begins the job of cutting out the main label from the transfer paper. This is what John calls, "the most time consuming part of the job." He also masks over the mask remaining on the tank, so the lines in his sketch aren't covered by paint. The actual painting starts with black followed by two coats of basecoat white.

Now the mask of the main label is re-applied to the tank and the mask for the label on the neck is cut out, pulled off, and the area painted white over black.

Continued on page 166

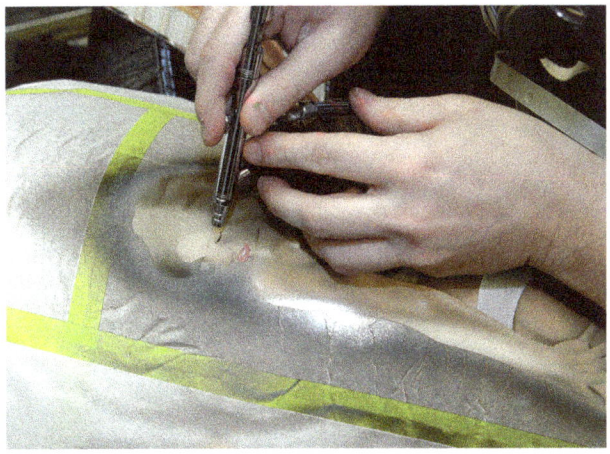

Holding the brush close, shading black is used to create eyeliner.

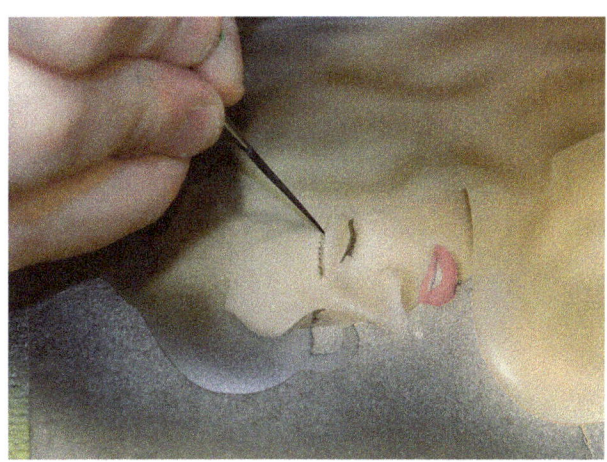

Water-based black paint and a steady hand are used to fill in the eyebrows…

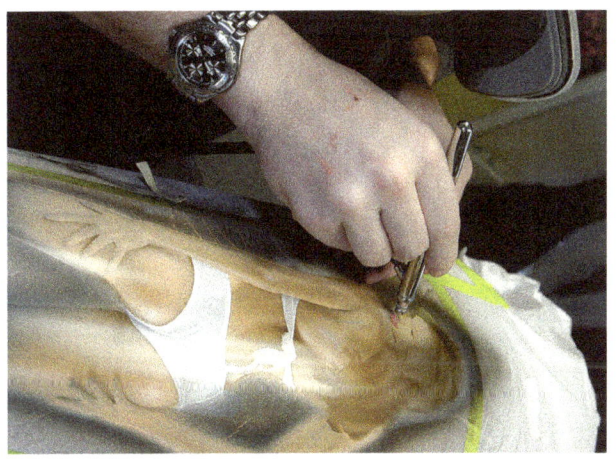

Details are created by holding the airbrush very close. "I use less air pressure, thinner paint and a few hand made stencils."

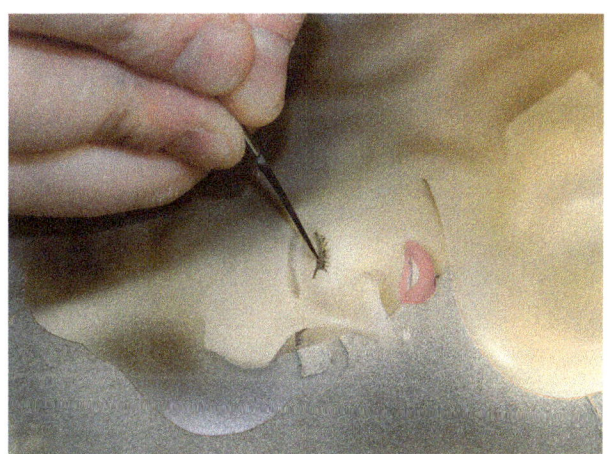

…the long eyelashes…

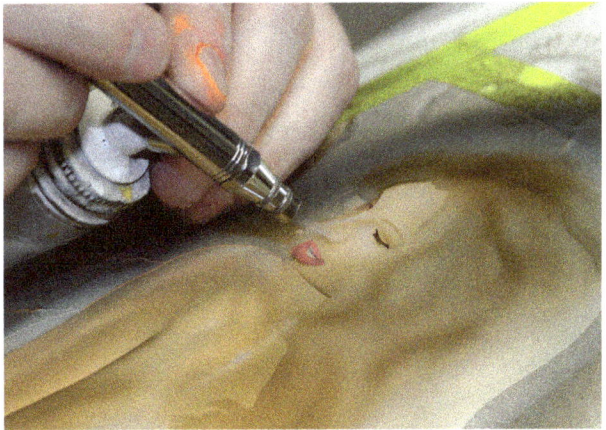

White is used to create highlights on the nose. "Get in close but make sure you spray a fat mist of paint through the airbrush off to the side first. This lessens the chance of spitting and having an 'oops.'"

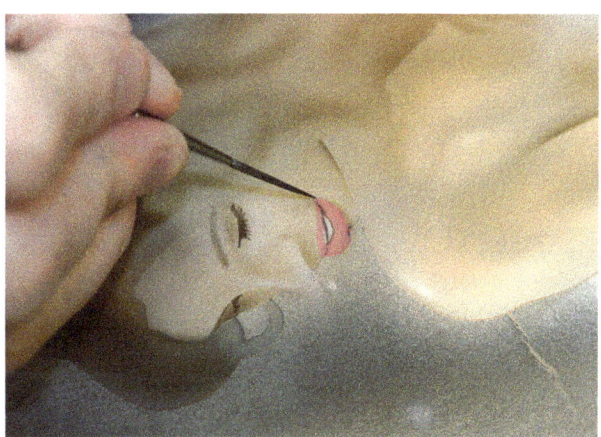

…and the fine details around her mouth.

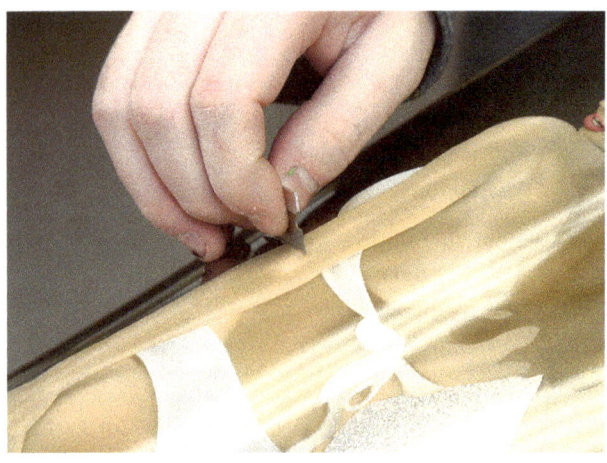

A razor blade is run carefully along the edges to minimize their thickness and make clearcoating easier.

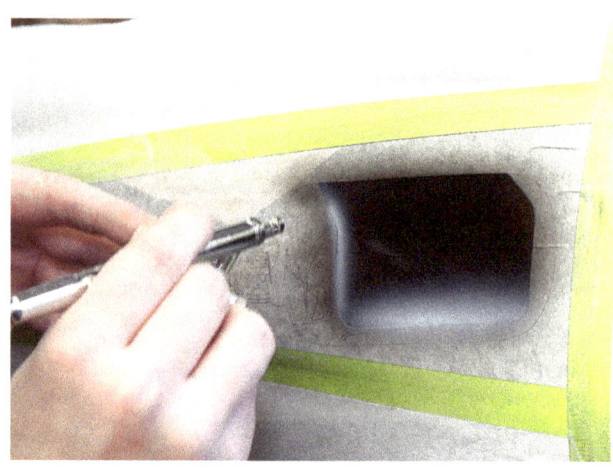

After cutting out the main label, John applies two coats of basecoat white.

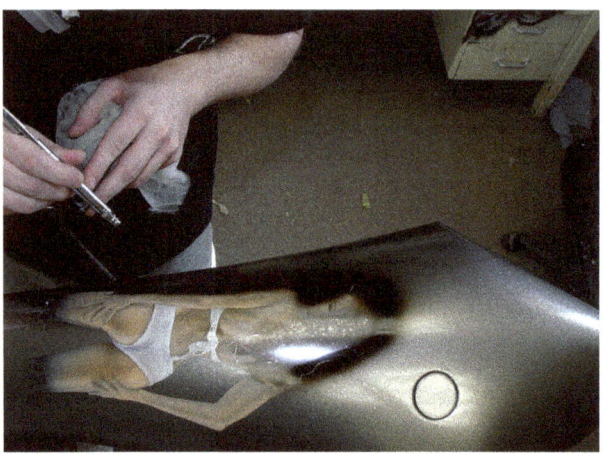

After putting a clear mask over the pinup, John sprays black around the figure, allowing the black to fade toward the outer edges.

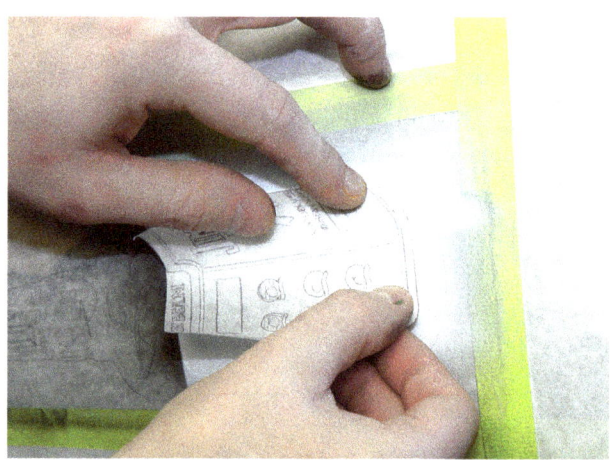

John puts the main label back on the Jim Beam bottle before cutting and removing another area of mask.

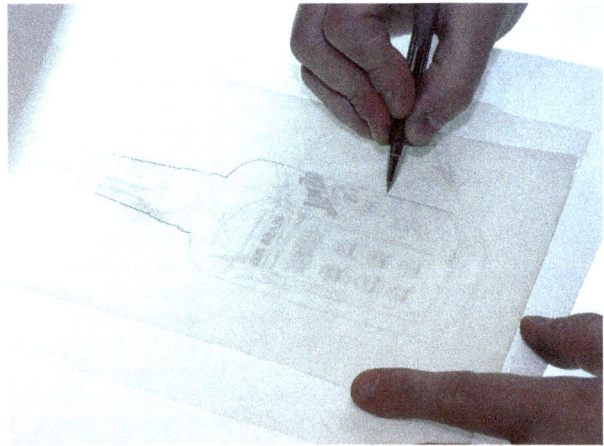

The next part of the image, the Jim Beam bottle, is traced onto a piece of Frisket paper before being applied to the tank.

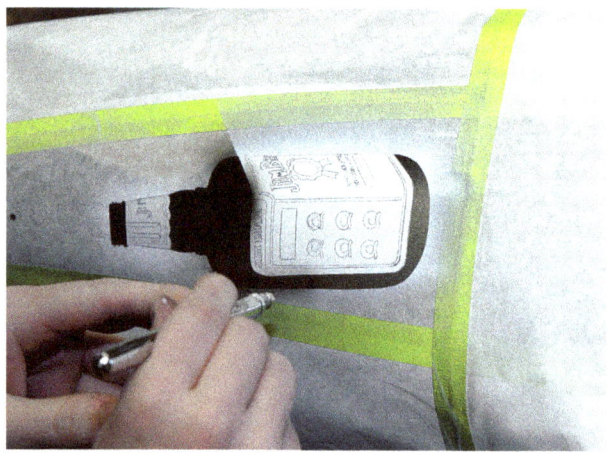

The special color, bourbon-in-glass, starts as black with highlights in silver followed by a mist of trans-red-oxide and more white for highlights.

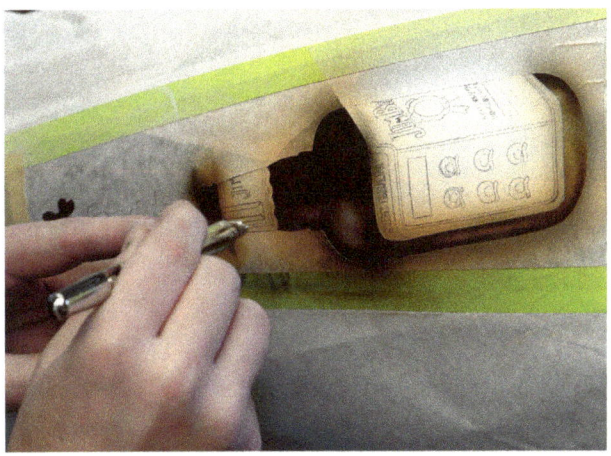

The final touch for the main part of the bottle is to make the highlights brighter with white basecoat applied to the brightest part of each highlight.

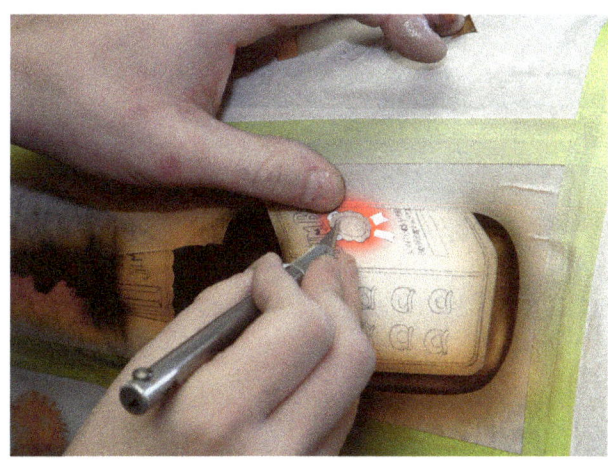

Then the mask for the center seal is replaced...

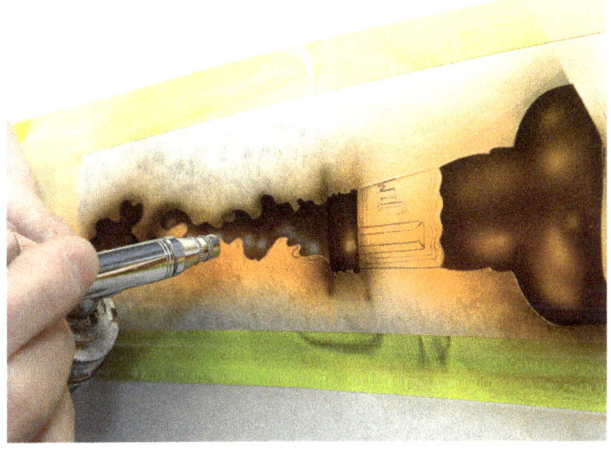

The spilled hooch is created in much the same way as the bottle, with the same basic set of colors and highlights in silver, (shown) with white used later.

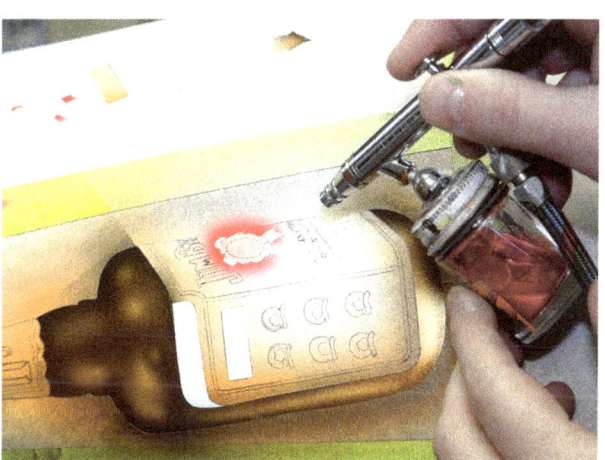

... and the ribbon area is cut out and painted red over white, making the red bright without too much buildup.

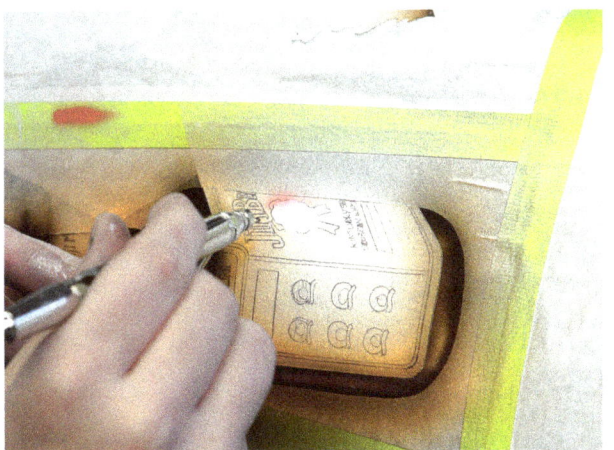

To duplicate the center part of the mask John cuts out the inner label and applies white followed by red.

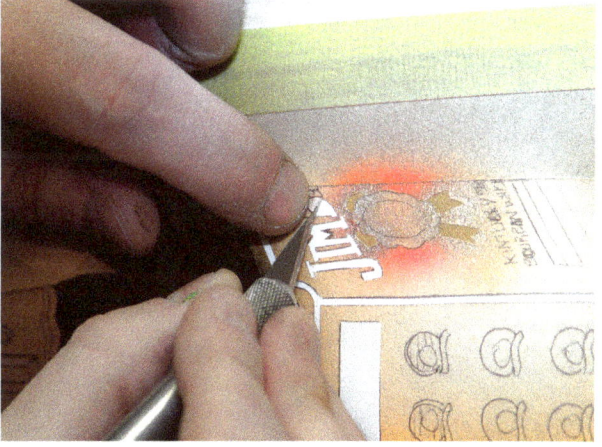

With a steady hand and a sharp knife, John cuts out the letters on the main label.

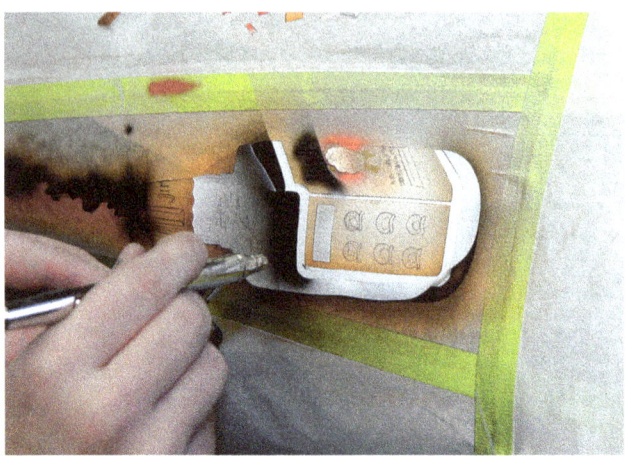

Now the letters and part of the side label are painted with solid black basecoat (DMD 683).

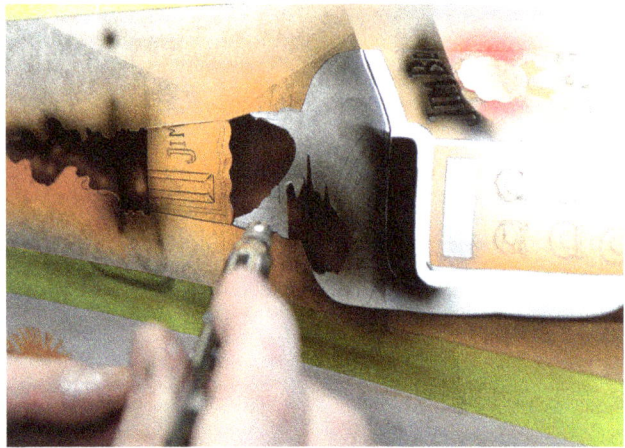

To duplicate the look of glass without any bourbon behind it, John cuts out that area and applies silver over the trans-red-oxide.

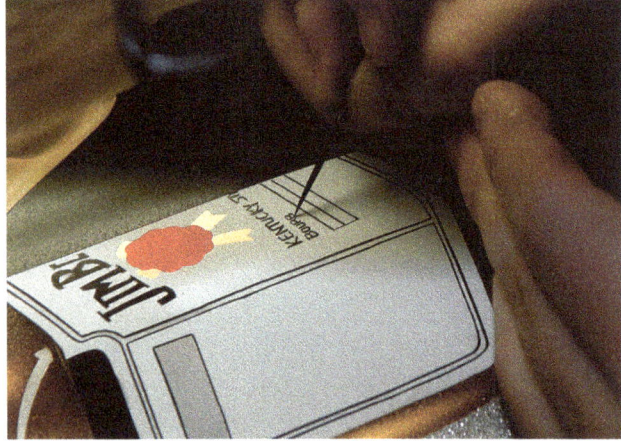

All the small letters and lines are done by hand, following lines left in the paint earlier by the knife.

With both label areas painted white and back-masked, John pulls the mask for the amber colored bottle. The bottle area is painted black, highlights are added in silver, the whole area is toned with trans-red-oxide, then a little white is added to the highlights. The color of the spilled whiskey is created by spraying black around the edges (after pulling the masks), then going over that with two light applications of trans-red oxide, and eventually the highlights (later).

Creating a life-like label with all the necessary detail required many small cutouts, painting, and back masking followed by a considerable amount of brush work. Much of this work it better explained by the photos on nearby pages.

"For much of this cutting out, I do want cut lines," explains John. "I want the Xacto knife to leave a line in the paint underneath, because I will use that as a guide when I come in later and do the pinstripes and letters by hand. In this situation, with water-based paint and such a fine line, the scriptwriter type brush is a better choice than a standard pinstriping brush."

"The other nice thing about this water-based paint is the fact that it dries flat, with very little film build up or edge. It makes the later clearcoating process easier . When I get to a part where I feel like I might mess it up by going too far, I lock it in with an application of clear."

At this point John starts on the deck of cards, a section we've left out due to space limitations, and it's also the simplest part of the paint job.

After creating the deck of cards, John switches back to the Jim Beam bottle. First a mask is made from clear material, then slits are cut where John wants highlights in the neck. Now he sprays the area with silver. At the very end of the bottle John creates highlights on the threads, following the same procedure. While he's in the neighborhood, John adds highlights to the spilled liquid.

At the bottom of the tank John applies clear masking material, then draws out more spilled liquid, then cuts it out. The idea is to have the spilled liquor at the bottom of the tank and have it catch fire with reality flames. "People say, 'why didn't you add those bubbles of the liquor when

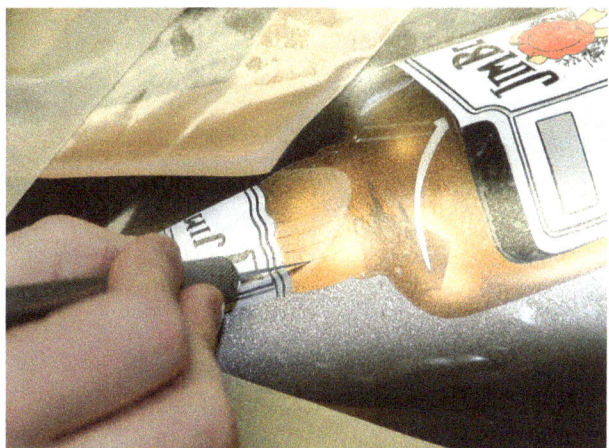

A clever way to create highlights: first apply clear masking material and cut a series of slits that reach around the neck.

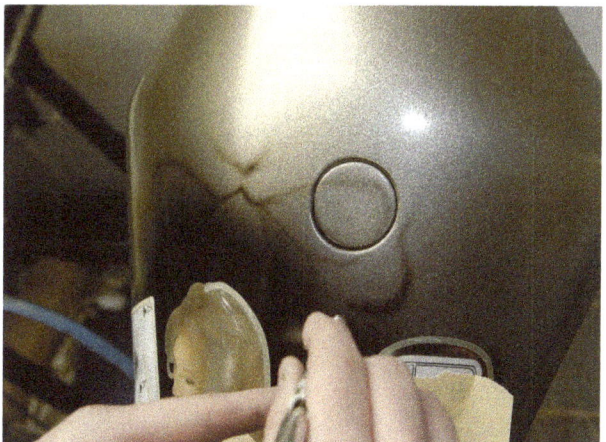

The third part of this montage, the skull, is formed freehand, starting with thinned down black basecoat.

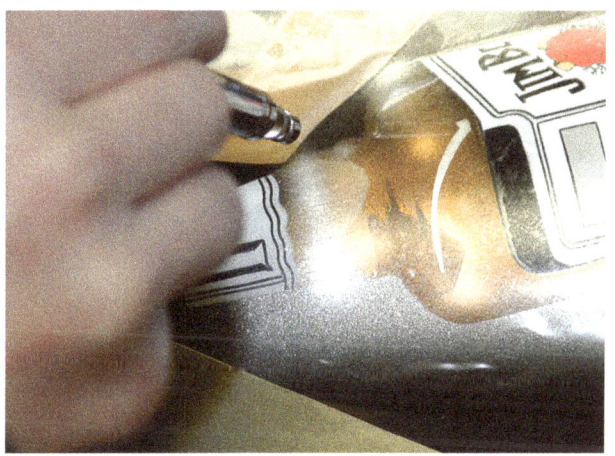

Then apply silver paint for highlights.

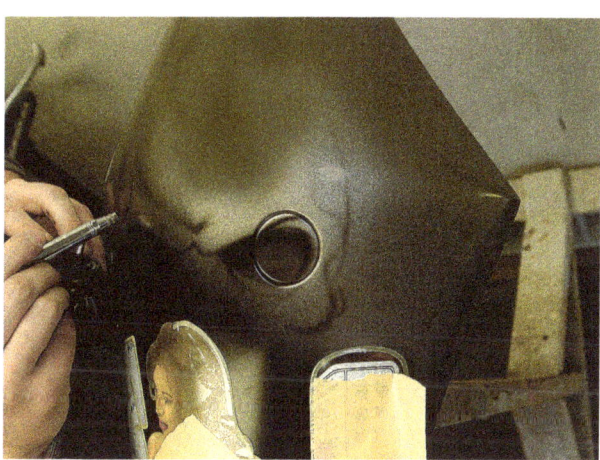

The eyes come first, followed by the beginning outlines of the skull.

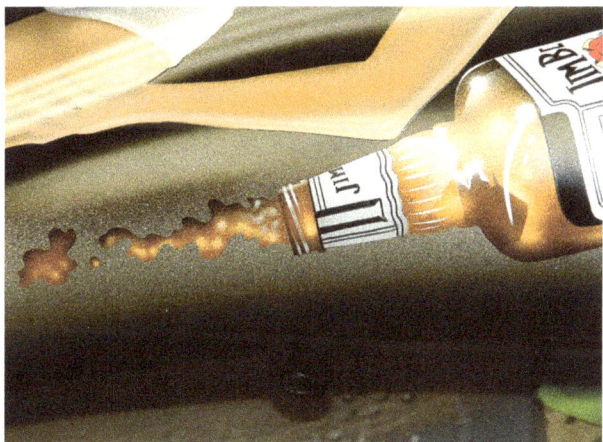

Here you can see the finished area, complete with hand painted details and highlights in white and silver (note, a few small areas of the bottle were further detailed later).

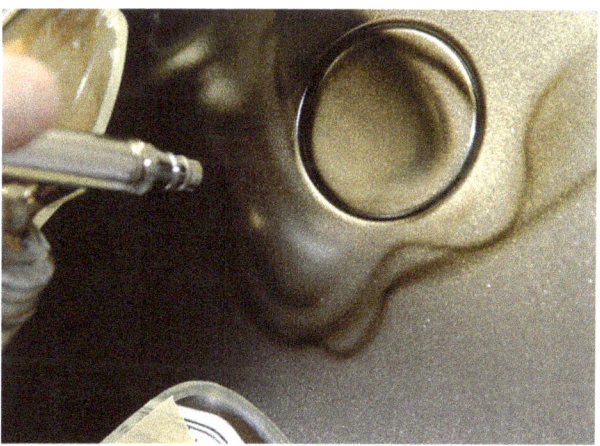

Highlights in silver are added all through the project, rather than at the very end.

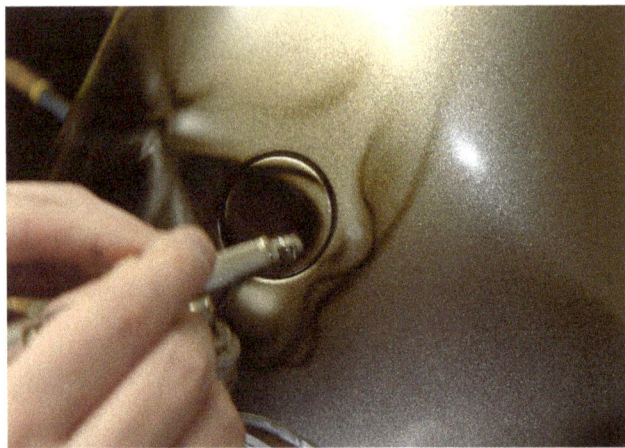

More silver is added to form the curved area just outside the eye socket.

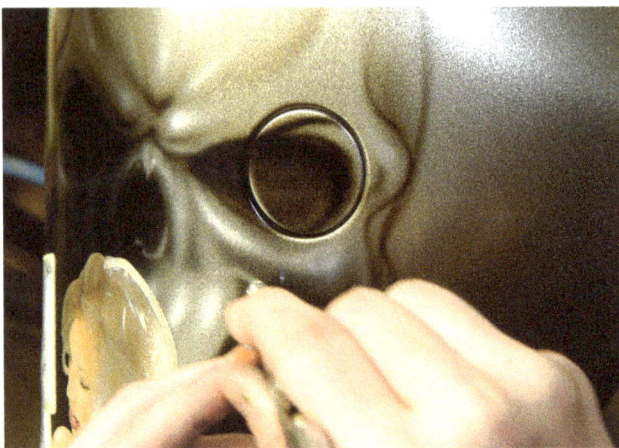

The shape of the cheekbones is likewise formed with silver highlights.

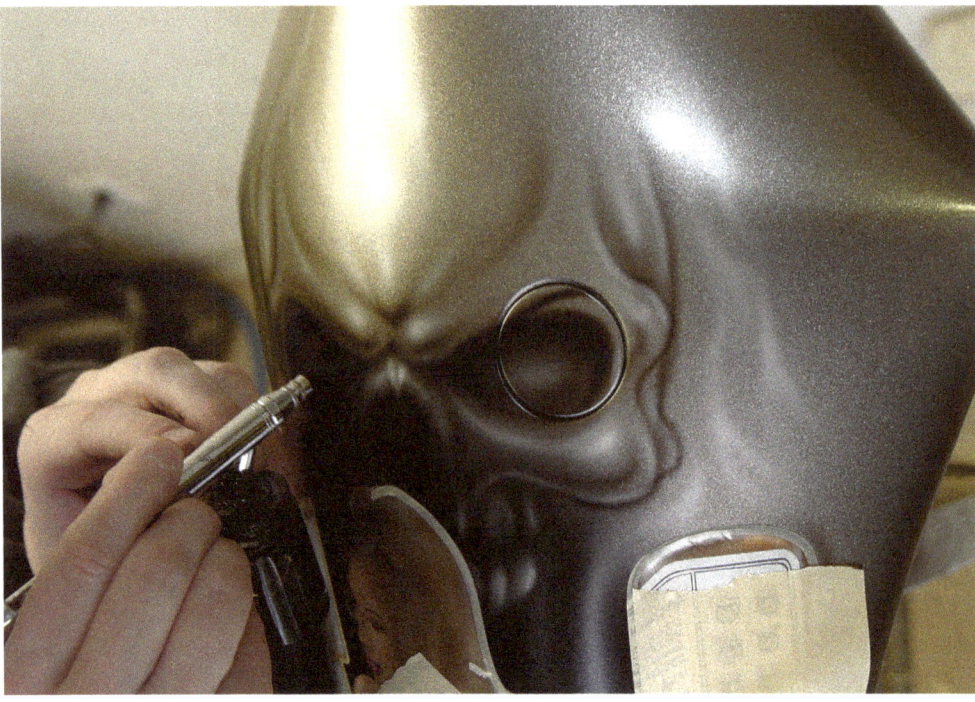

you did the bottle,?'" says John. "But at that time I didn't know how everything was going to fit together. It's easier to do it way, the piece comes together better, and the masking isn't as complicated."

THE SKULL

I've done a lot of skulls," says John, "and I always do the eyes first. The first color is basecoat black, thinned down. I start by going light to dark, then from dark to light." The job requires the use of basecoat black, candy black, silver for highlights and at the very end, blue pearl. This is another sequence where the photos do a better job of telling the story than writing does.

JOHN'S REALITY FLAMES

The formula for these reality flames is a little different than some others and actually starts with white.

The white is applied freehand to the edges of the spilled whiskey. John applies the paint with the tip close to the work, so it appears the wispy flames are coming off the top of the liquid. Medium chrome-yellow (DMD 639), thinned down, is the next color, applied on top of the white.

Basecoat orange is next. John keeps the tip close and free-hands the licks, one at a time. John decides to put a little more black on the bottom of

Now candy black is used to make a shadow just under some of the highlights.

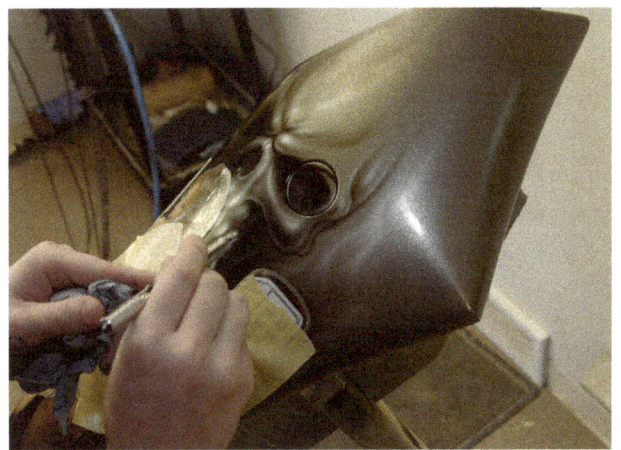

The same silver paint is used to form the evil teeth.

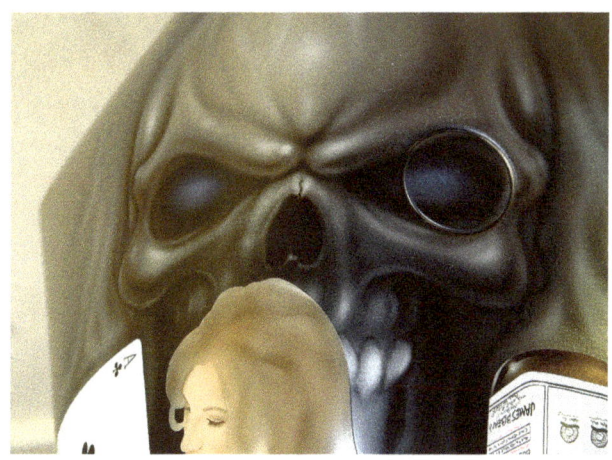

A quick look at the finished skull.

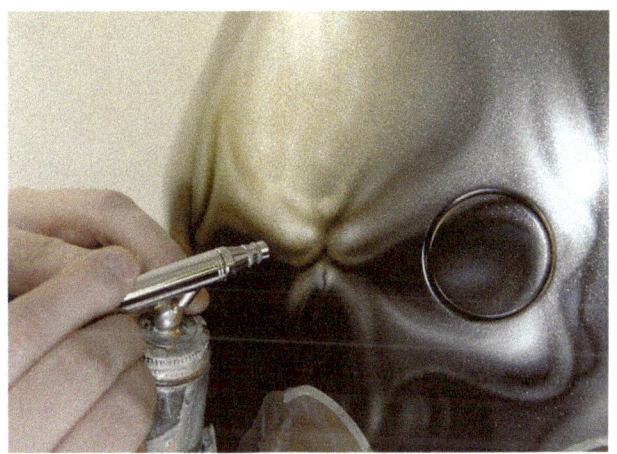

Highlights are developed further with the application of more silver to specific small areas.

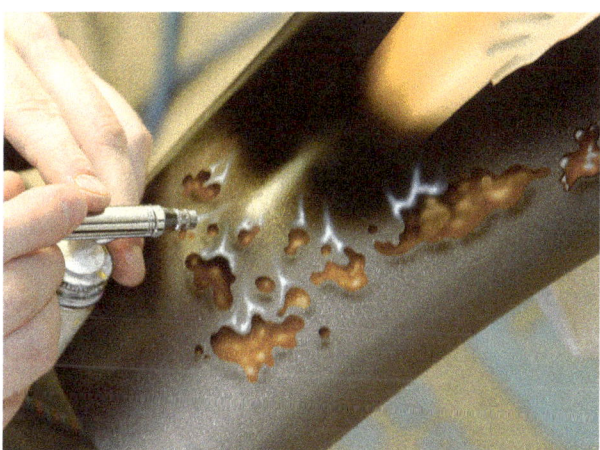

The reality flames emerge from the spilled bourbon, as though someone put a match to the firewater. John starts with white highlights on the spilled liquid.

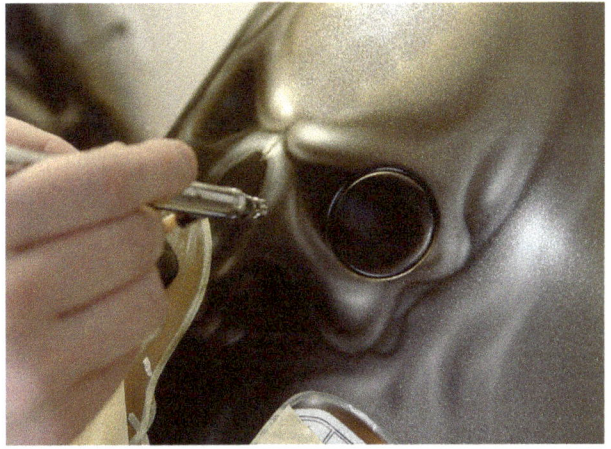

The piece 'de résistance, an evil gleam from deep in the sockets, is done in blue pearl.

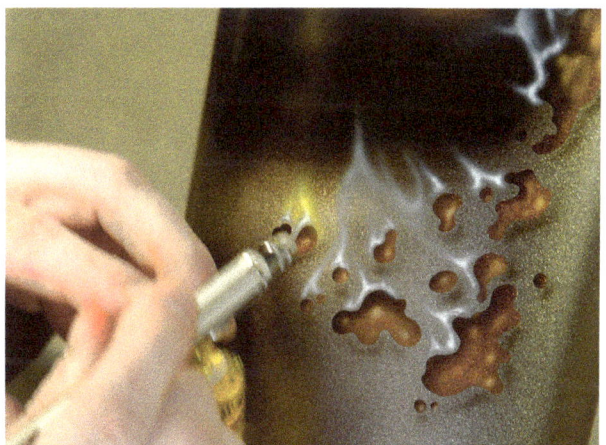

The next step is thinned-down, medium chrome yellow, applied on top of the white.

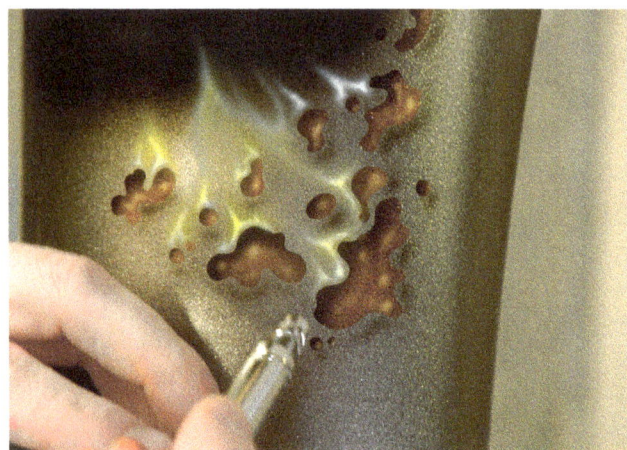

Each of the white wisps is topcoated with thinned-down yellow (medium chrome yellow DMD 639) to form what will be the hottest part of the fire.

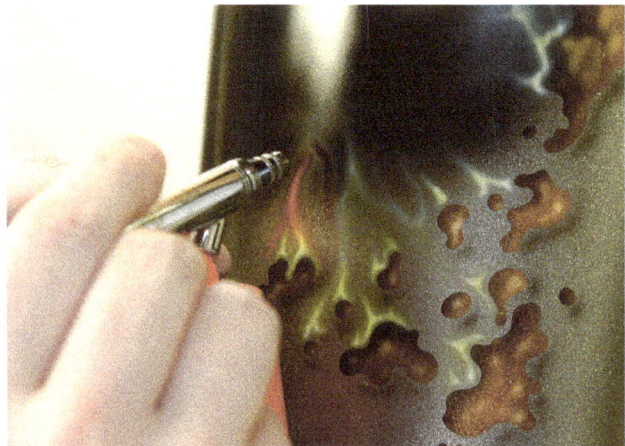

The next step is basecoat orange (or molly orange)...

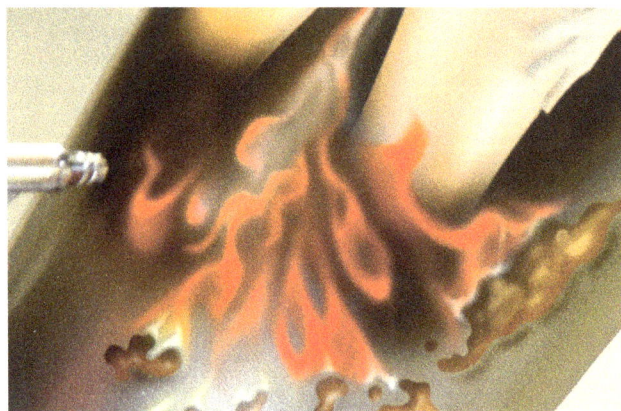

...which John applies "freehand like a free-flowing ribbon, the way it flips and twists."

the tank, followed by more orange licks. "Flames are a lot like painting liquids," explains John, "but the shiny spots are reversed."

Candy red is applied next, over all the orange. Followed by more orange again to highlight hot spots, and highlight the tips of the flames, and the area where the fire is coming from, "those are the hottest spots."

The next color is yellow, applied in much the same way as the preceding coat of orange. The yellow adds heat and helps to define each flame lick.

A little candy orange makes it all brighter. "Then I go back in with white to create the white hot spots, where it originates." Now a little yellow, on top of the white. John finishes with a few silver details added to the base of the fire for shine in the blobs of whiskey.

Continued on page 173

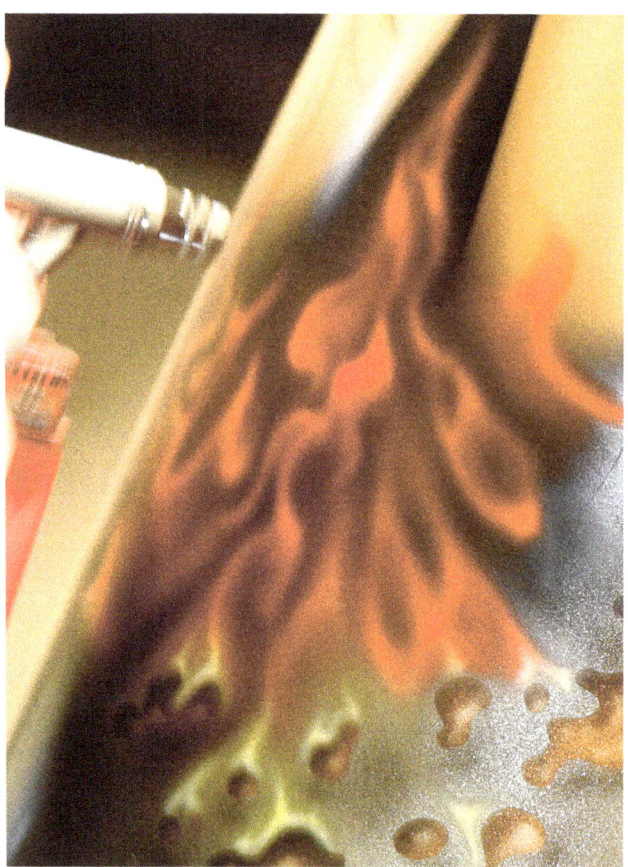

"Candy red is applied to orange parts of fire only. Be careful at this point not to get any candy red on the skin tones or they will become pink and look very wrong."

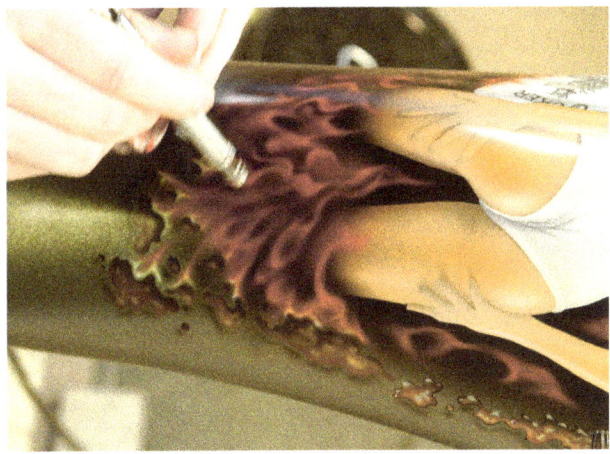

"More candy apple red is applied over the orange - just enough to make the orange red. This gives more depth than straight red."

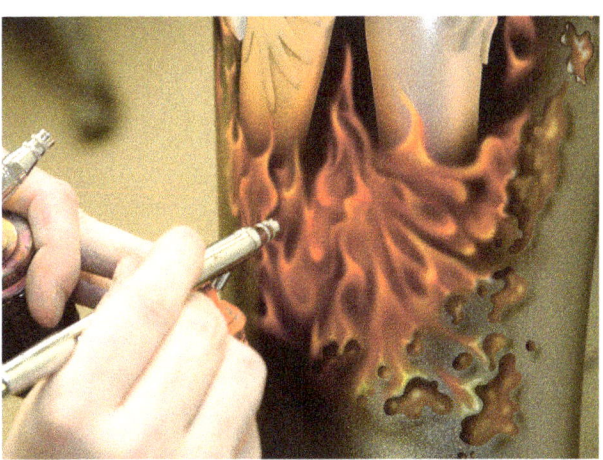

...close up shows how the yellow gives each lick more definition and makes them all much brighter.

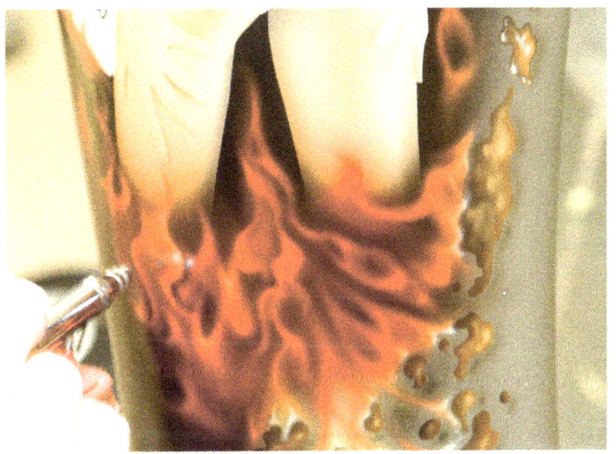

The red is followed by more orange, applied this time to just the tips.

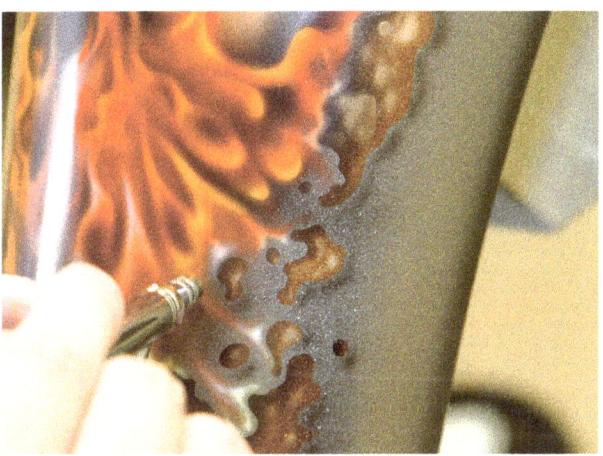

A little white is used to make hot spots at the base of the fire...

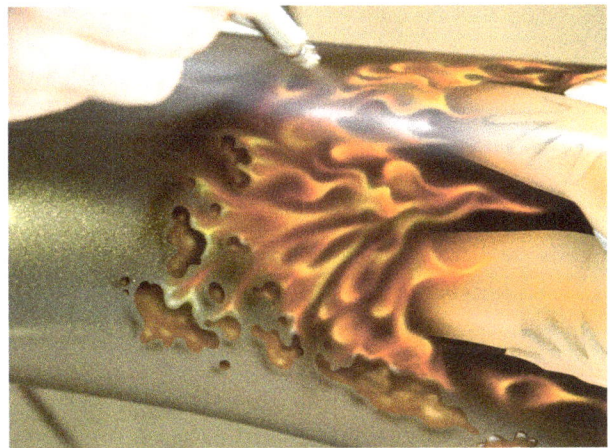

A little yellow is added to the upper part of the licks...

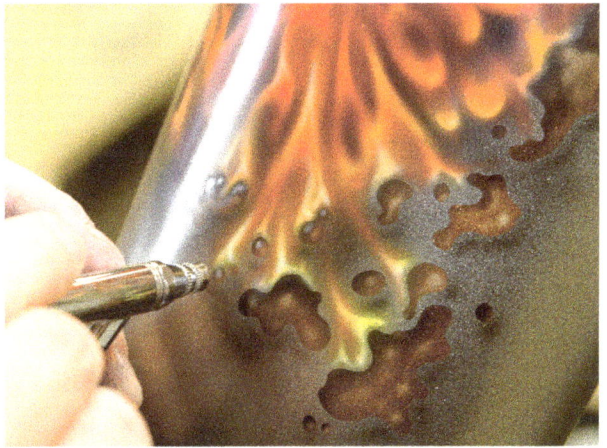

...which is followed by the same yellow used earlier in the sequence.

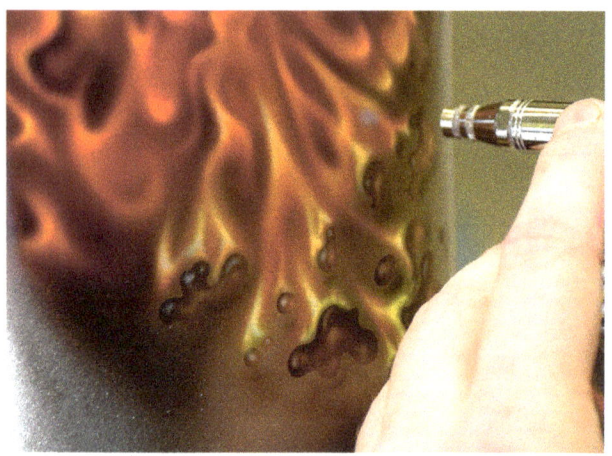

John even uses a little silver in small precise areas to create just the right color.

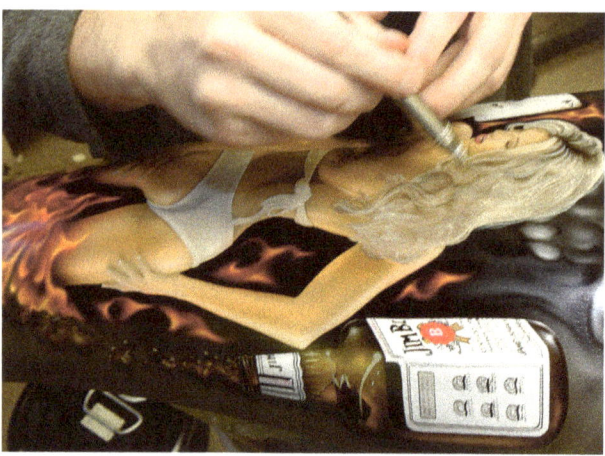

"Once I have the texture right I use some black to blend everything together so it isn't too bright.

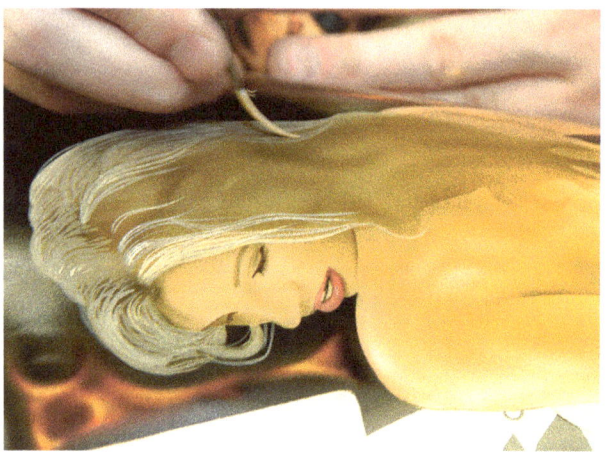

To create realistic hair John mixes up white, yellow, red and a little green (the basic flesh-tone formula) with the water-based paints.

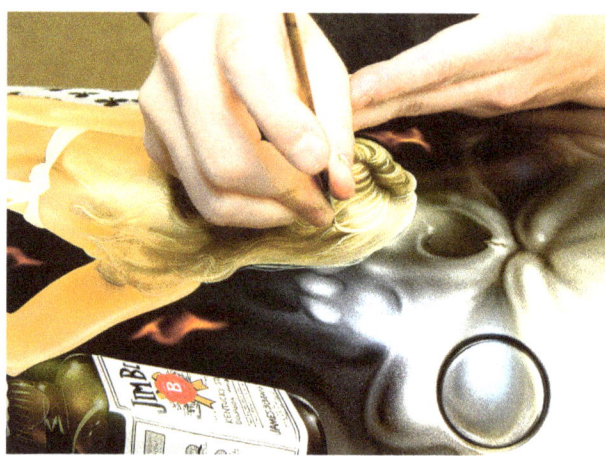

Next step - spray some yellow and TRO to make her blonde (not shown), followed by more brush work with yellow water-based, tinted with a little white.

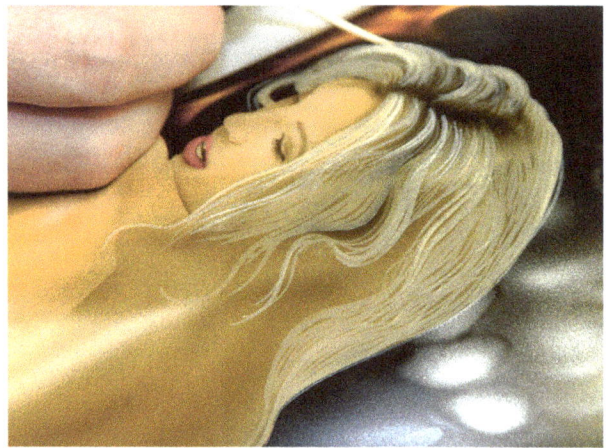

The paint is applied by hand, "It all comes together one brush stroke at a time."

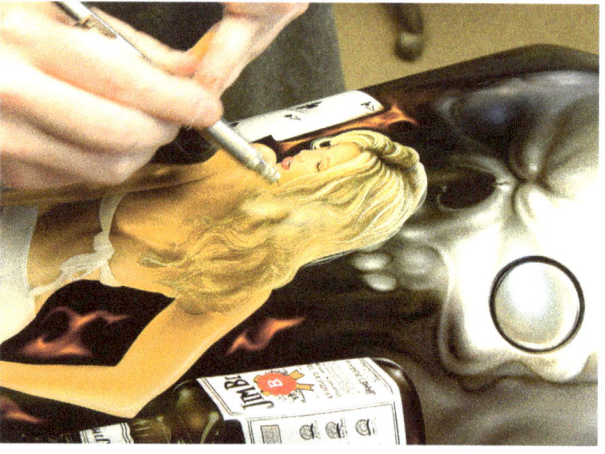

A little black is used again to create shadows. This is thinned-down black mixed with a little trans-red-oxide.

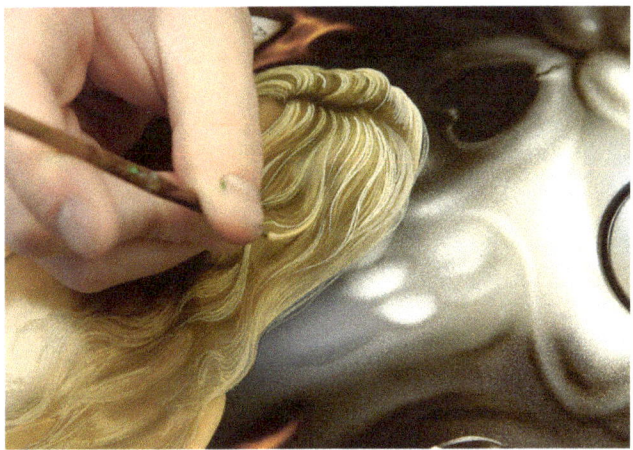

Creating the hair with realistic texture is a matter of multiple details added over time.

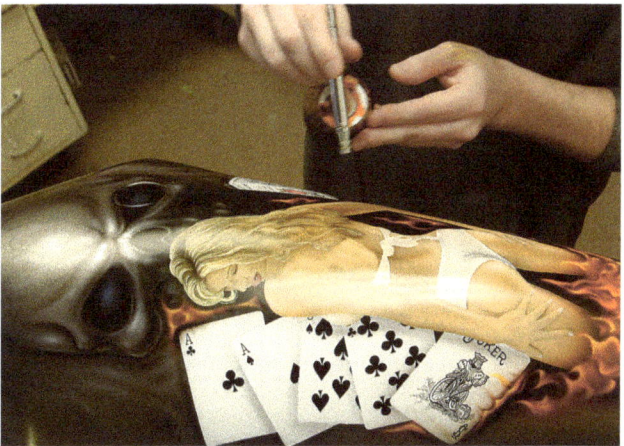

The final step is to give the hair a rich sheen with a light mist of trans-red-oxide.

FINAL DETAILS

The only thing left are a few details on the hands and the hair. To make a flesh tone paint John mixes white, yellow, red, and a little green. Using a brush and the flesh-tone mix, John adds details like fingernails to the hands (not shown).

Using the same paint and another brush, John actually paints in the hair by hand. To blend it all together he adds a mist of black with the airbrush. Next, from the airbrush, comes the chrome yellow basecoat (diluted).

Using the airbrush, John does a mist of yellow and trans-red oxide (not shown) followed by more brush work using white mixed with a little yellow.

"I have to be careful that the color I use for the hair isn't too yellow." explains John. Occasionally John does a mist of black to tone it down and blend it together. The final coat of color is a mist of trans-red oxide which gives the hair just the right tone.

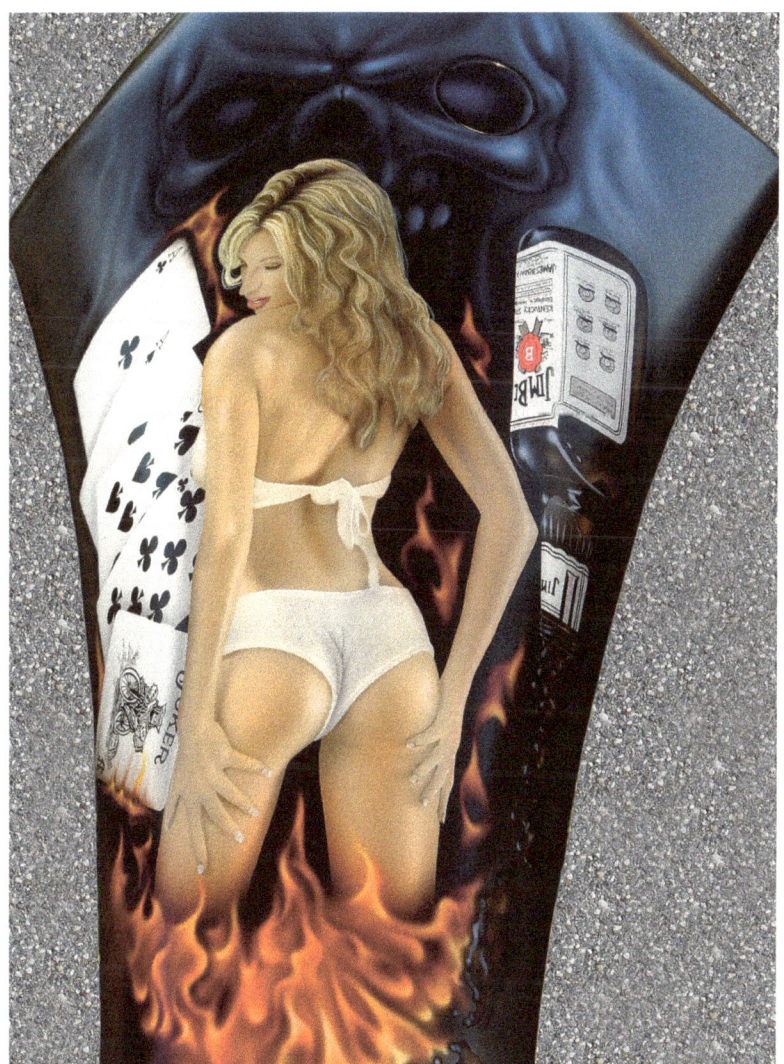

The finished piece. "But before putting everything away be sure to put a thin wet coat of intercoat clear on all the work so the water-based details won't be damaged during final wipe down."

Wolfgang Books On The Web
http://www.wolfpub.com

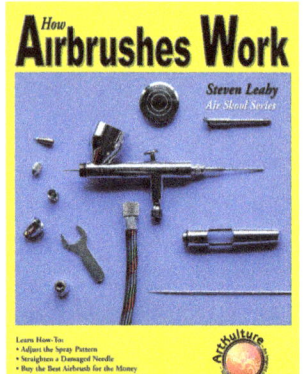

HOW AIRBRUSHES WORK

This is a comprehensive look at airbrush use, maintenance and repair. The book begins with a brief look at airbrush history, then moves to a discussion of the various airbrush types.

Too many first-time airbrush users have trouble because they don't know how to clean and maintain the airbrush. This book explains how to disassemble, clean and repair all the major brands. Even the best airbrush in the world isn't any good without a source of air. Steve discusses different compressor types and the advantages or disadvantages of each.

Two chapters explain airbrush painting basics - from types of paint to trigger control, and the three basic strokes all painters need to know. Steve closes the book with a gallery of airbrush art, and an airbrush buyer's guide to help readers choose wisely when they buy their first, or their fifth, airbrush.

Nineteen Chapters   144 Pages $27.95   Over 400 photos, 100% color

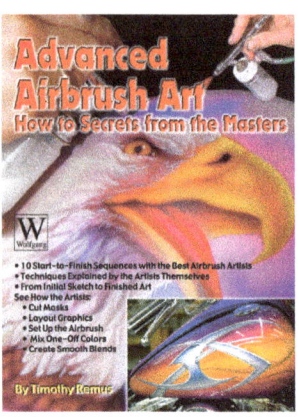

ADVANCED AIRBRUSH ART

Like a video done with still photography, this book is made up entirely of photo sequences that illustrate each small step in the creation of an airbrushed masterpiece. Watch as well-known masters like Vince Goodeve, Chris Cruz, Steve Wizard and Nick Pastura start with a sketch and end with a NASCAR helmet or motorcycle tank covered with graphics, murals, pinups or all of the above.

Interviews explain each artist's preference for paint and equipment, and secrets learned over decades of painting. Projects include a chrome eagle surrounded by reality flames, a series of murals, and a variety of graphic designs.

This is a great book for anyone who takes their airbrushing seriously and wants to learn more.

Ten Chapters   144 Pages $27.95   Over 400 photos, 100% color

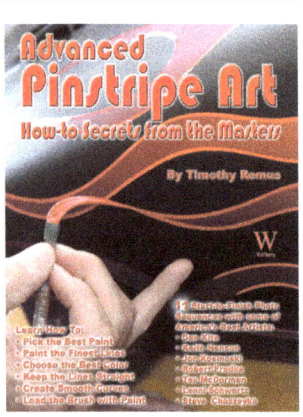

ADVANCED PINSTRIPE ART

Since the days of Von Dutch, hot rod and motorcycle enthusiasts have used pinstripes both as stand-alone art, and as a compliment to a flame or graphic paint job.

Each chapter presents one start-to-finish project and an interview with the artist. The photo sequences take the viewer from the initial sketch to the finished design. Text explains each step of the artwork; the interviews explain the artist's choice for paint and brushes. The artwork, often complimented with gold leaf or airbrush colors, is done on panels as well as various vehicles and components.

Advanced Pinstripe Art brings the reader into the shop of some of this country's best pinstripe artists, for an intense and intimate how-to lesson. This is pinstripe school, taught by masters, brought to your own home or shop.

Eleven Chapters   144 Pages $27.95   Over 400 photos, 100% color

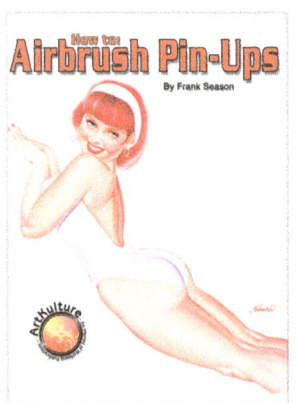

HOW TO AIRBRUSH PIN-UPS

How to Airbrush Pinups is a collection of 9 sequences done by well-known and experienced airbrush artists. The individuals included here include Edward Reed, Steve Nunez, Susan Heidi, Liz Austin, and Tom Nguyen. Each photo sequence starts with the artist's sketch, before moving, step-by-step, to the finished panel.

The human form, the human face, and skin tones, are three topics that beginning artists struggle to get right. And it is these three topics that make up much of the discussion in this new book. Each chapter includes a Q&A with the artist. These interviews allow the reader to experience the artist, one-on-one. This is a chance to learn not only which airbrush the artist prefer, but also how they learned their skills, who inspires them and how to avoid the typical mistakes.

Seven Chapters   144 Pages $27.95   Over 400 photos, 100% color

Wolfgang Publication Titles

For a current list visit our website at www.wolfpub.com

ILLUSTRATED HISTORY
Triumph Motorcycles — $32.95

BIKER BASICS
Sheet Metal Fabrication — $27.95
How to FIX American V-Twin MC — $27.95

COMPOSITE GARAGE
Composite Materials — $27.95

HOP-UP EXPERT
How to Hop & Customize Your Bagger — $27.95
How to Hop & Customize Your Softail — $27.95

OLD SKOOL SKILLS
Barris: Grilles, Scoops, Fins and Frenching (Vol. 2) — $24.95
Barris: Flames Scallops, Paneling and Striping (Vol. 4) — $24.95

HOT ROD BASICS
How to Air Condition Your Hot Rod — $27.95
How to Chop Tops — $24.95
How to Wire your Hot Rod — $27.95

MOTORCYCLE RESTORATION SERIES
Triumph Resotoration - Unit 650cc — $29.95
Triumph MC Restoration Pre-Unit — $29.95
Harley-Davidson Panhead Restoration — $34.95

AIR SKOOL SKILLS
How Airbrushes Work — $27.95
How to Airbrush Pin-Ups — $27.95
Air Brushing 101 — $27.95
Airbrush Bible — $27.95

PAINT EXPERT
Adv. Custom Motorcycle Painting — $27.95
Advanced Airbrush Art — $27.95
Advanced Custom Painting Techniques — $27.95
Advanced Pinstripe Art — $27.95
Kustom Painting Secrets — $19.95
Custom Paint & Graphics — $27.95
Pro Airbrush Techniques — $27.95

SHEET METAL
Advanced Sheet Metal Fabrication — $27.95
Ultimate Sheet Metal Fabrication — $24.95

CUSTOM BUILDER SERIES
Adv Custom Motorcycle Wiring — $27.95
Adv Custom Motorcycle Assembly & Fabrication — $27.95
Adv. Custom Motorcycle Chassis — $27.95
How to Build a Cheap Chopper — $27.95
How to Build a Chopper — $27.95

TATTOO U Series
Body Painting — $27.95
Tattoo- From Idea to Ink — $27.95
Tattoos Behind the Needle — $27.95
Advanced Tattoo Art — $27.95
Tattoo Bible Book One — $27.95
Tattoo Bible Book Two — $27.95

HOME SHOP
How to Paint Tractors & Trucks — $27.95

NOTEWORTHY
Guitar Building Basics
Acoustic Assembly at Home — $27.95

CALENDARS
Classic Triumph 2010 — $14.95

Sources

Art Essentials of New York Inc.
P.O Box 38, Tallman, NY 10982-0038
(800) 283-5323
Artessentialsofnewyork.com

Bear Air Express
20 Hampden Drive #2
S. Easton, MA 02375
(800) BearAir
Bearair.com

Blick Art Materials
P.O. Box 1267
Galesburg, IL 61402-1267
800-828-4548
309-343-6181 (International)
Dickblick.com

Steve Chaszeyka (Wizard)
11497.5 Youngstown-Pittsburgh Rd
New Middletown, OH 44442
(330) 542-4444
www.wizardgraphics.us

Coates & Best Inc.
883 2nd Avenue East
Owen Sound, ON N4K 2H2
519-376-5499

Mark Daniels
www.Psychoticair.com
630-896-1982

Devil's Candy Customs
Brian Boan
254 State Street
Daytona Beach, FL 32117
386-852-7984

District Auto Paint
7500 S. Archer Road
Justice, IL 60458
708-496-1000

Finishline
21725 County Rd. 10
Corcoran, MN 55374
763-416-4371
www.finishlineinc.com

Leah Gall
Finishline Design
21725 Co Rd 10
Corcoran, MN 55374
763-416-4371 *651-439-7052
Touchstone468@aol.com

Vince Goodeve
123003 Story Book Park Rd.
RR4 Own Sound, ON
Canada N4K 5N6
goodevestudios@aol.com

Graftobian Make-up Company
www.graftobian.com

Keith Hanson
233 Canton
Stoughton, MA 02072
78-344-9166
www.hansoncustom.net

Susan Heidi
Susan Heidi Art Studios
P.O. Box 115
Garrison, NY 10524
www.susanheidi.com
845-424-6016

House of Kolor
Division of Valspar Refinish
210 Crosby St.
Picayune, MS 39466
Tech-line: 601-798-4229
www.houseofkolor.com

Krazy Kolors
Lenni Schwartz
5413 Helena
Oakdale, MN 55128
krazykolors@msn.com
www.krazykolors.net

Logic Motorcycles
www.logicmotors.com
10359 W. South Range Rd.
Salem, OH 44460
330-332-2323

Psymonsen Airbrush
Ken Simonsen
966 Villa Street
Elgin, IL 60120
www.psymonsen.com
kensimonsen@earthlink.net
847-741-6632

Sid Moses Art Supplies
10456 Santa Monica Blvd.
Los Angeles, CA 90025
310-475-1111
www.moseart.com

Notablesigns
3112 Braley Road
Ransomville, NY 14131
716-751-3708
notablesigns@aol.com

Tom Nguyen
Tom Nguyen Art
2084 12th Ave. W.
Shakopee, MN 55379
www.TomNguyenArt.com
tom@tomnguyenart.com

Luca Paganico
Pittsburgh, PA 15235
412-607-6363
lucapaganico@yahoo.com

PPG World Headquarters
One PPG Place
Pittsburgh, PA 15272
412-434-3131
PPG.com

Scenic City Automotive
1010 9th Avenue West
Owen Sound, ON N4K 5R7
519-376-7310

Sign Gold Corporation
53 Smith Road
Middletown, NY 10941
845-692-6565
Signgold.com

Transfer Rite Ultra
American Biltrite Inc.
www.abitape.com

WJT Graphic supplies
WJT Distributing Inc.
160 Bentley St.
Markham, Ontario
L3R-3L2, Canada
800-465-8650

X-otic paint
www.xoticcolours.com

www.ingramcontent.com/pod-product-compliance
Lightning Source LLC
Chambersburg PA
CBHW040540220526
45473CB00016B/2989